SHELL STRUCTURES

Stability and Strength

Related titles

BEAMS AND BEAM COLUMNS: STABILITY AND STRENGTH
edited by R. Narayanan

1. Elastic Lateral Buckling of Beams   D. A. NETHERCOT
2. Inelastic Lateral Buckling of Beams   N. S. TRAHAIR
3. Design of Laterally Unsupported Beams   D. A. NETHERCOT and N. S. TRAHAIR
4. Design of I-Beams with Web Perforations   R. G. REDWOOD
5. Instability, Geometric Non-linearity and Collapse of Thin-Walled Beams   T. M. ROBERTS
6. Diaphragm-Braced Thin-Walled Channel and Z-Section Beams   T. PEKÖZ
7. Design of Beams and Beam Columns   G. C. LEE and N. T. TSENG
8. Trends in Safety Factor Optimisation   N. C. LIND and M. K. RAVINDRA

PLATED STRUCTURES: STABILITY AND STRENGTH
edited by R. Narayanan

1. Longitudinally and Transversely Reinforced Plate Girders   H. R. EVANS
2. Ultimate Capacity of Plate Girders with Openings in Their Webs   R. NARAYANAN
3. Patch Loading on Plate Girders   T. M. ROBERTS
4. Optimum Rigidity of Stiffeners of Webs and Flanges   M. ŠKALOUD
5. Ultimate Capacity of Stiffened Plates in Compression   N. W. MURRAY
6. Shear Lag in Box Girders   V. KŘISTEK
7. Compressive Strength of Biaxially Loaded Plates   R. NARAYANAN and N. E. SHANMUGAM
8. The Interaction of Direct and Shear Stresses on Plate Panels   J. E. HARDING

STEEL FRAMED STRUCTURES: STABILITY AND STRENGTH
edited by R. Narayanan

1. Frame Instability and the Plastic Design of Rigid Frames   M. R. HORNE
2. Matrix Methods of Analysis of Multi-Storeyed Sway Frames   T. M. ROBERTS
3. Design of Multi-Storey Steel Frames to Sway Deflection Limitations   D. ANDERSON
4. Interbraced Columns and Beams   I. C. MEDLAND and C. M. SEGEDIN
5. Elastic Stability of Rigidly and Semi-Rigidly Connected Unbraced Frames   G. J. SIMITSES and A. S. VLAHINOS
6. Beam-to-Column Moment-Resisting Connections   W. F. CHEN and E. M. LUI
7. Flexibly Connected Steel Frames   K. H. GERSTLE
8. Portal Frames Composed of Cold-Formed Channel- and Z-Sections   G. J. HANCOCK
9. Braced Steel Arches   S. KOMATSU
10. Member Stability in Portal Frames   L. J. MORRIS and K. NAKANE

SHELL STRUCTURES

Stability and Strength

Edited by

R. NARAYANAN

M.Sc.(Eng.), Ph.D., D.I.C., C.Eng., F.I.C.E., F.I.Struct.E., F.I.E.
Reader in Civil and Structural Engineering,
University College, Cardiff, United Kingdom

ELSEVIER APPLIED SCIENCE PUBLISHERS
LONDON and NEW YORK

ELSEVIER APPLIED SCIENCE PUBLISHERS LTD
Crown House, Linton Road, Barking, Essex IG11 8JU, England

Sole Distributor in the USA and Canada
ELSEVIER SCIENCE PUBLISHING CO., INC.
52 Vanderbilt Avenue, New York, NY 10017, USA

British Library Cataloguing in Publication Data

Shell structures: stability and strength.
1. Shells (Engineering)
I. Narayanan, R.
624.1'7762   TA660.S5

ISBN 0-85334-343-8

WITH 15 TABLES AND 178 ILLUSTRATIONS

Filmset and printed in Northern Ireland by The Universities Press (Belfast) Ltd.

PREFACE

I have great pleasure in writing a short preface to this book on *Shell Structures*, the fifth in the planned set of volumes on the stability and strength of structures.

The energy crisis of the seventies and the consequent search for oil under the deep sea bed have precipitated extensive theoretical and experimental investigations into the many forms of shell structures to enable better and safer marine installations to be built. The inspiration for this book comes from a wealth of new knowledge that has been generated in the last decade or so.

The policy of inviting internationally recognised specialists to contribute the various chapters in their fields of expertise has been continued in producing this volume; sufficient background material has been included in each topic to enable a reader with a fundamental understanding of structural mechanics to follow the most recent advances in the subject.

The book begins with a general introduction to the problem of shell stability and thereafter discusses various specialist applications to be found in stiffened shells, pressure vessels, tubular structures, cold-formed shells, submarine pipelines and torispherical shells. To stimulate new concepts on shell construction, a treatment of tensegric shells, consisting of a cable net and tensioned bars, has been included as the final chapter.

The book is written in SI units generally; the steadily increasing permeability of national boundaries and scientific thought have resulted in the inclusion of some material in Imperial units; I trust that the readers do not find this too distracting.

As editor, I wish to express my gratitude to all the contributors for the willing cooperation they extended in producing this volume. I sincerely hope that the book will be stimulating to the practising engineer and to the researcher.

R. NARAYANAN

CONTENTS

LIST OF CONTRIBUTORS

G. ABDEL-SAYED

Professor of Civil Engineering, University of Windsor, 401 Sunset Avenue, Windsor, Ontario, Canada N9B 3PA.

A. CHAJES

Professor, Department of Civil Engineering, University of Massachusetts, Amherst, Massachusetts 01003, USA.

W. F. CHEN

Professor and Head of Structural Engineering, School of Civil Engineering, Purdue University, West Lafayette, Indiana 47907, USA.

J. G. A. CROLL

Reader in Structural Engineering, Department of Civil and Municipal Engineering, University College, London WC1 6BT, UK.

G. D. GALLETLY

Professor of Applied Mechanics, Department of Mechanical Engineering, University of Liverpool, PO Box 147, Liverpool L69 3BX, UK.

D. KAVLIE

Division of Structural Mechanics, Norwegian Institute of Technology, Rich. Berkelands vei 1a, N-7034 Trondheim-NTH, Norway.

S. KENDRICK

Admiralty Marine Technology Establishment, St. Leonard's Hill, Dunfermline, Fife, Scotland KY11 5PW, UK.

P. MONTAGUE

Professor of Civil Engineering, Simon Engineering Laboratories, University of Manchester, Oxford Road, Manchester M13 9PL, UK.

T. H. SØREIDE

Professor, Division of Structural Mechanics, Norwegian Institute of Technology, Rich. Berkelands vei 1a, N-7034 Trondheim-NTH, Norway.

J. W. B. STARK

Head of the Department of Steel Structures, TNO Institute for Building Materials and Building Structures, PO Box 49, 2600 AA Delft, The Netherlands; Eindhoven University of Technology, Department of Building Structures and Architectural Design, PO Box 513, 5600 MB Eindhoven, The Netherlands.

H. SUGIMOTO

Initial Design Department, Ship Group, Kawasaki Heavy Industries, Kobe, Japan.

O. VILNAY

Lecturer, Department of Civil and Structural Engineering, University College, Newport Road, Cardiff CF2 1TA, UK.

P. E. DE WINTER

TNO Institute for Building Materials and Building Structures, PO Box 49, 2600 AA Delft, The Netherlands.

J. WITTEVEEN

TNO Institute for Building Materials and Building Structures, PO Box 49, 2600 AA Delft, The Netherlands; Delft University of Technology, Department of Civil Engineering, PO Box 5049, 2600 GA Delft, The Netherlands.

Chapter 1

STABILITY AND COLLAPSE ANALYSIS OF AXIALLY COMPRESSED CYLINDRICAL SHELLS

ALEXANDER CHAJES

Department of Civil Engineering, University of Massachusetts, Amherst, USA

SUMMARY

A review is made of the present state of knowledge of the buckling of axially compressed cylindrical shells. Both the theory and design procedures are summarised. The material deals primarily with shells of intermediate length.

1.1 INTRODUCTION

The type of buckling to which an axially compressed cylinder is susceptible depends on the ratio of its length to its radius, L/R, and on the ratio of its radius to its thickness, R/t. Very short cylinders with large diameters behave like flat plates that are supported along the loaded edges and free along the unloaded edges. They buckle into a single half sine wave in the axial direction and no waves in the circumferential direction (Fig. 1.1a). By comparison, very long cylinders with small diameters, i.e. tubes, buckle like Euler columns with no distortion of the circumferential cross-section occurring (Fig. 1.1b). A third group consists of moderately long cylinders that fail by local buckling. The surface of these cylinders buckles into a series of diamond-shaped dimples (Fig. 1.1c). The single most important characteristic of moderately long cylinders is that they fail at loads

1

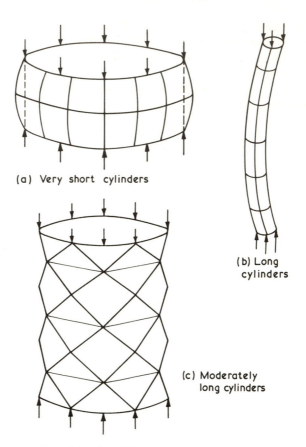

(a) Very short cylinders

(b) Long cylinders

(c) Moderately long cylinders

FIG. 1.1.   Buckling of cylindrical shells.

significantly below the critical load obtained using linear theory. It is with this last group that the chapter is mainly concerned.

1.2   LINEAR THEORY

Within the limits of elastic small-deformation theory, the behaviour of unstiffened axially compressed cylindrical shells is governed by the equation

$$D\nabla_w^8 + \sigma t \nabla^4 \frac{\partial^2 w}{\partial x^2} + \frac{Et}{R^2} \frac{\partial^4 w}{\partial x^4} = 0 \qquad (1.1)$$

where D = bending stiffness = $Et^3/12(1-\mu^2)$, E = Young's modulus of elasticity, t = shell thickness, R = shell radius, σ = axial stress, x = coordinate in axial direction, w = displacement in radial direction, ∇ = biharmonic operator.

A parameter which can be used to separate short cylinders from moderately long cylinders is

$$Z = \left(\frac{L}{R}\right)^2 \left(\frac{R}{t}\right)\sqrt{(1-\mu^2)} \tag{1.2}$$

where L = length of shell, μ = Poisson's ratio.

For short cylinders ($Z < 2 \cdot 85$), the critical stress obtained by solving eqn (1.1) is

$$\sigma_{cr} = \frac{k\pi^2 E}{12(1-\mu^2)}\left(\frac{t}{L}\right)^2 \tag{1.3}$$

For simply supported edges the constant k in eqn (1.3) is given by

$$k = \frac{1 + 12Z^2}{\pi^4} \tag{1.4}$$

and for fully clamped edges

$$k = \frac{4 + 3Z^2}{\pi^4} \tag{1.5}$$

For cylinders of intermediate length ($Z > 2 \cdot 85$), the critical stress is

$$\sigma_{cr} = \frac{E}{\sqrt{[3(1-\mu^2)]}}\left(\frac{t}{R}\right) \tag{1.6}$$

or

$$\sigma_{cr} = 0 \cdot 6E\left(\frac{t}{R}\right) \quad \text{for} \quad \mu = 0 \cdot 3 \tag{1.7}$$

Only the surface adjacent to the loaded edges of the cylinder is affected by the rotational restraint along these edges. Hence the critical stress for cylindrical shells of intermediate length, given by eqn (1.6), is valid for clamped as well as simply supported edges.

Since eqn (1.1) applies only to surface or local buckling it cannot be used to obtain the critical load for long tubes that buckle like Euler columns with no distortion of the surface.

1.3 BEHAVIOUR OF MODERATELY LONG SHELLS

The most significant fact about shells of intermediate length is that they tend to fail at loads well below those given by the linear theory. Failure loads as low as 30 per cent of the critical load are not uncommon. The cause of this discrepancy between linear theory and actual failure is generally believed to be the unstable post-buckling behaviour of the shell, which causes the shell to be extremely sensitive to even small initial imperfections of shape.

Using a large deflection theory, but limiting the analysis to initially perfect shells, Karman and Tsien (1941) were the first to discover the unstable post-buckling behaviour of axially compressed cylindrical shells. They found that, subsequent to reaching the critical load, the load that an initially perfect shell can support drops sharply with increasing deformations. As indicated in Fig. 1.2, the post-buckling behaviour of the shell is in sharp contrast to the way a simple column buckles. Whereas the load that a column can support subsequent to the onset of buckling remains fairly constant, in the case of the shell the load drops precipitously once buckling begins.

The unstable post-buckling behaviour of cylindrical shells discovered by Karman and Tsien indicates that equilibrium is possible in a slightly

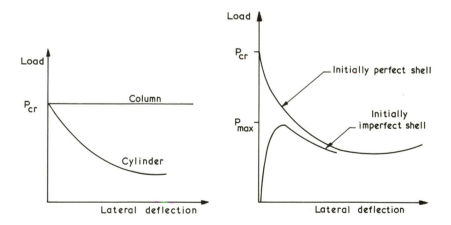

FIG. 1.2. Post-buckling curves for column and axially compressed cylindrical shell.

FIG. 1.3. Behaviour of initially imperfect shell.

deformed configuration at loads well below the critical load. These results by themselves do not, however, demonstrate why the applied load never reaches the critical load in the first place. The answer to this all-important question came several years later when Donnell and Wan (1950) included initial imperfections in their large deflection analysis and found that the presence of these imperfections resulted in a maximum load below the critical load obtained for the initially perfect shell. As shown in Fig. 1.3, the initially imperfect shell never reaches the critical load given by the linear theory for a perfect shell. Instead, the initially imperfect shell exhibits a maximum load that is considerably lower than the critical load of the perfect shell.

Working independently of the aforementioned investigators, Koiter (1945) developed a general theory of post-buckling behaviour which substantiates the conclusions reached by Donnell and Wan, namely that initial imperfections of shape are responsible for the fact that failure loads are significantly lower than the critical load. Based on the work of Koiter and that of Budiansky and Hutchinson (1966), the concept of imperfection sensitivity has been developed. In accordance with this theory one is able to calculate a parameter which is a measure of the steepness of the post-buckling curve. This parameter can then be used to estimate the degree to which initial imperfections reduce the strength of a structural element below its critical load. In other words, the steeper the post-buckling curve the greater will be the imperfection sensitivity of the member and the farther below the critical load will be the maximum load that the member can support. Using an analysis of this type it can be shown that axially compressed cylindrical shells are highly imperfection sensitive. Even very small initial imperfections can cause these shells to fail at loads well below the critical load given by the linear theory.

Prior to 1960, the conclusion that initial imperfections are responsible for the discrepancy between linear theory and actual buckling loads was based primarily on theoretical studies. However, in recent years experimental verification of the role that imperfections play has been obtained as well. Tennyson (1964) and several other investigators, by exercising extreme care, have for the first time been able to manufacture near perfect shells and thus minimise the effect of initial imperfections. Using these nearly imperfection-free shells, they were able to obtain experimental buckling loads that are close to the critical load predicted by linear theory.

Two additional aspects of the behaviour of axially compressed

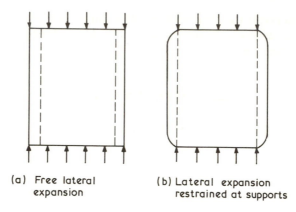

(a) Free lateral expansion   (b) Lateral expansion restrained at supports

Fig. 1.4.   Pre-buckling deformations.

cylindrical shells should be considered. These are the effect of pre-buckling deformations and the effect of boundary conditions. The linear theory of cylindrical shells assumes that only membrane stresses and no bending stresses exist in the shell prior to buckling. This assumption implies that the shell is free to expand laterally along its entire length prior to buckling and will consequently have the shape shown in Fig. 1.4a. Actually, however, cylindrical shells are usually prevented from expanding at their ends by the supports. As a consequence the shape of the shell is as shown in Fig. 1.4b and bending stresses do exist prior to buckling. It has been shown that the effect of these pre-buckling bending stresses is small and that their omission in the classical linear theory is therefore not a primary reason for the difference between the predictions of that theory and actual collapse loads.

Regarding the effect of boundary conditions on the behaviour of axially compressed cylindrical shells, it was previously mentioned that eqn (1.6) is valid for all edge conditions. This statement is correct with one exception. The linear theory which leads to eqn (1.6) tacitly assumes zero displacements at the edges not only in a direction normal to the shell but also in the tangential direction. It has been shown by Almroth (1966) that cylinders, whose edges are free to move in the tangential direction, buckle at a stress one half as large as that given by eqn (1.6). Since this edge condition rarely exists in actual shells, initial imperfections and not boundary conditions are believed to be responsible for the discrepancy between classical theory and test results.

Many aspects of the theory of axially compressed cylinders referred to above are reviewed in survey articles by Hoff (1966) and Hutchinson and Koiter (1970).

1.4 STIFFENED SHELLS

Cylindrical shells are often stiffened by the use of axial or ring stiffeners as shown in Fig. 1.5. Whereas unstiffened shells of intermediate length always fail by local buckling of the shell surface, stiffened shells can fail either by local buckling of the shell between stiffeners or by overall buckling, in which case both shell and stiffener buckle together.

The specific effects that stiffeners have on the buckling behaviour of axially compressed cylindrical shells is relatively complex. As a consequence it is difficult to summarise the behaviour of these shells in a concise and straight-forward manner. Nevertheless, the research that has been carried out during the past two decades allows one to note certain general behaviour patterns. Based on the work of Singer *et al.* (1967) and that of Hutchinson and Amazigo (1967), it is apparent that longitudinal stringers are more effective than ring stiffeners in increasing the strength of axially compressed cylinders. Whereas longitudinally stiffened cylinders may buckle at loads in the vicinity of the classical buckling load, cylinders with ring stiffeners tend to buckle at

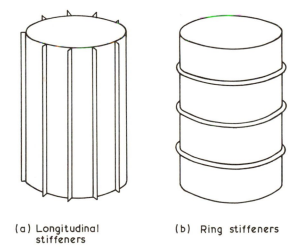

(a) Longitudinal   (b) Ring stiffeners
stiffeners

FIG. 1.5. Stiffened cylinders.

loads well below the linear critical load. Singer *et al.* (1967) do point out that ring stiffeners become more effective when used in conjunction with longitudinal stiffeners.

One of the most significant observations regarding the behaviour of longitudinally stiffened cylindrical shells subject to axial compression was made by van der Neut (1947). Using a theoretical analysis he discovered that shells with stiffeners attached to their outer surface exhibited buckling loads twice as large as those obtained for similar shells with the stiffeners attached to the inside of the shell. This superiority of outside stiffened shells over inside stiffened ones has since been verified experimentally. The difficulty in applying the above conclusion is that the behaviour of stiffened shells varies considerably with changes in the geometry of the shell. For example, Singer *et al.* (1967) show that whereas outside stiffened shells are twice as strong as inside stiffened shells at $Z = 300$, the former are only 20 per cent stronger than the latter at $Z = 3000$.

1.5 DESIGN CRITERIA

The behaviour of real shells deviates from that predicted by linear theory mainly because of the presence of initial imperfections of shape and inelastic stresses. A procedure commonly employed in the formulation of design criteria is to take the critical load of the elastic, initially perfect shell and to modify this relation by employing knockdown factors that account for initial imperfections and inelastic behaviour. Whereas the critical load can be obtained using theoretical calculations, the effects of initial imperfections and inelastic behaviour usually require the use of at least some experimental results. As a consequence, design criteria are as a rule semi-empirical in nature.

Making use of eqn (1.6), the local buckling stress of an unstiffened cylinder can be written in the form

$$\sigma_f = \frac{\eta CE}{(R/t)} \tag{1.8}$$

in which σ_f = the stress at which a real shell fails because of buckling, η = a plasticity reduction factor, and C = a knockdown factor that accounts for initial imperfections.

In the 1950s, Donnell and Wan (1950), using a theoretical analysis, demonstrated that C decreases with increasing values of R/t, as shown

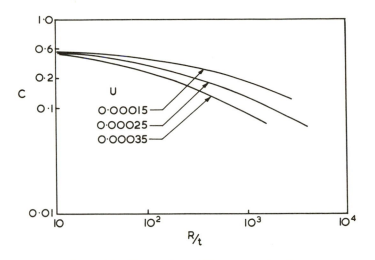

FIG. 1.6. Donnell and Wan curves for C.

in Fig. 1.6. It is evident from these results that the reduction in the failure load of the shell caused by initial imperfections increases as the shell becomes thinner. In other words thin shells are more imperfection sensitive than thick shells. Donnell and Wan (1950) also found that C decreases as the magnitude of the imperfection increases, the parameter U in Fig. 1.6 being proportional to the size of the imperfection. Numerous experimental investigations have since been carried out and their results are in general agreement with the theory developed by Donnell and Wan. Based on one such experimental study, Clark and Rolf (1964) obtained the following empirical relation for C:

$$C = \frac{0 \cdot 612}{[1 + 0 \cdot 02\sqrt{(2R/t)}]^2} \tag{1.9}$$

Gerard (1956) indicates that several investigators, using both theory and experiments, have concluded that a suitable plasticity reduction factor for axially compressed cylinders is

$$\eta = \frac{\sqrt{(E_s/E_t)}}{E} \tag{1.10}$$

in which $E_s =$ the secant modulus and $E_t =$ the tangent modulus.

Although C given by eqn (1.9) is relatively easy to obtain, the use of eqn (1.10) to calculate η requires either a trial and error process or a separate design curve for every variation in material properties caused by changes in alloys or residual stresses. As a consequence most specifications have chosen not to employ eqns (1.8), (1.9) and (1.10). Some, like the AISI specification (AISI, 1968), rely almost entirely on empirical data, while others, such as the ASME and ECCS (ECCS, 1981) specifications, combine both theory and experimental results.

1.5.1 AISI Design Criteria

One of the most commonly employed design criteria for local buckling of unstiffened shells made from sharp yielding steel is the empirically obtained Plantema relation depicted in Fig. 1.7. Based on a systematic evaluation of a large number of tests, Plantema determined that the ratio of the failure stress to the yield stress σ_f/σ_y can be expressed as a function of the parameter $\alpha = (E/\sigma_y)(t/D)$. The resulting design curve consists of three linear segments as shown in the figure. The first of these, which corresponds to elastic buckling, is given by the equation

$$\frac{\sigma_f}{\sigma_y} = 0.33\alpha \qquad \alpha < 2.5 \qquad (1.11)$$

If the expression for α given in the foregoing paragraph is substituted

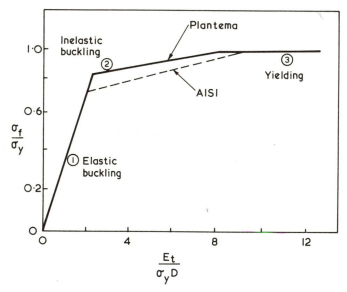

FIG. 1.7. Plantema and AISI design criteria.

into eqn (1.11), it can be rewritten in the form

$$\sigma_f = 0 \cdot 165 Et/R \qquad (1.12)$$

Comparison of eqn (1.12) with eqn (1.8) indicates that the two are identical if in eqn (1.8) η is equated to unity and C is taken as $0 \cdot 165$. The value of C used in eqn (1.12), namely $0 \cdot 165$, is in good agreement with the value of C given by the Donnell and Wan curve, in Fig. 1.6, for thin shells with large R/t ratios. It is of course in this range of R/t values that elastic buckling occurs.

The second line in Fig. 1.7 corresponds to inelastic buckling. It can be expressed analytically as

$$\frac{\sigma_f}{\sigma_y} = 0 \cdot 75 + 0 \cdot 031 \alpha \qquad 2 \cdot 5 < \alpha < 8 \cdot 0 \qquad (1.13)$$

This expression is entirely empirical and no theoretical relation exists with which it can be compared.

When α exceeds $8 \cdot 0$, failure takes place as a result of yielding and not because of buckling. This range of behaviour is represented by the third line segment in the figure.

The dashed line in Fig. 1.7 represents the design criteria recommended by the American Iron and Steel Specifications for inelastic buckling (AISI, 1968). It is evident that the AISI design criteria are somewhat more conservative than the Plantema expression. The AISI curve is given by the expression

$$\frac{\sigma_f}{\sigma_y} = 0 \cdot 665 + 0 \cdot 368 \alpha \qquad 2 \cdot 17 < \alpha < 9 \cdot 1 \qquad (1.14)$$

The AISI specifications make no recommendations for elastic buckling. It can be inferred from this that very few steel tubes are thin enough to fall into the elastic range.

1.5.2 Aluminium Design Criteria

Clark and Rolf (1964) propose the following design procedure for unstiffened aluminium alloy shells. In the elastic range the buckling stress is given by eqn (1.8) with $\eta = 1 \cdot 0$. In the inelastic range the buckling stress can be obtained from

$$\sigma_f = B_t - D_t(R/t)^{1/2} \qquad (1.15)$$

in which

$$B_t = \sigma_2 \left[1 + 4.6 \left(\frac{1000\sigma_2}{E} \right)^{0.2} \left(\frac{\sigma_2}{\sigma_1} - 1 \right) \right] \qquad (1.16)$$

and

$$D_t = \frac{B_t}{0.9} \left(\frac{B_t}{E} \right)^{1/3} \left(\frac{\sigma_2}{\sigma_1} - 1 \right)^{1/2} \qquad (1.17)$$

The quantities σ_1 and σ_2 are the values of the compressive yield strength at 0·1 and 0·2% offset respectively. In order to avoid inelastic design curves that do not intersect the elastic design curve, the ratio σ_2/σ_1 is taken to be 1·06 for those cases where the actual ratio exceeds this value. One of the advantages of the design criteria given by eqns (1.15), (1.16) and (1.17) is that they are given in a form which makes them applicable to materials other than aluminium alloys. Before these expressions are used in this manner it would, however, be prudent to obtain some experimental verification.

Both the design criteria given by AISI for steel cylinders and those recommended by Clark and Rolf for aluminium alloy shells are limited to local buckling of unstiffened cylinders. The reason for not considering stiffened shells is that these design criteria are meant to be applied to thin-walled tubes which, unlike large-diameter shells, are not reinforced with stiffeners. However, owing to the fact that the walls of these tubes are relatively thin, they fail by local buckling of the surface and not by column buckling, and are consequently considered in this chapter.

1.5.3 ECCS Design Criteria

The design curve depicted in Fig. 1.8 is recommended by the European Convention for Constructional Steelwork (ECCS, 1981). It applies to local buckling of unstiffened cylindrical shells.

If $\alpha\sigma_{cr} < \frac{1}{2}\sigma_y$, buckling takes place in the elastic range and the failure stress is given by

$$\sigma_f = 0.75\alpha\sigma_{cr} \qquad (1.18)$$

For $\alpha\sigma_{cr} \geq \frac{1}{2}\sigma_y$, buckling occurs in the inelastic range and the failure stress is

$$\sigma_f = \sigma_y \left[1 - 0.4123 \left(\frac{\sigma_y}{\alpha\sigma_{cr}} \right)^{0.6} \right] \qquad (1.19)$$

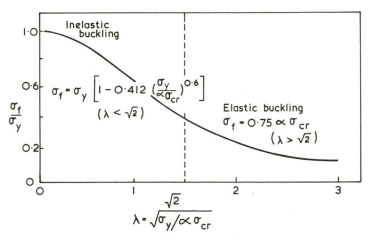

FIG. 1.8. ECCS design criteria.

In these expressions σ_{cr} = the critical stress and α = a reduction factor which accounts for initial imperfections. The following expressions for α have been obtained by using a lower bound for a larger number of test results

$$\alpha = \frac{0\cdot83}{(1+0\cdot01R/t)} \qquad R/t < 212 \qquad (1.20)$$

$$\alpha = \frac{0\cdot70}{(0\cdot1+0\cdot01R/t)} \qquad R/t > 212 \qquad (1.21)$$

The elastic buckling criterion given by eqn (1.18) is similar to that recommended by most specifications in that the failure stress is obtained by applying a knockdown factor α, which accounts for initial imperfections, to the critical stress. As is done with the corresponding factor C for aluminium alloy shells in Section 1.5.2, α is expressed as a function of R/t. By comparison, the Plantema criterion in Section 1.5.1 ignores the variation of C with R/t and uses a single value of C for the entire elastic range.

The ECCS criterion differs from other design recommendations in that it takes cognisance of the fact that α varies with the magnitude of the initial imperfections. This is accomplished by limiting the applicability of the design criterion to a given range of imperfection magnitudes. A second difference between the ECCS design relationships and those given by other specifications is that ECCS applies a reduction factor, in addition to α, to the failure load. This factor, which is equal to 0·75 in the elastic range and varies from 0·75 to 0 for the inelastic range, accounts for the high imperfection sensitivity displayed by the axially compressed shells. The factor is larger for elastic buckling than for inelastic buckling because thin shells are more imperfection sensitive than thick ones.

1.5.4 ASME Design Criteria

The following design criteria for steel shells were developed by Miller (1981) and his associates, and are currently being used by the American Society of Mechanical Engineers. They apply to stiffened as well as unstiffened shells. Whereas unstiffened shells always fail by local buckling, stiffened shells can fail either by local buckling of the shell between stiffeners or by overall buckling of both shell and stiffeners.

Local Buckling

The local buckling stress for stiffened or unstiffened shells is given by

$$\sigma_f = \eta \alpha \sigma_{cr} \tag{1.22}$$

in which σ_{cr} = the critical stress, η = a plasticity reduction factor, and α = a knockdown factor that accounts for initial imperfections.

To determine α the larger of the values given by eqns (1.23) or eqns (1.24) is used

$$
\begin{aligned}
&\alpha = 0·207 && R/t > 600 \\
&\alpha = 1·52 - 0·473 \log_{10}(R/t) && \left.\begin{array}{l}\text{Use smaller value} \\ \text{for } R/t < 600\end{array}\right. \\
&\alpha = 300(\sigma_y/E) - 0·033 &&
\end{aligned}
\tag{1.23}
$$

$$
\begin{aligned}
&\alpha = 0·826/(M)^{0·6} && 1·73 < M < 10 \\
&\alpha = 0·207 && M > 10
\end{aligned}
\tag{1.24}
$$

in which $M = L/\sqrt{(Rt)}$.

The plasticity reduction factor, η, is given by

$$
\begin{aligned}
&\eta = 1·0 && \Delta < 0·55 \\
&\eta = \frac{0·45}{\Delta} + 0·18 && 0·55 < \Delta < 1·6 \\
&\eta = \frac{1·31}{1·0 + 1·15\Delta} < \frac{1}{\Delta} && \Delta > 1·6
\end{aligned}
\tag{1.25}
$$

in which $\Delta = \alpha\sigma_{cr}/\sigma_y$.

Overall Buckling

The stress at which a ring-stiffened cylinder fails because of combined buckling of shell and stiffeners is given by

$$\sigma_f = \sigma_{crs}\alpha_s\eta \qquad (1.26)$$

in which σ_{crs} = the critical stress of a ring-stiffened cylinder, α_s = a knockdown factor that accounts for initial imperfections in ring-stiffened cylinders, and η = a plasticity reduction factor.

The knockdown factor α_s is given by

$$
\begin{aligned}
\alpha_s &= 0.72 & A &> 0.2 \\
\alpha_s &= (3.6 - 5.0\alpha)A + \alpha & 0.06 &< A < 0.2 \\
\alpha_s &= \alpha & A &< 0.06
\end{aligned}
\qquad (1.27)
$$

in which $A = A_r/L_r t$, A_r = area of ring stiffener, L_r = distance between ring stiffeners, and α is obtained from eqns (1.23) or (1.24).

The critical stress of a ring-stiffened cylinder is given by

$$\sigma_{crs} = 0.6E\frac{t}{R}\left(1 + \frac{A_r}{L_r t}\right)^{1/2} \qquad (1.28)$$

The plasticity reduction factor η is independent of loading or geometry and is obtained from eqn (1.25).

1.6 CONCLUSIONS

Aside from relatively minor differences, the design criteria presented in the previous sections all adhere to the same general pattern. In each instance, the failure stress is obtained by means of a semi-empirical relationship which incorporates the critical stress and knockdown factors that account for initial imperfections and inelastic behaviour. The critical stress is obtained from theoretical calculations while the knockdown factors are based on experimental results.

In most instances the factor used to account for the effects of initial imperfections varies inversely with the parameter R/t. In other words, the thinner the shell, the greater the reduction in carrying capacity due to initial imperfections. This is of course the conclusion that Donnell and Wan arrived at in their pioneering study, the results of which are depicted in Fig. 1.6. A second conclusion formed by Donnell and Wan was that the failure stress is also reduced as the magnitude of the initial imperfection increases. None of the design criteria considered herein include this factor in their equations. The main reason for this omission appears to be the difficulty of obtaining accurate measurements of initial imperfections. Nevertheless, several specifications are planning to include a factor that accounts for the magnitude of initial imperfections in future revisions of the design equations.

The second knockdown factor, which accounts for the reduction of the failure stress because of inelastic behaviour, varies with the parameter σ_y/σ_{cr}. The larger the ratio σ_y/σ_{cr}, the lower will be the ratio of the failure stress to the critical stress.

The design criteria presented in the preceding sections range from very simple, empirically obtained expressions, like the Plantema curve in Section 1.5.1, to relatively detailed formulations such as the aluminium alloy criteria in Section 1.5.2 and the ASME equations in Section 1.5.4. Since design relations should never be under-conservative, simplifications made by omitting parameters from the governing equations are usually compensated for by making the design criteria more conservative. In other words, the more detailed a design criterion is and the more it explicitly accounts for the variables involved, the less conservative does it have to be. It would thus appear, at first, that the more detailed and consequently the less conservative a design criterion is, the more desirable it is. This is, however, not necessarily true. Design criteria are as a rule used by practising engineers who are not entirely familiar with the theoretical basis of the criteria. As a consequence, involved design relationships are sometimes used incorrectly and this can lead to far more serious problems than slightly over-conservative design.

The most desirable design criterion would thus appear to be the one which accounts for the most important variables in an explicit manner but takes care of the remaining, less significant variables in a conservative empirical fashion.

REFERENCES

AISI (1968) Specification for the design of cold-formed steel structural members. American Iron and Steel Institute.
ALMROTH, B. O. (1966) Influence of edge conditions on the stability of axially compressed cylindrical shells. *American Institute of Aeronautics and Astronautics Journal*, **4**(1), 134–40.

BUDIANSKY, B. and HUTCHINSON, J. W. (1966) A survey of some buckling problems. *American Institute of Aeronautics and Astronautics Journal*, **4**(9), 1510–10.

CLARK, J. W. and ROLF, R. L. (1964) Design of aluminum tubular members. *Journal of Structural Division, ASCE*, **90**(ST3), 259–89.

DONNELL, L. H. and WAN, C. C. (1950) Effects of imperfections on buckling of thin cylinders and columns under axial compression. *Journal of Applied Mechanics*, **17**, 73.

ECCS (1981) European Recommendations for Steel Construction, Buckling of Shells, Section 4.6. European Convention for Constructional Steelwork.

GERARD, G. (1956) Compressive and Torsional Buckling of Thin-walled Cylinders in Yield Region. NACA, Technical Note 3726.

HOFF, N. J. (1966) The perplexing behavior of thin circular cylindrical shells in axial compression. *Israel Journal of Technology*, **4**(1), 1–28.

HUTCHINSON, J. W. and AMAZIGO, J. C. (1967) Imperfection sensitivity of eccentrically stiffened cylindrical shells. *American Institute of Aeronautics and Astronautics Journal*, **5**, 392–401.

HUTCHINSON, J. W. and KOITER, W. T. (1970) Post-buckling theory. *Applied Mechanics Reviews*, **23**, 1353–66.

KARMAN, T. von and TSIEN, H. S. (1941) The buckling of thin cylindrical shells under axial compression. *Journal of the Aeronautical Sciences*, **8**, 43–50.

KOITER, W. T. (1945) On the stability of elastic equilibrium, Thesis, Technical High School Delft, J. H. Paris, Amsterdam, The Netherlands.

MILLER, C. D. (1981) Buckling design methods for steel structures, a state of the art. *Integrity of Offshore Structures*, Proc. Second International Symposium, Glasgow, Scotland, July 1981, (Ed. by D. Faulkner, M. J. Cowling and P. A. Frieze), Applied Science Publishers, London.

SINGER, J., BARUCH, M. and HARARI, O. (1967) On the stability of eccentrically stiffened cylindrical shells under axial compression. *International Journal of Solids and Structures*, **3**, 445–470.

TENNYSON, R. C. (1964) An Experimental Investigation of the Buckling of Circular Cylindrical Shells in Axial Compression Using the Photoelastic Technique, Institute of Aerospace Sciences, University of Toronto, Report No. 102, Toronto, Canada.

VAN DER NEUT, A. (1947) General Instability of Stiffened Cylindrical Shells under Axial Compression, Report S-314, National Luchvaart Laboratory, Amsterdam, The Netherlands.

Chapter 2

STIFFENED CYLINDRICAL SHELLS UNDER AXIAL AND PRESSURE LOADING

JAMES G. A. CROLL

Department of Civil Engineering, University College, London, UK

SUMMARY

A reduced stiffness analysis is used to provide a convenient basis for predicting lower bounds to the elastic non-axisymmetric general buckling of orthotropically stiffened cylinders subjected to arbitrary combinations of axial and pressure loading. An imperfect form of this elastic model is used to provide lower bounds for elastic–plastic collapse. This allows design collapse to be represented in a form closely related to the Ayrton–Perry–Robertson column equation, and provides a simple but rational basis for future design against this form of general buckling collapse.

NOTATION

a_x, a_θ	Coefficients for axial and hoop incremental stresses (cf. eqns (2.26) and (2.32))
d_s, d_r	Depth of stringer and ring stiffeners
e_x, e_θ	Coefficients for axial and hoop fundamental strains (cf. eqn (2.3))
i	Number of circumferential waves in critical mode
j	Number of axial half-waves in critical mode
l	Length of orthotropic cylinder
l_s, l_r	Spacing between adjacent stringers and adjacent rings
m_x, m_θ, m_{x_θ}	Axial, hoop and twist moment stress resultants
n_x, n_θ, n_{x_θ}	Axial, hoop and shear stress resultants

p	External radial pressure loading
r	Radius of midsurface of cylinder skin
s_x, s_θ	Coefficients for axial and hoop fundamental stresses in cylinder plating (skin) (cf. eqn (2.5))
t	Thickness of cylinder plating (skin)
t_{eq}	Thickness of equivalent weight isotropic cylinder
t_s, t_r	Thickness of stringer and ring stiffeners
t_x, t_θ	Average thickness in axial and hoop directions
u, v, w	Midsurface (x, θ, z) displacements in shell plating (skin)
x, z	Axial and surface normal coordinates
A_{ij}	Elements of linear components in eigenvalue matrix eqn (2.11)
C_j	$j = 0, 1, \ldots, 4$ coefficients used in plating yield criterion, eqn (2.34)
E	Modulus of elasticity for shells skin and stiffeners
P	Axial compression force
Q_{ij}	Elements of linearised components in eigenvalue matrix eqn (2.11)
U_{ij}, V_{ij}	Normalised (x, θ) displacements in critical mode (i, j)
U_{2M}, U_{2B}	Strain energy from membrane and bending actions
$\hat{V}_{2M}, \tilde{V}_{2M}$	Linearised strain energies from fundamental stresses and strains
Z_{s_t}, Z_{r_t}	Non-dimensional eccentricity of stringer and ring tips
Z_{s_p}, Z_{r_p}	Non-dimensional eccentricity of cylinder plate surface from stringer and ring
$\alpha_x, \alpha_\theta, \alpha_{x_\theta}$	Orthotropic membrane stiffness coefficients (cf. Fig. 2.1)
α, β	Coefficients defined in eqn (2.35) and approximately in eqn (2.37)
$\beta_x, \beta_\theta, \beta_{x_\theta}$	Orthotropic bending stiffness coefficients (cf. Fig. 2.1)
$\gamma_x, \gamma_\theta, \gamma$	Measures of fundamental membrane axial and hoop stress ratios
$\varepsilon_x, \varepsilon_\theta, \varepsilon_{x_\theta}$	Membrane strains
η_e	Lower bound elastic knockdown factor $(\equiv \sigma_{cm}^*/\sigma_{cm})$
η_{ij}	Modal elastic knockdown factor $(\equiv \sigma_c^*/\sigma_c)$
θ	Circumferential angular coordinate
λ	Non-dimensional axial wave number $(\equiv j\pi r/l)$
Λ	Stress normalised by plastic (squash) stress
μ	Poisson's ratio

$\chi_x, \chi_\theta, \chi_{x_\theta}$ Bending curvature strains
ρ Generalised imperfection parameter
ρ_x, ρ_θ Axial and hoop imperfection parameters
σ Stress parameter ($\equiv \sigma_x^F$ for axial and $\equiv \sigma_\theta^F$ for radial pressure)
σ_p Plastic (squash) stress
σ_x, σ_θ Axial and hoop stresses
σ_y Uniaxial yield stress of stiffener and shell plating

Subscripts

c   Belonging to critical state
cm   Belonging to minimising critical state
eq   Associated with equivalent weight isotropic cylinder
fy   First yield state
ij Belonging to critical mode (i, j)
s, r, p   Associated with stringer, ring, or shell plating
t, p   Yield associated with stiffener tip or shell plate surface
x, θ Associated with axial or hoop direction

Superscripts

$', ''$ Associated with linear or quadratic incremental strain–displacement relation
$(\overline{\ldots})$ Evaluated at orthotropic centroid
*   Associated with reduced stiffness model
F   Belonging to fundamental pre-buckling state
°   Geometric imperfection
s, r, p   Associated with stringer, ring, or shell plating
x, θ Associated with axial or hoop direction

2.1 INTRODUCTION

Cylinders are frequently fabricated with closely spaced longitudinal (stringers) and circumferential (rings) stiffeners. For some load cases, and particularly where radial pressure dominates the loading, there are well-recognised stiffness and strength advantages in adopting ring stiffening. Improved material efficiency in these circumstances may compensate the additional costs involved in forming and fabricating the possibly complex geometric forms. For other loading cases and stiffening geometries, the direct economic benefits of using integrally stiffened cylinders may not be so obvious. There have recently been questions raised concerning the practice of using stringer stiffening to improve the performance of axially loaded cylinders. However, whatever the reasons might be for their adoption, it is apparent that the presence of ring and stringer stiffening greatly complicates the estimation of buckling capacity.

Compared with an equivalent unstiffened cylinder, the buckling of an integrally stiffened cylinder is complicated by the many and varied forms that it might take. Where an incipient buckling mode has wavelengths considerably longer than the inter-stiffener spacing, it is possible to model the stiffened shell as basically an homogeneous and orthotropic system. In this case the so-called 'general buckling' behaviour has a close resemblance to that of the isotropic cylinder. Indeed, as this chapter will show, it is possible to interpret the behaviour of the unstiffened cylinder as but a special case of the characteristics exhibited by orthotropic cylinder buckling. As if this were not difficult enough, the stiffened cylinder has the added complications of permitting many possible forms of 'local buckling' to precipitate collapse. These local modes involve interactions between the shell plating (skin) and the torsional properties of the stiffeners. For systems having fairly squat stiffeners it is the shell plating which is responsible for the major destabilisation in the local modes, whereas for slender stiffeners, it is the local torsional buckling (tripping) which may provide the controlling influence on local buckling.

In reality of course it is not possible to separate the effects of torsional buckling of stiffeners from those of skin buckling, but behaviours dominated by each have their own separate forms of buckling collapse behaviour. That this local buckling is itself a complicated matter may be appreciated by considering what happens between adjacent stiffeners in a ring stiffened shell. This shell plating, while interacting with the torsional properties of the rings, effectively forms an unstiffened cylinder with all its attendant complications.

But even this multitude of different possible forms of buckling mode is not the end of the possible complications. If a general and local buckling were to occur simultaneously a strong and potentially disastrous form of mode interaction may become possible. In this interaction the development of say a local inter-stiffener buckle would significantly weaken the shell's orthotropic stiffness against the longer wavelength general buckling. In turn, the growth of general buckling deformations throws additional membrane forces onto the plating and stiffeners which would accelerate the rate of growth of local deformations. For both reasons the interaction between local and general buckling modes could seriously reduce the characteristic strength and stiffness of the shell system.

It is to avoid these potentially disastrous situations, as well as to avoid our inability to properly analyse them, that design guidance documents usually insist on a wide separation between local and general collapse loads. In proportioning stiffening, ASME (1980), DnV (1981) and ECCS (1983) Rules recommend that these be sufficiently squat that local torsional buckling (tripping) effects would become important only at loads well above the characteristic strength. In contrast, the local plate (skin) buckling is made to control design for pressure loaded ring stiffened cylinders by insisting that the general collapse strength is many times greater than the local strength (see BS 5500, 1982). Although the philosophy adopted shows considerable variability, the effects are usually the same: namely, to ensure that no strong interaction between local and general modes is possible. Only rarely does a recommended design approach allow the local and general collapse modes to occur nearly simultaneously, and where this is permitted · (ASME, 1980) an allowance is made for the effects coming from interactive buckling.

Whether design is based upon a policy of avoiding local–general interaction, or whether it is based upon an analysis of its effects, it is imperative that methods should be available to designers so that they may properly estimate the resistance to general collapse modes.

This chapter is concerned with the prediction of elastic–plastic collapse for arbitrary axial and pressure load buckling into general modes that have a non-axisymmetric form. As the method described includes isotropic cylinder buckling as a special case of orthotropic cylinder buckling, the treatment allows consideration of local buckling between adjacent ring stiffeners. It does not, however, include local buckling between stringer stiffeners, nor does it include general buckling into axisymmetric modes.

2.2 APPROACHES TO THE ANALYSIS OF GENERAL COLLAPSE

Much of the current theoretical work on buckling of cylindrical shell components is focused on the use of large-scale numerical facilities. An aim of these works is to reproduce test results with such accuracy that numerical experimentation could eventually be accepted as providing an alternative to the relatively more costly physical testing of these components. Clearly the prospect of being able to use this inherently more controllable form of empirical approach has considerable attraction. But it must be admitted that the degree of reliability so far achieved by these computer-based algorithms certainly does not warrant the degree of optimism that many presently invest in them. For a number of important classes of behaviour, and especially where dimensions are such that elastic buckling deformations have an important controlling influence upon collapse, numerical solutions are manifestly incapable of reproducing physical observation.

For what is probably the most densely researched topic of shell buckling, that of the axially loaded isotropic cylinder, it is still probably safe to assert that none of the many large-scale numerical codes available to designers can satisfactorily account for elastic buckling behaviour, especially where initial imperfections are moderately large. For example, the independent observations of Arbocz and Babcock (1969), Arbocz and Sechler (1974) and those at University College London (Batista, 1979; Batista and Croll, 1979a), show that the mode which is amplified just prior to buckling of axially loaded cylinders has a shape consisting of a single axial half-wave and a well-defined circumferential wavenumber. This characteristic circumferential wavenumber is determined by the shell geometry and support conditions rather than the precise imperfection geometry. It contrasts strongly with the short axial wavelength modes that are characteristic of the advanced post-buckled configurations; and yet, numerical analyses do not appear to have been able to capture this essential feature of buckling behaviour.

Since it is this long axial wavelength triggering mode that largely controls the form of the short wavelength post-buckled dimples, it follows that, equally, there has been no satisfactory explanation of their characteristic shape. Naturally, a very lightly stiffened cylinder would be expected to show buckling characteristics similar to those of the unstiffened cylinder. Yet the fact that lightly stiffened cylinders buckle into long axial wavelength general collapse modes, and therefore apparently display discontinuities of behaviour with their unstiffened counterparts, also remains unaccounted for in purely numerical simulations. Certainly, there would not yet appear to be a case for supplanting the present reliance on physical empiricism with an inevitably less certain form of numerical empiricism.

But even when numerical solutions allow more accurate reproduction of physical tests, there will remain considerable problems for design based upon purely numerical empiricism. How, for example, will the results be summarised for designers? One of the reasons for seeking numerically based design curves is that instead of just one or two curves as at present, it may be possible to sharpen-up on the relative importance of all the parameters that affect buckling collapse. At one extreme this could mean that designers will be faced with many hundreds of tables and figures showing all the different parametric relationships; for the numbers of apparently independent geometric, material, imperfection, boundary support, etc., variables involved in the buckling of orthotropically stiffened cylinders, not to mention the differences arising from variations in combined loading, such a document could be very large indeed, while at the other extreme design documents may increasingly be found to incorporate clauses exhorting designers to base calculations on some suitably validated numerical code. As an indication of the adequacy of these two extremes it is only necessary to contemplate how much less satisfactory would be beam design were it based on either of these approaches without the unifying framework of engineering beam theory.

There are clear signs that what is now required in shell buckling design is the equivalent of engineering beam theory. This would provide a more effective framework for interpreting physical test data, and also numerical test data when they are proven sufficiently reliable. Adoption of classical shell buckling theory as the unifying framework is proving problematic on account of the extreme difficulties of adequately accounting for the effects of geometric imperfections. For this reason much of our own recent work has been directed towards the evolution of an alternative to, or at least modification of, classical theory. The resulting 'reduced stiffness theory' allows parameters affecting buckling collapse to be explicitly delineated, and automatically provides a safe but reliable assessment of the knockdowns produced by practical levels of tolerance control. It could provide the equivalent of engineering beam theory for shell buckling. But like beam design it would provide only the parametric framework, and for adoption in design practice would need to be calibrated against physical tests, and eventually, perhaps, numerical tests.

The following sections outline the essential features of the reduced stiffness philosophy, for the specification of both elastic and elastic–plastic knockdown factors for the general buckling of orthotropic stiffened cylinders. Because the method has already been extensively described and compared with test data by the author and his colleagues (Batista, 1979; Batista and Croll, 1979a,b; Croll, 1981; Ellinas *et al.*, 1981) the presentation takes on a summarised and descriptive form rather than validatary tone. Among other important features the method shows that isotropic cylinder buckling emerges as merely a special case of orthotropic cylinder buckling. Furthermore, initiation of elastic–plastic collapse is shown to be representable in a highly compact form closely related to the Ayrton–Perry–Robertson formulation for columns.

2.3 ELASTIC BUCKLING

One aspect of buckling behaviour that most rotationally symmetric shells have in common is that elastic deformations about their classic critical states are unstable. In a practical context this means that the buckling has a high degree of sensitivity to imperfections in the form of the gravest of the critical modes, to the extent that the buckling loads often possess little direct relationship with the classical critical loads. Of course it is towards trying to elucidate the analytically complicated relationship between the critical loads and these imperfection-sensitive buckling loads that has preoccupied much of classical elastic buckling research.

However, fortunately, the physics underlying this highly complex behaviour is often more straightforward than its detailed analysis. Basically, the loss of stiffness in the post-buckled response of cylinders is all to do with the loss of the initial stabilising membrane stiffness of the shell. As is well known, the shell derives many of its inherent advantages from the presence of this membrane stiffness (or energy). It plays the crucial role of forcing the shell to take-up short wavelength buckling modes, within which the bending resistance is considerably increased over and above that in the longer wavelengths characteristic of equivalent flat structures. In addition, the membrane energy usually provides a significant additional stiffness contribution within these short wavelength modes. It is these influences of membrane energy that give the shell its weight-for-weight advantage over, say, an equivalent flat-plate structure. But equally, it is the presence of the membrane energy in the initial stabilisation of the shell that is responsible for its subsequent loss of stiffness in the post-buckled regime. For it is the erosion of this initial membrane stiffness in the buckling mode that allows imperfect shells to buckle at loads so much less than the classical critical loads.

As lower bound to the potential loss of stiffness in a given critical mode would be a shell modelled in such a way that those membrane energy components at risk, due to the combined effects of imperfections and mode coupling, are simply eliminated. It is this 'reduced stiffness model' that will be used in the following analysis as an adjunct to classical theory for the specification of safe elastic buckling loads for design formulations.

2.3.1 Design Analysis for Upper Bounds

For an orthotropically stiffened cylinder, with geometric notation and sign convention indicated in Fig. 2.1, a fundamental pre-buckled state may be approximated in terms of the average membrane stresses $(\sigma_x^F, \sigma_\theta^F)$ given as

$$\sigma_x^F = \gamma_x \sigma = n_x^F/t_x$$
$$\sigma_\theta^F = \gamma_\theta \sigma = n_\theta^F/t_\theta \tag{2.1}$$

where the average thicknesses (t_x, t_θ) in the (x, θ) coordinate directions

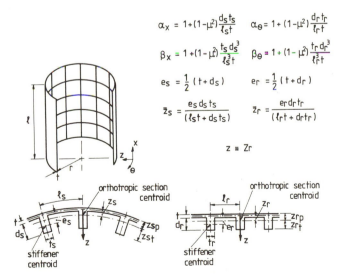

FIG. 2.1. Notation and convention for geometry of orthotropically stiffened cylinders.

are

$$t_x = t + \frac{d_s t_s}{l_s}$$

$$t_\theta = t + \frac{d_r t_r}{l_r}$$

Stress σ is a characterising stress, the choice of which will govern the relative stress ratios $(\gamma_x, \gamma_\theta)$. If, for example, the axial stress is dominant, then $\gamma_x = 1$ would be the appropriate choice, whereas for pressure dominated loading $\gamma_\theta = 1$ might be more suitable. In either case the ratios $(\gamma_x, \gamma_\theta)$ would allow arbitrary combinations of axial compression, P, and radial pressure, p, to be defined such that

$$\frac{\gamma_x}{\gamma_\theta} = \frac{P}{2\pi r^2 p} \frac{t_\theta}{t_x} \tag{2.2}$$

These averaged, or nominal, stresses would not represent the stresses actually occurring in either the shell plating or the stiffeners. On the assumption of uniform membrane strains throughout the orthotropic sections, the fundamental axial and hoop strains would be

$$\varepsilon_x^F = \frac{(\alpha_\theta \gamma_x t_x - \mu \gamma_\theta t_\theta)(1 - \mu^2)}{(\alpha_x \alpha_\theta - \mu^2)t} \left(\frac{\sigma}{E}\right) \equiv e_x \left(\frac{\sigma}{E}\right)$$

$$\varepsilon_\theta^F = \frac{(\alpha_x \gamma_\theta t_\theta - \mu \gamma_x t_x)(1 - \mu^2)}{(\alpha_x \alpha_\theta - \mu^2)t} \left(\frac{\sigma}{E}\right) \equiv e_\theta \left(\frac{\sigma}{E}\right) \tag{2.3}$$

with the uniform stresses in the stringers and rings given, respectively, as

$$\sigma_{x_s}^F = E\varepsilon_x^F = e_x \sigma$$

$$\sigma_{\theta_r}^F = E\varepsilon_\theta^F = e_\theta \sigma \tag{2.4}$$

and those for the plating

$$\sigma_{x_p}^F = \frac{E}{(1 - \mu^2)}(\varepsilon_x^F + \mu\varepsilon_\theta^F) = \frac{(e_x + \mu e_\theta)}{(1 - \mu^2)}\sigma \equiv s_x \sigma$$

$$\sigma_{\theta_p}^F = \frac{E}{(1 - \mu^2)}(\varepsilon_\theta^F + \mu\varepsilon_x^F) = \frac{(e_\theta + \mu e_x)}{(1 - \mu^2)}\sigma \equiv s_\theta \sigma \tag{2.5}$$

For a perfect shell undergoing no bending deformations it would be these stiffener and plating stresses of eqns (2.4) and (2.5) that would control 'squash' collapse. This is treated in eqns (2.23) and (2.24).

Classical elastic critical loads can be formulated in terms of the quadratic form for the change in total potential energy

$$V_2 = U_{2B} + U_{2M} + \tilde{V}^x_{2M} + \tilde{\tilde{V}}^x_{2M} + \tilde{V}^\theta_{2M} + \tilde{\tilde{V}}^\theta_{2M} \qquad (2.6)$$

about the perfect membrane fundamental state. In this quadratic form the linear bending and membrane stiffnesses are represented by their quadratic strain energies (U_{2B}, U_{2M}); in any mode they will both contribute positive stiffness, or equivalently positive energy of resistance, to critical deformations. Destabilisation is produced by the linearised stiffness terms $(V^x_{2M}, V^\theta_{2M})$ which represent the interactions between the fundamental stresses and strains and the first non-linear contributions to the incremental stresses and strains. This interaction has been described in greater details by Batista (1979), Ellinas et al. (1981) and Croll and Ellinas (1983), where it has been pointed out that these linearised membrane stiffness terms (or strictly quadratised membrane energy terms) are part of the non-linear membrane energy.

For simplicity, the following analysis is based upon a Donnell–von Karman type approximate shell theory, for which the membrane strain displacement relations are taken in the form

$$\varepsilon_x \equiv \varepsilon'_x + \varepsilon''_x \qquad \varepsilon'_x = \frac{\partial u}{\partial x} \qquad \varepsilon''_x = \frac{1}{2}\left(\frac{\partial w}{\partial x}\right)^2$$

$$\varepsilon_\theta \equiv \varepsilon'_\theta + \varepsilon''_\theta \qquad \varepsilon'_\theta = \frac{1}{r}\left(\frac{\partial v}{\partial \theta} - w\right) \qquad \varepsilon''_\theta = \frac{1}{2r^2}\left(\frac{\partial w}{\partial \theta}\right)^2 \qquad (2.7a)$$

$$\varepsilon_{x\theta} \equiv \varepsilon'_{x\theta} \qquad \varepsilon'_{x\theta} = \frac{1}{2}\left(\frac{\partial v}{\partial x} + \frac{1}{r}\frac{\partial u}{\partial \theta}\right)$$

and those for bending as

$$\chi'_x = \frac{\partial^2 w}{\partial x^2} \qquad \chi'_\theta = \frac{1}{r^2}\frac{\partial^2 w}{\partial \theta^2} \qquad \chi'_{x\theta} = \frac{1}{r}\frac{\partial^2 w}{\partial x\,\partial \theta} \qquad (2.7b)$$

The single prime indicates that the strain or stress comes from the linear part of the strain–displacement relation, while a double prime denotes a quadratic relation. These strains and displacements are measured at the midsurface of the shell plating, so that membrane strains at the centre of bending for the orthotropic section are given by

$$\bar{\varepsilon}_x = \varepsilon_x - z_s\chi'_x \qquad \bar{\varepsilon}_\theta = \varepsilon_\theta - z_r\chi'_\theta \qquad (2.8)$$

On this basis the individual contributions to the total potential energy eqn (2.6) are

$$U_{2M} = \frac{1}{2} \int_0^l \int_0^{2\pi} [\overline{n'_x \varepsilon'_x} + \overline{n'_\theta \varepsilon'_\theta} + 2\overline{n'_{x\theta} \varepsilon'_{x\theta}}] r \, d\theta \, dx$$

$$U_{2B} = \frac{1}{2} \int_0^l \int_0^{2\pi} [\overline{m'_x \chi'_x} + \overline{m'_\theta \chi'_\theta} + \overline{(m'_{x\theta} + m'_{\theta x}) \chi'_{\theta x}}] r \, d\theta \, dx$$

$$\tilde{V}_{2M}^x = \frac{1}{2} \int_0^l \int_0^{2\pi} \overline{n_x^F \varepsilon''_x} r \, d\theta \, dx \qquad \tilde{\tilde{V}}_{2M}^x = \frac{1}{2} \int_0^l \int_0^{2\pi} \overline{n''_x \varepsilon_x^F} r \, d\theta \, dx \quad (2.9)$$

$$\tilde{V}_{2M}^\theta = \frac{1}{2} \int_0^l \int_0^{2\pi} \overline{n_\theta^F \varepsilon''_\theta} r \, d\theta \, dx \qquad \tilde{\tilde{V}}_{2M}^\theta = \frac{1}{2} \int_0^l \int_0^{2\pi} \overline{n''_\theta \varepsilon_\theta^F} r \, d\theta \, dx$$

where the overbar implies that the terms are evaluated at the ortho-tropic centroids.

For incremental deformation of the form

$$u = u_{ij} \cos j\pi x/l \cos i\theta$$
$$v = v_{ij} \sin j\pi x/l \sin i\theta \qquad (2.10)$$
$$w = w_{ij} \sin j\pi x/l \cos i\theta$$

stationarity of the total potential energy of eqn (2.6) corresponds with the eigenvalues of the equation

$$[A]\{u\} - \left(\frac{\sigma_c}{E}\right)[Q]\{u\} = 0 \qquad (2.11)$$

where σ_c is the critical reference stress, $\{u\}^T \equiv \{u_{ij}, v_{ij}, w_{ij}\}$ is the critical mode, and $[A]$, $[Q]$ are symmetric 3×3 matrices defined by the non-zero coefficients

$$A_{11} = \alpha_x \lambda^2 + \frac{\alpha_{x\theta}}{2} (1 - \mu) i^2$$

$$A_{12} = -\frac{\alpha_{x\theta}}{2} (1 - \mu) i\lambda = A_{21}$$

$$A_{13} = \mu\lambda - \alpha_x Z_s \lambda^3 = A_{31} \qquad (2.12)$$

$$A_{22} = \alpha_\theta i^2 + \frac{\alpha_{x\theta}}{2} (1 - \mu) \lambda^2$$

$$A_{23} = -\alpha_\theta i + Z_r i^3 = A_{32}$$

$$A_{33} = [\alpha_x Z_s^2 \lambda^4 + \alpha_\theta (1 - Z_r i^2)^2] + \frac{1}{\alpha} [\beta_x \lambda^4 + 2\mu i^2 \lambda^2 + \beta_\theta i^4$$

$$+ (\beta_{x\theta} + \beta_{\theta x})(1 - \mu^2) i^2 \lambda^2]$$

$$\equiv A_{33}'' + A_{33}'$$

$$Q_{33} = \frac{1}{2} \left[(\alpha_x \lambda^2 + \mu i^2) \varepsilon_x^F + \frac{\lambda^2 n_x^F}{K} + \frac{i^2 n_\theta}{K} \right]$$

$$+ \left[\frac{1}{2} (\alpha_\theta i^2 + \mu \lambda^2) \varepsilon_\theta^F \right]$$

$$= Q_{33}' + Q_{33}''$$

for a mode having j axial half-waves and i circumferential waves. Orthotropic membrane and bending stiffness parameters are derived by Ellinas and Croll (1981) and Ellinas $et\ al.$ (1981) and are specified in Fig. 2.1. Where local buckling between stiffeners occurs these coefficients may be adjusted to allow for the loss of effective flange width. Solution of the first two equations of eqn (2.11) allows specification of the normalised eigen-mode

$$u_{ij} = \frac{(A_{12} A_{23} - A_{13} A_{22})}{(A_{11} A_{22} - A_{12}^2)} \cdot w_{ij} \equiv U_{ij} w_{ij}$$

$$v_{ij} = \frac{(A_{13} A_{12} - A_{23} A_{11})}{(A_{11} A_{22} - A_{12}^2)} \cdot w_{ij} \equiv V_{ij} w_{ij}$$

(2.13)

which upon substitution in the third of eqns (2.11) permit the associated critical stress to be represented as

$$\frac{\sigma_c}{E} = \frac{\{A_{33}' + [A_{11} U_{ij}^2 + A_{22} V_{ij}^2 + A_{33}'' + 2(A_{12} U_{ij} V_{ij} + A_{13} U_{ij} + A_{23} V_{ij})]\}}{[Q_{33}' + Q_{33}'']}$$

(2.14)

In this expression the A_{33}' term represents that part of the linear stiffness coming from bending action, while the second term in the numerator reflects the linear membrane contributions. The reason for splitting-up the strain energies in this way, as well as the breaking down of the non-linear terms into the two parts (Q_{33}', Q_{33}'') will become clear in our following discussion of elastic lower bounds.

Critical stresses expressed in the form of eqn (2.14) are closely related to those adopted in recent design guidance documents of ASME (1980) and DnV (1981). But it is well known that the critical stresses given by eqn (2.14) are unreliable upper bounds of observed elastic buckling loads. How the classical critical stress spectrum of eqn (2.14) may by modified to yield the appropriate elastic knockdown factors is treated in the following sections.

2.3.2 Lower Bounds for Axially Dominated Loading

One of the considerable benefits of breaking down the energy of resistance to critical deformations in the way described in eqn (2.6), is that it elucidates the reasons why axially loaded cylinders behave so differently to their pressure loaded counterparts. The explanation all centres on the term $\tilde{V}_{2M}^{\theta}$ which from eqn (2.9) arises from the interaction between the fundamental hoop strain ε_{θ}^{F} and the non-linear hoop stress n_{θ}'' associated with the non-linear hoop strains for the critical, incremental, deformations. Why this term is so important is that unlike all the other linearised energy terms it is positive when the fundamental stress is dominated by axial compressive stress; that is, when the Poisson bulging associated with axial compression is not nullified by hoop compressions resulting from radial pressure loading. Not only is the term $\tilde{V}_{2M}^{\theta}$ positive, and therefore contributing to the initial stabilisation of the shell, but for long axial wavelength modes it often provides the single most important contribution to the stabilisation. Moreover, it is this same term that will be eroded in the mode coupling action so clearly described by Donnell as long ago as 1934 (Donnell, 1934). More recent descriptions of this mode coupling, and specifically how it may be used to define a reduced stiffness model, may be found in the studies of the author and his colleagues at University College London (see, for example, Batista and Croll, 1979a; Croll and Ellinas, 1983).

A lower bound to the loss, through mode coupling, of the non-linear membrane energy term $\tilde{V}_{2M}^{\theta}$ is provided by a modelling based upon the reduced total potential energy

$$V_2^* = U_{2B} + U_{2M} + \tilde{V}_{2M}^{x} + \tilde{\tilde{V}}_{2M}^{x} + \tilde{V}_{2M}^{\theta} \qquad (2.15)$$

In the present approximate modelling the in-plane deformations (u_{ij}, v_{ij}) would continue to be given by eqn (2.13), while the third equation would yield the reduced stiffness critical stress, σ_c^*, which may be expressed in the form

$$\frac{\sigma_c^*}{E} = \frac{(Q_{33}' + Q_{33}'')}{Q_{33}'} \cdot \frac{\sigma_c}{E} \equiv \eta_{ij}\sigma_c \qquad (2.16)$$

With Q_{33}', Q_{33}'' identified in eqn (2.12) it is a relatively straightforward matter to derive an explicit form for these modal reduction factors, η_{ij}; for modes in which the axial half-wave length is considerably greater than the circumferential half-wave length, so that $(i/\lambda)^2 \gg 1$, the modal reduction factor can be approximated as

$$\eta_{ij} = \frac{1}{\left[1 + \frac{1}{2}\left(\frac{\mu}{\alpha_x}\right)\left(\frac{i}{\lambda}\right)^2\right]} \tag{2.17}$$

Comparing this with the modal reduction factor for an isotropic cylinder (see eqn (12) of Croll and Ellinas, 1983) allows the effects of orthotropic stiffening on the knockdown for a given mode to be interpreted on the basis of an equivalent Poisson's ratio (μ/α_x). For design purposes it is the mode (i^*_{cm}, j^*_{cm}) producing the minimum reduced stiffness critical stress σ^*_{cm} that will determine the potentially most sensitive buckling. A lower bound, σ_e, to the elastic buckling would then be given as

$$\sigma_e = \eta_e \sigma_{cm} \tag{2.18}$$

where the elastic knockdown factor η_e is defined by

$$\eta_e = \frac{\sigma^*_{cm}}{\sigma_{cm}} \tag{2.19}$$

For three shell examples the predictions from eqns (2.14) and (2.16) are shown in Fig. 2.2. An isotropic cylinder displays the well-known classical buckling behaviour of non-uniqueness of critical mode at the minimum classical stress, σ_{cm}. In contrast the present reduced stiffness theory predicts that there will be a certain unique mode $(i, j) \equiv (i^*_{cm}, 1)$ in which loss of the linearised membrane stiffness $\tilde{V}^\theta_{2M}$ is likely to have its most severe consequences. Recent tests carried out at University College London (Batista, 1979; Batista and Croll, 1979a) as well as independent earlier observations by Arbocz and Babcock (1969) have shown that it is this unique mode which triggers the snap buckling when shells contain moderate levels of imperfection. Additionally, the scatter of observed buckling stresses is reliably bounded from below by the above reduced stiffness predictions of eqns (2.16) and (2.14). Close agreement has also been found between the predictions and tests for stringer stiffened and ring stiffened cylinders (Ellinas and Croll, 1983a,b).

The way in which the addition of stiffeners modifies the behaviour of

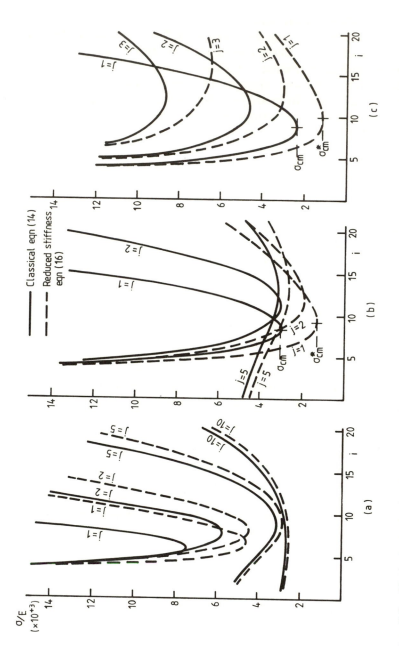

FIG. 2.2. Typical classical and reduced stiffness critical stress spectrum for axially loaded cylinders having $l/r = 1 \cdot 0$. $r/t_{eq} = 200$, and (a) ring stiffening with $n_r = 19$, $d_r/t_r = 5$ and $\alpha_\theta = 1 \cdot 2$; (b) isotropic cylinder $\alpha_\theta = \alpha_x = 1 \cdot 0$; and (c) stringer stiffening with $n_s = 40$, $d_s/t_s = 10$ and $\alpha_x = 1 \cdot 2$.

the unstiffened cylinder is illustrated in Figs 2.2(a) and (c) for examples of, respectively, typical ring and stringer stiffened cylinders. With the total volume of material held constant for the three shells of Fig. 2.2, and hence equivalent thickness, t_{eq}, fixed, it is possible to interpret the modifications to behaviour which result from stiffening in the form of a strength optimisation. In mode $j = 1$, for example, the major source of stiffness, or energy of resistance, is derived for an isotropic cylinder from hoop bending and axial membrane action. Moving material from the plating to rings, as indicated in Fig. 2.2(a), results in a dramatic increase in hoop bending stiffness. Since this increased hoop bending stiffness is accomplished with moderately little change in the axial membrane resistance, there is a lengthening of the circumferential wavelength and a marked increase in the minimum critical stress for the long axial wavelength modes $j = 1, 2, \ldots$ For the shorter axial wavelength modes, $j \geq 5$, the isotropic cylinder of Fig. 2.2(b) derives much more of its resistance to critical deformations from axial bending energy.

The reductions in axial bending stiffness will, when ring stiffening is heavy, that is α_θ is sufficiently large, more than compensate the increased resistance provided by hoop bending action. This is seen to be the case for the example of Fig. 2.2(a), where for the short axial wavelength modes, $j \geq 5$, there is a reduction in critical stresses compared with the equivalent weight unstiffened cylinder. As discussed by Ellinas and Croll (1981), moving material from shell plating into ring stiffeners initially produces substantially increased elastic buckling resistance. However, beyond a certain critical level of α_θ the extent of the knockdowns in mode $j = 1$, as measured by σ^*_{cm}, will be such that a short axial wavelength mode might be expected to initiate buckling. Usually, this short axial wavelength buckling takes the form of axisymmetric modes, analysis of which has recently been described by Croll and Ellinas (1984) in a form similar to that outlined herein. This transition from imperfection-sensitive, long axial wavelength buckling, to imperfection-insensitive short axial wavelength elastic buckling is more clearly depicted in Fig. 2.3. It might be added that such a transition behaviour has also been noted in past test programmes of Singer et al. (1971).

The effects of transferring material from the skin to stringer stiffeners can be interpreted in a similar way. Reductions in the all-important hoop bending stiffness initially result in a reduction of load-carrying capacity and it is only when the orthotropic stiffness parameter α_x

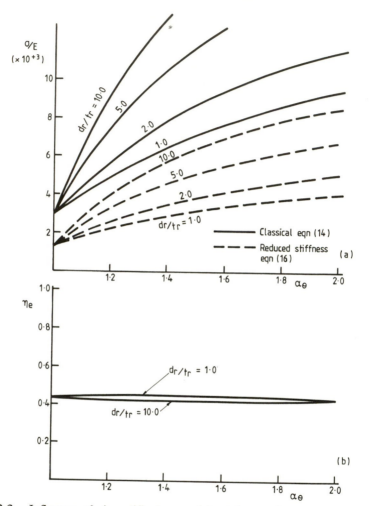

FIG. 2.3. Influence of ring stiffening on (a) minimum classical and reduced stiffness axial critical stresses and (b) elastic knockdowns. Cylinders have $l/r = 1 \cdot 0$, $r/t_{eq} = 200$, $t_\theta = t_{eq}$, $n_r = 19$ and $\mu = 0 \cdot 3$.

becomes very large that the increased axial bending stiffness starts to compensate the loss of hoop bending.

For the example of Fig. 2.2(c) there is a loss of resistance to buckling in the long axial wavelength, $j = 1$, mode. Figure 2.4 shows that this loss of elastic resistance persists over a wide range of stringer stiffener geometries. However, because of the increased importance of axial

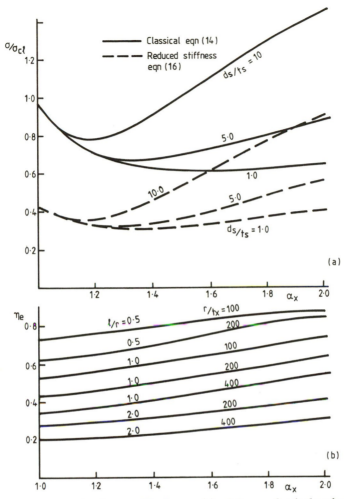

FIG. 2.4.   Influence of stringer stiffening on (a) minimum classical and reduced stiffness axial critical stresses and (b) elastic knockdowns. Cylinders have $l/r = 1\cdot0$, $r/t_{eq} = 200$, $t_x = t_{eq}$, $n_s = 40$ and $\mu = 0\cdot3$.

bending when isotropic cylinders buckle into shorter axial wavelength modes, the movement of material into stringers has the effect, illustrated in Fig. 2.2(c), of greatly enhancing elastic buckling resistance in these modes. Use of stringer stiffeners has the effect of making buckling much more well defined, in the sense that there is a unique classical as well as reduced stiffness minimum critical mode. Although there is some reduction in the extent of the imperfection sensitivity, as measured by η_e in Fig. 2.4(b), it is evident that stringer stiffened cylinders retain the property of high imperfection sensitivity. An important consideration to emerge from parametric studies like those shown in Figs 2.3(b) and 2.4(b) is the dependence of the elastic knockdown factor on the precise shell and stiffener geometries. This and other consequences of moving material from the shell skin into rib stiffening are discussed by Ellinas et al. (1981).

2.3.3 Lower Bounds for Pressure Dominated Loading

In contrast with loading dominated by axial compression, the term $\tilde{V}^\theta_{2M}$ ceases to provide stabilising effects upon critical deformations once γ_θ becomes large in comparison with γ_x. This occurs when the radial pressure produces hoop compression strains greater than the hoop tensile strains arising from the Poisson bulging associated with the axial compressive force. For pressure dominated loading the only initially stabilising terms which are at risk in the non-linear post-buckling behaviour are the linear membrane energy terms U_{2M}. For the long axial wavelengths which characterise pressure dominated buckling, the linear membrane energy is itself dominated by that resulting from the periodic axial stresses. Lower bounds to this post-buckling loss of stiffness would therefore be predicted on the basis of a reduced total potential energy

$$V_2^{**} = U_{2B} + \tilde{V}^x_{2M} + \tilde{\tilde{V}}^x_{2M} + \tilde{V}^\theta_{2M} + \tilde{\tilde{V}}^\theta_{2M} \qquad (2.20)$$

An approximation to the reduced stiffness critical stresses σ^*_c may be obtained on the basis of a classical critical mode, in which case

$$\sigma^*_c = \frac{U_{2B}}{(U_{2B} + U_{2M})} \cdot \sigma_c \equiv \eta_{ij}\sigma_c \qquad (2.21)$$

In this form of buckling the full energy plays the important role of biasing the shell to buckle into the mode $(i, j) \equiv (i_{cm}, 1)$ associated with the minimum of the σ_c spectrum. Within this mode the minimum post-buckled stiffness will be given by the reduced stiffness critical stress

$$\sigma^*_{cm} = \left[\frac{U_{2B}}{(U_{2B} + U_{2M})} \right] \Bigg|_{\substack{i=i_{cm} \\ j=1}} \sigma_{cm} \equiv \eta_e\sigma_{cm} \equiv \sigma_e \qquad (2.22)$$

where η_e represents the elastic knockdown factor as defined in eqn (2.19). For the case of pure radial pressure loading Fig. 2.5 illustrates

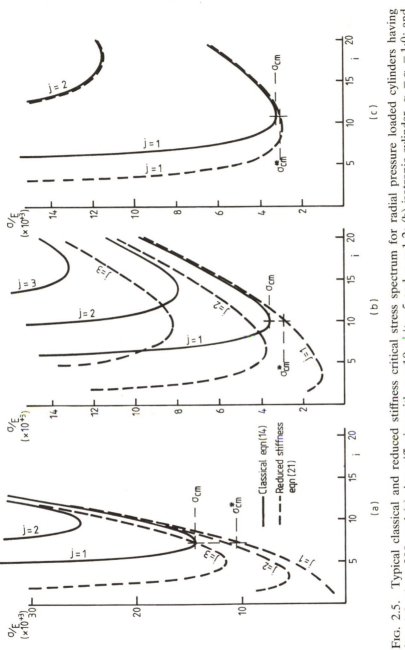

FIG. 2.5. Typical classical and reduced stiffness critical stress spectrum for radial pressure loaded cylinders having $l/r = 1.0$, $r/t_{eq} = 200$, and (a) ring stiffening with $n_r = 19$, $d_r/t_r = 5$ and $\alpha_\theta = 1.2$; (b) isotropic cylinder, $\alpha_\theta = \alpha_x = 1.0$; and (c) stringer stiffening with $n_s = 40$, $d_s/t_s = 10$ and $\alpha_x = 1.2$.

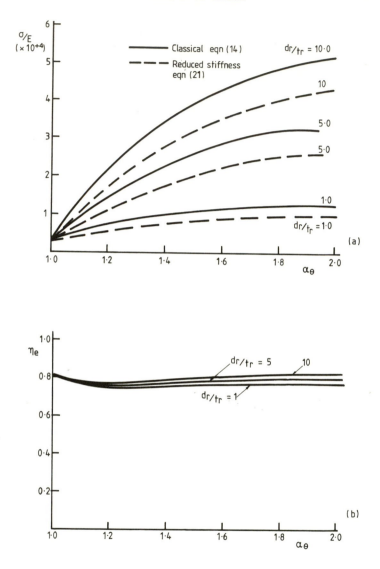

FIG. 2.6. Influence of ring stiffening on (a) minimum classical and reduced stiffness radial pressure critical spectrum and (b) elastic knockdowns. Cylinders have $l/r = 1 \cdot 0$, $r/t_{eq} = 200$, $t_\theta = t_{eq}$, $n_r = 19$ and $\mu = 0 \cdot 3$.

the consequences of moving material from the skin into either ring or stringer stiffening. Changes in critical stress spectrum can once again be interpreted in terms of the relative changes in hoop and axial bending strain energy.

Use of the ring stiffening as illustrated in Fig. 2.5(a) greatly enhances the hoop bending stiffness with concomitant increases in critical stresses for the long axial wavelength modes, $j = 1, 2, \ldots$.

Conversely, there is a loss of hoop bending stiffness and, consequently, critical stress capacity, when material is moved from the skin into stringers, as in Fig. 2.5(c). Interestingly, although the level and form of ring stiffening has a pronounced beneficial influence on critical pressure loadings as illustrated in Fig. 2.6(a), it has little effect on the extent of potential elastic knockdowns as shown in Fig. 2.6(b).

2.3.4 Lower-Bound Interaction Curves

The effects of moving material from the cylinder plating to stiffeners are further illustrated by the load interaction studies of Figs 2.7 and 2.8. In Fig. 2.7 the tendency for elastic buckling resistance to be reduced for light to moderate levels of stringer stiffenings compared with the equivalent weight unstiffened cylinder is seen to remain true for all load combinations. For radial pressure loading the results of Fig. 2.7 indicate that even with very heavy stringer stiffening there is a loss of load carrying capacity compared with the equivalent isotropic cylinder.

In contrast, Fig. 2.8 shows that for all axial and pressure load combinations there is a considerable enhancement to be gained from the use of ring stiffening. Not included in Fig. 2.8 are the elastic buckling loads associated with the short axial wavelength axisymmetric buckling modes. For loadings dominated by axial components these short axial wavelength modes will control the elastic buckling resistance for the present stiffener geometry once the orthotropic stiffness parameter α_θ exceeds $\simeq 1 \cdot 1$. When plasticity effects are taken into account the short axial wavelength buckling modes are likely to control buckling over even wider parametric ranges.

2.4 PLASTIC SQUASH

A cylinder having no initial imperfection would in the present context reach an upper bound to its plastic strength when in the assumed

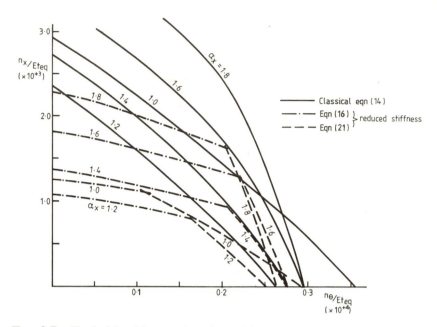

FIG. 2.7. Typical load interactions for minimum classical and reduced stiffness elastic critical stress for stringer stiffened shells having $l/r = 1\cdot0$, $r/t_{eq} = 200$, $t_x = t_{eq}$, $n_s = 40$ and $d_s/t_s = 10$.

membrane state either the stiffeners or the shell plating commence yielding. With the stringer and ring stresses given by eqn (2.4), the appropriate uniaxial yield conditions provide estimates for plastic collapse of stringer and ring $(\sigma_{p_s}, \sigma_{p_r})$ as

$$\sigma_{p_s} = \frac{1}{e_x} \cdot \sigma_y$$
$$\sigma_{p_r} = \frac{1}{e_\theta} \cdot \sigma_y$$
(2.23)

while the biaxial stress state in the plating, given by eqn (2.5), would begin yielding on the basis of a von Mises yield criterion when

$$\sigma_{p_p} = \frac{\sigma_y}{(s_x^2 - s_x s_\theta + s_\theta^2)^{1/2}}$$
(2.24)

These upper bounds of plastic strength will be significantly reduced by elastic deformations and imperfections.

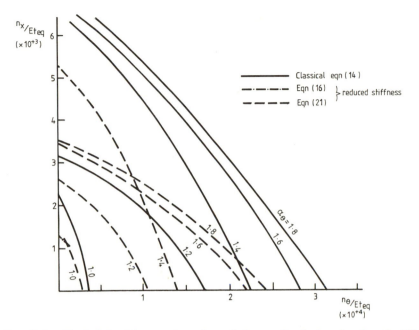

FIG. 2.8. Typical load interactions for minimum classical and reduced stiffness elastic critical stress for ring stiffened shells having $l/r = 1 \cdot 0$, $r/t_{eq} = 200$, $t_\theta = t_{eq}$, $n_r = 19$ and $d_r/t_r = 5$.

2.5 ELASTIC–PLASTIC BUCKLING

From a theoretical standpoint it has been the prediction of the appropriate allowance for this interaction between elastic and plastic behaviours that has proved most difficult to incorporate into shell collapse analysis. The present reduced stiffness approach enables this to be achieved in a particularly convenient fashion. For an imperfection introduced into the reduced stiffness modelling of elastic buckling will at a given load level automatically provide upper bounds of the incremental, buckling deflections, and therefore stresses. This means that a first material yield criterion of plastic collapse based upon the reduced stiffness method would provide lower bounds of the 'exact' first yield state predicted on the basis of a fully non-linear elastic theory. These lower bounds would be as reliable as are the present lower bounds to elastic buckling for a given imperfection level. Since the elastic lower bounds have been shown by Batista *et al.* (1979), Ellinas *et al.* (1981) and Ellinas and Croll (1983*a*, *b*) to be reliable over a wide range of shell geometries for elastic buckling it is likely that the following should prove equally reliable and provide a simple approach for lower bounds to plastic collapse. The method has been described more fully in relation to the specific buckling problems of isotropic (Croll, 1981, 1982) and pressure-loaded ring-stiffened shells (Ellinas and Croll, 1983*c*).

Depending upon the nature of the loading, and the form and size of stiffening employed, first material yield may occur in the stiffeners or the shell skin. Each is therefore considered separately.

2.5.1 First Stiffener Yield

The total stress occurring at the tips of stringer and/or ring stiffeners on the meridians associated with maximum and minimum stress may be expressed as

$$\sigma_{x_s} = e_x \sigma \pm E a_{x_s} \left(\frac{w_{cm}}{r} \right)$$

$$\sigma_{\theta_r} = e_\theta \sigma \pm E a_{\theta_r} \left(\frac{w_{cm}}{r} \right)$$

(2.25)

where w_{cm} represents the amplitude of the incremental deformation in the mode associated with the minimum reduced stiffness elastic critical stress. The membrane strain parameters (e_x, e_θ) are specified in eqn (2.3), while parameters (a_{x_s}, a_{θ_r}) are defined as

$$a_{x_s} = c_p(\lambda U_{cm} - Z_{s_t}\lambda^2) - \lambda^2 Z_{s_t}$$

$$a_{\theta_r} = c_p(-i_{cm}V_{cm} + 1 - Z_{r_t}i_{cm}^2) - i_{cm}^2 Z_{r_t}$$

(2.26)

and provide the membrane and bending contributions in the axial and hoop directions respectively. Coefficient c_p is taken as unity for axially dominated buckling, since at the instant of buckling it is assumed that incremental membrane stresses are developed. For pressure dominated buckling, in which the reduced stiffness analysis is based on the assumption that the linear incremental membrane stresses have been eroded through modifications in mode form, c_p is taken as zero.

On the basis of the reduced stiffness theory an imperfection w_{cm}° in the form of the most critical of the elastic deformations will induce an incremental displacement

$$w_{cm} = \frac{\sigma}{(\sigma_{cm}^* - \sigma)} w_{cm}^\circ$$

(2.27)

so that the limiting of total stresses $(\sigma_{x_s}, \sigma_{\theta_r})$ to the material uniaxial yield stress σ_y may be written in the forms

$$
\left(1 - e_x \frac{\sigma_{fy}^s}{\sigma_y}\right)\left(\frac{\sigma_e}{\sigma_y} - \frac{\sigma_{fy}^s}{\sigma_y}\right) = \pm \rho_{x_s} \frac{\sigma_{fy}^s}{\sigma_y}
$$

$$
\left(1 - e_\theta \frac{\sigma_{fy}^r}{\sigma_y}\right)\left(\frac{\sigma_e}{\sigma_y} - \frac{\sigma_{fy}^r}{\sigma_y}\right) = \pm \rho_{\theta_r} \frac{\sigma_{fy}^r}{\sigma_y}
$$

(2.28)

for the stringers and rings respectively. Imperfection parameters $(\rho_{x_s}, \rho_{\theta_r})$ are defined as

$$
\rho_{x_s} = a_{x_s}\left(\frac{E}{\sigma_y}\right)\left(\frac{w_{cm}^\circ}{r}\right)
$$

$$
\rho_{\theta_r} = a_{\theta_r}\left(\frac{E}{\sigma_y}\right)\left(\frac{w_{cm}^\circ}{r}\right)
$$

(2.29)

and can be seen to incorporate the effects of shell and stiffener geometry, critical buckling mode shape, as well as the material elastic–plastic properties and the critical imperfection amplitudes. Normalised first yield stresses $(\sigma_{fy}^s, \sigma_{fy}^r)$ depend upon the appropriate imperfection parameters $(\rho_{x_s}, \rho_{\theta_r})$, the fundamental strain distribution (e_x, e_θ) and the ratio of the lower bound elastic to yield stresses σ_e/σ_y. Whether first yield will occur at the meridian $\theta = 0$ or at $\theta = \pi/i_{cm}^*$ depends upon the sign of (e_x, e_θ). In eqns (2.25) and (2.28) the upper sign refers to the stresses at the tip of an inward stiffener for a positive imperfection; the lower sign refers to the $\theta = \pi/i_{cm}^*$ meridian. It is evident that the present approach enables first yield to be formulated in an identical fashion to that often employed for columns.

An even more compact summary of stiffener yield may be obtained by normalising with respect to the plastic squash stresses $(\sigma_{p_s}, \sigma_{p_r})$ rather than the material yield σ_y. In this case the two separate criteria for stringers and rings may be encapsulated into the single column-type expression

$$
(1 - \Lambda_{fy})(\Lambda_e - \Lambda_{fy}) = \pm \rho \Lambda_{fy}
$$

(2.30)

where for stringer $\Lambda_{fy} \equiv \sigma_{fy}^s/\sigma_{p_s}$, $\Lambda_e \equiv \sigma_e/\sigma_{p_s}$ and $\rho \equiv \rho_{x_s}$; while for rings $\Lambda_{fy} = \sigma_{fy}^r/\sigma_{p_r}$, $\Lambda_e \equiv \sigma_e\sigma_{p_r}$ and $\rho \equiv \rho_{\theta_r}$. The great beauty of such a formulation is that stiffener yield in the general buckling of any ring or stringer stiffened cylinder may be summarised in a single plot such as that of Fig. 2.9. All that need be calculated for design are the appropriate values of Λ_e and ρ.

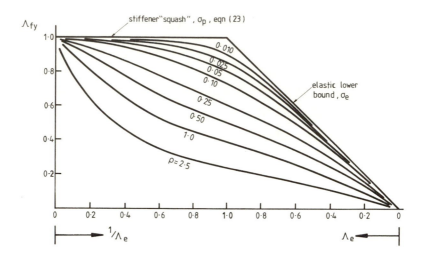

FIG. 2.9. Summarised first stiffener yield for rings and/or stringers; eqn (2.30).

Such an approach has close relationships with many existing code formulations. By putting these procedures on a rational footing and providing explicit relationships for the composite geometric, material and generalised imperfection parameters ρ, the present approach should enable factors of safety to be more consistently chosen in future design. Since stiffener yield usually precedes the onset of first plate yield, these important practical features of eqn (2.30) should normally be able to be taken advantage of in design. However, in circumstances where very small and stocky stiffeners are used and/or where primary loading is normal to the direction of the stiffening, yielding may sometimes be initiated in the shell plating.

2.5.2 First Shell Plate Yield

Total stresses in the shell plating may be written as

$$\sigma_{x_p} = s_x \sigma \pm E a_{x_p} \left(\frac{w_{cm}}{r} \right)$$

$$\sigma_{\theta_p} = s_\theta \sigma \pm E a_{\theta_p} \left(\frac{w_{cm}}{r} \right)$$

(2.31)

where the plate stress parameters are given as

$$a_{x_p} = c_p[(\lambda U_{cm} - \lambda^2 Z_{s_p}) + \mu(-i_{cm}V_{cm} + 1 - Z_{r_p}i_{cm}^2)]/(1-\mu^2)$$
$$+ \lambda^2 Z_{s_p} + \mu i_{cm}^2 Z_{r_p}$$
$$a_{\theta_p} = c_p[(-i_{cm}V_{cm} + 1 - Z_{r_p}i_{cm}^2) + \mu(\lambda U_{cm} - \lambda^2 Z_{s_p})]/(1-\mu^2)$$
$$+ i_{cm}^2 Z_{r_p} + \mu\lambda^2 Z_{s_p}$$

$$(2.32)$$

Again the upper sign refers to stresses on the outside face at $\theta = 0$ for an inward displacement; the lower sign refers to $\theta = \pi/i_{cm}^*$. Coefficient c_p has the meaning discussed in relation to eqn (2.26). On the basis of a von Mises yield criterion

$$\sigma_{x_p}^2 - \sigma_{x_p}\sigma_{\theta_p} + \sigma_{\theta_p}^2 = \sigma_y^2 \qquad (2.33)$$

and making use of the reduced stiffness incremental displacements of eqn (2.27), first surface yield of shell plate may be represented in terms of the lowest solution of the quartic

$$\sum_{i=0}^{i=4} C_i (\Lambda_{fy}^P)^i = 0 \qquad (2.34)$$

Stresses are all normalised with respect to the plate squash stress σ_{P_p} of eqn (2.24) so that $\Lambda_{fy}^P \equiv \sigma_{fy}^P/\sigma_{P_p}$ and $\Lambda_e \equiv \sigma_e/\sigma_{P_p}$. Coefficients C_i take the form

$$C_0 = -\Lambda_e^2$$
$$C_1 = +2\Lambda_e$$
$$C_2 = \Lambda_e^2 + \alpha\Lambda_e + \beta - 1$$
$$C_3 = -2\Lambda_e - \alpha$$
$$C_4 = +1$$

where

$$\alpha = \frac{(2s_x\rho_{x_p} - s_x\rho_{\theta_p} - s_\theta\rho_{x_p} + 2s_\theta\rho_{\theta_p})}{(s_x^2 - s_x s_\theta + s_\theta^2)^{1/2}}$$

$$(2.35)$$

$$\beta = \rho_{x_p}^2 - \rho_{x_p}\rho_{\theta_p} + \rho_{\theta_p}^2$$

and generalised axial and hoop imperfection parameters are

$$\rho_{x_p} = a_{x_p}\left(\frac{E}{\sigma_y}\right)\left(\frac{w_{cm}^\circ}{r}\right)$$

$$(2.36)$$

$$\rho_{\theta_p} = a_{\theta_p}\left(\frac{E}{\sigma_y}\right)\left(\frac{w_{cm}^\circ}{r}\right)$$

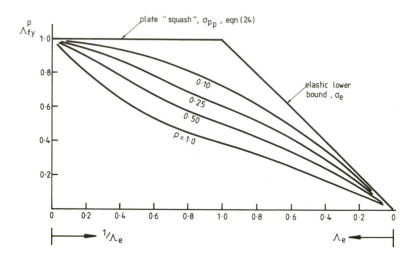

FIG. 2.10.   Summarised first shell plate yield for ring and/or stringer stiffened and/or unstiffened cylinders using eqn (2.34) and approximation of eqn (2.37).

In contrast with the case of stiffeners, plate yield can be seen explicitly to involve two imperfection parameters $(\rho_{x_p}, \rho_{\theta_p})$ as well as the normalised fundamental stress ratios (s_x, s_θ). For shells in which plate yield is likely to occur prior to stiffener yield it is usual for one of the imperfection parameters $(\rho_{x_p}, \rho_{\theta_p})$ to dominate over the other. Furthermore, it has been shown by Croll (1982) for the case of isotropic cylinders that the stress ratio (s_x/s_θ) is a secondary variable. In these circumstances the solution of eqn (2.33) can, like that for stiffeners, be represented in terms of the elastic-to-plastic stress ratio Λ_e and a single imperfection parameter ρ, where ρ would represent whichever of either ρ_{x_p} or ρ_{θ_p} is dominant. Which of $(\rho_{x_p}, \rho_{\theta_p})$ will dominate depends upon the nature of both load and stiffening. The composite parameters (α, β) needed in eqn (2.34) would then be given by

$$\alpha \simeq \rho \frac{(2-\gamma)}{(1-\gamma+\gamma^2)^{1/2}}$$

$$\beta \simeq \rho^2 \qquad\qquad\qquad\qquad (2.37)$$

where γ represents the stress ratio s_θ/s_x or s_x/s_θ, depending upon whether ρ is associated with ρ_{x_p} or ρ_{θ_p}. In this form the first plate yield is represented in a way identical with that recently described by Croll (1982) for isotropic cylinders. Since $\gamma = 0$ provides the most severe knockdown, and since the knockdown is only marginally affected by variations in γ, plots of the solution to eqn (2.34) may be presented in the form shown in Fig. 2.10. As for stiffener yield, just the two independent parameters (Λ_e, ρ) are involved. Even if the more exact description of eqn (2.34) needs to be used, and this can sometimes be the case when stiffening and loading are mutually orthogonal, it is a simple matter to programme the entire procedure on any of the now widely accessible desk top computers. Indeed, all the studies reported in this chapter have been obtained on such computing devices.

2.5.3 Typical Parametric Studies

Figures 2.11 and 2.12 illustrate typical examples of axially loaded stringer stiffened cylinders and radial pressure loaded ring stiffened cylinders, respectively. Although these have been obtained on the basis of solutions to eqns (2.30) and (2.34), they could equally have been obtained directly from Figs 2.9 and 2.10. Apart from shells having very low levels of stiffening, $\alpha_x < 1 \cdot 06$ in the case of axially loaded stringer stiffened shells of Fig. 2.11 and only unstiffened shells in the case of ring stiffened shells of Fig. 2.12, first yield is governed by yielding at the stiffener tip. What is striking about Fig. 2.11 is that even the elastic–plastic axial collapse strengths tend to be reduced by the use of stringers. Depending upon the imperfection level, the use of stringers to improve weight-for-weight general buckling strength only becomes economical at very high levels of stiffening. For squat stringers, $d_s/t_s < 10$, the situation is even worse; this mirrors a similar pattern observed by Ellinas et al. (1981) for the elastic buckling resistance. In contrast, Fig. 2.12 shows that there is generally a considerable radial pressure strength advantage to be gained through use of ring stiffener.

These relative advantages of using rings rather than stringers prevail for collapse under varying combinations of axial and pressure loading. Figures 2.13 and 2.14 summarise typical collapse loads for examples of stringer- and ring-stiffened geometries, respectively. What these plots demonstrate is that stiffener yield tends to govern the first yield criterion. It is only when the loading is dominated by components normal to the direction of stiffening, for example axial load on ring stiffened shells, that plate yield initiates plastic behaviour.

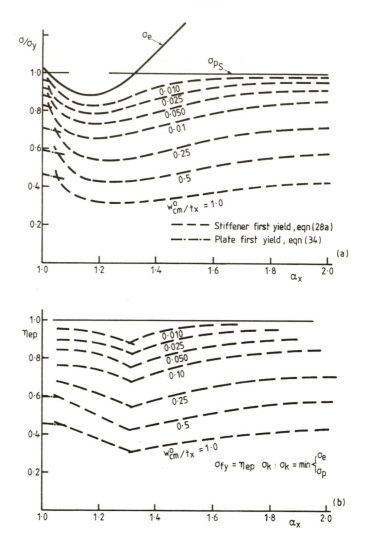

FIG. 2.11. Typical (a) first yield stresses and (b) elastic–plastic knockdown factors, η_{ep}, for axially loaded cylinders ($\gamma_x = 1$, $\gamma_\theta = 0$) with stringer stiffeners; $l/r = 1$, $r/t_{eq} = 200$, $t_x = t_{eq}$, $n_s = 40$, $d_s/t_s = 10$, $\sigma_y/E = 0.001\,25$, and variable critical imperfection amplitude w_{cm}°.

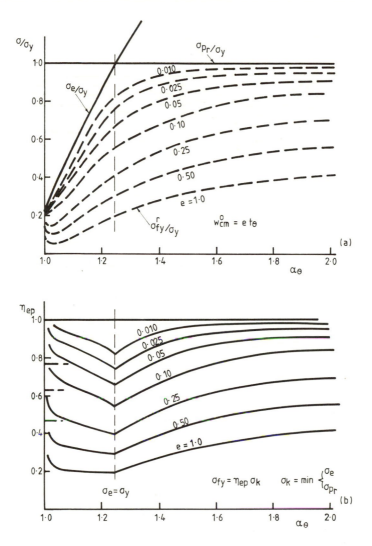

FIG. 2.12. Typical (a) first yield stresses and (b) elastic–plastic knockdown factors, η_{ep}, for radial pressure loaded cylinders ($\gamma_\theta = 1$; $\gamma_x = 0$) with ring stiffeners; $l/r = 1\cdot0$, $r/t_{eq} = 200$, $t_\theta = t_{eq}$, $n_r = 19$, $d_r/t_r = 5$, $\sigma_y/E = 0\cdot00125$, and variable critical imperfection amplitude w°_{cm}.

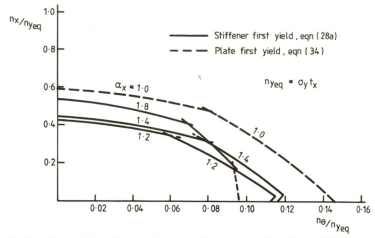

FIG. 2.13. Typical load interactions for lower bounds to first yield for stringer stiffened cylinders having $l/r = 1\cdot0$, $r/t_{eq} = 200$, $t_x = t_{eq}$, $n_s = 40$, $d_s/t_s = 10$, $\sigma_y/E = 0\cdot00125$ and $w^{\circ}_{cm}/t_{eq} = 0\cdot5$.

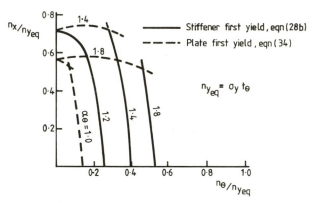

FIG. 2.14. Typical load interactions for lower bound to first yield for ring stiffened cylinders having $l/r = 1\cdot0$, $r/t_{eq} = 200$, $t_\theta = t_{eq}$, $n_r = 19$, $d_r/t_r = 5$, $\sigma_y/E = 0\cdot00125$ and $w^{\circ}_{cm}/t_{eq} = 0\cdot5$.

2.6 DISCUSSION

The explicit relationships derived for the elastic–plastic general buckling collapse relate to orthotropic cylinders having end diaphragm supports that are effectively simply supported. Many practical shell components do not possess such analytically convenient end conditions. In these cases the critical load calculations of eqn (2.14) might be more conveniently performed using some suitable numerical facility. Equally, the composite imperfection, material and geometric parameters entering into the calculation of elastic–plastic knockdowns would need to be adjusted in accordance with the results of suitable numerical calculations. However, even with these boundary-induced complications, the basic parameters identified in the above analysis would remain essentially unchanged. In these situations the analytical framework described could still provide the parametric basis of numerically calibrated design curves.

A further limitation of the analysis described in the present chapter is that it is restricted to just the prediction of non-symmetric collapse modes. When buckling is symmetric, a different set of parameters control collapse. Even so, the approach used to predict axisymmetric collapse can be very similar to that adopted above for non-axisymmetric collapse. For unstiffened cylinders these similarities have been elaborated by Croll (1983), while for the general axisymmetric collapse of orthotropically stiffened cylinders Croll and Ellinas (1984) have shown that collapse can be formulated in a way identical to that described above for non-axisymmetric collapse. Particularly for ring stiffened shells under axial loading, this form of general axisymmetric collapse can for some imperfection distributions occur at loads lower than those for the non-symmetric general collapse described above. In a properly conceived design approach both forms of collapse would need to be checked.

Whether it is axisymmetric or non-axisymmetric collapse, another aspect that can have important influence on collapse behaviour is the local buckling of shell plating and stiffener tripping. As discussed earlier many design codes adopt the philosophy that stiffeners are designed so that local buckling controls the load-carrying capacity. In these cases parametric limits on stiffener size are introduced to ensure that general buckling is sufficiently high such that no interaction is possible. But even in this extreme situation it remains imperative that the prediction of general collapse is provided with a rational base. A more general approach to design would aim at producing adequate margins against all possible collapse modes. Whatever design approach is used it is possible that reductions to general collapse resistance caused by local buckling may have to be estimated. Use of the reduced effective widths of shell plating and/or reduced effective depths of stiffeners when local buckling modes occur, can be relatively easily incorporated into the analysis described above. But it must be admitted that the appropriate choice of reduced stiffness properties in these circumstances is as yet a far from certain process. Adoption of this approach should therefore proceed cautiously until adequate empirical evidence becomes available. An interim measure might be the adoption of reduced effective widths for stiffness and strength calculations like those adopted by ASME (1980). If such an approach is adopted it becomes even more essential that general collapse prediction be provided with a simplified but reliable basis of the type outlined above.

2.7 CONCLUSIONS

A reduced stiffness method for the analysis of lower bounds to the elastic general buckling of stringer and ring stiffened cylinders under arbitrary combinations of axial and radial pressure loading is described. Using this approach a straightforward extension of classical critical load analysis allows specification of elastic knockdowns which are at once simple to obtain and yet capable of accurately representing all the important and independent influences arising from shell and stiffening geometry, loading, and end boundary support conditions. Within this analysis the isotropic cylinder, so often treated as having distinctive behaviour, emerges as merely a special case of orthotropic cylinder buckling.

An imperfect form of the reduced stiffness elastic modelling is then adopted as the basis of a first yield criterion for incipient plastic collapse. While first yield can sometimes be rather conservative for eventual collapse, there are many important reasons why it should not be exceeded in practice. Adopting the reduced stiffness modelling as a basis for predicting first yield ensures that the lower bound nature of this criterion is maintained. For a given level of initial imperfection the elastic–plastic collapse predictions described above will be as reliable as lower bounds as those for purely elastic buckling. Since recent comparisons have shown that the reduced stiffness method provides accurate lower bounds to the elastic buckling of widely varying classes of orthotropically stiffened and unstiffened cylinders, it is suggested that the present design expressions should likewise provide accurate lower bounds of first surface yield. This, combined with the simplicity and compactness of the present approach, as well as its close relationships with much of existing design practice, should recommend the method as a serious alternative for future design.

REFERENCES

ARBOCZ, J. and BABCOCK, C. D. (1969) The effects of general imperfections on the buckling of cylindrical shells. *J. Appl. Mech.*, **36**, 28–38.

ARBOCZ, J. and SECHLER, E. E. (1974). On buckling of axially compressed imperfect cylindrical shells. *J. Appl. Mech.*, **41**, 737–55.

ASME (1980) *1980 Code Case, Nuclear Components*, Case N-284, American Society of Mechanical Engineers, New York, USA.

BATISTA, R. C. (1979) Lower bound estimates for cylindrical shell buckling, PhD Dissertation, University of London.

BATISTA, R. C. and CROLL, J. G. A. (1979a) A design approach for axially compressed unstiffened cylinders. In: *Stability Problems in Engineering Structures and Components* (Eds T. H. Richards and P. Stanley), Applied Science Publishers Ltd, London.

BATISTA, R. C. and CROLL, J. G. A. (1979b) Design approach for unstiffened cylindrical shells under external pressure. In: *Thin Walled Structures* (Ed. J. Rhodes), Crosby-Lockwood, Glasgow.

BS 5500 (1982) *Specifications for Unfired Fusion Welded Pressure Vessels*, British Standards Institution,

CROLL, J. G. A. (1981) Lower bound elasto-plastic buckling of cylinders. *Proc. Inst. Civ. Engrs*, Part 2, **71**, 235–61.

CROLL, J. G. A. (1982) Elastic–plastic buckling of pressure and axial loaded cylinders. *Proc. Inst. Civ. Engrs*, Part 2, **72**, 633–52.

CROLL, J. G. A. (1983) Axisymmetric collapse of cylinders including deformations of ring stiffening. In: *Behaviour of Thin Walled Structures* (Ed. by J. Rhodes and J. Spence), Elsevier Applied Science Publishers, London, pp. 211–233.

CROLL, J. G. A. and ELLINAS, C. P. (1983) Reduced stiffness axial load buckling of cylinders. *Int. J. Solids and Structures*, **19**, 461–77.

CROLL, J. G. A. and ELLINAS, C. P. (1984) A design formulation for axisymmetric collapse of stiffened and unstiffened cylinders. *3rd Int. Symp. on Offshore Mechanics and Arctic Engineering*, ASME, New Orleans.

DnV (1981) Rules for the Design Construction and Inspection of Offshore Structures, Appendix C—Steel Structures, Det Norske Veritas, Norway.

DONNELL, L. H. (1934) A new theory for the buckling of thin cylinders under axial compression and bending. *Trans. ASME*, **56**, 795.

ECCS (1983) European Recommendations for Steel Construction—Draft Recommendations for Stringer Stiffened Cylinders, European Convention for Constructional Steelwork. The Construction Press, London.

ELLINAS, C. P. and CROLL, J. G. A. (1981) Overall buckling of ring stiffened cylinders. *Proc. Inst. Civ. Engrs*, Part 2, **71**, 637–61.

ELLINAS, C. P. and CROLL, J. G. A. (1983a) Experimental and theoretical correlations for elastic buckling of axially compressed stringer stiffened cylinders. *J. Strain Analysis*, **18**, 41–67.

ELLINAS, C. P. and CROLL, J. G. A. (1983b) Experimental and theoretical correlations for elastic buckling of axially compressed ring stiffened cylinders. *J. Strain Analysis*, **18**, 81–93.

ELLINAS, C. P. and CROLL, J. G. A. (1983c) Elastic–plastic general buckling of ring stiffened cylinders. In: *Collapse: The Buckling of Structures in Theory and Practice*, Proc. of IUTAM Symposium (Ed. by J. M. T. Thompson and G. W. Hunt), Cambridge University Press, Cambridge, pp. 93–109.

ELLINAS, C. P., BATISTA, R. C. and CROLL, J. G. A. (1981) Overall buckling of stringer stiffened cylinders. *Proc. Inst. Civ. Engrs*, Part 2, **71,** 479–512.

SINGER, J., ARBOCZ, J. and BABCOCK, C. D. (1971) Buckling of imperfect stiffened cylindrical shells under axial compression. *AIAA J.*, **9,** 68–75.

Chapter 3

RING-STIFFENED CYLINDERS UNDER EXTERNAL PRESSURE

S. KENDRICK

Admiralty Marine Technology Establishment, Dunfermline, Scotland, UK

SUMMARY

The chapter deals with the fundamentals of axisymmetric stress analysis particularised to the case of ring-stiffened cylinders. Simple buckling formulae are presented and compared with results from a general shell buckling program. The effect of shape imperfections on stresses and overall collapse is treated. The chapter ends with sections on semi-empirical collapse prediction methods, design criteria and computer-aided design.

NOTATION

a Mean radius of shell
a_f Radius of stiffener flange
a_s Radius of stiffener centre of gravity
a_t Radius of toe
b Width of faying flange of stiffener (Fig. 3.2)
d Depth of web of stiffener
f Width of flange of stiffener
h Shell thickness
h_b Thickness of faying flange
h_f Thickness of standing flange
h_w Thickness of web
n Number of circumferential waves

57

p Applied external pressure
p_e Axisymmetric buckling pressure
p_{eb} Bifurcation buckling pressure
p_{sy} Pressure causing yield stress in stiffener flange allowing for out-of-roundness
p_{ys} Pressure causing yield stress in stiffener flange with zero out-of-roundness
q Load/unit circumferential length on ring stiffener
u Longitudinal displacement
v Tangential displacement
w Radial displacement
x Distance in longitudinal direction
z Distance in radial direction

A_s Cross-sectional area of stiffener
D $Eh^3/12(1-\mu^2)$
E Young's modulus
I_z Second moment of area of stiffener about z-axis
L Unsupported length of shell between stiffeners
L_c Overall length of cylinder
L_s Stiffener spacing
V Elastic strain energy
W Work done by external load

α $3(1-\mu^2)/a^2h^2$
β $pa^3/2Eh$
ε Departure from mean circle or strain
θ Angular coordinate
λ $\pi a/L_c$
σ Yield stress of shell
σ_{ys} Yield stress of stiffener

3.1 INTRODUCTION

The analysis of ring-stiffened cylinders was treated extensively in Germany at the time of the First World War and the classic references of that period are those of von Sanden and Gunther (1921) and von Mises (1929). These references were reviewed and extended by Windenburg and Trilling (1934) and a large effort carried out at the David Taylor Model Basin was reviewed by Wenk (1961).

The subject was covered extensively in the book edited by Gill (1970). Since that time many papers have been published concerned with elasto-plastic theoretical analysis and with the use of generalised computer codes for carrying out buckling and design analysis. This chapter is concerned with summarising the more significant analyses. A comprehensive set of design criteria are set down which arise naturally from the information presented. These criteria are essentially those used in the Design Code for Pressure Vessels issued by British Standards (1976).

The chapter starts with elastic stress analysis followed by elastic buckling analysis and the effect of shape imperfections on stresses. This leads on to the theoretical treatment of elasto-plastic collapse and the prediction of collapse pressures using a semi-empirical approach. The chapter ends with a section on design criteria and computer-aided design.

3.2 THE ELASTIC DEFORMATION OF CYLINDERS

3.2.1 The Equations of Deformation

With reference to Fig. 3.1 the conditions of equilibrium give the following equations:

$$\frac{dQ}{dx} = P + N_\theta/a \qquad (3.1)$$

$$\frac{dM}{dx} = Q + N_x \frac{dw}{dx} \qquad (3.2)$$

where N_θ is the circumferential membrane force (tension positive) and

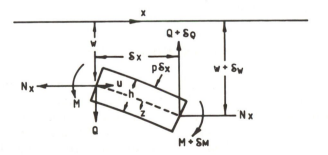

FIG. 3.1. Element forces and displacements

N_x is the axial membrane force (tension positive). The strain expressions are as follows:

$$\varepsilon_\theta = -w/a \tag{3.3}$$

$$\varepsilon_x = \frac{du}{dx} - z\frac{d^2w}{dx^2} \tag{3.4}$$

The membrane forces are given by

$$N_\theta = \frac{hE}{(1-\mu^2)}\left\{\frac{-w}{a} + \frac{\mu}{} \frac{du}{dx}\right\} \tag{3.5}$$

$$N_x = \frac{hE}{(1-\mu^2)}\left\{\frac{du}{dx} - \frac{\mu w}{a}\right\} \tag{3.6}$$

giving

$$\frac{du}{dx} = \frac{N_x(1-\mu^2)}{Eh} + \frac{\mu w}{a} \tag{3.7}$$

$$N_\theta = \frac{-Ehw}{a} + \mu N_x \tag{3.8}$$

Using the relationship $M = D\, d^2w/dx^2$ where $D = Eh^3/12(1-\mu^2)$ the differential equation in w is as follows:

$$\frac{d^2}{dx^2}\left\{h^3\frac{d^2w}{dx^2}\right\} - \left\{\frac{12(1-\mu^2)N_x}{E}\right\}\frac{d^2w}{dx^2} + \left\{\frac{12(1-\mu^2)h}{a^2}\right\}w$$

$$= \frac{12(1-\mu^2)}{E}\left(p + \frac{\mu N_x}{a}\right) \tag{3.9}$$

For a cylinder of uniform thickness the following equations hold:

$$\frac{d^4w}{dx^4} + 4\alpha^4\beta^2\frac{d^2w}{dx^2} + 4\alpha^4w = \left(\frac{1}{D}\right)\left(p - \frac{\mu N_x}{a}\right) \tag{3.10}$$

where

$$\alpha^4 = 3(1-\mu^2)/a^2h^2$$

$$\beta^2 = -N_x a^2/Eh$$

$$Q = D\frac{d^3w}{dx^3} + -N_x\frac{dw}{dx} = D\left[\frac{d^3w}{dx^3} + 4\alpha^4\beta^2\frac{dw}{dx}\right]$$

$$u - u_0 = \frac{N_x(1-\mu^2)x}{Eh} + \frac{\mu}{a}\int_0^x w\, dx$$

$$= \frac{N_x(1-\mu^2)x}{Eh} + \frac{\mu}{4a\alpha^4}\int_0^x\left\{\left(\frac{1}{D}\right)\left(p + \frac{\mu N_x}{a}\right) - \frac{d^4w}{dx^4} - 4\alpha^4\beta^2\frac{d^2w}{dx^2}\right\}dx$$

using the differential equation

$$= x\left\{\frac{pa\mu}{Eh}+\frac{N_x}{Eh}\right\}-\frac{\mu a}{Eh}\{[Q]_{x=x}-[Q]_{x=0}\} \tag{3.11}$$

For the case of uniform external pressure $N_x = -pa/2$, the differential equation in w reduces to

$$\frac{\mathrm{d}^4w}{\mathrm{d}x^4}+4\alpha^4\beta^2\frac{\mathrm{d}^2w}{\mathrm{d}x^2}+4\alpha^4w = p(1-\mu/2)/D \tag{3.12}$$

where $\alpha^4 = 3(1-\mu^2)/a^2h^2$ and $\beta^2 = pa^3/2Eh$.

Methods of solving eqn (3.12) for quite general boundary conditions are discussed by Kendrick (1961) and a general computer program based on this reference is available and described by Kendrick and McKeeman (1961). An alternative computer program for carrying out this type of analysis is described by Bushnell (1974).

3.2.2 Equally-Spaced Stiffeners

A case of particular interest is the uniform thickness cylinder with equally-spaced stiffening rings for which closed-form solutions are available. The term in β arises due to the end pressure and produces 'beam–column' type non-linearity. The inclusion of this term in the analysis leads to considerable complication and produces expressions for stresses and deflections which are virtually linear for low pressures, become more and more non-linear as the pressure increases and eventually increase indefinitely at the axisymmetric elastic buckling pressure. This buckling pressure is invariably very much greater than the working pressure so that non-linearity is small enough to be neglected in most cases. Neglecting the β term simplifies the analysis and equations for the more important stresses derived by Wilson (1956) are as follows:

$\sigma_3 = (pa/h)(1+\gamma H)$—circumferential stress on outside surface
of shell midway between stiffeners

$\sigma_5 = (pa/h)(1+\gamma G)$—mean circumferential stress midway
between stiffeners

$\sigma_7 = (pa/2h)\{1+[12/(1-\mu^2)]^{1/2}\}\gamma R$—maximum longitudinal stress in
the shell (inside surface of
shell adjacent to the stiffener)

$\sigma_s = pa^2\left(1-\frac{\mu}{2}\right)\bigg/ha_f\left\{1+\frac{A}{bh+(2Nh/\alpha)}\right\}$—circumferential stress in
standing flange of stiffener

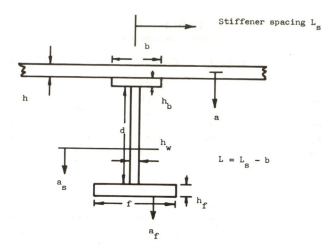

FIG. 3.2.   Geometry definition.

where (see Fig. 3.2):

$$N = \frac{\cosh \alpha L - \cos \alpha L}{\sinh \alpha L + \sin \alpha L}$$

$$\gamma = \frac{A\left(1 - \dfrac{\mu}{2}\right)}{(A + bh)(1 + B)}$$

$$A = \frac{a^2 A_s}{a_s^2}$$

$$B = \frac{2hN}{\alpha(A + bh)}$$

$$H = \frac{-2\left[1 + \sqrt{\left(\dfrac{3\mu^2}{1 - \mu^2}\right)}\right] \sinh \dfrac{\alpha L}{2} \cos \dfrac{\alpha L}{2} + \left[1 - \sqrt{\left(\dfrac{3\mu^2}{1 - \mu^2}\right)}\right] \cosh \dfrac{\alpha L}{2} \sin \dfrac{\alpha L}{2}}{\sinh \alpha L + \sin \alpha L}$$

$$G = \frac{-2\left[\sinh \dfrac{\alpha L}{2} \cos \dfrac{\alpha L}{2} + \cosh \dfrac{\alpha L}{2} \sin \dfrac{\alpha L}{2}\right]}{\sinh \alpha L + \sin \alpha L}$$

$$R = \frac{\sinh \alpha L - \sin \alpha L}{\sinh \alpha L + \sin \alpha L}$$

The radial deflection at frame w_f and midbay w_5 can be obtained

TABLE 3.1
STRESS PARAMETERS

	Case 1	Case 2	Case 3	Case 4
h (mm)	25	25	25	25
L_s (mm)	750	500	500	750
f (mm)	100	100	100	100
h_f (mm)	16	20	16	16
d (mm)	190	250	190	190
h_w (mm)	8	12	8	8
b (mm)	8	12	8	8
h_b (mm)	0	0	0	0
a (mm)	2 700	2 700	2 700	2 700
σ_y (N/mm^2)	430	430	430	900
σ_{ys} (N/mm^2)	400	400	400	900
E (N/mm^2)	207 000	207 000	207 000	207 000
μ	0·3	0·3	0·3	0·3
p_{y3} (N/mm^2)	3·997	4·712	4·464	8·365
p_{y5} (N/mm^2)	4·189	5·078	4·693	8·768
p_{y7} (N/mm^2)	4·457	4·298	4·943	9·329
σ_y (h/a)	3·981	3·981	3·981	8·333
p_{ys} (N/mm^2)	5·284	6·016	5·334	11·89
p_{y3}^* (N/mm^2)	3·895	4·626	4·411	7·856
p_{y5}^* (N/mm^2)	4·116	5·030	4·667	8·387
p_{y7}^* (N/mm^2)	4·252	4·166	4·791	8·370
p_e (N/mm^2)	25·51	25·51	40·51	41·66

Note: Geometry definitions are given in Fig. 3.2.

from these stress expressions as follows:

$$w_f = a_f \sigma_f / E \tag{3.13}$$

$$w_s = a\sigma_s / E - \mu p a^2 / 2Eh \tag{3.14}$$

Examples of the stresses arising in uniformly stiffened cylinders are given in Table 3.1 using the notation p_{y3} as the stress at which σ_3 reaches the yield stress of the shell σ_y, etc. Case 1 is a design usable at a working external pressure of 2 N/mm^2 (for exception see Section 3.7.1) and has fairly wide stiffener spacing for a high external pressure requirement. For this reason p_{y5} is only 5% higher than the unstiffened value, $\sigma_y(h/a)$; p_{y3} is lower than p_{y7} but this is not always as shown by Case 2. Case 3 shows the effect of closer stiffener spacing.

The asterisk values, p_{y3}^*, etc., are obtained by including the beam–column effect due to the term in β. It can be seen that for Case 1 the lowest yield pressure p_{ys} is only reduced by 3%. For the higher yield stress, Case 4, the lowest yield pressure p_{y3} is reduced by 6%. The axisymmetric elastic buckling pressure p_e is included in Table 3.1 and is seen to be more than 10 times the maximum working pressure for Case 1.

3.2.3   End Bay Effects

The previous section dealt with the stresses and deflections in a typical section between uniformly spaced stiffening rings and away from heavy flanges or dome ends. It is noteworthy that the incorporation of a heavy stiffener or flange can lead to a weakening by increasing the circumferential membrane stress to values higher than σ_5. Bending stresses can be greatly increased by the presence of heavy stiffeners or their equivalent, but are unlikely to affect the collapse pressure as discussed later.

The increase in circumferential membrane stress is due to the fact that the differential equation (3.12) is the same as for a beam on an elastic foundation and has the characteristic that the deflection response to a concentrated load is a damped cosine. This is illustrated in Fig. 3.3. The reduced radial deflection at a heavy stiffener is equivalent to a radially outwards load and will usually result in an increased circumferential mean stress compared to that in the typical bay unless the stiffener spacings near to the heavy stiffener are slightly reduced. The effect is usually only a few per cent in cylinders but can be larger near to cone–cylinder intersections. Uniformly framed cylinders will almost invariably collapse near to the ends owing to this effect unless overall collapse occurs earlier owing to inadequate stiffener size. The deformations and stresses near to heavy ends can easily be calculated using the general analysis programs described in Kendrick and Mc-Keeman (1961) and Bushnell (1974).

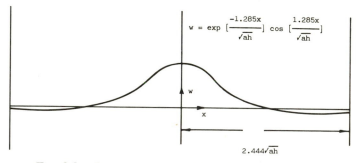

FIG. 3.3.   Response to concentrated axisymmetric load.

3.2.4   Non-Axisymmetric Loading

When the loading is not axially symmetric the stress analysis is best carried out by breaking the loading down into its modal components. The analysis can be carried out for modal components as a 2D problem and then superimposed to give the total stress distribution and deformation pattern. The program described in Bushnell (1974) does this extremely conveniently and efficiently. An alternative approach requiring much more computing time and not recommended for axisymmetric structure is to use a general 3D finite element program such as NASTRAN described in McCormick (1982).

3.3   ELASTIC BIFURCATION BUCKLING

3.3.1   The Form of Bifurcation Buckling

Ring-stiffened cylinders of perfect axial symmetry will deform under external pressure in the way described in Section 3.2. However, in all practical cases the axisymmetric asymptotic buckling discussed previously will be preceded by bifurcation buckling as shown in Fig. 3.4, occurring either elastically or plastically, depending upon the geometry and the ratio of yield stress to Young's modulus. Elastic buckling will be considered first.

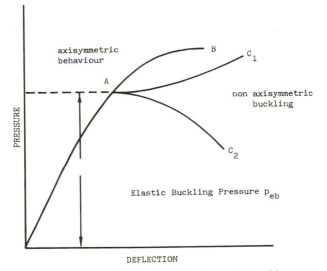

FIG. 3.4.   Possible load–deflection relationship.

Figure 3.4 illustrates a case where a considerable degree of non-linearity in the axisymmetric behaviour occurs before bifurcation is possible. This is unlikely in practical cases where the non-linearity will usually be only a few per cent at the bifurcation pressure.

Figure 3.4 illustrates that for $p < p_{eb}$ only one deflection corresponds to one value of p. In this region the deformation is axisymmetric and a small disturbance from axial symmetry, such as could be caused by a vibration, would merely produce oscillations about the axially symmetric equilibrium position. As the pressure is increased the response to a given non-axisymmetric force would increase until at $p = p_{eb}$ the shell would become unstable and, for pressures greater than p_{eb}, the curve AB is only possible theoretically since an infinitesimal disturbance would cause a sudden dynamic motion.

The rising form of post-buckling curve, labelled C_1, is possible but yielding will usually result in a drop of pressure except for cylinders which buckle at extremely low values of strain. The bifurcation buckling is associated with the shell developing departures from the circular which are in the form of pure sine waves in the circumferential direction as illustrated in Fig. 3.5. The shape in the longitudinal direction can be very varied and for any cylinder there are a doubly infinite number of buckling modes associated with $n = 1, 2, 3, 4. . .$, since for each n there is an infinite number of longitudinal mode shapes and there is no limit to the size of n. In practice, the meaningful number of buckling modes is finite because wavelengths in the circumferential or longitudinal direction must be several times the shell thickness for them to be meaningful in terms of thin shell theory. It is worth noting that only buckling shape is meaningful since the magnitude is indeterminate.

MODE SHAPE N=2   MODE SHAPE N=3   MODE SHAPE N=4

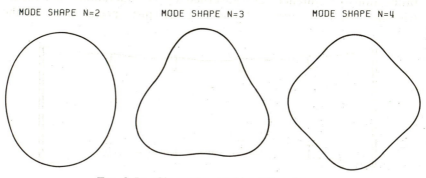

FIG. 3.5.   Circumferential buckling shapes.

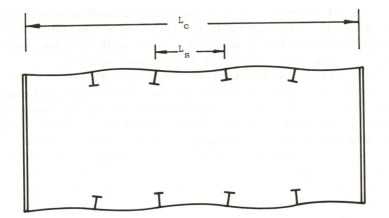

FIG. 3.6.   Interstiffener buckling.

Although the innumerable elastic buckling modes described above are real, it is possible to design cylinders by considering only three simple cases designated:

(a) interstiffener buckling (Fig. 3.6);
(b) overall buckling   (Fig. 3.7);
(c) stiffener tripping   (Fig. 3.8).

This is because for a cylinder of a given radius and thickness the stiffener spacing is governed by considerations of interstiffener buckling. The size of stiffeners is governed by considerations of overall buckling and has a secondary effect on interstiffener buckling. The proportions of stiffeners are governed by considerations of stiffener tripping. All three types of buckling are just special cases of the

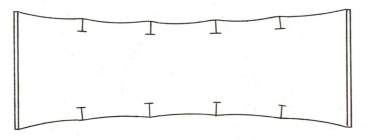

FIG. 3.7.   Overall buckling.

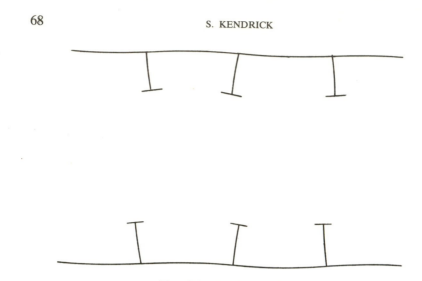

Fig. 3.8.   Stiffener tripping.

general buckling modes but each can be calculated more simply as a special case.

The theory of all three types of buckling is treated extensively in Gill (1970) but only the simpler formulae will be repeated here because they are the only ones needed in design.

3.3.2 Interstiffener Buckling

A good approximation to the interstiffener buckling pressure is given by the following assumptions:

- (a) The effect of stiffeners on pre-buckling stress in the shell can be neglected.
- (b) The rotational and axial restraint to shell buckling due to the stiffeners can be neglected.
- (c) The stiffening rings remain circular during buckling.

With these assumptions the following buckling displacement pattern can be shown to be an exact solution.

$u = A \cos n\theta \cos (\pi x/L)$ (longitudinal buckling displacement)

$v = B \sin n\theta \sin (\pi x/L)$ (tangential buckling displacement)   (3.15)

$w = C \sin n\theta \sin (\pi x/L)$ (radial buckling displacement)

A third-order matrix equation can be derived for calculating the buckling pressure (eigenvalue) and the mode shape (in this case the

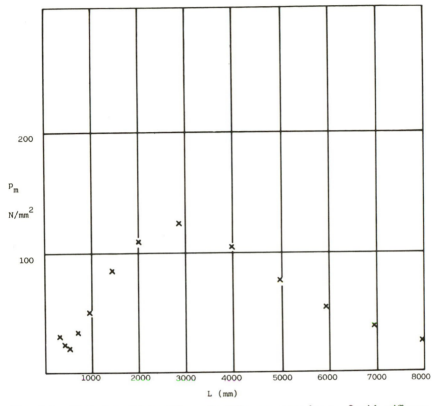

FIG. 3.9. Variation of interstiffener buckling pressure for $n = 2$ with stiffener spacing.

ratio $A : B : C$). An approximation to the lowest root of this matrix equation was derived by von Mises (1929) and is given in Timoshenko and Gere (1961). With a small modification to give correct answers for low values of n the buckling pressure is as follows

$$p_m = \left(\frac{Eh}{a}\right) \frac{1}{\left[n^2 - 1 + \frac{1}{2}\left(\frac{\pi a}{L}\right)^2\right]}$$

$$\times \left\{\frac{1}{[n^2(L/\pi a)^2 + 1]^2} + \frac{h^2}{12a^2(1 - \mu^2)}[n^2 - 1 + (\pi a/L)^2]^2\right\} \qquad (3.16)$$

The variation of p_m with both L and n is of interest and is shown in Figs 3.9 and 3.10 for the Case 1 of Table 3.1.

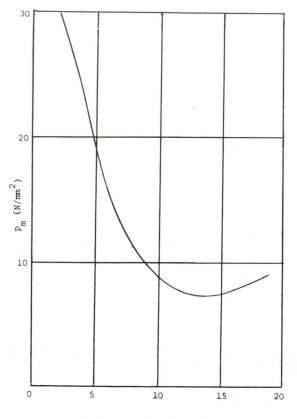

n   Number of Circumferential Lobes

FIG. 3.10   Variation of interstiffener buckling pressure with the number of circumferential lobes.

The value of n at which the minimum occurs is given in Fig. 3.6(1) of British Standards (1976). The minimum value of p_m can also be obtained from ε which is given graphically in Fig. 3.6(2) of British Standards (1976). The parameter ε is the circumferential buckling strain and the following relationship holds:

$$p_m = (Eh/a)\varepsilon \qquad (3.17)$$

3.3.3 Overall Buckling

A good approximation to the overall buckling pressure is derived in Gill (1970), p. 454, and is as follows:

$$p = (Eh/a)\lambda^4/(n^2 - 1 + \lambda^2/2)(n^2 + \lambda^2)^2 + (n^2 - 1)EI_c/a^3L_s \qquad (3.18)$$

TABLE 3.2

L_c (mm)		3 750	6 750	8 250	9 750	11 250	21 600
L_e (mm)							
p_2 (N/mm^2)	457	112·0	43·7	27·0	17·6	12·2	4·07
p_3 (N/mm^2)	443	32·4	13·4	11·0	9·90	9·34	8·59
p_4 (N/mm^2)	427	22·3	16·9	16·3	16·1	16·0	15·9

where $\lambda = \pi a/L_c$ and I_c is the second moment of area of the combined section of stiffener plus effective length L_e of the shell. Values of L_e/L_s are given as Table 3.6(1) in British Standards (1976). Equation (3.18) is obtained by the addition of the buckling pressure for the unstiffened cylinder to the buckling pressure for a combined section of one ring stiffener plus one bay of shell with a reduced effective length L_e. Numerical values obtained from eqn (3.18) for Case 1 of Table 3.1, but with variation of L_c are given in Table 3.2.

The results of Table 3.2 illustrate the following features which are common to overall buckling pressures:

(1) p_n reduces with increasing L_c;
(2) the variation of p_n with L_c reduces rapidly for increasing n;
(3) the value of n for which p_n is a minimum increases as L_c decreases;
(4) L_e is not a function of L_c.

3.3.4 Stiffener Tripping

Both external and internal stiffeners can undergo local instability but internal stiffeners buckle at much lower applied stresses. A conservative buckling stress for internal stiffeners is easily derived if a condition of zero rotational restraint is assumed at the toe. With reference to Fig. 3.11 the circumferential strain can be written by inspection in terms of the radial displacement w and tripping angle β as follows:

$$\varepsilon = [-w + (Z + z)(1 - \cos \beta) + x \sin \beta]/[a - (Z + z)]$$

$$\approx \frac{1}{a}\left[-w + \frac{(Z+z)}{2}\beta^2 + x\beta\right] \tag{3.19}$$

The above equation for ε is derived on the assumption that the stiffener retains its cross-sectional shape and rotates about its toe.

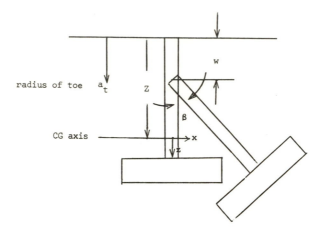

FIG. 3.11.   Geometry definition for stiffener tripping.

The elastic strain energy is given by

$$V = \pi a E \iint \varepsilon^2 \, dA \qquad \text{taken over the stiffener cross-section}$$

$$= (\pi E/a) \iint [w^2 - w(Z+z)\beta^2 + x^2\beta^2] \, dA \qquad \begin{array}{l}\text{for a section symmetrical} \\ \text{about the } z\text{-axis}\end{array}$$

$$= (\pi E/a)(w^2 A_s - w A_s Z\beta^2 + I_z\beta^2) \qquad \begin{array}{l}\text{if terms in } \beta^3 \text{ and above} \\ \text{are neglected} \qquad\qquad (3.20)\end{array}$$

where I_z is the second moment of area about the z-axis. The work done by the external load/unit length q is given by

$$W = \pi a q w \qquad\qquad\qquad (3.21)$$

Equations (3.20) and (3.21) yield

$$E(w^2 A_s - w A_s Z\beta^2 + I_z\beta^2) = q a^2 w$$

The trivial solution is $\beta = 0$, $w = qa^2/EA_s$. A solution $\beta \neq 0$ is also possible if

$$w = qa^2/EA_s \quad \text{and also} \quad w = I_z/A_s Z \qquad (3.22)$$

This gives

$$q = EI_z/a^2 Z \qquad\qquad\qquad (3.23)$$

$$\sigma_e = EI_z/aZA_s \qquad\qquad\qquad (3.24)$$

For the stiffener geometry given in Case 1, Table 3.1, eqn (3.24) gives $\sigma_e = 224 \, \text{N/mm}^2$ which is approximately one-half of the yield stress. Equation (3.24) is used in British Standards (1976) for the design of flanged stiffeners in spite of its extreme pessimism in most cases. The true buckling stress for geometry of Case 1, Table 3.1, is many times higher than that given by eqn (3.24) due to rotational restraint provided by the shell plating. This will be discussed later.

For flat bar stiffeners, eqn (3.24) gives extremely low buckling stresses and the assumption of zero rotational restraint cannot be used in design. An alternative approach is adopted in British Standards (1976) of fixing a lower bound for the buckling stress associated with zero rotational restraint for the value of n at which p_m is a minimum. Fortunately the buckling of flat bar stiffeners for the range of n of interest can be tabulated in terms of two non-dimensional parameters so that exact theory can be used. Such a tabulation is given in British Standards (1976).

A rigorous theory for sideways tripping is given in Gill (1970), p. 455, and developed further in Kendrick (1983a). The earlier theory treats only the stiffener and needs to be given a value for the rotational stiffness at the toe. The later theory treats shell and stiffener simultaneously and hence calculates the correct rotational restraint. It also treats interstiffener instability of the shell subject to the rotational restraint of the stiffener which is a refinement of the theory given in Section 3.3.2.

Numerical results for the geometry of Case 1, Table 3.1, are given in Table 3.3. The following comparisons can be made between the results of the various theories which illustrate general features of these analyses.

(1) For low n, when $p_m > \text{N9B}$ (clamped) the stiffener is effectively clamped at the toe, i.e. E1 $\simeq$ N9B (clamped). Also E2 and p_m are similar showing that the stiffener cannot effectively restrain the shell rotation.

(2) For higher values of n (in this case $n \geqslant 6$), E2 and N9B (clamped) are very similar showing that the shell effectively clamps the stiffener provided that N9B (clamped) and p_m are not similar in value.

(3) In the intermediate range of n (around $n = 5$ in this case) the value of E1 is significantly lower than either N9B (clamped) or p_m. This shows an interaction between sideways tripping and interstiffener buckling where p_m is similar to N9B (clamped).

S. KENDRICK

TABLE 3.3
ELASTIC BUCKLING PRESSURES (N/mm^2)

n	N9E		N9B		p_m	BOSOR 4				
						Branched shell			Discrete ring	
	E1	E2	Clamped	Zero rotational restraint		$\bar{E}1$	$\bar{E}2$	$\bar{E}3$	$\bar{E}1$	$\bar{E}2$
0			16·8	2·45						
1			17·1	2·94						
2	16·6	31·3	16·8	3·76	30·3	3·37(0)	15·7(3)	24·0(2)	3·54(0)	399·0(1)
3	16·4	27·6	16·6	4·89	26·8	8·59(0)	15·4(3)	22·9(2)	9·69(0)	189·0(1)
4	16·6	23·6	16·9	6·25	22·9	14·8 (0)	15·5(3)	22·2(2)	18·2 (0)	104·0(1)
5	16·9	20·1	17·7	7·84	19·2	16·0 (3)	17·9(2)	20·1(4)	27·4 (2)	64·3(1)
6	15·5	19·5	19·1	9·70	15·9	15·5 (4)	17·1(2)	18·6(3)	33·8 (2)	42·8(1)
7	13·0	21·2	21·0	11·8	13·2	13·3 (4)	15·9(2)	19·9(3)	30·6 (1)	34·8(2)
8	11·0	23·6	23·5	14·2	11·1	11·4 (4)	14·8(2)	22·0(3)	23·3 (1)	31·9(2)
9	9·55	26·5	26·4	16·7	9·62	9·94(1)	13·8(2)	24·5(3)	18·8 (1)	28·0(2)
10	8·52	29·9	29·8	19·2	8·57	8·91(1)	13·0(2)	27·3(3)	16·1 (1)	24·5(2)
11	7·84	33·6	33·5	21·7	7·89	8·24(1)	12·3(2)	30·1(3)	14·4 (1)	21·8(2)
12	7·45	37·5	37·4	23·9	7·49	7·85(1)	11·8(2)	32·8(3)	13·5 (1)	19·7(2)
13	7·28	41·4	41·3	25·8	7·32	7·70(1)	11·5(2)	35·0(5)	13·0 (1)	18·1(2)
14	7·27	45·0	45·0	27·2	7·31	7·71(1)	11·3(2)	36·3(5)	12·8 (1)	17·0(2)
15	7·40	48·2	48·1	28·1	7·44	7·86(1)	11·3(2)	37·1(5)	12·8 (1)	16·2(2)
16	7·63	50·5	50·5	28·7	7·67	8·13(1)	11·3(2)	37·5(5)	12·9 (1)	15·7(2)

Notation:
N9B   Theory of Gill (1970)
N9E   Theory of Kendrick (1983a)
E1   First eigenvalue
E2   Second eigenvalue
p_m Equation (3.16)
BOSOR 4   Bushnell (1974)

(0) Overall
(1) Interstiffener
(2) Interstiffener, symmetrical about stiffener
(3) Local instability, little shell deformation
(4) Local instability, significant shell deformation
(5) Local instability, significant $(m = 2)$ shell deformation

(4) For higher values of n, E1 and p_m are very similar showing once again that the stiffener provides little rotational restraint to the shell.

The five last columns headed BOSOR 4 will be discussed later.

3.3.5 Analysis by General Computer Program

All of the types of elastic buckling treated in Sections 3.3.2 to 3.3.4, and many more besides, can be analysed by the powerful computer program BOSOR 4 written by Bushnell (1974). This program can analyse any axisymmetric stiffened shell, but it is for the sophisticated and experienced user unless simplified input formats are used for special problems. BOSOR 4 can be used with varying degrees of approximation. For example, stiffening rings can either be treated as discrete rings, in which case engineering approximations are made in the formulation of stiffnesses, or treated as branched shells with the only approximations those of thin shell theory. BOSOR 4 uses a finite difference solution to the differential equations and the mesh size is completely variable. Use of a fine mesh gives high accuracy but sometimes at the expense of allowing many unwanted modes of buckling to arise and complicate the output.

The use of BOSOR 4 will be illustrated for the geometry of Table 3.1, Case 1. In principle one idealisation could be used to find all modes of buckling. In practice the limitation on the number of shell segments and the number of mesh points means that several idealisations need to be used to find all modes of interest. For Case 1, Table 3.1, the number of stiffeners is too great for them to be treated as branched shells. The stiffeners have to be treated as discrete rings which involve engineering approximation and cannot give the local instability modes.

An analysis of Case 1, Table 3.1, has been carried out using discrete rings for the stiffeners and two values of N the number of mesh points in each shell bay between stiffeners. The first three eigenvalues for $n = 2, 3, 4$ are given in Table 3.4 and the various types of mode shape are given in Fig. 3.12. The first eigenvalue mode shapes are all close to

TABLE 3.4
BOSOR 4 BUCKLING PRESSURES (N/mm^2)

n	$N = 4$			$N = 10$			Equation (3.18)
	E1	E2	E3	E1	E2	E3	
	(0, 1)	(0, 2)	m	(0, 1)	(0, 2)	i	
2	4·461	13·24	27·1	4·485	13·21	22·92	4·07
	(0, 1)	(0, 2)	(0, 3)	(0, 1)	(0, 2)	(0, 3)	
3	9·74	10·56	13·04	9·721	10·53	12·99	8·59
	(0, 1)	(0, 2)	(0, 3)	(0, 1)	(0, 2)	(0, 3)	
4	18·30	18·36	18·65	18·15	18·20	18·49	15·9
				(i)	(i)	(i)	
14				9·565	9·582	9·598	

Notation:
i   Interstiffener buckling
(0, r)   Overall buckling with mode shape $w = A \sin n\theta \sin (r\pi x/L_b)$
m   Mixed mode buckling involving stiffener deformation and interstiffener deformation
N   Number of mesh points between stiffeners

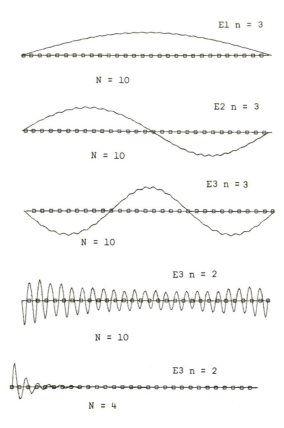

FIG. 3.12.   Longitudinal mode shapes.

one-half sine wave between the ends with small interstiffener deformations. The $r = 2$, 3 mode shapes are close to that given by

$$w = A \sin n\theta \sin (r\pi x/L_c)$$

where x is measured from one end.

The results from the simple eqn (3.18) for the appropriate value of L_c are also included in Table 3.4 and can be seen to give a good approximation to the E1 values. The $r = 2$ values are close to those obtained from eqn (3.18) using $L_c/2$ instead of L_c. The results from eqn (3.18) are closer to the correct values for the structure because the use of discrete rings in BOSOR 4 introduces errors. This will be shown later in the discussion on single stiffener calculations using BOSOR 4.

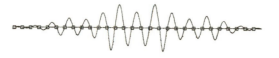

Mode 1

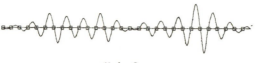

Mode 2

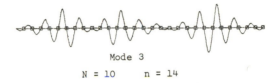

Mode 3

N = 10   n = 14

FIG. 3.13.   First three longitudinal mode shapes.

The value of E3 and the associated mode shape for $n = 2$ is very sensitive to the value of N as illustrated in Fig. 3.12. If the value of N in any bay of shell plating is increased from 10, the buckling deformation will be concentrated in that bay to the exclusion of elsewhere. Unless values of N are taken everywhere so large that further increases do not affect the mode shape then the latter are meaningless. For E1 $n = 2$ the mode shape and eigenvalue are little affected by increasing from $N = 4$ to $N = 10$ so that they are both meaningful.

The first three eigenvalues for $N = 10$ $n = 14$ are also included in Table 3.4 and are illustrated in Fig. 3.13. The eigenvalues are seen to be very close in value in spite of the considerable variation in mode shapes. The value of $9 \cdot 6 \, \text{N/mm}^2$ is considerably above the correct value of $7 \cdot 70 \, \text{N/mm}^2$ owing to the incorrect rotational restraint provided by the stiffener idealisation. This will be discussed further in the discussion on single stiffener calculations.

In order to examine local instability stiffener modes of buckling and the inaccuracies associated with discrete ring idealisation a number of single stiffener results are given in Table 3.3. The idealisation required symmetry about midbay as the only imposed boundary condition. The mode shapes notation 0–5 are all illustrated in Fig. 3.14. The

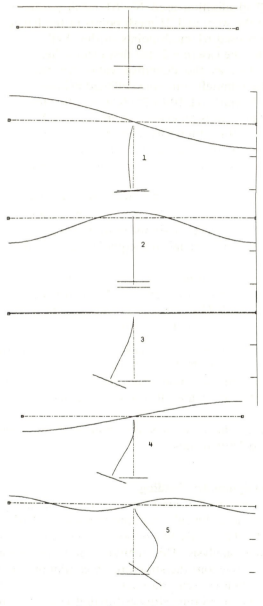

Number denotes Mode Type

Fɪɢ. 3.14.   Single stiffener buckling modes.

branched shell idealisation used $N = 61$ mesh points in the shell, 21 mesh points in the web, and 21 mesh points in the flange. The discrete ring idealisation used 61 mesh points in the shell.

First, consider the case $n = 2$; the first eigenvalue is $3 \cdot 37$ N/mm^2 and this can be taken as the definitive value for the overall buckling pressure for the infinitely long ring stiffened cylinder. The discrete ring value is $3 \cdot 54$ N/mm$^2 = (1 \cdot 10)(3 \cdot 37)$ N/mm^2 showing that the use of discrete rings introduces an erroneous increase in buckling pressure of 10%. It is interesting therefore that, from Table 3.4, $N = 10$ gives $E1 = 4 \cdot 49$ which is 10% higher than the value given by eqn (3.18). This suggests strongly that the latter value is accurate to much better than 10%.

Let us now consider $n = 14$ where the branched shell value of $7 \cdot 71$ N/mm^2 is close to the value $7 \cdot 31$ N/mm^2 given by the von Mises equation (eqn (3.16)). This shows that the error introduced by the assumptions used in deriving the equation is only about 5% in this case.

Comparing discrete ring with branched shell for all values of n shows that the former is only meaningful for overall modes of buckling. Comparing BOSOR 4 branched shell with N9E, N9B and p_m values the following points may be made.

(a) The lowest non-overall buckling pressure is always predicted accurately using N9E.

(b) The interstiffener mode buckling pressures (type 1) obtained from BOSOR 4 are all in good agreement with N9E and p_m values.

(c) The type 3 buckling pressures from BOSOR 4 agree well with clamped N9B results.

3.3.6 Non-Axisymmetric loading

When the loading is non-axisymmetric the calculation of buckling pressures is far more difficult. An approximate method is available as an option in BOSOR 4. By this option a stress analysis is first carried out using Fourier analysis. This analysis is not approximate and produces stresses throughout the structure by combining modal solutions. A generator is then chosen and buckling calculations are carried out assuming that the membrane stresses for that generator are applied to all generators. By varying the generator chosen a lower bound to the true buckling pressure can usually be found.

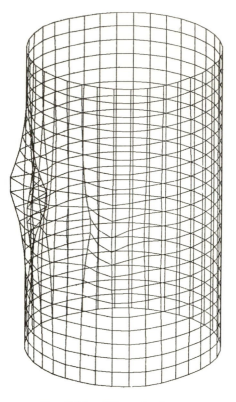

FIG. 3.15.   3D mode shape.

It is possible to use general finite element programs such as NAS-
TRAN, described in McCormick (1982). Such calculations require
large times on large computers and checking the adequacy of the mesh
size employed is difficult and expensive. The shape associated with the
lowest buckling load for a saddle support problem calculated by
NASTRAN is shown in Fig. 3.15. Considerable expertise is required to
get reliable answers using this very powerful facility.

3.4   THE EFFECT OF SHAPE IMPERFECTIONS ON ELASTIC DEFORMATION

3.4.1   Axisymmetric Shape Imperfections

The fabrication of ring-stiffened cylinders usually produces a degree of
concertina-type distortion in which internal stiffeners stand out. The

opposite is true for external stiffeners. Axisymmetric analysis using the general computer programs described in Section 3.2 shows that 'shell inwards' initial distortions increase the circumferential stresses in the shell, whereas an initial outward bulging of the shell reduces these stresses. Not surprisingly this leads to a reduction in strength in the former case and an increase in strength in the latter case. An effect of ±5% is fairly common and this will be discussed further in Section 3.6.

3.4.2 Non-Axisymmetric Shape Imperfections

The analysis of non-axisymmetric shape imperfections is treated in Gill (1970) but a simplified 'one-mode' approach can be used for design purposes. The shape of any bifurcation buckling mode can be expressed as

$$w_b = f(x) \sin n\theta \qquad (3.25)$$

where $f(x)_{max} = 1$.

Under applied pressure any initial shape imperfection in the shape of this buckling mode but with a maximum amplitude A will give rise to normal displacements of magnitude

$$w = A \cdot f(x) \sin n\theta[p/(p_n - p)] \qquad (3.26)$$

where p_n is the elastic buckling pressure associated with mode n. The change of curvature in the circumferential direction is

$$\Delta K = \pm[(w + w_{\theta\theta})/a^2] \qquad (3.27)$$

and the stress in a stiffener flange due to this change of curvature is

$$\sigma_{sb} = Ee_f\Delta K \qquad (3.28)$$

where e_f is the distance of the stiffener flange from the neutral axis. This leads to the following expression for the stress in the stiffener flange:

$$\sigma_{sb} = (n^2 - 1)(Ee_f/a^2)A \cdot f(x)[p/(p_n - p)] \sin n\theta \qquad (3.29)$$

where x is the axial coordinate at the position of the stiffener under consideration. The term $A \cdot f(x)$ in eqn (3.29) shows that initial shape imperfections in the shape of interstiffener buckling modes play an insignificant part in producing stiffener bending stresses. This is because for interstiffener modes $A \cdot f(x)$ is very small compared to the maximum departure from the mean circle.

A conservative estimate of stiffener bending stresses can be obtained by assuming that $A \cdot f(x)$ is equal to ε_m, the maximum allowed departure from the mean circle.

TABLE 3.5

STIFFENER YIELD AND COLLAPSE PRESSURES

ε_m/a	L_c (mm)	n	p_n (N/mm^2)	p_{sy} (N/mm^2)	p_c (ZRS) (N/mm^2)	p_c (RS2) (N/mm^2)
0	nr	nr	nr	5·28		
0·0025	21 600	2	4·07	2·66	2·64	2·32
0·005	21 600	2	4·07	2·15	2·21	2·03
0·01	21 600	2	4·07	1·61	1·73	1·66
0·0025	11 250	2	12·25	4·48	4·42	4·56
0·0025	21 600	3	8·594	3·14	3·14	2·80
0·005	21 600	3	8·594	2·40	2·44	2·28
0·01	21 600	3	8·594	1·68	1·70	1·62
0·0025	11 250	3	9·342	3·28	3·33	3·12

nr, not relevant.

The maximum total stress in the stiffener can now be written as

$$\sigma_{sT} = \sigma_s + (n^2 - 1)(Ee_f/a^2)\varepsilon_m[p/(p_n - p)] \qquad (3.30)$$

Equating σ_{sT} to σ_{ys} leads to a quadratic in $p = p_{sy}$ for the pressure at which the stiffener first yields assuming zero residual stresses.

Values of p_{sy} are given in Table 3.5 for the geometry of Table 3.1, Case 1, and for one shorter overall length. Four values of initial departure from the mean circle are taken: namely, 0%, $\frac{1}{4}$%, $\frac{1}{2}$% and 1% on radius. The values of p_c are discussed later in Section 3.5. The following points can be made.

(a) The yield pressure is greatly reduced (factor of 0·3) by an out-of-roundness of 1%. It is reduced by a factor of 0·60 on going from $\frac{1}{4}$% to 1% out-of-roundness.

(b) The yield pressure is very sensitive to overall length L_c.

(c) The ratio (yield pressure/p_n) varies greatly.

It will be shown in Section 3.7 that eqn (3.30) is a very useful design equation.

3.5 ELASTO-PLASTIC COLLAPSE

3.5.1 Shell Collapse

The elastic deformation analysis given in Section 3.2 can be extended into the elasto-plastic range using a general axisymmetric analysis program such as BOSOR 5 as described in Bushnell (1976). This program is capable of bifurcation analysis of axisymmetric structure as well as being capable of calculating asymptotic axisymmetric collapse. The effect on collapse of axisymmetric shape imperfections and residual stresses can be investigated.

Until more research has been carried out it is not certain that such analysis would give better predictions of interstiffener collapse than the semi-empirical method described in Section 3.6. For ratios p_m/p_{y5} greater than 1·5 empirical predictions can be made within 10% provided that shape imperfections are kept within acceptable limits. For lower ratios of p_m/p_{y5}, shape imperfections are known to produce greater scatter and the non-axisymmetric components can be expected to be significant.

Programs are available for general 3D elastic–plastic shell analysis. Two of the better known ones are ASAS N/L by Atkins (1982) and STAGS by Almroth et al. (1980). These programs require much computing time and preparation time as well as expert use and are not practicable for design use. They can, however, prove very useful in special cases: for example in examining the effect of localised damage, unusual shape imperfections, etc. An example of the use of ASAS N/L is given in Kendrick (1983b).

3.5.2 Overall Collapse

The computing time necessary to use ASAL N/L or STAGS to analyse overall collapse would be much greater than for interstiffener collapse because much more structure needs to be included in the analysis. A far simpler approach based on a number of simplifying physical assumptions is described in Kendrick (1979) and summarised below.

First, considering a ring with an initial departure from circularity w_0 the bending moment can be written

$$M = -pa(w + w_0) \tag{3.31}$$

the change of curvature is

$$\Delta K = (w + w_{\theta\theta})/a^2 \tag{3.32}$$

Given a relationship between M and ΔK, the problem is easily solved even when the M–ΔK relationship is non-linear.

In the elastic case when $M = EI\,\Delta K$, eqns (3.31) and (3.32) lead to

$$w_{\theta\theta} + w + \frac{pa^3}{EI}(w + w_0) = 0 \tag{3.33}$$

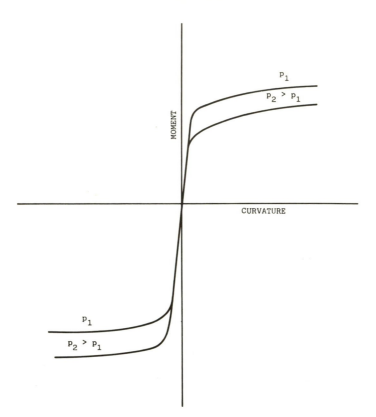

FIG. 3.16.   Effect of circumferential membrane force on moment/curvature
relationship.

for $w_0 = \varepsilon_m \cos n\theta$ this gives

$$w = p\varepsilon_m \cos n\theta/(p_n - p) \qquad (3.34)$$

where $p_n = (n^2 - 1)(EI/a^3)$. Equation (3.34) is a particular case of eqn
(3.26) with p_n the well-known Föppl formula for the buckling of a ring.

Provided that the effect of plastic unloading is neglected, it is
possible to derive a one-to-one relationship

$$M = f(\Delta K, p)$$

allowing for the effects of residual stresses due to the method of
fabrication. The form of this relationship is given in Fig. 3.16. It can be
seen that the mean compressive force in the circumferential direction

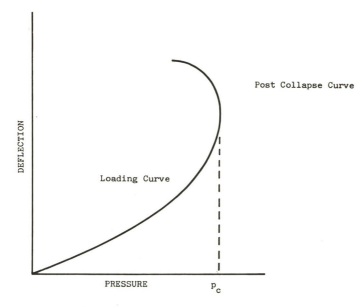

FIG. 3.17.   Form of calculated collapse curve.

due to external pressure reduces the maximum moment for one direction of bending but increases it in the other direction.

The simple method of solution described in Kendrick (1979) leads to a load–deflection relationship of the form shown in Fig. 3.17. The method of solution gives two deflections for each value of applied pressure except at the collapse pressure when the two solutions coincide.

Because of the assumption of zero plastic unloading there is no need to calculate the entire load–deflection curve in order to find the collapse pressure. Without this assumption an incremental approach would be necessary with greatly increased computer time. It has been shown that although plastic unloading does occur it has a very small effect on the collapse pressure and can be ignored.

The theoretical approach described above can be used to give first approximation answers for the collapse of very long cylinders reinforced with equally spaced stiffeners. The collapse pressures calculated by this approach would be in error for two reasons, as follows:

(a)   The axisymmetric stress distribution in a ring-stiffened cylinder is such that the ring stiffeners are appreciably less stressed than the plating. This is partly due to the ring stiffeners being stressed uniaxially whereas the plating is stressed biaxially. This leads to the ring stiffener stresses being reduced by a factor $(1 - \mu/2)$. The other factor is that the plating deforms between the ring stiffeners thus reducing the radial deformation at the stiffeners.

(b)   The elastic buckling pressure for a ring-stiffened cylinder will usually be less than that for a ring composed of one ring stiffener plus a full bay length of shell. This is because the effective length of shell is usually less than the full frame space.

These two effects usually act in opposite directions with neglect of the true axisymmetric stress distribution leading to an underestimate of the collapse pressure whereas the assumption of full effective breadth leads to an overestimate.

The effect (a) can be allowed for by adding a compressive stress to the plating and subtracting a compressive stress from the ring stiffener so that the total circumferential load is unchanged but the stress in the ring stiffener is exactly that from axisymmetric theory. The compressive stress which is subtracted from the ring stiffener is as follows:

$$\sigma_f = paL/(A_f + A_p) - p\sigma_{ys}/p_{ys}$$

where A_f is the area of the stiffener, A_p is the area of the shell, and p_{ys} is the pressure at which the stiffener stress in a perfect elastic cylinder reaches the yield stress of the stiffener σ_{ys}. The compressive stress which is added to the shell plating is

$$\sigma_p = \sigma_f(A_f/A_p)$$

It is to be noted that these additional stresses vary with the external pressure.

The effect (b) can be allowed for by adding to the function $f(\Delta K, F)$ a term $A \, \Delta K$ where

$$A = a^3 L p_n/(n^2 - 1) - EI$$

p_n is the elastic overall buckling pressure allowing for reduced effective length of plating, and EI is the elastic flexural rigidity of the combined section of stiffener plus a length L_s of plating.

For very long cylinders the constant A will usually be negative and this has the effect of reducing the bending stiffness. It is necessary to limit the effect of the term $A \, \Delta K$ to prevent negative stiffnesses occurring. This is done by keeping M constant at the value at which $dM/d\,\Delta K = 0$.

Using this approach it is necessary to consider initial departures from the mean circle in the form of pure buckling modes. This is because p_n varies with mode and a correct value of p_n could not be assigned for a general initial shape made up of many modal components. A finite length cylinder can be treated by using the appropriate value of p_n.

Numerical results for the collapse pressures obtained from this simplified approach are given in Table 3.5 and are denoted by p_c (ZRS) for the condition of zero residual stress. It is notable that collapse occurs very soon after reaching p_{sy} which is the value at which yielding first occurs. This is due to the use of Tee-bar stiffeners which have little reserve of stiffness once the flange is yielded. The cases where p_c values are slightly less than p_{sy} result from a slight error in the theory. This error is because an elastic neutral axis position appropriate to full effective breadth in the plastic analysis is used whereas p_{sy} is calculated using the position appropriate to a reduced effective breadth L_e.

3.5.3 The Effect of Residual Stresses

The theory described in Kendrick (1979) can allow for the effect of residual stresses due to fabrication. A common form of fabrication is to cold roll the shell plating and stiffeners separately giving the stress distribution shown in Fig. 3.18 for Table 3.1, Case 1, and the collapse pressures denoted by p_c (RS2) in Table 3.5. It can be seen that the residual stresses reduce the collapse pressure by 13% for $\frac{1}{4}$% out-of-roundness but by only 4% for 1% out-of-roundness. The reason for this is that the more out-of-roundness the greater the importance of bending effects and hence the lesser importance of residual stresses. In the limit of, say, a square cross-section, rigid plastic analysis would hold and residual stresses would have no effect.

3.6   COLLAPSE PREDICTION

Collapse under external pressure is almost always implosive in nature and precipitated at small values of deflection. Under dead loading the collapse will usually involve both shell and stiffeners even when the collapse initiates in either the shell or the stiffeners. This is because

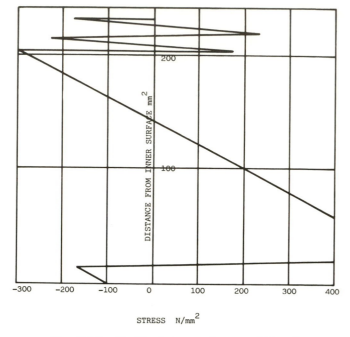

FIG. 3.18.   Residual stresses due to cold bending.

economical designs are such that the stiffeners have insufficient strength to remain circular when the shell has lost stiffness owing to collapse. Collapse can be arrested in several ways experimentally. For example, if a cylinder is tested in a pressure chamber, collapse is usually accompanied by a drop in pressure with equilibrium being reached at a lower pressure. The more the cylinder fills the chamber the smaller the deformation before equilibrium is reached. An effective way of limiting collapse deformation still further is by filling the cylinder with water with minimum air pockets and raising the differential pressure by bleeding off internal water.

To predict collapse pressures it is necessary to differentiate between collapse modes which initiate collapse and those which occur due to the occurrence of another mode of collapse. The first of these former modes is interstiffener collapse.

3.6.1 Collapse Between Stiffeners

When p_m is much smaller than p_{y5} and p_{ys} and the out-of-circularity is very small, as in machined cylinders, the collapse pressure will be close

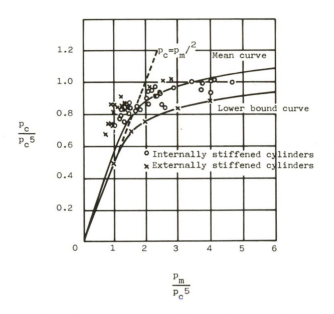

FIG. 3.19.   Plot of interstiffener collapse results.

to p_m. When p_m is greater than $6p_{y5}$ and appreciably smaller than p_{ys}, the collapse pressure will be close to $1\cdot15p_{c5}$. The factor of $1\cdot15$ is due to the influence of the end compression on the yield criteria (von Mises–Henky criterion). Collapse at pressures close to p_m will be lobar in appearance. Collapse at pressures close to $1\cdot15p_{c5}$ will be axisymmetric in appearance. For intermediate geometries the collapse is influenced by geometry, E and σ_y and out-of-circularity. As discussed in Gill (1970) there is a universal curve in terms of the non-dimensional parameters p_c/p_{y5} and p_m/p_{y5} which fits experimental data closely for $p_m/p_{y5} \geqslant 1\cdot5$ and provides a useful design curve over the whole range of geometries. Figure 3.19 shows a plot of well-documented experimental data and it can be seen that externally stiffened cylinders are significantly stronger than internally stiffened cylinders due to the favourable direction of axisymmetric welding distortion associated with the former. This distortion is likely to diminish as cylinder size increases so that the difference in collapse pressure could well diminish for cylinders larger than those used in the plot which were usually less than 1500 mm in diameter.

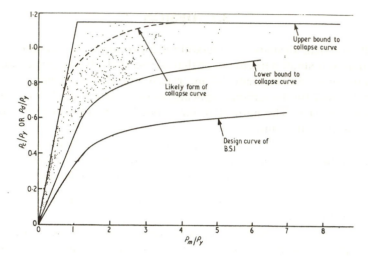

FIG. 3.20.   Plot of all experimental results.

For a variety of reasons, which are discussed in Gill (1970), the lower-bound collapse curve is taken as in Fig. 3.20 and with the ordinate reduced by a factor of 1·5 this curve is used as the design curve in British Standards (1976). The lower-bound curve is known to be appreciably pessimistic for cylinders which are of a high degree of circularity and for which $p_m/p_y < 1$. Such cylinders will usually collapse at pressures close to p_m. However fabricated cylinders with departures from perfect circularity of less than $\frac{1}{2}\%$ on radius can collapse at pressures close to $p_m/2$ and this determines the initial slope of the design curve. A fuller discussion of the choice of design curve is given in Kendrick (1983b).

3.6.2 Overall Collapse

The prediction of overall collapse for general shape imperfection is in principle possible using general programs such as described in Atkins (1982) and Almroth et al. (1980). Very few such calculations have been performed because they make very large demands on computer time. For idealised shape imperfections in the form of an overall buckling mode the theory described in Section 3.5.2 can be used. The latter theory has been found to give good agreement with experimental results as discussed in Kendrick (1979).

3.7 DESIGN

In all practical designs of ring-stiffened cylinders the weight of the stiffeners is a small percentage of that of the shell. For a given external pressure requirement, material and radius, the shell thickness is determined mainly by the stiffener spacing and to a much smaller extent by the stiffener size. The natural design procedure is therefore to aim for the required minimum collapse pressure for interstiffener collapse and to ensure that the stiffening rings are adequate to avoid premature overall collapse. Arranging for the pressures for overall collapse and interstiffener collapse to coincide is not good practice because:

(a) The collapse mechanisms would then interact making the calculation more complex.
(b) Slight over-design of the stiffeners so as to avoid rather than predict overall collapse is inexpensive in terms of weight or cost.
(c) Overall collapse pressures are far less predictable due to their extreme sensitivity to the degree of lack of circularity which is not known in advance.

The approach adopted in British Standards (1976) is to ensure that interstiffener collapse cannot occur at less than 1·5 times the design pressure. Overall collapse is not allowed to occur at less than 1·8 times the design pressure. For stress-relieved vessels this is achieved by the requirement

$$p_{sy} \geqslant 1 \cdot 8 p_d$$

For cold fabricated vessels the requirement is

$$p_{sy} \geqslant 2 \cdot 0 p_d$$

where p_{sy} is evaluated for $n = 2$–6 for $\varepsilon = (0 \cdot 005)a$. The reduction in overall collapse caused by residual stresses is allowed for by using $2 \cdot 0 p_d$ instead of $1 \cdot 8 p_d$. The need for elastic–plastic calculations is avoided by this procedure.

Stiffener proportions can be checked by the requirement that the lowest instability pressure associated with local stiffener instability is at least four times the design pressure. The factor of 4 is chosen because the design curve for interstiffener collapse requires that $p_m \geqslant 3 p_d$ and it is desirable to avoid interaction between the various buckling modes.

Using the N9E program (Section 3.3.4) which can be run on a small microcomputer an additional criterion for the limiting aspect ratio of the flange is required. A suitable criterion is given in British Standards (1976). Using a BOSOR 4 single stiffener, branched shell idealisation (Section 3.3.5), no additional criterion is required provided that sufficient mesh points are used in both web and flange to pick up web or flange buckling. Much simpler criteria for stiffener proportions suitable for hand computing are presented in British Standards (1976).

3.7.1 Computer-Aided Design

The design procedure outlined above is well suited to computer-aided design using the fact that all collapse pressures increase monotonically with the shell thickness h. A very useful design program [AMTE(S)/PDOO9] is available which takes as fixed parameters the radius, material properties, design pressure, stiffener proportions,

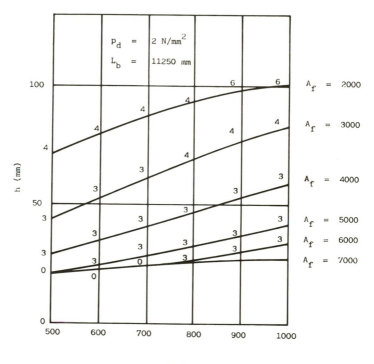

FIG. 3.21. Variation of required shell thickness with stiffener spacing and area.

shape tolerance and overall length. Ranges of values of stiffener spacing and area are then specified and the program calculates the shell thickness required for $n = 0$ (interstiffener collapse) and $n = 2, 3, 4, 5, 6$ (adequate p_{sy} value for $n = 2, 3, 4, 5, 6$). For a particular value of the stiffener area A_f a curve of required h against L_f can be drawn as shown in Fig. 3.21 for Table 3.1, Case 1, except for shell thickness and stiffener area. Cold forming is assumed so that p_{sy} must exceed $2p_d = 4$ for each value of n. The stiffener proportions are the same as those of Table 3.1.

The curves of Fig. 3.21 are labelled with the value of n which is critical. When $n = 0$, p_{sy} is greater than 4 for all values of n and the stiffener area is adequate. For any other value of n the shell thickness is determined by the need to achieve $p_{sy} = 4$ for that value of n. It can be seen that A_f needs to be at least 6000 mm^2 for $L_s = 750$ mm before the shell thickness is not determined by overall collapse rather than interstiffener collapse.

For $A_f < 6000$ mm^2, $L_s = 750$ mm, the structure is inefficient for the required external pressure loading. It may however be efficient for combinations of loading. For example many pressure vessels are designed for a high internal pressure but only need to withstand one atmosphere externally. For such cylinders the shell thickness is usually much thicker than the optimum for external pressure only.

3.8 SHAPE MEASUREMENT

The design procedures outlined in Section 3.7 require the cylinders to be manufactured to within a specified out-of-circularity. The measurement of shape is not always straightforward and a discussion of the available methods is given in Kendrick (1980).

3.9 CONCLUDING REMARKS

The analysis and design of ring-stiffened cylinders for external pressure loading can be carried out to high accuracy using the methods given above. The treatment of the effect of shape imperfections is idealised to shapes which are pure buckling modes. The presence of imperfections of more general shape will not affect the accuracy of collapse pressure prediction provided that the conditions used in Section 3.7 are satisfied.

When these conditions are not met overall collapse could occur first and 3D elasto-plastic analysis would be required for the prediction of collapse pressure. Little research has been done in this area and the use of suitable computer programs would need extensive checking against experimental results before they could be used with confidence. The assessment of the strength of damaged cylinders is a case in point and needs to be studied theoretically and experimentally.

REFERENCES

ALMROTH, B. O., BROGAN, F. A., STANLEY, G. M. (1980) Structural Analysis of General Shells. User Instructions for STAGSC-1, Lockheed Palo Alto Research Laboratory, California.

ATKINS RESEARCH AND DEVELOPMENT LTD (1982) ASAS/NL User Manual, Version 6, 1st edn.

BRITISH STANDARDS (1976) Specification for Unfired Fusion Welded Pressure Vessels, British Standards Institution, London, Section 3.6, pp. 3/43–3/52.

BUSHNELL, D. (1974) Stress, stability and vibration of complex branched shells of revolution. Computers and Structures, 4.

BUSHNELL, D. (1976) Program for buckling of elastic–plastic complex shells of revolution including large deflections and creep. Computers and Structures, 6.

GILL, S. S. (1970) The Stress Analysis of Pressure Vessels and Pressure Vessel Components, Pergamon Press, Oxford, pp. 405–511.

KENDRICK, S. (1961) The Deformation of Axisymmetric Shells, Report No NCRE/R457, July, pp. 1–17.

KENDRICK, S. (1979) The influence of shape imperfections and residual stresses on the collapse of stiffened cylinders. I. Mech. E. Conf. on Significance of Deviations from Design Shape, March. pp. 25–36.

KENDRICK, S. (1980) The measurement of shape in pressure vessels. 4th Int. Conf. Pressure Vessel Technology, London, May. pp. 261–267.

KENDRICK, S. (1983a) Developments in Pressure Vessel Technology—4 (Ed. by R. W. Nicholls), Applied Science Publishers, London, pp. 197–233.

KENDRICK, S. (1983b) The technical basis of the external pressure section of BS 5500. American Soc. Mech. Engrs, 83-PVP-6.

KENDRICK, S. and MCKEEMAN, J. L. (1961) Pegasus Computer Specifications—Axisymmetric Stress Analysis, Report No. NCRE/R452, March.

MCCORMICK, C. W. (Ed.) (1982) MSC/NASTRAN, Version 62A. Users Manual—Vols 1 and 2, MacNeal–Schwendler Corporation Report MSR-39.

VON MISES, R. (1929) Stodola Festschrift, Zurich, p. 418.

VON SANDEN, K. and GUNTHER, K. (1952) The strength of cylindrical shells stiffened by frames and bulkheads under uniform external pressure on all sides, 1920 and 1921. Translation 38, David Taylor Model Basin, Carderock, Maryland.

TIMOSHENKO, S. P. and GERE, J. M. (1961) *Theory of Elastic Stability*, McGraw-Hill, New York.

WENK, E. (1961) Pressure vessel analysis of submarine hulls. *The Welding Journal*, **40** (6).

WILSON, L. B. (1956) The Deformation Under Uniform Pressure of a Circular Cylindrical Shell Supported by Equally Spaced Circular Ring Frames, Reports, Nos NCRE/R337A, R337B and R337C, December.

WINDENBURG, D. and TRILLING, C. (1934). Collapse by instability of thin cylindrical shells under external pressure. *ASME Trans*, **56**.

Chapter 4

COMPOSITE, DOUBLE-SKIN SANDWICH PRESSURE VESSELS

PETER MONTAGUE

*Department of Civil Engineering, Simon Engineering Laboratories,
University of Manchester, UK*

SUMMARY

The first experiments on double-skinned composite cylinders under external pressure were done at the University of Manchester in 1975 using five and a half inch diameter steel cylinders with an epoxy-resin mixture between the skins. It was found that the steel skins attained their full yield strength without shell buckling occurring but, more than this, the cylinders continued to withstand increasing pressure with fully-yielded skins and collapsed only when the filler broke down in compression.

The resin filler was replaced by concrete, which is stiffer and cheaper, and numerous tests have been conducted under external pressure to investigate variations in geometric and material properties, end closures, penetrations, long-term loading and so on.

This chapter describes the results of these investigations and relates them to the simple analytical procedures developed to predict the stresses in the composite shells, their deformations and failure.

NOTATION

a_1	$d_1^2 + d_2^2$
a_2	$d_1^2 - d_2^2$
b	Thickness of filler
d	Mean diameter of shell

d_1, d_2 Outside, inside diameter of filler

d_o, d_i Outside, inside diameter of composite shell

d_n Diameter of nozzle

f_c Compressive strength of 6 in. diameter $\times$ 12 in. long solid cylinder of concrete

f_{cu} Characteristic cube strength of concrete

h Wall thickness of shell

$\bar{h}$ Thickness of equivalent homogeneous wall

$m_x, n_{\phi x}, m_{\phi x}, m_z, m_\theta, m_{\theta z}$ Stress resultants in the vicinity of the cylinder–nozzle intersection, see Fig. 4.9

p_1, p_2 Radial pressure at outside, inside interface, see Fig. 4.4

p_{c1} Elastic instability pressure of the (all-elastic) composite shell

p_{c2} Instability pressure of the partially-plastic composite shell

p_d Design (working) pressure of shell

p_f Failure pressure of the composite shell

p_f' Factored value of p_f

p_{f1} Empirical failure pressure, $p_{f1} < p_p$, see eqn (4.23)

p_{f2} Empirical failure pressure, $p_{f2} > p_{pp}$, see eqn (4.24)

p_i, p_o Inside, outside pressure on shell

p_{ln} Limit pressure of nozzle

p_{lsh} Limit pressure of shell

p_p Value of p_o at which the inside skin reaches yield

p_p' Factored value of p_p

p_{pp} Value of p_o at which the outside skin reaches yield

p_{th} Theoretical (strength) failure pressure of composite shell

r Radius of shell

t Thickness of skin

t_i, t_o Thickness of inside, outside skin

t_n Wall thickness of nozzle

w Mean radial displacement

w_i, w_o Inside, outside radial displacement

E_{c0} Concrete modulus at zero strain

E_f Elastic modulus of filler

E_p Instantaneous slope of stress versus plastic strain for steel (uniaxial test)

E_s Elastic modulus of skins

$\bar{E}$ Elastic modulus of the equivalent homogeneous wall

E'	Instantaneous modulus of fictitious 'biax-concrete'
L	Length of shell
P	Yield function
P_x	Longitudinal load on shell
α	d_o/h
γ	Percentage of skin area in composite wall cross-section
Δ	Maximum deviation from a true circle
ε	Strain
$\varepsilon_1, \varepsilon_2, \varepsilon_3$	Principal strains
$\varepsilon_x, \varepsilon_\theta$	Longitudinal strain, circumferential strain
$\varepsilon_{xsi}, \varepsilon_{xso}$	Longitudinal strain of inside, outside skin
$\varepsilon_{\theta_1}, \varepsilon_{\theta_2}$	Circumferential strain at interface 1, 2 (Fig. 4.4)
$\varepsilon_{\theta si}, \varepsilon_{\theta so}$	Circumferential strain of inside, outside skin
ε_{unimax}	Concrete strain at f_c, see Fig. 4.3c and 4.3d
λ	Instantaneous scalar multiplier
ν	Poisson's ratio
ν'	Poisson's ratio of fictitious 'biax-concrete'
ν_f, ν_s	Poisson's ratio of filler, skin
$\sigma_1, \sigma_2, \sigma_3$	Principal stresses
σ_{0f}	Uniaxial strength of resin filler
σ_{xf}	Mean longitudinal stress in filler
$\sigma_{xf1}, \sigma_{xf2}$	Longitudinal stress at outside, inside face of filler
$\sigma_{xsi}, \sigma_{xso}$	Longitudinal stress in inside, outside skin
σ_y	Yield stress of steel
$\sigma_{\theta f1}, \sigma_{\theta f2}$	Circumferential filler stress at outside, inside surface
$\sigma_{\theta si}, \sigma_{\theta so}$	Circumferential stress in inside, outside skin

4.1 INTRODUCTION

The idea of the double-skin shell to withstand external pressure, see Montague (1975), was born out of the frustration of trying to predict the collapse of ring-stiffened steel shells subjected to this kind of loading.

The ring-stiffened shell, Fig. 4.1a, is the conventional structure for resisting external pressure. Its analysis and design have attracted the attention of numerous illustrious investigators, from von Mises' (1914) classic elastic instability analysis to the distinguished work of Kendrick embodied in the recommendations of BS 5500 (1976).

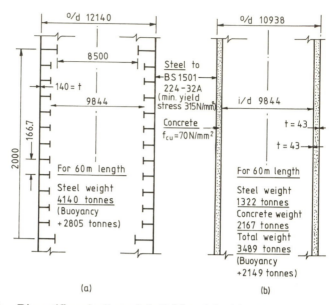

FIG. 4.1.   Ring-stiffened, all-steel shell (a) and double-skin composite shell (b) with similar inside clearance diameters, both designed to withstand 5 N/mm² (500 m water depth) working external pressure. (Approx. material cost ratio (a) : (b) = 2·5 : 1).

For short, relatively thick-walled single-skin steel shells, a rigid–plastic analysis, see Hodge (1959) or Montague (1969), or, more conservatively, a simple membrane yield analysis (giving the so-called boiler pressure), will furnish an adequate estimate of failure between stiff, radial diaphragms. For long, slender shells of good initial circularity, the collapse pressure will approach the von Mises prediction. Practical shells fall between these two extremes and their failure occurs as a result of interaction between strength and stability. Initial stresses and, more significantly, initial shape deviations from true circularity are important factors affecting the behaviour of the shell under load. The real shape of any shell can be determined only after fabrication is completed and, even with such detailed information, its analysis would be a difficult and complex operation. The BS 5500 design guidelines to avoid interstiffener failure are therefore based upon the empirical evidence from numerous tests and suggest that the initial out-of-circularity of the shell, $2\Delta/d$, should not exceed 0·5%. This is a tolerance which can be assured by experienced fabricators.

The stiffeners must retain their structural integrity beyond the failure load of the interstiffener shell length and considerable attention is therefore devoted to good stiffener design in BS 5500. During the course of loading by external pressure, a ring-stiffened shell will experience a mean radial displacement of its circumference plus local variations of radial displacement which represent the growth of initial shape imperfections. It is this local growth, with the consequent bending stresses adding to the general membrane stresses to eventually cause regions of plasticity, which will cause the shell to become geometrically unstable. The pre-collapse displacement at any point is therefore difficult to predict. However, the sudden increase of such displacements is the immediate prelude to failure, so that this too is difficult to predict.

The most important characteristic of the double-skin composite shell is that it can be designed on the basis of strength calculations. As will be demonstrated, a shell of practical dimensions will never show any sign of instability before the full strength of the skins has been achieved.

4.1.1 The Double-Skinned Sandwich (Composite) Shell

The composite shell (Fig. 4.1b) uses a wall construction made very simply by pouring a filling material (filler) between two concentrically-placed, thin membranes. The filler sets, cures and acts as the 'web' to the membrane 'flanges'. Stiffeners are not used.

The membranes, or skins, must be of relatively high stiffness and strength (compared with the filler) and are usually steel. The filler must be sufficiently stiff to keep the skins apart and strong enough to continue to accept load after the skins have reached their yield condition. Assuming that slip does not occur at the filler–skin interfaces (and this will be discussed in Section 4.4.3) this arrangement can provide the wall with a high bending stiffness, reduce the sensitivity of the shell to initial shape imperfections and give the vessel a high instability pressure.

This construction has the advantage of using individual skin thicknesses each less than half of the single interbay single skin thickness required in a conventional shell of comparable performance, with a consequent reduction of rolling and welding problems. The fabrication costs and initial stress raisers associated with ring stiffeners are therefore traded for the necessity to roll two (thinner) cylindrical shells (instead of one) and the filling procedure. Generally, for a given performance, and similar effective inside diameters of the two types of shell (i.e. across the stiffener flanges in one case and across the inside skins in the other) the ring-stiffened shell will have a bigger outside diameter. However, the use of thinner steel plate and the absence of stiffeners, together with the fact, as will be demonstrated later, that very high quality steels are neither efficient nor required in the sandwich wall, will allow the design of a composite shell for pressures which the conventional shell would find difficulty in achieving. For example, it is relatively easy to design a steel–concrete composite vessel to operate at 1000 m of water depth with appropriate partial material safety factors on the steel and concrete and an acceptable load factor, using 70 N/mm^2 concrete and Grade 50 steel. A ring-stiffened shell of similar performance would require the use of very high quality steel. Of course, most applications do not require such pressure capacity and the composite shell can be designed to withstand low pressure differences. The comparison shown in Fig. 4.1 will be discussed more fully in Section 4.4.6.

4.1.2 The Structural Behaviour of the Composite Shell Under External Pressure

This is best described by considering the behaviour of the mid-length section of the shell away from the influence of boundary induced stress perturbations. (The effects of end closures and radial diaphragms will be described in Section 4.3.3.) This mid-section can be regarded, therefore, as acting like a long cylinder subjected to external pressure. Figure 4.2 shows typical variations of the mean radial displacements at the mid-sections of two composite shells. Both have linear-elastic, perfectly-plastic steel skins, but they have different filler materials.

The line $Oa_1b_1c_1$ is the response of a shell filled with a mixture of epoxy resin and glass microspheres (Fillite), which is isotropic and displays virtually linear stress–strain relations in a uniaxial compressive test, a compressive breakdown stress of 62·5 N/mm^2 and an elastic modulus of 4·26 kN/mm^2. Along Oa_1 the entire shell is elastic with the longitudinal and circumferential loads shared between the filler and the skins. The skin stresses are high compared with the filler stresses to reflect their difference in extensional stiffness. The shell behaves with almost complete axisymmetry (as will be shown in Sections 4.3.3 and 4.4.2); that is, there is very little growth of initial circularity imperfection, so that the mean radial displacement represents the displacement at every point around the circumference to a close approximation. Due

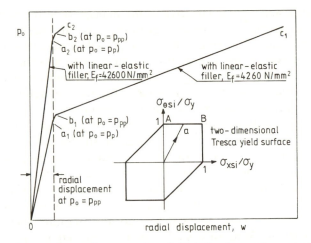

FIG. 4.2. Comparison of composite shell behaviour when steel skins are combined with a 'soft' filler ($Oa_1b_1c_1$) and a 'hard' filler ($Oa_2b_2c_2$).

to the high circumferential and longitudinal stresses (by comparison with the radial stress) in the filler, the Poisson's ratio effect causes the filler (and, therefore, the wall itself) to get thicker. There is a positive radial interface stress at the filler–skin interfaces of the same order of magnitude as the outside pressure on the shell. This positive interface pressure and the absence of any significant longitudinal or circumferential curvature change (except the secondary effect due to change of mean radius) is associated with no slip at the interfaces.

At the point a_1 ($p_o = p_p$) one of the skins, generally the inside one, will yield and its capacity for accepting further stress is reduced. Its theoretical acceptance of more stress beyond this point depends upon the yield surface assumed and whether the material has strain-hardening properties (see Section 4.3.2). For the sake of simplicity at this stage, let us suppose that the two-dimensional form of Tresca is assumed (i.e. the radial stress in the steel is ignored, see Fig. 4.2) and that the steel has no strain-hardening capacity. Under these circumstances, the stress state in the inside skin will have reached a point such as point a (Fig. 4.2) and is not capable of accepting further circumferential stress, although its longitudinal stress can continue to rise.

The stiffness of the wall is now reduced by the circumferential plasticity of the inside skin and is further reduced when the outside skin also reaches the yield surface at $p_o = p_{pp}$, i.e. at point b_1. At $p_o > p_{pp}$ all increase in circumferential load is carried by the filler alone and, due to its low stiffness, the radial displacement increases at a higher rate than previously, with the circumferential stress in the filler rising rapidly until it crushes at c_1. Interestingly, the rate of increase in axial compressive strain is smaller at $p_o > p_{pp}$ than at $p_o < p_p$, due to the increased growth rate of the circumferential strain in the filler at $p_o > p_{pp}$ and the consequent increased Poisson's ratio effect in the axial direction. (This statement must be qualified when the filler is concrete because, in this case, there is a reduction in filler volume as micro-cracking spreads through the filler. This reduction in volume can overcome the reduced rate of compressive strain increase described above for the resin filler.) The curve $Oa_1b_1c_1$ demonstrates a typical performance of a practical resin-glass filled shell (using skins of yield stress of about $200\,N/mm^2$), with collapse occurring at about $p_o = 2p_p$; that is, it carries about twice as much pressure as that required to cause first steel yield.

By contrast, the curve $Oa_2b_2c_2$ in Fig. 4.2 refers to a shell with similar steel skins and a filler with similar strength (as $a_1b_1c_1$) but a modulus ten times as big, viz. $42 \cdot 6\,kN/mm^2$, comparable with the initial modulus of a good concrete. Because of this higher stiffness, the stress level in the filler is much higher when the steel yields than in the previous case and the post-p_{pp} 'cushion' of shell capacity is thereby reduced.

The curves in Fig. 4.2 describe the essential nature of the response of composite shells to external pressure. Many aspects of this be-haviour will be described, but they all fall within this simple, basic concept.

4.2 MATERIALS

4.2.1 The Skins

All the experimental tests to date have been on vessels with mild steel skins varying from CR4 and HR4 (to BS 1449) all-purpose mild steel sheet (with a yield stress of about $200\,N/mm^2$) to mild steel plate satisfying BS 1501-224-32A (with a yield stress of about $350\,N/mm^2$). However, there is no reason why lighter materials, such as an aluminium alloy or a stiff, strong plastic, should not be used for relatively low performance vessels.

When using steel skins, the total load-life of the shell, i.e. from zero pressure to collapse, takes the steel through its entire stress–strain range so that elastic, elastic–plastic and, where appropriate, plastic–strain hardening constitutive relations are required. A full discussion of stress–strain relations, for both steel skins and concrete fillers, is given by Choate (1984) but, in the present context, it is more appropriate to be brief.

Suppose that the skins are made from an isotropic material which, when subjected to increasing stress, displays elastic behaviour until yield occurs, this being defined by P, which is a function of the stress vector and strain hardening. If the elastic modulus of the skins is E_s and, in a uniaxial test, the instantaneous slope of the stress versus plastic strain characteristic is E_p, then, invoking the normality hypothesis (associated plasticity) and assuming that the total strain increment is divisible into elastic and plastic components, the total stress–strain relations can be expressed in terms of the principal stress and strain increments (signified by a dot) as

$$\begin{Bmatrix} \dot{\varepsilon}_1 \\ \dot{\varepsilon}_2 \\ \dot{\varepsilon}_3 \\ 0 \end{Bmatrix} = \begin{bmatrix} 1/E_s & -\nu_s/E_s & -\nu_s/E_s & \partial P/\partial\sigma_1 \\ -\nu_s/E_s & 1/E_s & -\nu_s/E_s & \partial P/\partial\sigma_2 \\ -\nu_s/E_s & -\nu_s/E_s & 1/E_s & \partial P/\partial\sigma_3 \\ \partial P/\partial\sigma_1 & \partial P/\partial\sigma_2 & \partial P/\partial\sigma_3 & -E_p \end{bmatrix} \begin{Bmatrix} \dot{\sigma}_1 \\ \dot{\sigma}_2 \\ \dot{\sigma}_3 \\ \lambda \end{Bmatrix} \quad (4.1)$$

where λ is an instantaneous scalar multiplier.

Both the Tresca and the von Mises yield criteria have been used within the function P to compare the experimental behaviour of steel composite shells with theoretical predictions and, as will be demonstrated later, Tresca has proved to give the closer correlation.

4.2.2 The Filler

Two types of filler have been used between the steel skins: an epoxy resin (Ciba Geigy 219 System) mixed with hollow glass microspheres (Fillite), and concrete. The epoxy resin-based filler displays isotropic stress–strain characteristics under compressive stress and is almost linear up to failure, which is adequately predicted by Tresca (see Montague, 1975, 1978a).

Concrete, on the other hand, is a complex material and its response to multiaxial stress systems remains an area of active research. The works of Kupfer and Gerstle (1973), Newman (1973), Kotsovos (1974, 1980), Cedolin et al. (1977), Kotsovos and Newman (1979),

Gerstle *et al.* (1980), represent only a sample of the research done in recent years. Because of this continuing research and the fact that concrete provides a stiffer and cheaper filler than resin mixes, the remainder of this section is devoted to a discussion of its properties.

Prompted by the need to understand the behaviour of the concrete filler in a composite shell, this topic has been studied by Choate (1984) and Qazzaz (1984) at Manchester. Their work has included testing of relatively thin-walled plain concrete shells subjected to external hydrostatic pressure and combinations of axial load with radial pressure. The reason for such tests is as follows.

The numerous multiaxial stress tests on concrete which have been conducted in various parts of the world to study failure (breakdown) criteria, e.g. Richart *et al.* (1928), Bresler and Pister (1958), McHenry and Karmi (1958), Bellamy (1961), Rosenthal and Glucklick (1970), Hannant (1974), Hobbs *et al.* (1977), Olsen (1978), Haynes (1979), show considerable scatter and inconsistency. Of course, a non-homogeneous material such as concrete, with inevitable variations in the properties of its constituents and in its curing conditions, etc., is bound to display some inconsistency. But there are two major factors which are also important, both of which can be controlled. One is the type of specimen tested and the other is the method of testing. The majority of the tests have been conducted on relatively short, thick specimens (cubes or solid cylinders) or on relatively thick-walled hollow cylinders and boundary (load–transfer) arrangements have varied considerably. Under such conditions, the only certain stresses are the directional mean values and the particular stress combinations at the point of failure initiation can hardly be known with any precision. When such tests have been used to deduce stress–strain relations by measurement of surface strains, again it is difficult to see how the stress at the point of strain measurement can be known with confidence. A wide variation of results, particularly with respect to failure, even on similar samples but tested in different machines, is therefore not surprising.

The recent stress–strain and breakdown studies at Manchester by Qazzaz (1984) have been carried out on plain, hollow concrete cylinders with relatively thin walls ($\alpha = 12$ to 24) and sufficiently high L/d_o ratios ($\simeq 2$) to ensure that the middle length region of the shell is free from end effects (bending perturbations). Experimental monitoring of circumferential profiles during testing has shown that their deformation response was axisymmetric and yet the walls were sufficiently thin to induce only small variations of stress across the thickness. The stresses in the wall could therefore be deduced to a good approximation by simple equilibrium. The tests were all conducted under hydrostatic external pressure and the validity of the resulting stress–strain relations and breakdown criteria must therefore be restricted to a principal compressive stress ratio of $2:1:S$, where S is a small value, varying from zero at the inside surface to about 0.1 at the outside (and depending upon the diameter to wall thickness ratio). The stress state therefore approximates to a $2:1$ ratio of principal stresses in a state of plane stress, a condition which closely resembles that of the filler in a composite shell.

In the approach which Qazzaz adopted to the use of his experimental results, it is stipulated that the non-homogeneous, fracturing concrete behaves during its first loading history like a fictitious non-linear, incrementally isotropic material (labelled biax-concrete for the sake of convenience) whose incremental stress–strain relationship, under $2:1:S$ principal stress ratios, can be expressed by a simple Hookean relationship of the form:

$$\begin{Bmatrix} \dot{\varepsilon}_1 \\ \dot{\varepsilon}_2 \end{Bmatrix} = \begin{bmatrix} 1/E' & -v'/E' \\ -v'/E' & 1/E' \end{bmatrix} \begin{Bmatrix} \dot{\sigma}_1 \\ \dot{\sigma}_2 \end{Bmatrix} \tag{4.2}$$

By taking incremental measurements of $\varepsilon_\theta (= \varepsilon_1)$ and $\varepsilon_x (= \varepsilon_2)$ at the inside and outside of the plain concrete shell wall at eight equally spaced locations around the mid-length circumference and averaging the results, values of E' and v' were obtained at each value of the applied pressure. The values of E' were then normalised against the initial uniaxial modulus E_{c0} (derived from the standard compression test on a solid 6 in. diameter $\times$ 12 in. long cylinder of the concrete) and plotted against the ratio of the maximum principal strain during the hollow shell test (ε_1) to the maximum uniaxial strain, $\varepsilon_{\text{unimax}}$ (see Figs. 4.3c and 4.3d). Various different strengths of concrete were used and the results are shown on Fig. 4.3, together with the variation of v' against $\varepsilon_1/\varepsilon_{\text{unimax}}$.

The relationships on Fig. 4.3 can apply only to the particular case of the so-called biaxial concrete ($\sigma_1 : \sigma_2 = 2 : 1$) but, for this case, provide a useful total constitutive relationship for the macroscopic behaviour of the concrete, and derive credibility from the small amount of scatter in spite of the use of different concrete strengths, ranging from $f_{\text{cu}} = 25$ to $81\ \text{N/mm}^2$.

The relationships of Fig. 4.3 serve for the (long shell) analysis of a

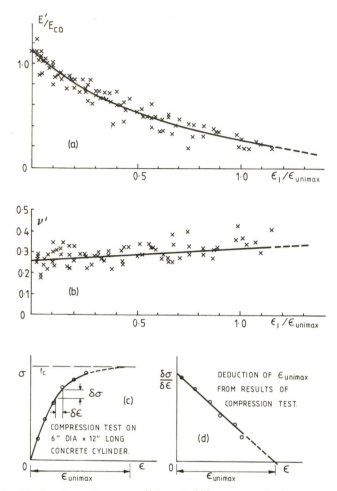

FIG. 4.3.   Deduction of ε_{unimax} ((c) and (d)) and equivalent properties of 'biaxial concrete' ((a) and (b)).

concrete-filled vessel subjected to hydrostatic pressure, but to deal with a short plain concrete shell (and, therefore, with the concrete filler in a short composite shell) to include the effects of boundary conditions, which cause longitudinal bending and a consequent range of principal stress ratios throughout the thickness, a more sophisticated approach to the stress–strain relations is required.

Such a study has been completed by Choate (1984) who has used the initial stress method to incorporate the elastic non-linear concrete model of Kotsovos and Newman (1979) and Kotsovos (1980) into a new finite element program (DOMCOM) for the analysis of plain concrete and concrete-filled composite shells, which takes account of end closures and radial diaphragms. More will be said about this analysis in Section 4.3.3.

Although a great deal of effort has been spent upon the constitutive relations for concrete, their importance in the context of composite shell behaviour must be put into perspective. At load levels below p_p (i.e. before yielding of the skins occurs), the concrete will usually contribute less than half of the total extensional stiffness of the wall at zero load, and this contribution will diminish as the concrete stiffness reduces more quickly than that of the steel (which will not fall at all if the steel is linear-elastic up to yield). Thus, theoretical changes in the pre-p_p performance of the shell consequent upon small differences in the concrete constitutive relations, are not significant. For this reason, the results of analyses using a tangent modulus approach based upon the uniaxial stress–strain characteristic of concrete, see Montague (1979), and analyses using either the Kotsovos–Choate model or the relations of Fig. 4.3, will be very little different at the working load of the shell.

This is not true, of course, at post-p_{pp} pressures, when the stiffness of the shell becomes more dependent upon the stiffness of the concrete but, by this stage, initial circularity imperfections are beginning to magnify and local stress patterns are becoming more complex than those assumed in an axisymmetric analysis.

With regard to the breakdown of concrete, the inconsistencies observed in the results of various investigators have already been mentioned, but under a $2 : 1 : 0$ compressive principal stress ratio, the evidence available indicates that an enhancement in strength of $1 \cdot 2$ over the uniaxial breakdown stress is a safe estimate.

4.3 ELASTIC–PLASTIC THEORY OF DOUBLE-SKIN COMPOSITE SHELLS

The analytical treatment of the composite shell can vary from simple to complex depending upon the characteristics of the materials being used, the type of end closure employed, the absence or presence of such features as large penetrations, the nature of the loading and the degree of approximation which is acceptable.

The simplest materials to deal with are linear-elastic, perfectly-plastic skins combined with a linear-elastic, isotropic filler material with a well-defined breakdown criterion. The behaviour of mild steel often fits (or can be approximated to) the first description and the epoxy resin-glass mentioned earlier closely resembles the second. Less amenable materials, such as plastic strain-hardening steel and concrete, do not, in themselves, make the long shell analysis more difficult, but the full analysis (including boundaries) becomes more complex and, whenever non-linear materials are involved, it is generally necessary to use an incremental approach.

Theoretical analysis of the composite shell has progressed to the consideration of the aspects to be described below. Various problems remain to be tackled and some of these will be mentioned at the end of the chapter.

4.3.1 Long Cylinder Analysis with Linear-Elastic, Perfectly-Plastic Skins and a Linear Elastic-Breakdown Filler

The assumptions made in this analysis are that there is no longitudinal bending (i.e. any end perturbation has dissipated), no circumferential bending (i.e. deformations are axisymmetrical and second-order bending, due to change of radius, may be neglected), the radial stress in the skins may be ignored but is recognised in the filler, the stress distribution is uniform across the skins and the axial strain is uniform across the wall. The notation is defined in Fig. 4.4.

The isotropic nature of the filler permits it to be treated as a thick cylinder using the Lamé equations to define its circumferential equilibrium. Thus,

$$\sigma_{\theta f1} = (p_1 a_1 - 2p_2 d_2^2)/a_2 \qquad \sigma_{\theta f2} = (2p_1 d_1^2 - p_2 a_1)/a_2 \qquad (4.3)$$

Circumferential equilibrium of the outside and inside skins gives

$$2t_o\sigma_{\theta so} + p_1 d_1 - p_o d_o = 0 \qquad 2t_i\sigma_{\theta si} + p_i d_i - p_2 d_2 = 0 \qquad (4.4)$$

With the longitudinal strain assumed to be constant with r across the filler and equal to ε_x, it follows that, for an isotropic filler, its longitudinal stress is also constant with r. Therefore,

$$\sigma_{xf} = \sigma_{xf1} = \sigma_{xf2} = E_f \cdot \varepsilon_x + 2\nu_f(p_1 d_1^2 - p_2 d_2^2)/a_2 \qquad (4.5)$$

Longitudinal equilibrium in the shell wall demands that

$$d_o t_o \sigma_{xso} + d_i t_i \sigma_{xsi} + a_2 \sigma_{xf}/4 - P_x/\pi = 0 \qquad (4.6)$$

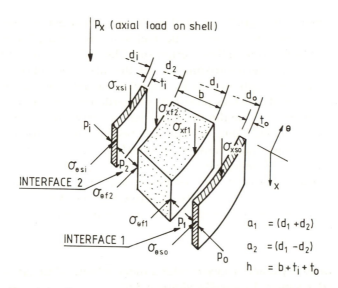

FIG. 4.4.   Stresses on an element of the composite shell wall.

Longitudinal compatibility of strain between the filler and the skins is implicit in the imposed condition of constant longitudinal strain across the wall thickness. Circumferentially, there will be equal strains in the filler and the respective skins at interfaces 1 and 2 (Fig. 4.4). Incorporating these conditions into the constitutive relations, it follows that, whilst both skins and filler remain elastic,

$$\varepsilon_x = \{\sigma_{xso} - \nu_s \sigma_{\theta so}\}/E_s = \{\sigma_{xf} - \nu_f(\sigma_{\theta f1} + p_1)\}/E_f \qquad (4.7a)$$

$$\varepsilon_x = \{\sigma_{xsi} - \nu_s \sigma_{\theta si}\}/E_s = \{\sigma_{xf} - \nu_f(\sigma_{\theta f2} + p_2)\}/E_f \qquad (4.7b)$$

(The equality of the right-hand sides of eqns (4.7a) and (4.7b) is not an independent relationship; it follows from eqn (4.3).) Also,

$$\varepsilon_{\theta 1} = \{\sigma_{\theta so} - \nu_s \sigma_{xso}\}/E_s = \{\sigma_{\theta f1} - \nu_f(\sigma_{xf} + p_1)\}/E_f \qquad (4.8a)$$

$$\varepsilon_{\theta 2} = \{\sigma_{\theta si} - \nu_s \sigma_{xsi}\}/E_s = \{\sigma_{\theta f2} - \nu_f(\sigma_{xf} + p_2)\}/E_f \qquad (4.8b)$$

For any given values of P_x, p_o and p_i, eqns (4.3) to (4.8), when solved simultaneously, give the corresponding values of σ_{xsi}, σ_{xso}, σ_{xf}, $\sigma_{\theta so}$, $\sigma_{\theta si}$, $\sigma_{\theta f1}$, $\sigma_{\theta f2}$, p_1 and p_2. The strains follow from eqns (4.7) and (4.8) and the radial displacements at the outside and inside of the shell wall, viz. w_o and w_i, are then given by

$$w_o = \varepsilon_{\theta so} d_o/2 \qquad w_i = \varepsilon_{\theta si} d_i/2 \qquad (4.9)$$

The change in the thickness of the filler is $(w_o - w_i)$. If the shell is subjected to external hydrostatic pressure p_o, with $p_i = 0$, then $P_x = \pi d_o^2/4$ and the quantity $(w_o - w_i)$ will be negative, indicating that the wall of the shell has become thicker, with p_1 and p_2 both positive. The positive interface pressure between the filler and the skins is an important feature of the composite shell action and, as will be discussed later, p_1 provides an effective barrier against the spread of fluid pressure (p_o) at the interface 1 if there should be a hole in the outside skin.

Equations (4.3) to (4.8) describe the behaviour of the long shell (and that of the mid-length region of a shorter shell) whilst the skins and the filler remain linear-elastic. In a well-designed shell, the skins will reach their plastic condition before the filler becomes plastic or breaks down. This is consequent upon the high ratio of the skin modulus to the filler modulus (which causes a correspondingly high ratio of stresses between the two materials) overcoming the ratio of their respective yield or breakdown strengths. It will be seen later that a high steel (skin) strength combined with a filler of relatively low strength can have the undesirable effect of causing the filler to break down before the steel skins have achieved their full (yield) strength.

Normally, the inside skin will reach the specified yield condition (whatever that might be) before the outside skin. From this point, the analysis will become incremental. If it is assumed that changes of strain in the inside skin are now divisible into elastic and plastic components, then the left-hand sides of eqns (4.7b) and (4.8b) become, respectively,

$$\dot{\varepsilon}_x = \dot{\varepsilon}_{xsi} = \{\dot{\sigma}_{xsi} - \nu_s \dot{\sigma}_{\theta si}\}/E_s + \dot{\varepsilon}_{xsi}^P \qquad (4.10)$$

$$\dot{\varepsilon}_{\theta 2} = \dot{\varepsilon}_{\theta si} = \{\dot{\sigma}_{\theta si} - \nu_s \dot{\sigma}_{xsi}\}/E_s + \dot{\varepsilon}_{\theta si}^P \qquad (4.11)$$

where the superscript p identifies the plastic component of the total strain increment. These changes in the inside skin constitutive equations are the only ones necessary to proceed with the analysis at $p_o > p_p$ (but prior to yielding of the outside skin) apart, of course from the use of all the other equations in an incremental form. Equation (4.1) contains eqns (4.10) and (4.11) and includes an explicit statement of the plastic strain increment $\dot{\varepsilon}^P$ which will depend upon the yield criterion P used in the analysis. For elastic, perfectly-plastic skins (no strain hardening) E_p in eqn (4.1) will be zero.

At $p_o > p_p$, the other skin (usually the outside) will also reach the yield condition and, at $p_p > p_{pp}$, equations of the form of eqns (4.10) and (4.11) must therefore replace the left-hand sides of eqns (4.7a) and (4.8a).

The two most commonly-used yield criteria for steel are Tresca (maximum shear stress) and von Mises (critical shear strain energy). Montague (1975) gives a complete description of the analysis presently being considered, using Tresca, which has proved to be a better predicter of skin yield than von Mises in the many tests conducted by Montague (1978a,b), Goode and Fatheldin (1980) and Montague et al. (1983) on composite shells subjected to external hydrostatic pressure. With this kind of loading, which produces a ratio $\sigma_{\theta s}$ to σ_{xs} of approximately 2 to 1, the von Mises yield surface predicts yield at a value of σ_θ about 15% higher than that predicted by Tresca.

Figure 4.5 illustrates the results of the long shell analysis with linear-elastic, perfectly plastic skins and a linear filler. Figure 4.5a shows $\sigma_{\theta si}$ reaching yield first, at $p_o = p_p$, whereupon there is an increase in the rate of increase of $\sigma_{\theta so}$ until it reaches yield at $p_o = p_{pp}$, when the stress states of both skins will be on the side AB of the Tresca yield criterion on Fig. 4.2. The longitudinal skin stresses σ_{xsi} and σ_{xso} carry stresses approximately half the size of $\sigma_{\theta si}$ and $\sigma_{\theta so}$ until $p_o = p_{pp}$, after which they increase together at a reduced rate. From $p_o = p_{pp}$ until failure (by crushing of the filler at stress values also calculated using Tresca in this case), p_2 remains constant (the inside skin not being able to withstand any further increase in $\sigma_{\theta si}$) and the increase in p_1 is carried entirely by the filler, causing corresponding increases in the growth rates of $\sigma_{\theta f1}$ and $\sigma_{\theta f2}$. As can be seen, at all points of the loading history the third principal stresses in the skins and the filler (viz. the radial components p_o, p_1 and p_2) are truly small compared with the circumferential and longitudinal stresses. Figure 4.5b shows the strain growths, with $\varepsilon_{\theta 2}$ greater than $\varepsilon_{\theta 1}$ and therefore indicating that the shell wall is becoming thicker.

4.3.2 Long Cylinder Analysis for a Shell with a Concrete Filler and Either Linear-Elastic, Perfectly-Plastic or Plastic Strain-Hardening Steel Skins

The procedure of analysis is basically similar to that outlined in Section 4.3.1. Due to the non-linear nature of the concrete, the analysis must be carried out incrementally. The equations of equilibrium and compatibility remain as before but the constitutive equations for the filler and for the post-yielded skins must be changed. For the general loading case, the concrete constitutive equations due to Kotsovos

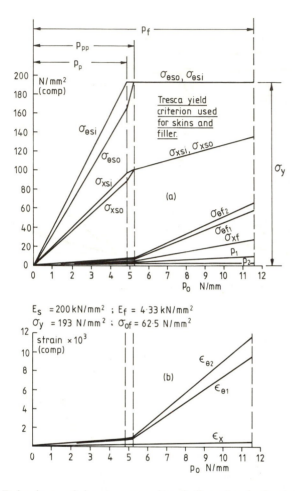

FIG. 4.5. Behaviour of long, composite shell under hydrostatic pressure ($\alpha = 14\cdot6$, $\gamma = 16\cdot6$). Skins, linear-elastic, perfectly plastic steel. Filler, linear-elastic to breakdown, resin-glass.

(1980) and transformed to the incremental form by Choate (1984) are appropriate. For the hydrostatic pressure case, the particular relations derived by Qazzaz (1984) and illustrated in Fig. 4.3 can be used. In fact, Montague (1979) used the tangent modulus values from the uniaxial concrete stress–strain curve as an approximation justified by the reasoning presented in Section 4.2.2. For a non-isotropic material with known directional values of the elastic modulus, modified versions

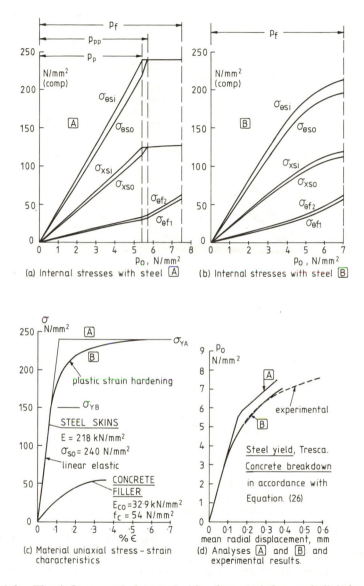

(a) Internal stresses with steel $\boxed{A}$

(b) Internal stresses with steel $\boxed{B}$

(c) Material uniaxial stress – strain characteristics

(d) Analyses $\boxed{A}$ and $\boxed{B}$ and experimental results.

FIG. 4.6. The influence of the steel skin characteristic on shell behaviour $(\alpha = 24, \gamma = 17)$.

of the Lamé equations, see Choate (1984) and Qazzaz (1984), can be used.

In order to demonstrate the differences in behaviour due to the replacing of the relatively 'soft' (resin-glass) filler in Fig. 4.5, with a concrete filler about $7\frac{1}{2}$ times stiffer, the analyses illustrated in Fig. 4.6 again refer to a shell subjected to hydrostatic, external pressure. Figures 4.6a and 4.6b are the results of using the concrete of Fig. 4.6c combined with steel A and steel B respectively, i.e. an elastic, perfectly-plastic steel (A) and an elastic, strain-hardening steel (B).

The immediate point of contrast between the stress patterns of Figs 4.5 and 4.6 is the relatively low value of p_f/p_{pp} for the concrete-filled shell compared with the resin-filled shell. This is because of the higher stiffness of the concrete which takes higher stresses than the resin and therefore delays the growth of stress in the steel. The slightly non-linear responses of the steel stresses in Fig. 4.6a is a consequence of the concrete non-linearity shown in Fig. 4.6c. At $p_o > p_{pp}$, the concrete filler must carry all increases in the circumferential load which has the effect of reducing the circumferential stiffness of the shell and increasing the Poisson's ratio strain in the longitudinal direction. The filler therefore becomes effectively stiffer in the longitudinal direction and takes a higher share of the longitudinal load. The longitudinal stress growth in the skins is reduced.

Figure 4.6b shows the results of analysing the same shell using the same concrete (Fig. 4.6c) but with skins displaying the strain-hardening characteristic B in Fig. 4.6c. In this case, the initial yield surface is associated with the skin stress σ_{yB} and the yield surface continues to expand with increasing strain. The skins continue to accept increases of stress until breakdown of the concrete occurs. It will be noted from Fig. 4.6b that $\sigma_{\theta si}$ has not reached σ_{yA} (240 N/mm^2) when the shell fails. This is because the reducing stiffness of the steel puts a higher proportion of load into the concrete at similar values of p_o and, as would be expected, the predicted failure of the shell (based upon concrete stress levels—see Section 4.4.1) occurs at a lower value of p_o using steel B rather than steel A. This is shown in Fig. 4.6d where the measured experimental performance of this particular shell is compared with the two theoretical predictions.

The example illustrated in Fig. 4.6 shows the behaviour of a shell fabricated from a relatively low-yield steel (240 N/mm^2) combined with a relatively strong concrete ($f_c = 54$ N/mm^2). The performance of the shell can be improved by increasing the strength of the steel to the point when steel yielding will still occur before concrete breakdown. If the steel yield stress is so high that its full strength cannot be realised before the concrete fails then the full potential of the steel is not being realised. If, therefore, readily available concrete strengths are used, there is no advantage in using very high steel strengths in the composite shell.

4.3.3 The Short Composite Shell; the Effects of Boundaries

So far, the discussion has been concerned entirely with the long shell with the implication that this applies to the central region of a shell with end restraints, i.e. in the region remote from the effects of such boundaries. In this section the effects on the cylindrical shell of end closures and radial stiffening are investigated. It is important to assess the degree of approximation which would be involved by assuming that the shell's behaviour is adequately described by the long shell analysis.

Palaninathan and Montague (1981) considered the problem of the composite shell with hemispherical and torispherical end closures, using steel skins and a concrete filler, and subjected to external hydrostatic pressure. Two approaches were used.

In the first analysis, thin shell equations were employed after converting the double-skin composite wall into an equivalent wall of single thickness $\bar{h}$ and elastic modulus $\bar{E}$.

By comparing the extensional stiffness of the composite wall with that of an equivalent homogeneous wall of thickness $\bar{h}$ and elastic modulus $\bar{E}$, and then making a similar comparison between the bending stiffness of the real and equivalent walls, the values of $\bar{h}$ and $\bar{E}$ were deduced to be

$$\bar{h} = \{12D_1(1 - \nu_{\mathrm{f}}^2)/B_1(1 - \nu_{\mathrm{e}}^2)\}^{1/2} \tag{4.12}$$

$$\bar{E} = B_1(1 - \nu_{\mathrm{e}}^2)/\bar{h} \tag{4.13}$$

where

$$D_1 = E_{\mathrm{s}}\{(b + 2t)^3 - b^3\}/12(1 - \nu_{\mathrm{s}}^2) + E_{\mathrm{f}}b^3/12(1 - \nu_{\mathrm{f}}^2) \tag{4.14}$$

$$B_1 = 2tE_{\mathrm{s}}/(1 - \nu_{\mathrm{s}}^2) + E_{\mathrm{f}}b/(1 - \nu_{\mathrm{f}}^2) = B_{\mathrm{s}} + B_{\mathrm{f}} \tag{4.15}$$

$$\nu_{\mathrm{e}} = (B_{\mathrm{s}}\nu_{\mathrm{s}} + B_{\mathrm{f}}\nu_{\mathrm{f}})/B_1 \tag{4.16}$$

and

$$t = t_{\mathrm{o}} = t_{\mathrm{i}}$$

This was, of course, an elastic analysis and could only be applied at load levels at which the uniaxial concrete stress–strain characteristic

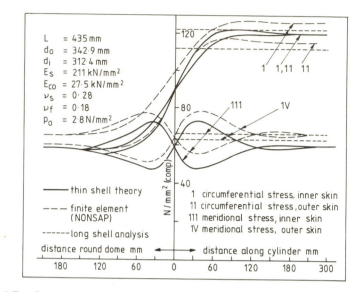

FIG. 4.7. Stresses in composite cylinder with hemispherical dome (Palaninathan and Montague, 1981).

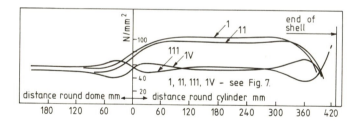

FIG. 4.8. Stresses in composite cylinder of Fig. 4.7 with hemispherical dome and rigid end closure from finite element program DOMCOM (Choate, 1984).

could be approximated to a straight line of slope E_f. Within this approximation was the assumption that the concrete could be treated as an isotropic material in this stress regime.

The second analysis by Palaninathan and Montague used the NON-SAP finite element program to study the end-closure problem. In this case, because of the limitations of the constitutive models available in the program, the stress–strain relations for the concrete were based upon a bilinear approximation to the uniaxial stress–strain curve.

The results of these two analyses are shown on Fig. 4.7 for a particular shell with a hemispherical end closure at an external pressure of 2·76 N/mm². Also shown in Fig. 4.7 are the results of the long shell analysis.

In examining Fig. 4.7, two points are worthy of note. The first is that within about one-radius distance from the dome–cylinder intersection on this shell ($\alpha = 22, \gamma = 15·7$), the stress perturbations have disappeared and the circumferential and meridional stresses from all three analyses agree to within about 10%; the agreement between the finite element analysis and the long shell analysis is within 3%. Secondly, the perturbations themselves are quite gentle and particularly so in the larger, circumferential stresses.

More recently, Choate (1984) has analysed the same shell using his finite element program DOMCOM, which incorporates the Kotsovos (1980) constitutive relations for concrete. In addition to the hemispherical end closure, Choate introduced a radially rigid diaphragm at the other end of the shell. Some of the results are shown in Fig. 4.8. They show somewhat smaller skin stresses than those of Fig. 4.7, probably due to the fact that the Kotsovos constitutive relations give a slightly higher concrete stiffness than the relations used for Fig. 4.7. Choate's analysis indicates that, in the region close to the rigid diaphragm (a component which would be unnecessary in a composite shell) longitudinal bending would cause local yielding of the outside skin at a pressure below p_p. However, the restraint provided by the diaphragm and the continued elastic stiffness of the main barrel of the shell prevents the formation of a failure lobe associated with this local yielding. Experimental evidence supports this reasoning and indicates that skin yielding over the central region of the shell (which can be calculated by the long shell analysis) is the condition which leads to failure.

4.3.4 Large Penetrations in the Composite Shell Wall

The problem of a single penetration in the side of a composite cylinder (Fig. 4.9) presents particular difficulties because of its non-axisymmetry and the presence of two materials. Figure 4.9 represents an all-steel nozzle penetrating the composite wall of the main shell and welded to both the outside and inside skins. The loading is externally hydrostatic so that the z-direction load in the nozzle is $\pi d_n^2 p_o/4$. The analysis presented by Horne and Choo (1979) and summarised by Montague and Choo (1981) uses thin shell theory which approximates the three-dimensional stress state around the intersection to a statement in terms

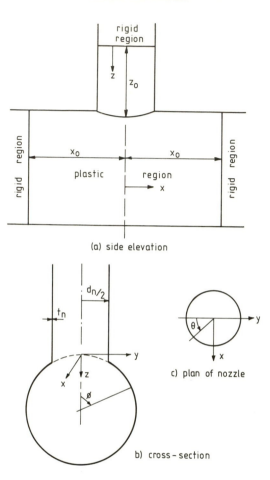

FIG. 4.9.   Intersection between composite vessel and steel nozzle.

of two-dimensional stress resultants. It is a lower-bound solution and hence only equilibrium and yield are considered.

A plastic region around the intersection is postulated as shown in Fig. 4.9. This extends to distances x_o in each direction along the shell and to z_o along the nozzle. There are nine unknown stresses but only six equilibrium equations for the main vessel. This is also true for the nozzle, so there remain three independent stress resultants for each component. The three for the vessel (m_x, $n_{\phi x}$, $m_{\phi x}$) are expressed in terms of trigonometric series in x and ϕ, and those for the nozzle (m_z,

m_θ, $m_{\theta z}$) in terms of trigonometric and polynomial series in θ and z. The coefficients of these form the components of a vector $\mathbf{x}$ which also include the limit pressure p_l and the coefficients of all the other stress resultants for both the vessel and the nozzle. The vector $\mathbf{x}$ is then varied so as to maximise p_l subject to the yield constraints being satisfied at a finite set of points around the intersection. Also, a good approximation to equilibrium is achieved between the actions at the vessel–nozzle junction.

The yield condition used for the composite shell was derived by Horne and Choo (1979) and is based upon the von Mises yield criterion for the steel skins and an approximate square yield criterion for the concrete core defined, in two dimensions, by $\sigma_c < \bar{f}_c$ where $\bar{f}_c = 1 \cdot 2 f_c$. The composite yield criterion is expressed as

$$Y = Q_t/l + Q_m/m^2 + n/lm \, |Q_{tm}| \qquad (4.17)$$

where l, m and n are coefficients optimised for a particular shell wall cross-section and Q_t, Q_m, Q_{tm} are respectively the yield conditions for the shell under direct force, bending moment and interaction between direct force and bending moment. The Ilyushin (1948) yield criterion is used for the all-steel nozzle.

The analysis described above is formalised in a computer program and in Section 4.4.4 its predictions of collapse will be compared with some experimental results on shells with d_n/d_o equal to $0 \cdot 2$ and $0 \cdot 26$ (see Table 4.2).

4.3.5 Interaction Between Strength and Stability for the Composite Shell

The main purpose of the composite construction is to avoid instability problems, i.e. to enable the shell to make full use of the strength of its component materials (and especially its steel skins) without encountering instability problems. However, it is of interest to inquire how slender a composite shell must be (with a given combination of skin and filler materials) before an interaction between strength and stability becomes important.

To investigate this question conceptually, Montague (1978b) proposed that the shell could be considered in each of two states: first, as an all-elastic structure at $p_o < p_p$ and, secondly, as an elastic–plastic structure at $p_o > p_{pp}$. (The pressure interval between p_p and p_{pp} is small and, for this purpose, was ignored).

For the first, all-elastic state, the equivalent homogeneous wall, defined by eqns (4.12) and (4.13), was adopted. These values of $\bar{h}$ and $\bar{E}$ were used in the von Mises (1914) expression for the elastic instability pressure p_{c1} of the (equivalent) all-elastic simply-supported shell when subjected to hydrostatic pressure, i.e.

$$
p_{c1} = \left(\frac{\bar{E}\bar{h}}{r}\right) \frac{1}{\left[n^2 - 1 + \frac{1}{2}\left(\frac{\pi r}{L}\right)^2\right]} \left\{ \frac{1}{\left[n^2\left(\frac{L}{\pi r}\right)^2 + 1\right]^2} \right.
$$
$$
\left. + \frac{\bar{h}^2}{12r^2(1 - \nu^2)}\left[n^2 - 1 + \left(\frac{\pi r}{L}\right)^2\right] \right\} \tag{4.18}
$$

where n, the number of half-waves in the buckling mode, is a positive integer chosen to minimise eqn (4.18) and ν is a mean value of Poisson's ratio.

To find the instability pressure p_{c2} of the shell in its second state (at $p_o > p_{pp}$) a concept is invoked which is akin to the reduced or double modulus theory of Considère (1891), Engesser (1895) and von Karman (1910). Without claiming any direct connection with the reduced modulus theory, and notwithstanding Shanley's (1947) tangent modulus theory, the concept is interpreted as follows in the context of the composite shell moving into a lobar buckling mode when both skins are plastic (due to compression). The skins are considered to follow an elastic, perfectly plastic stress–strain path (no strain hardening), so that when both are plastic and the shell moves from perfect circularity into a lobar buckling mode at constant load, the consequent changes of curvature cause an increase of compressive strain on one face of each half wave ($E_s = 0$) and a reversal of strain on the other side where, therefore, the elastic modulus E_s is recalled. Thus, the elastic skin alternates between the inner face and the outer face with each half wavelength of the buckling mode. In these circumstances, eqns (4.12) and (4.13) can still be used if D_1 and B_1 are replaced by D_2 and B_2 where

$$
D_2 = E_s t(3e^2 - 3et + t^2)/3(1 - \nu_s^2) + E_f(b^3 + 3b^2 t
$$
$$
+ 3bt^2 - 3b^2 e + 3be^2 - 6bte) \tag{4.19}
$$

$$
B_2 = E_s t/(1 - \nu_s^2) + bE_f(1 - \nu_f^2) \tag{4.20}
$$

$$
e = \{E_f(b^2 + 2bt) + E_s t^2\}/2(bE_f + tE_s) \tag{4.21}
$$

Hence, the instability pressure of the filler-elastic, skins-plastic shell, viz. p_{c2}, can be found.

The Rankine strength–stability interactive line may be expressed as

$$\frac{\lambda_f}{\lambda_p} + \frac{\lambda_f}{\lambda_c} = 1 \qquad (4.22)$$

where λ_f, λ_p and λ_c are load factors associated with experimental failure, rigid–plastic collapse and elastic instability respectively.

Using eqn (4.22) as the basis of his reasoning, Montague (1978b) argued to the following results for the interactive failure pressures p_{f1} and p_{f2} of the composite shell:

$$p_{f1} = (p_{th} \cdot p_{c1})/(p_{th} + p_{c1}) \qquad p_{f1} < p_p \qquad (4.23)$$

$$p_{f2} = (p_{th} \cdot p_{c2})/(p_{th} + p_{c2} - p_p) \qquad p_{f2} > p_p \qquad (4.24)$$

These empirical expressions have been tested against experimental results and the comparison is shown in Fig. 4.15.

4.4 THE EXPERIMENTAL BEHAVIOUR OF COMPOSITE SHELLS

Some two hundred tests have been completed by the Manchester group on double-skin composite shells subjected to external pressure. The shells have ranged in diameter from less than 150 mm to 1500 mm (see Montague and Collard, 1983) and lengths have varied from 220 mm to 4000 mm, with L/d_o ratios usually between 2 and 3, but reducing to less than unity in some tests. The α-value has varied between about 10 and 100 (the higher values being associated with an experimental study of strength–stability interaction for very slender shells—see Section 4.4.5), but most tests have involved α-values between 18 and 24. The skins have always been fabricated from steel, ranging from 0·8 mm-thick CR4 or HR4 all-purpose mild steel sheet with a yield stress of approximately 200 N/mm², to 9·5 mm-thick plate (BS 1501) with a yield stress of about 350 N/mm². The percentage of steel in the wall has been typically between 10% and 20%.

Two kinds of filler have been used; epoxy resin-Fillite mixes, with a uniaxial compressive strength of 55–65 N/mm² and elastic modulus 4–4·5 kN/mm², and concrete, with cube strengths varying from about 50 to 70 N/mm² and corresponding initial moduli (E_{c0}) from about 28 to 34 kN/mm².

Aspects of shell behaviour which have been investigated experimentally have included deformation patterns over the entire inside surface of the shell (including circumferential and longitudinal profiles), surface strains along circumferential and meridional lines on both surfaces of the shell wall, the effects of various kinds of bonding between the filler and the skins, the influence of rigid, radial diaphragms and hemispherical end closures, variations in the parameters α, γ and L/d_o, repeated loading, long-term loading and the measurement of creep deformations, the effects of severe damage (holes in the outside skin and large 'dents' in the wall) and the influence of large lateral penetrations through the composite wall. In addition, extensive testing has been conducted on plain concrete shells under external hydrostatic pressure in order to simulate the loading conditions experienced by the filler in a composite shell.

The examples of experimental results quoted below have therefore been selected merely as illustrations of the information available, but every effort has been made to make them representative. One general point can be made with regard to size effects. The independent geometric parameters of the shell cross-section in the analytical treatment of shells with given material properties, are α and γ. Throughout the large range in the absolute size of the shells tested, there has never been any indication that these parameters lose their independence in practice, i.e. no size effect has been observed in the shells' behaviour.

4.4.1 Deformation of the Composite Shell

Figure 4.10 shows a comparison between mean radial displacements measured at the mid-lengths of four concrete-filled composite shells and the long-shell analysis predictions (using the tangent modulus approach for the concrete constitutive relations) reported by Montague and Choo (1981). The details of the shells are given in Table 4.1. The radial displacements recorded in Fig. 4.10 are the mean of eighteen readings taken around the inside circumference of the shell (i.e. at 20° intervals) at each increment of p_o. It is characteristic of such theoretical–experimental comparisons to find excellent agreement up to $p_o = p_p$, with some divergence after skin yield, but not more than about 10% on the vertical ordinate. Shell number 1 in Fig. 4.10 is an example of such a result. These curves refer to the middle of the shell length, but many tests have demonstrated that these lines will describe the mean deformation of a typical shell ($\alpha = 16$–24, $L/d_o >$ about 1) to within a radius of a radially stiff diaphragm. The rapid deflection growth near the end of the shell is generated by bending and shear. (The finite element analysis DOMCOM suggests that, in a typical

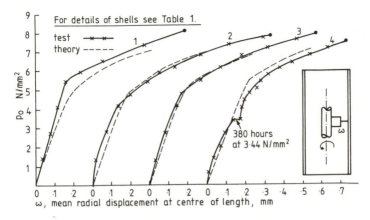

FIG. 4.10. Typical behaviour of concrete-filled shells.

concrete-filled shell, the shear deformation near the ends of the shell will contribute about 10% of the total radial displacement required to achieve compatibility with the central region of length).

In Fig. 4.10, the termination of the dashed line in each case marks the failure of the shell by filler (concrete) breakdown in accordance with the form of the criterion suggested by Hobbs et al. (1977). This criterion suggests that failure of concrete occurs when

$$\sigma_1 = 0 \cdot 67 f_{cu} + 3\sigma_3 \qquad (4.25)$$

where σ_1 and σ_3 are the maximum and minimum principal stresses in the concrete (corresponding to $\sigma_{\theta f2}$ and p_2, respectively). Hobbs et al. (1977) proposed eqn (4.25) as a design guide, with the implication that it is conservative. Test results, such as those in Fig. 4.10 (where theoretical breakdown was predicted using eqn (4.25) with $0 \cdot 67 f_{cu}$

TABLE 4.1

Specimen[a]	σ_y (N/mm^2)	E_s (kN/mm^2)	f_{cu} (N/mm^2)	Mechanical bond	h_{min} (mm)	$\dfrac{200\Delta}{d_i}$
1	189	202	63·2	none	21·2	1·8
2	183	194	64·8	studs	20·8	0·64
3	191	194	67·0	bolts	20·7	0·64
4	188	205	66·7	none	20·7	0·58

[a] For all specimens: $L = 1100$ mm, $d_o = 495$ mm, $h = 22 \cdot 5$ mm, $t = 1 \cdot 95$ mm, $\alpha = 22$ and $\gamma = 17 \cdot 3$.

replaced by $0.8f_{cu}$), have demonstrated that this is true. Qazzaz (1984) has carried out a comprehensive survey of the failure criteria for concrete proposed by numerous investigators and they show considerable variations which reflect, among other things, differences in testing techniques. Qazzaz himself, using the evidence from his tests on plain concrete shells, has suggested that, for the particular case of a plain concrete shell subjected to external hydrostatic pressure, concrete breakdown occurs when

$$\sigma_1^n + \sigma_2^n - m(\sigma_1\sigma_2)^{n/2} - f_c^n = 0 \qquad (4.26)$$

where $n = 2.9 \exp[-0.00054 f_c^{1.6}] + 0.015\alpha$

$$m = 0.995 + 0.0061 f_c - 0.007\alpha$$

In the composite shell, σ_1 and σ_2 would correspond to $\sigma_{\theta f2}$ and σ_{xf2} respectively. Application of eqn (4.26) to composite shell tests has shown good agreement.

From Table 4.1 it will be noted that the shells of Fig. 4.10 combine a relatively weak steel ($\sigma_y \simeq 190 \text{ N/mm}^2$) with a relatively strong concrete ($f_{cu} > 60 \text{ N/mm}^2$). This accounts for the large pressure capacities of the shells at $p_o > p_p$. This post-p_p capacity reduces as the steel strength increases or the concrete strength decreases.

4.4.2 Circumferential Profile Development with Increasing Pressure

Figure 4.11 is a typical illustration of profile growth. (Profiles are deduced by applying a simple Fourier analysis to the radial displacement readings taken at 10° or 20° intervals around the circumference, see Montague (1975).) In Fig. 4.11, Δ is the deviation from the current mean perfect circle at any value of p_o, represented by the horizontal axis. The two profiles drawn are at $p_o = 0$ (the initial imperfection from true circularity) and at $p_o = 10 \text{ N/mm}^2$, i.e. just prior to failure. The first striking point about these two lines is that one is a simple exaggeration of the other, with the points of zero deviation remaining stationary. This is absolutely characteristic.

The second point of interest is the manner of this growth with respect to the increase in p_o. This is demonstrated on the inset diagram by reference to the increase of Δ at the peak deviation points A and B. The theoretical value of p_{pp} (at which both skins become plastic) for this specimen is 6.1 N/mm^2. It will be noted that the deviation from circularity increases very little below this pressure, i.e. at $p_o < p_p$ the shell is deforming virtually axisymmetrically. The profile at 6.1 N/mm^2

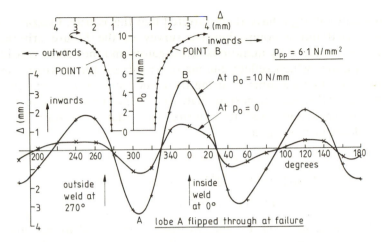

FIG. 4.11. Typical circumferential profile development of a composite shell.

is very little different from the initial (zero load) profile. This insensitivity to initial out-of-roundness is entirely characteristic of the composite shell behaviour. For this shell $200\Delta/d_i$ (the BS 5500 measure of out-of-roundness) was initially 0.58 and values up to 1.5 have been recorded without causing any significant reduction in shell performance. (It will be recalled that the BS 5500 recommendation is that $200\Delta/d_i$ should not exceed 0.5.)

After the skins have become plastic, there is severe reduction in the stiffness of the wall and original deviations from circularity increase quickly (the rate of growth being dependent to some degree on the work-hardening properties of the skins) and lead to failure. In the case shown in Fig. 4.11, the inward-facing lobe B grew rapidly at $p_o > p_{pp}$ and at failure (which is always sudden) caused lobe A to flip through and to join B to form one large inward-facing failure lobe.

4.4.3 Bond, Repeated Loading and Long-Term Loading (Creep)

In the vast majority of shells which have been tested, no special arrangement has been made to create bonding between the skins and the filler, not even cleaning of the steel surfaces before the concrete is poured between the skins. However, the shells in Table 4.1 (illustrated in Fig. 4.10) formed part of a series to examine the effects of different kinds of mechanical bond. Specimens 1 and 4 were cast without any mechanical bonding device between the concrete and the steel skins. Specimen 2 had self-tapping screws into both the inside and outside

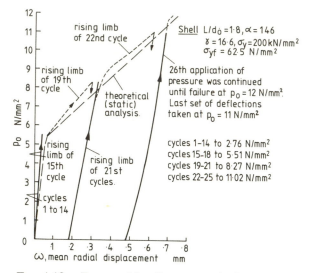

FIG. 4.12.   Repeated loading on a resin-filled shell.

skins on a 100 mm orthogonal grid, with the screw heads embedded in the concrete filler and Specimen 3 had bolts passed right through the wall, also on a 100 mm grid pattern. In addition, shells were tested with a concrete–steel glue at both interfaces. None of these devices made a significant difference to the performances of the shells.

Obviously associated with the bond between the filler and the skins is the behaviour of the composite shell under repeated loading. Does repeated loading break the bond and cause a deterioration in performance? Figure 4.12 shows the results of 26 applications of pressure to a resin-filled shell: 14 cycles below p_p, 4 cycles at p_{pp}, 3 cycles at $p_{pp} < p_o < p_f$, then 4 cycles with p_o just below p_f and the 26th loading taken to failure. The theoretically predicted (static) behaviour of the shell is also shown in Fig. 4.12. The repeated loading did not have an adverse effect.

The lack of experimental evidence to indicate either an enhancement of performance due to mechanical bonding or a reduction in performance with repeated loading is interesting. Both fillers used, viz. resin and concrete, suffer some shrinkage during curing and it might therefore be concluded that the filler will retreat from the outside skin to leave no bond at all at interface 1 (Fig. 4.4). There is no evidence to suggest that this happens, although neither has it been positively established that it does not occur. When shells are cast (i.e. the filler

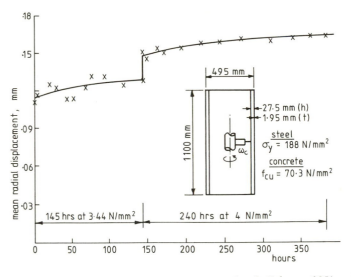

FIG. 4.13.   Creep of a steel–concrete composite shell ($p_{pp} = 6$ N/mm^2).

poured between the skins) with their longitudinal axes placed verti-
cally, shrinkage of the filler is always evident by the drop in the surface
level during setting and top-up is required. If a space should exist at
interface 1 at zero load, the application of external pressure to the
shell will immediately close the gap and create a positive interface
pressure because, on application of the load, the outside skin would
carry the entire radial pressure and the inside skin and filler would
carry only longitudinal load. The separate components would therefore
rapidly come together.

The long-term behaviour of the composite shell is clearly a matter of
vital importance in view of the presence of filler materials which suffer
creep (although, of course, the percentage of steel in the steel–concrete
wall is likely to be at least five times greater than that in conventionally
reinforced structural concrete, so there is a good deal more capacity
for load transfer in the composite shell wall). Figure 4.13 shows the
results of a test carried out on a steel–concrete composite shell under
external pressure sustained for 385 h, the first 145 h at $p_o =
3 \cdot 44$ N/mm^2 and the remaining 240 h at 4 N/mm^2. The vertical ordi-
nate is the mean radial displacement of the shell. During this test, the
mean circumferential stress in the concrete filler at $p_o = 3 \cdot 44$ N/mm^2
(which approximately represents the design working pressure for this

shell) is $0{\cdot}24f_{cu}$ and at $p_o = 4\,\text{N/mm}^2$ the mean circumferential concrete stress is $0{\cdot}28f_{cu}$. In uniaxial compression, it is considered acceptable (from the point of view of creep) to allow a compressive stress of $f_{cu}/3$ in concrete. This is a conservative criterion when the concrete is subjected to multiaxial compressive stress (as in the composite shell wall), but is nevertheless regarded as prudent. The decaying creep rate illustrated on Fig. 4.13 seems to support this proposition. A different criterion, but a very simple one, would be to stipulate that the working pressure of the shell should not result in a (short-term) circumferential concrete stress-resultant which could not be totally accommodated by the steel skins without exceeding the minimum steel yield stress. This point is mentioned again in Section 4.4.6.

4.4.4 The Behaviour at Domed Ends and at Large Penetrations
The results of one of the tests reported by Palaninathan and Montague (1981) on steel–concrete composite shells with hemispherical end closures is shown on Fig. 4.14. Further tests have been conducted by Montague and Kormi (1982) and by Montague et al. (1983). The experimental stress patterns (deduced from measured strains) in Fig. 4.14 indicate that the theoretically predicted values are approximately correct with the obvious conclusion that the skin thickness in the

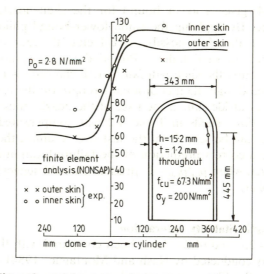

FIG. 4.14. Circumferential stresses from measured strains and from finite element analysis in steel–concrete shell.

TABLE 4.2

Specimen	L (mm)	d_o (mm)	d_o/h	t (mm)	d_n/d_o	t_n (mm)	p_{ln}/p_{lsh}	p_f (N/mm^2)
5	900	331	21·5	1·22	0·2	1·22	1·08	7·6 in shell
6	900	331	21·5	1·22	0·2	1·63	1·05	8·6 in shell
7	1100	495	18·0	1·95	0·26	1·95	0·91	7·7 at intersection

hemispherical dome can safely be reduced to (say) two-thirds of the cylinder skin thickness provided the total wall thickness remains the same.

Experimental testing of composite shells with large penetrations (Fig. 4.9) has been limited to a small number of specimens subjected to hydrostatic pressure; two tests on large (1·5 m diameter) shells by Montague *et al.* (1983) and three at a smaller scale by Montague and Choo (1981) which are listed in Table 4.2. All have been constructed as described in Section 4.3.4, viz. an all-steel nozzle penetrating the wall of the composite shell and welded to both skins. The design objective is to ensure that, under external pressure, failure does not occur at the shell–nozzle intersection (or, of course, in the nozzle itself) before the shell itself fails. The analysis of Choo (1981), described in Section 4.3.4, gives a lower bound for the shell–nozzle intersection limit pressure. By applying the same lower-bound philosophy to the shell itself, it is therefore possible to calculate the ratio of intersection (nozzle) failure to shell failure. Provided that this ratio (p_{ln}/p_{lsh}) is greater than unity, the shell will fail first. If the ratio is less than unity for a proposed design, then additional strength (in the form of a collar welded to the outside skin at the base of the nozzle) must be provided. None of the three shells in Table 4.2 was compensated with such a collar and, as can be seen from the last two columns, the p_{ln}/p_{lsh} ratio proved to be a correct prediction of the failure location in every case. However, even when $p_{ln}/p_{lsh} < 1$, prudence would suggest the addition of such a collar.

4.4.5 Strength–Stability Interaction

Equations (4.23) and (4.24) have been compared with the results of a series of tests conducted by Nash and Montague (1984) on resin-filled steel-skin shells. The experimental results are compared with the predictions of eqns (4.23) and (4.24) in Fig. 4.15.

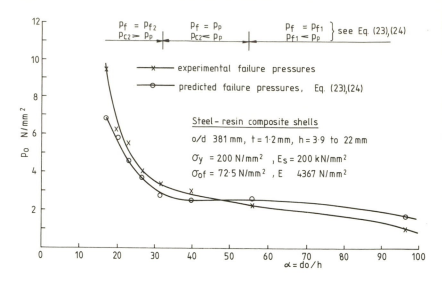

FIG. 4.15. Strength–stability interaction failure predictions and experimental results (Nash and Montague, 1984).

4.4.6 Comparison Between Ring-Stiffened and Composite Shells

As an example of the comparative dimensions and weights of a conventional ring-stiffened, all-steel shell designed in accordance with BS 5500 and a concrete-filled, steel-skinned composite shell designed to the same working pressure, Nash (1985) has produced the details shown in Fig. 4.1.

In both cases, steel to BS 1501–224-32A ($\sigma_y = 315 \, \text{N/mm}^2$) has been used, with a concrete strength of $f_{cu} = 70 \, \text{N/mm}^2$ in the composite shell. The same inside clearance diameter (across the flanges of the light stiffeners in the all-steel shell) has been stipulated and both shells are designed to operate at an external pressure of $5 \, \text{N/mm}^2$ (equivalent to 500 m of water depth).

The allowable factored yield stress is in accordance with BS 5500 in both shells ($238 \, \text{N/mm}^2$ for the all-steel shell and $274 \, \text{N/mm}^2$ for the composite shell: this higher value arising because of the smaller thickness of the composite's steel skins). The material factor applied to the characteristic concrete strength is 1·5.

Having incorporated these material safety factors on the steel and concrete of the composite shell, the corresponding values of p_p' and p_f' are calculated, p_f' being in accordance with the conservative criterion of eqn (4.25), but with $0·67f_{cu}$ replaced by $0·8f_{cu}$. To calculate the design (working) pressure, p_d, of the composite shell, a load factor has been applied according to the most conservative of the three following criteria:

(i) $p'_p/p_d = 1·2$,
(ii) $p'_f/p_d = 1·5$, or
(iii) p_d is such that the short-term circumferential load in the concrete (at p_d) can be carried entirely by the steel skins without causing them to reach the (unfactored) yield stress in that direction.

The resulting composite shell shows considerable savings in steel weight over the all-steel shell and a smaller total weight. It seems likely also that the cost saving on steel would be complemented by further savings on fabrication costs, the comparison here being between the fabrication and filling of two 43 mm-thick membranes and the fabrication of a single membrane of thickness 140 mm with the addition of ring stiffeners at 1·7 m centres.

The circularity specification for the composite membranes could be relaxed to 50% above the BS 5500 value of 0·5% for the ring-stiffened shell.

4.5 CURRENT RESEARCH ON COMPOSITE SHELLS

Recent and continuing work at Manchester is concerned with the behaviour of composite shells subjected to independently applied axial load and radial pressure, corresponding studies of the stress–strain characteristics of concrete under varying principal stress ratios, the residual strength of composite shells after suffering severe damage and the response of steel–concrete composite members when subjected to bending.

The study of concrete constitutive relations is not, of course, a new field of investigation. But, as was discussed in Section 4.2.2, the relatively slender plain concrete cylinder provides the opportunity for the measurement of strains at locations where the stresses are known with a good degree of confidence. It is hoped that further useful results might be obtained to supplement the particular 2 : 1 stress ratio values of E' and v' shown in Fig. 4.3.

Two forms of severe damage to composite shells are being studied experimentally; holes (e.g. weld faults) in the outside skin and deep 'dents' in the wall. Early results with both types of damage are encouraging. The presence of small holes (of the order of 1 mm diameter) in the outside skin (1 mm thick) of $\frac{1}{2}$ m-diameter shells has had no effect on their load-carrying capacity, because fluid entering through the holes is restricted from spreading to more than about 25 mm distance from the holes at interface 1 (Fig. 4.4) by the interface pressure p_1. It has yet to be seen whether shells with thicker (and therefore less flexible) skins will behave in a similar manner. Similarly, local dents of depths up to one-quarter of the wall thickness have not affected shell failure pressures.

Work is being conducted on the bending of composite members in which the concrete is totally confined within steel membranes. The basic idea is similar to that in the composite shells, viz. to realise the full yield strength of steel before buckling occurs and, at the same time, use the stiffness and strength of the concrete to enhance the overall performance of the member.

ACKNOWLEDGEMENTS

The work outlined in this chapter has been done in association with colleagues and research students, C. D. Goode, Y. T. Fatheldin, Y. S. Choo, T. Nash, P. R. Choate, R. Palaninathan and A. N. Qazzaz and with the help of research funds provided by the Science and Engineering Research Council through its Marine Technology Directorate. Also, although confidentiality has forbidden the discussion of results, the work done in fulfilling a research contract for Sir Robert McAlpine and Sons has added substantially to the understanding of composite shell behaviour.

REFERENCES

BELLAMY, C. J. (1961) Strength of concrete under combined stress. *ACI Journal, Proc.*, **58**(4), 367–81.

BRESLER, B. and PISTER, K. S. (1958) Failure of plain concrete under combined stress. *ACI Journal, Proc.*, **55**(3), 321–46.

BS 5500 (1976) *Specification for Unfired Fusion Welded Pressure Vessels*, British Standards Institution, London.

CEDOLIN, L. CRUTZEN, Y. R. J. and POLI, S. D. (1977) Triaxial stress–strain relationship for concrete. *Proc. ASCE*, **103** (EM3), 423–39.

CHOATE, P. R. (1984) Multiaxial behaviour of concrete in shells subjected to external pressure, PhD thesis, University of Manchester.

CHOO, Y. S. (1981) Limit analysis and experimental investigation of a double-skinned composite sandwich cylindrical vessel with a large penetration subject to external pressure, PhD thesis, University of Manchester.

CONSIDÈRE, A. (1891) Resistance des pièces comprimées. Congres International des Procédés de Construction, Paris, Vol. 3.

ENGESSER, F. (1895) Knickfragen. Schweizerische Bauzeitung, 26.

GERSTLE, K. H. et al. (1980) Behaviour of concrete under multiaxial stress states. Proc. ASCE, 106, 1383–1402.

GOODE, C. D. and FATHELDIN, Y. T. (1980) Sandwich cylinders (steel–concrete–steel) subjected to external pressure. ACI Journal, March/April, 109–115.

HANNANT, D. J. (1974) Nomograms for the failure of plain concrete subjected to short-term, multi-axial stresses. The Structural Engineer, 52(5), 151–65.

HAYNES, H. H. (1979) Design for Implosion of Concrete Cylinder Structures Under Hydrostatic Loading, Technical Report R-874, US Naval Civil Engineering Laboratory, Port Hueneme, California.

HOBBS, D. W., POMEROY, C. D. and NEWMAN, J. B. (1977) Design stresses for concrete structures subject to multiaxial stresses. The Structural Engineer, 55(4), 151–64.

HODGE, P. G. (1959) Plastic Analysis of Structures, McGraw-Hill, New York.

HORNE, M. R. and CHOO, Y. S. (1979) Large penetrations in the composite shell: Seminar on Double-Skin Composite Construction for Sub-sea Vessels, University of Manchester.

ILYUSHIN, A. A. (1948) Plasticity, Grostekhizdat, Moscow.

KARMAN, T. VON (1910) Untersuchungen uber knickfestigkeit: Mitteilungen uber Forschungsarbeiten auf dem Gebiete des Ingenieurwesens, Berlin, No. 81.

KOTSOVOS, M. D. (1974) Failure criteria for concrete under generalised stress states, PhD thesis, University of London.

KOTSOVOS, M.D. (1980) A generalised constitutive model for concrete based on fundamental material properties, Thesis submitted for Habilitation at the Institute of Fundamental Research of the Polish Academy of Sciences.

KOTSOVOS, M. D. and NEWMAN, J. B. (1979) A mathematical description of the deformational behaviour of concrete under complex loading. Mag. Conc. Res., 31(107), 77–90.

KUPFER, H. B. and GERSTLE, K. H. (1973) Behaviour of concrete under biaxial stresses. J. ASCE, 99(EM4), 852–66.

McHENRY, D. and KARMI, J. (1958) Strength of concrete under combined tensile and compressive stress. ACI Journal, Proc., 54(10), 829–39.

MISES, R. VON (1914) Critical external pressure on cylindrical pipes. Zeitschrift des vereines Deutscher Ingenieure, 58.

MONTAGUE, P. (1969) Experimental behaviour of thin-walled cylindrical shells subjected to external pressure. J. Mech. Eng. Sci., 11(1), 40–56.

MONTAGUE, P. (1975) A simple composite construction for cylindrical shells subjected to external pressure. J. Mech. Eng. Sci., 17(2), 105–113.

MONTAGUE, P. (1978a) The failure of double-skinned, composite circular, cylindrical shells under external pressure. J. Mech. Eng. Sci., 20(1), 35–48.

MONTAGUE, P. (1978b) The experimental behaviour of double-skinned composite, circular, cylindrical shells under external pressure. *J. Mech. Eng. Sci.*, **20**(1), 21–34.

MONTAGUE, P. (1979) The theoretical behaviour of steel–concrete, circular, cylindrical shells subjected to external pressure. *Proc. ICE Part II*, June, 483–98.

MONTAGUE, P. and CHOO, Y. S. (1981) Double-skin construction of large pressure vessels for sub-sea systems. Offshore Technology Conference, Houston, Paper OTC 4106.

MONTAGUE, P. and COLLARD, M. S. (1983) *The deep sea production systems*. *Proc. of the Engineering Section of the British Association for the Advancement of Science*, Liverpool, 1982. CIRS, UK, 25–47.

MONTAGUE, P. and GOODE, C. D. (1979) Some aspects of double-skin, composite construction for sub-sea pressure chambers. *2nd Inst. Conf. on the Behaviour of Offshore Structures*, London, August.

MONTAGUE, P. and KORMI, K. (1982) Double-skin composite vessels to withstand external pressure. *Buckling of Shells in Offshore Structures* (Ed. by J. E. Harding, P. J. Dowling and N. Agelidis), Granada, London, pp. 331–64.

MONTAGUE, P., GOODE, C. D. and NASH, T. (1983) 1/10-Scale Double Skin Composite and Reinforced Concrete Shells Subjected to External Pressure, A report on the tests undertaken at AMTE, Rosyth Naval Facilities for Sir Robert McAlpine and Sons Ltd.

NASH, T. (1985) Behaviour of large-scale double-skinned composite and reinforced concrete shells under external pressure, PhD thesis, University of Manchester (restricted access due to commercial secrecy).

NASH, T. and MONTAGUE, P. (1984) The strength–stability interaction for double-skin, composite shells. *Proc. Instn Mech. Engrs*, **198C**(16).

NEWMAN, J. B. (1973) Criterion for concrete strength, PhD thesis, University of London.

OLSEN, O. (1978) Implosion analysis of concrete cylinders under hydrostatic pressure: *ACI Journal*, **75**, 82–5.

PALANINATHAN, R. and MONTAGUE, P. (1981) Studies of dome-ended, composite construction, cylindrical vessels subjected to external pressure. *Proc. ICE Part II*, March, 83–105.

QAZZAZ, A. N. (1984) The behaviour and implosion of plain concrete cylindrical shells when subjected to external pressure, PhD thesis, University of Manchester.

RICHART, F. E., BRANTZAEG, A. and BROWN, R. L. (1928) A Study of The Failure of Concrete under Combined Compressive Stresses, Bulletin No. 185, University of Illinois, Engineering Experiment Station.

ROSENTHAL, I. and GLUCKLICK, J. (1970) Strength of plain concrete under biaxial stress. *ACI Journal, Proc.*, **67**(11), 903–14.

SHANLEY, F. R. (1947) Inelastic column theory. *Journal of the Aeronautical Sciences*, **14**(5), 261.

Chapter 5

FABRICATED TUBULAR COLUMNS USED IN OFFSHORE STRUCTURES

W. F. CHEN

School of Civil Engineering, Purdue University, West Lafayette, Indiana, USA

and

H. SUGIMOTO

Initial Design Department, Ship Group, Kawasaki Heavy Industries Ltd, Kobe, Japan

SUMMARY

This chapter is concerned with the analysis and design of fabricated tubular columns as used in offshore structures. It is divided into two parts.

In the first part, the ultimate strength study of large fabricated tubular beam–columns subjected to external hydrostatic pressure is presented. The study considers the effects of beam–column dimensions and materials such as slenderness ratios and diameter–thickness ratios, external hydrostatic pressure, and imperfections of columns such as out-of-roundness, out-of-straightness and residual stresses due to fabrication. As a result, column strength curves and beam–column interaction equations are proposed for practical use.

In the second part, post-buckling and cyclic behaviour of beam–columns and frames are studied using a finite segment model together with generalised cyclic stress–strain relationships and an automatic load control technique. Numerical examples of structural members and simple frames are given using the computer model developed. Comparisons are also made with available experimental data as well as the results of simple rigid–plastic analyses.

NOTATION

f	Shape factor
r	Radius of gyration
t	Thickness of pipe
u	Lateral displacement at mid-span
u	Axial shortening of column
u^b	Bowing component of axial shortening
u^e	Elastic component of the axial shortening
u^p	Plastic component of axial shortening
v	Vertical displacement at mid-span
x	Distance of given point in $x-y$ plane from y-axis
y	Distance of given point in $x-y$ plane from x-axis
z	Distance along the length of tube (z-axis)
A	Area of cross-section
C	Non-dimensional constant $= \sqrt{(2\pi^2 E/\sigma_y)}$
C_m	Equivalent moment factor used in the AISC specifications
D	Mean diameter
E	Young's modulus
E_{eff}	Effective Young's modulus
F_y	Yield stress of material (ksi)
$\{F_1\}$	Generalised stress for a biaxially loaded column
$\{F_2\}$	Generalised stress for a column subjected to hydrostatic pressure
$\{\dot{F}_1\}$	Generalised incremental stress for a biaxially loaded column
$\{\dot{F}_2\}$	Generalised incremental stress for a column subjected to hydrostatic pressure
I	Moment of inertia of cross-section
K	Effective column length factor
L	Column length
M	Bending moment
M_b	M_{pm} for $P<0$; and $-M_{pm}$ for $P>0$
M_p	Fully plastic moment of a cross-section
M_{pm}	Ultimate plastic moment by the axial force
M_{pQ}	Fully plastic moment of a cross-section including the effect of hydrostatic pressure
M_x	Bending moment with respect to x-axis
M_y	Bending moment with respect to y-axis
M_A	Bending moment at end A

M_B	Bending moment at end B
M_ξ	Circumferential bending moment due to pressure
$\dot{M}_x$	Incremental bending moment with respect to x-axis
$\dot{M}_y$	Incremental bending moment with respect to y-axis
$\dot{M}_\xi$	Incremental circumferential bending moment due to pressure
P	Axial force
P_e	Euler's buckling load
P_{ext}	Additional non-hydrostatic axial load
P_{extuQ}	Maximum additional non-hydrostatic axial load capacity of a column
P_{extyQ}	Additional non-hydrostatic yielding axial load for the given value of hydrostatic pressure
P_h	Axial compression force due to hydrostatic pressure
P_t	Total axial force
P_u	Ultimate axial capacity of a column
P_y	Yield axial capacity of a cross-section
P_z	Axial force in the direction of z-axis
P_ζ	Circumferential normal force due to hydrostatic pressure
$\dot{P}_z$	Incremental axial force in the direction of z-axis
$\dot{P}_\zeta$	Incremental circumferential normal force due to hydrostatic pressure
Q	Lateral load
Q	External hydrostatic pressure
Q_{cr}	Elastic critical buckling pressure at which perfect long pipe buckles
Q_p	Plastic limit lateral load
$[Q_1]$	Tangent stiffness matrix for a biaxially loaded column
$[Q_2]$	Tangent stiffness matrix for a column subjected to hydrostatic pressure
$\{\dot{X}_1\}$	Generalised strain for a biaxially loaded column
$\{\dot{X}_2\}$	Generalised strain for a column subjected to hydrostatic pressure
α	Degradation factor in a material model
α_m	Coefficient representing the effect of D/t on the relationship between moment capacity of cross-section and applied hydrostatic pressure
α_p	Coefficient representing the effect of D/t on the relationship between axial capacity of cross-section and applied hydrostatic pressure

α_u Coefficient representing the effect of D/t on the relationship between axial capacity of a column and applied hydrostatic pressure

β Yield growth factor in a material model

Δ Axial shortening

Δ_y Yield axial shortening

ε Axial strain

ε_{ave} Average compressive strain

ε_y Uniaxial axial yield strain

ε_z Axial strain along the length of tube (z-axis)

ε_ζ Circumferential strain due to hydrostatic pressure

$\dot{\varepsilon}_z$ Incremental axial strain along the length of tube (z-axis)

$\dot{\varepsilon}_\zeta$ Incremental circumferential strain due to hydrostatic pressure

η Distance of the given point in ξ–η plane from ξ-axis

θ Angle around the circumference of the tube cross-section

λ Non-dimensional slenderness ratio = $(1/\pi)(KL/r)\sqrt{(\sigma_y/E)}$

μ $0\cdot2(\lambda - 0\cdot2)$

ν Poisson's ratio

σ Stress

σ_{ave} Average compressive stress

σ_i Initial yield stress under biaxial state

σ_u Peak average compressive stress

σ_y Uniaxial yield stress

Φ Curvature under applied loadings

Φ_x Curvature with respect to x-axis

Φ_y Curvature with respect to y-axis

Φ_ξ Curvature due to hydrostatic pressure

$\dot{\Phi}_x$ Incremental curvature with respect to x-axis

$\dot{\Phi}_y$ Incremental curvature with respect to y-axis

$\dot{\Phi}_\xi$ Incremental curvature due to hydrostatic pressure

ABBREVIATIONS

AISC   American Institute of Steel Construction
AISI   American Iron and Steel Institute
API   American Petroleum Institute
CRC   Column Research Council
DNV   Det norske Veritas
ECCS   European Convention for Structural Steelwork
SSRC   Structural Stability Research Council

5.1 INTRODUCTION

Fabricated tubular members with annular shapes have been almost exclusively used as primary members in offshore structures because of their strength property of section and hydrodynamic force aspects.

Two primary design problems emerge with the use of these columns. On the one hand, the designer is faced with an immediate lack of reliable design guidance. The lack of experimental evidence on probable strength levels for these columns hinders specification writers in their attempts to provide designers with safe but relatively economical column design guidance (API, 1972). On the other hand, there is also a major lack of knowledge about the behaviour and strength of such fabricated tubes under various axial loading situations.

Realising the foregoing deficiencies, several designers of offshore platforms began a critical review of this situation in the early 1970s under the auspices of the API's Task Group on Fixed Platform Criteria. One of the major outgrowths of this review was the recognition of the need for more basic information regarding the probable ultimate strengths and corresponding design strengths of axially loaded, large fabricated tubular columns.

During the last decade, the ultimate strength and local buckling characteristics of structural tubing have been the subject of considerable research. A fabricated tubular steel column as commonly used in offshore structures contains imperfections that are far more complicated than the hot-rolled members such as channel, angle and wide flange, because it involves a more complicated manufacturing process than that of the hot-rolled members. A fabricated tubular column undergoes two main stressing processes: (i) rolling from a steel plate to form a cylinder; and (ii) welding of the longitudinal seam of the cylinder to form a 'can'. This results in significant circumferential and longitudinal residual stresses as well as out-of-roundness of the cross-section. Furthermore, the transverse welding of the 'cans' to form a long column results in a significant out-of-straightness of the column.

A realistic design of axially loaded fabricated steel tubular columns must, therefore, consider the fact that an actual tubular column is geometrically and materially imperfect, and is also frequently subjected to bending. Furthermore, a realistic design for tubular beam–columns in deep ocean must consider the fact that the tubes are sometimes subjected to high external hydrostatic pressure. Few studies have been made on this subject.

Another problem is that offshore towers are highly redundant structures where achieving the ultimate capacity of an individual member does not constitute failure of the structure. Tests have indicated that even after a member had 'failed', it still had considerable strength and stiffness so that it would continue to participate in carrying the total forces on the structure. Maintaining 'failed' members in an analytical model was important to determine realistic collapse conditions for structures subject to extreme dynamic, seismic or storm conditions. Current design practice is to have a highly redundant structure fully utilising the inelastic deformation capacity of individual members. Considerable research has been carried out not only on behaviour up to ultimate load but also on post-buckling, post-maximum and cyclic behaviour of members and structures.

5.2 SHORT TUBE

5.2.1 Plastic Moment Capacity
In the 1960s, an interest developed as to whether plastic design concepts could be applied to tubular beams. Plastic design or plastic analysis for collapse loads of tubular structures was very attractive, since tubes have a relatively high shape factor of 1·3. For tubes commonly used in offshore structures, the shape factor is approximately

$$f = \frac{4}{\pi} \left[1 + \left(\frac{t}{D} \right) \right] \qquad (D/t > 10) \qquad (5.1)$$

where f = shape factor; t = wall thickness; and D = mean diameter.

Sherman (1983) summarised various moment capacity data for tubular beams with different D/t ratios to investigate plastic moment capacity (Fig. 5.1). Several comments are made regarding the plastic capacity of tubular beams.

1. There were only a few instances when members with D/t less than $3300/F_y$ (where F_y = yield stress in ksi) did not quite achieve the mechanism load. These were generally simply supported beams with long constant moment regions. It should also be noted that these tests were terminated because of large deflections before the load actually began to decrease because of local buckling.

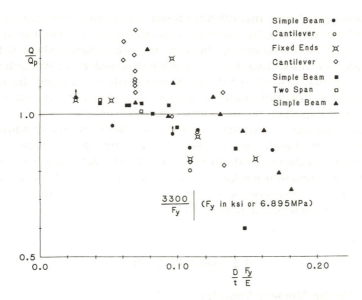

FIG. 5.1.   Ultimate strength of tubular beams based on D/t and F_y.

2. In all of the tests, no elastic local buckling was encountered and the moment that produced first yielding was exceeded.

3. Even though the restrained beams with D/t less than $3300/F_y$ achieved the mechanism load, there is still some reluctance to use plastic analysis up to this limit. This reluctance is because of the fact that mechanism loads were not achieved until the members had deflected over half the diameter and some of the load was carried by axial tension.

API (1972) and AISI (1976) indicate that tubular members may be considered compact and suitable for plastic design with full redistribution of moments when $D/t \leqslant 1300/F_y$, where F_y is the yield stress of material in ksi. For tubular members with $1300/F_y < D/t \leqslant 1900/F_y$ (semi-compact), the full plastic limit load and full plastic moment capacities may be developed, but the plastic rotational capacity may be limited. Where $D/t > 3300/F_y$, a reduced allowable stress considering local buckling is recommended.

DNV (1982) specifies that the tubular cross-section with $D/t \leqslant E/9F_y$ may be considered as compact. This value corresponds to $3300/F_y$ (ksi) in normal steel.

5.2.2 Moment–curvature Relationships

Toma and Chen (1979) extended the tangent stiffness method to the analysis of a fabricated tubular segment considering the biaxial stress state, based on the previous work by Santathadaporn and Chen (1977).

For a biaxially loaded column the appropriate set of generalised stresses are bending moments M_x and M_y, and axial force P_z and the corresponding generalised strains are curvatures Φ_x and Φ_y and axial strain ε_z (Fig. 5.2). Assuming that a plane section remains a plane after bending and introducing the effective Young's modulus concept for a material under biaxial yielding, we have the following incremental generalised stress–strain relationship for an elastic–plastic section in the $x–y$ plane.

$$\begin{Bmatrix} \dot{M}_x \\ \dot{M}_y \\ \dot{P}_z \end{Bmatrix} = \int_A E_{\text{eff}} \begin{bmatrix} y^2 & -xy & y \\ -xy & x^2 & -x \\ y & -x & 1 \end{bmatrix} \begin{Bmatrix} \dot{\Phi}_x \\ \dot{\Phi}_y \\ \dot{\varepsilon}_z \end{Bmatrix} dA \qquad (5.2)$$

or simply

$$\{\dot{F}_1\} = \int_A E_{\text{eff}}[Q_1]\{\dot{X}_1\}\, dA \qquad (5.3)$$

In a similar manner, we have the following incremental relationship in the $\xi–\eta$ plane that relates to hydrostatic pressure (Fig. 5.2).

$$\begin{Bmatrix} \dot{M}_\xi \\ \dot{P}_\zeta \end{Bmatrix} = \int_A E_{\text{eff}} \begin{bmatrix} \eta^2 & \eta \\ \eta & 1 \end{bmatrix} \begin{Bmatrix} \dot{\Phi}_\xi \\ \dot{\varepsilon}_\zeta \end{Bmatrix} dA \qquad (5.4)$$

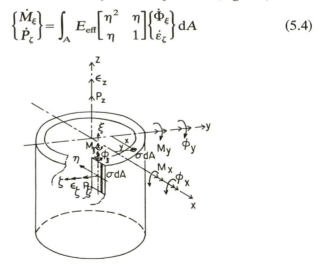

FIG. 5.2.   Column segment under axial load, external hydrostatic pressure and biaxial bending moment.

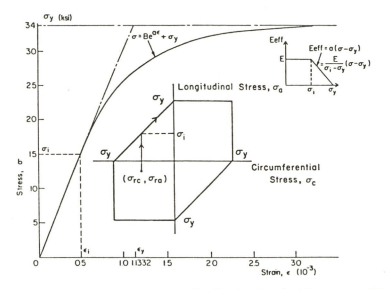

FIG. 5.3. Effective Young's modulus idealisation for biaxial stress condition.

or simply

$$\{\dot{F}_2\} = \int_A E_{\text{eff}}[Q_2]\{\dot{X}_2\}\,dA \qquad (5.5)$$

in which E_{eff} is the effective Young's modulus and dot ($\cdot$) denotes a rate of change of each of the quantities considered. Assuming a linear variation of Young's modulus with increasing stress after the initial yielding of an element (see inset, Fig. 5.3), the effective Young's modulus in the biaxial plastic range results in (see Chen and Atsuta (1977, Fig. 3))

$$E_{\text{eff}} = \frac{d\sigma}{d\varepsilon} = \frac{E}{\sigma_i - \sigma_y}(\sigma - \sigma_y) \qquad (5.6)$$

where σ_i is an initial yield stress under biaxial state and σ_y is a yield stress under uniaxial state.

Total equilibrium condition can be obtained iteratively using the tangent stiffness approach and maintaining equilibrium at the cross-section as

$$\{F_i\} = \int_A E_{\text{eff}}[Q_i]\{X_i\}\,dA \qquad i = 1, 2 \qquad (5.7)$$

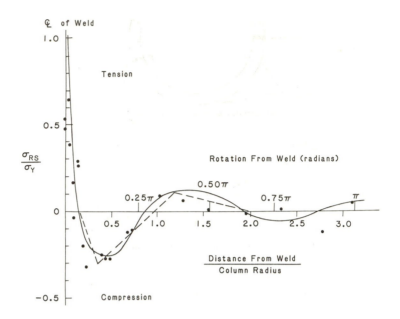

FIG. 5.4.   Longitudinal residual stress distribution obtained from slicing method (Lehigh Test).

Moment–curvature relationships for a tubular cross-section with residual stresses as shown in Figs 5.4 and 5.5 (both longitudinal and circumferential residual stresses, see Chen and Ross (1976)), geometric imperfections (initial out-of-roundness of 1%, shape of $\cos 2\theta$), hydrostatic pressures and a diameter–thickness ratio of 48 are shown in Fig. 5.6 for three values of $Q/Q_{cr} = 0\cdot 0$, $0\cdot 4$ and $0\cdot 6$. The axial intensity due to the additional non-hydrostatic axial load is varied from $P_{ext}/P_y = 0\cdot 0$ to $0\cdot 8$ (see Chen and Sugimoto (1983)).

It can be seen that the hydrostatic pressure, Q, has a major influence on the behaviour and strength of a tubular segment for all ranges of the additional non-hydrostatic axial load, P_{ext}. Also, residual stresses have an influence on the reduction of tangent stiffness of the cross-section, especially near the region immediately beyond the initial yielding point of a cross-section.

Other diameter–thickness ratios (D/t), are expected to have different curves. The effect of D/t on $M–\Phi–P_{ext}–Q$ relations can be approximately obtained by the axial compression forces due to the external

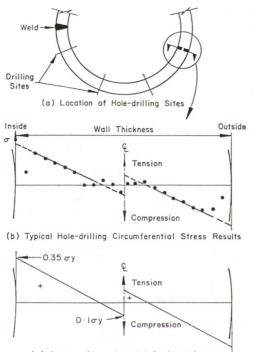

(a) Location of Hole-drilling Sites

(b) Typical Hole-drilling Circumferential Stress Results

(c) Average Circumferential Residual Stress Pattern

FIG. 5.5. Circumferential residual stress pattern (Lehigh Test).

hydrostatic pressure as follows

$$\frac{P_h}{P_y} = \frac{1}{4\sigma_y}\left(\frac{D}{t}\right)Q = \frac{E}{2\sigma_y(1-\nu^2)}\left(\frac{t}{D}\right)^2\left(\frac{Q}{Q_{cr}}\right) \qquad (5.8)$$

where Q_{cr} is the elastic buckling pressure for a perfect long cylinder and ν is Poisson's ratio. This critical pressure has the value (Timoshenko and Gere, 1961)

$$Q_{cr} = \frac{2E(t/D)^3}{(1-\nu^2)} \qquad (5.9)$$

From the above equation, a larger influence of the external hydrostatic pressure can be predicted for tubular sections with smaller diameter–thickness ratios having the same external hydrostatic ratio, Q/Q_{cr}.

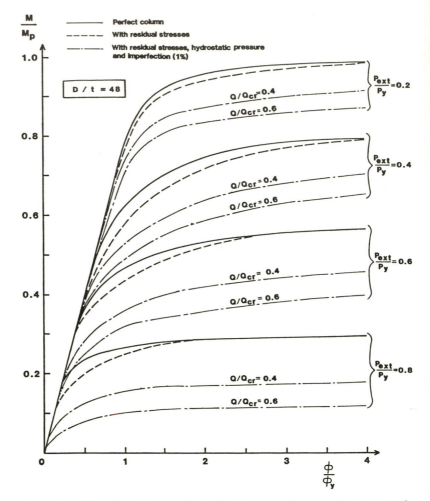

FIG. 5.6. M–P_{ext}–Φ–Q relationships for an imperfect tubular cross-section, $D/t = 48$.

Wagner *et al.* (1976, 1977) investigated the moment–curvature relationship for a thin-walled circular section with a somewhat different pattern of longitudinal residual stress distribution. For a perfect circular section without residual stresses, the curves computed from the computer program reported by Toma and Chen (1979) match closely the results of Wagner *et al.* However, for the circular section with the longitudinal residual stress distribution of the type adopted by Wagner *et al.* their results are found to be considerably lower than the results reported by Toma and Chen (1979). This is because the longitudinal residual stress distribution used in the analysis by Wagner *et al.* (1976, 1977) has a larger and more uniform compressive stress near the region away from the diametrical plane containing the longitudinal weld. Since in these regions the elements are far from the neutral axis, they result in an earlier yielding of the cross-section.

5.2.3 Interaction Curves for Cross-section

In Fig. 5.7, the maximum strength interaction curves between the ratio of the additional non-hydrostatic axial load, P_{ext}, to the maximum additional non-hydrostatic yielding load for each pressure, P_{extyQ} (with $M = 0$) by Chen and Sugimoto (1983) are shown for the tubular section with $D/t = 48$. It can be seen that the results for the hydrostatic pressures of $Q/Q_{cr} = 0.4$ and 0.8 are almost identical to the curve for $Q/Q_{cr} = 0$. Note that P_{ext}, P_{extyQ}, and M_{pQ} can be reduced to P, P_y, and M_p respectively in the special case of $Q/Q_{cr} = 0$.

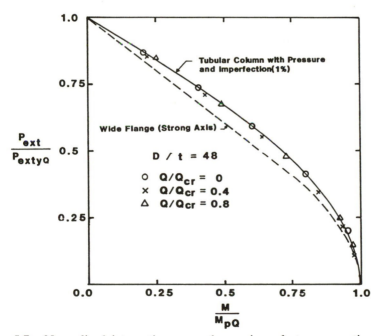

FIG. 5.7. Normalised interaction curve for an imperfect cross-section with residual stresses (1% out-of-roundness, $D/t = 48$).

A better representation for the interaction curve of a fabricated tubular cross-section can be made by the following equations, which are similar to the equations used for a wide flange shape:

$$\frac{M}{M_{pQ}} = 1 - 1 \cdot 18 \left(\frac{P_{ext}}{P_{extyQ}} \right)^2 \quad \text{for} \quad 0 \leqslant \frac{P_{ext}}{P_{extyQ}} \leqslant 0 \cdot 65$$

$$\frac{M}{M_{pQ}} = 1 \cdot 43 \left[1 - \left(\frac{P_{ext}}{P_{extyQ}} \right) \right] \quad \text{for} \quad 0 \cdot 65 \leqslant \frac{P_{ext}}{P_{extyQ}} \leqslant 1 \cdot 0$$

$$(5.10)$$

Equation (5.10) gives the maximum moment-carrying capacity of a tubular cross-section in the presence of an applied axial load including the effect of hydrostatic pressure. P_{extyQ} and M_{pQ} are the end points of the exact interaction curve where the curve crosses the P_{ext}/P_y and M/M_p axes corresponding to a given value of Q/Q_{cr}.

The effects of the diameter–thickness ratios on the P_{extyQ}/P_y versus Q/Q_{cr} relations can be approximately expressed as follows.

$$\frac{P_{extyQ}}{P_y} = 1 - \alpha_p \left(\frac{Q}{Q_{cr}} \right)^{1 \cdot 2} \tag{5.11}$$

The coefficient α_p is dependent on the D/t ratios and can be expressed conservatively as follows.

$$\alpha_p = \begin{cases} -\dfrac{1}{61} \left(\dfrac{D}{t} \right) + 1 \cdot 05 & (32 \leqslant D/t < 48) \\ -\dfrac{1}{348 \cdot 6} \left(\dfrac{D}{t} \right) + 0 \cdot 4 & (48 \leqslant D/t \leqslant 70 \cdot 5) \end{cases} \tag{5.12}$$

The effects of the diameter–thickness ratios on the M_{pQ}/M_p versus Q/Q_{cr} relations can be expressed approximately with a linear relation as follows

$$\frac{M_{pQ}}{M_p} = 1 - \alpha_m \left(\frac{Q}{Q_{cr}} \right) \tag{5.13}$$

An approximate relation can be expressed conservatively as follows.

$$\alpha_m = \begin{cases} -\dfrac{1}{91 \cdot 4} \left(\dfrac{D}{t} \right) + 0 \cdot 725 & (32 \leqslant D/t < 48) \\ -\dfrac{1}{514 \cdot 3} \left(\dfrac{D}{t} \right) + 0 \cdot 294 & (48 \leqslant D/t \leqslant 70 \cdot 5) \end{cases} \tag{5.14}$$

It should be noted that the external hydrostatic pressure, Q/Q_{cr}, can not exceed the pipe collapse pressure.

5.3 BEAM–COLUMNS

5.3.1 Analytical Model

For a long or intermediate length beam–column, the instability of the member arising from the magnification of the primary moments by the axial load acting on the laterally deflected beam–column must be considered. The instability of a beam–column may be classified in accordance with its load–deflection characteristic as being the bifurcation or non-bifurcation type. For the bifurcation type of instability, the beam–column deforms in the direction of the applied load as the load is increased from zero until a critical (or buckling) load is reached and the beam–column has two states of equilibrium. The beam–column prefers a stable configuration and changes its deformation suddenly from the unstable to the stable state. The buckling load or, more accurately, the bifurcation load can be determined conveniently by an eigenvalue analysis to an idealised member.

Biaxially loaded beam–columns exhibit the non-bifurcation type of instability in which the deflection increases until a maximum load is reached, beyond which static equilibrium can only be sustained by decreasing the load for a plastic beam–column. The problem must, therefore, be approached from the standpoint of a load–deflection analysis.

Any rigorous analysis which attempts to cover this behaviour is complicated. For the case of a long beam–column for which elastic analysis may be applied, the governing differential equilibrium equations may be solved rigorously by the use of formal mathematics. In the plastic or non-linear range, the differential equations are often intractable and recourse must be made to numerical methods to obtain solutions. The numerical methods which have been used by various investigators include the finite integral method, the numerical integration method and the finite difference method. The disadvantage of these methods is that they are efficient and successful only for isolated members or small structures.

For practical purposes, the differential equilibrium equations of a biaxially loaded plastic beam–column can be simplified considerably by introducing additional assumptions. The assumptions which have been used by various investigators include establishing equilibrium only at mid-height of the beam–column or at a number of stations along the length of the member, assuming the displacements of a beam–column to be given by known simple functions, and idealising the shape of the biaxial moment–curvature–thrust relationships. The accuracy of these assumptions can be checked by comparing them with more refined solutions. The approximate approaches are generally found quite adequate and satisfactory for many cases and, thus, can be used efficiently to generate a large volume of data from which practical design methods can be developed.

Recently, there has been an increasing number of applications of the finite element method to flexural–torsional buckling and to three-dimensional non-linear analysis of biaxially loaded thin-walled beam–columns. In this development, the beam–column is divided into a number of finite segments or finite elements and the assemblage of these elements is treated as a space structure. The matrix stiffness method is then applied to obtain solutions. The advantages of this method are that it can be used for large structures and it is systematic in obtaining solutions. Complex beam–column problems such as local buckling interaction and elastically restrained beam–columns subjected to biaxial loading can all be solved on the basis of this method.

The ultimate strength analysis by Newmark's method (see for example, Chen and Atsuta, 1976) considering the initial imperfections, residual stresses and external hydrostatic pressure is discussed in the following (Chen and Sugimoto (1983)).

The external hydrostatic pressure introduces an additional axial force and a lateral pressure on the member that will affect the moment–curvature–axial compression–external pressure behaviour of the tubular cross-section (M–Φ–P–Q behaviour), but it will not produce any secondary moment due to the additional axial hydrostatic forces along the column, because hydrostatic pressure is always in a self-equilibrium.

This behaviour can be explained using the following concepts by Peterson (1963). Consider an elastic column with a uniform cross-section, A, subjected to an end load of P_t which consists of the hydrostatic axial load, P_h, and an additional non-hydrostatic applied axial load, P_{ext}, and a lateral pressure, Q, (Fig. 5.8a). A consideration of the equilibrium equation of an element (Fig. 5.8b and Fig. 5.8c), together with the replacement of lateral pressure, Q, by an equivalent hydrostatic pressure (which is always in equilibrium) and an end-load (Fig. 5.8d) leads directly to the basic differential equation on, u, the lateral deflection

$$EI\frac{d^4u}{dz^4}+P_{ext}\frac{d^2u}{dz^2}=0 \qquad (5.15)$$

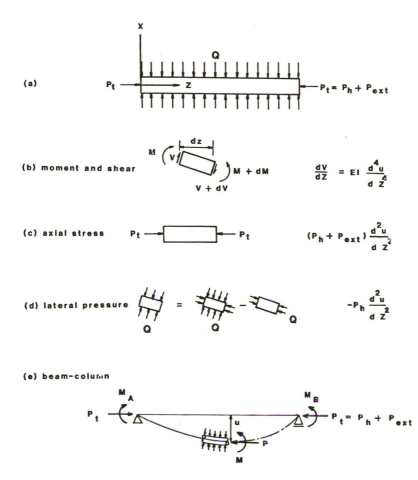

FIG. 5.8.   Hydrostatic forces entering into the equilibrium of an element of a
buckled column.

This equation leads directly to the conclusion that a uniform hydrostatic pressure field will not affect the theoretical buckling load. A column
in a pure hydrostatic field ($P_{ext} = 0$) will always be in a stable equilibrium state.

In the plastic-column case, a hydrostatic axial force, P_h, and a lateral
pressure, Q, will affect the M–Φ–P–Q behaviour significantly at the
section level that will indirectly influence the maximum load-carrying
capacity. Thus, P takes the value of $(P_h + P_{ext})$ for the sectional

response, while P_h does not produce any secondary moment along the column.

The Newmark's method is found to be a convenient numerical method for obtaining the maximum strength of a beam–column by first tracing out the load–deflection (or load–rotation) curve of a beam–column and then by determining the peak point from this curve.

The Newmark's integration method provides a useful means for computing the deflected shape from a given curvature distribution. The moment–curvature–axial compression–external hydrostatic pressure relationship for the cross-section must be known before applying this method. As the hydrostatic axial load component, P_h, does not produce any secondary moment along the beam–column, bending moment, M, and axial force, P, at an arbitrary section, z, may be expressed as follows (Fig. 5.8e).

$$\begin{Bmatrix} M \\ P \end{Bmatrix} = \begin{bmatrix} 1 & 0 \\ 0 & 1 \end{bmatrix} \begin{Bmatrix} M_A + \dfrac{M_B - M_A}{L} z \\ P_h \end{Bmatrix} + \begin{bmatrix} u \\ 1 \end{bmatrix} \{P_{ext}\} \qquad (5.16)$$

Sherman, Erzurumlu and Mueller (1979) solved this problem approximately by introducing a negative rotational spring with a constant stiffness at each station along the length of a beam–column model in order to account for the effect of hydrostatic pressure.

5.3.2 Column Curves

Recent tests by Chen and Ross (1977) conducted in the air, on ten large fabricated tubular columns with diameter–thickness ratios, $D/t = 48$ and 70 and slenderness ratios, $L/r = 39$ and 83 indicate that large fabricated tubular columns as used in offshore structures may be adequately designed using the present AISC–CRC column curve which is basically derived from tests of rolled wide-flange columns and those built-up by welding. Recently, Toma and Chen (1979) proposed the column strength curve for the design of large fabricated tubular columns with residual stresses, out-of-straightness (0.1%) and out-of-roundness (1%).

$$\frac{P_u}{P_y} = \begin{cases} 1.0 - 0.091\lambda - 0.22\lambda^2 & \text{for} \quad 0 \leqslant \lambda \leqslant 1.41 \\ 0.015 + \dfrac{0.84}{\lambda^2}. & \text{for} \quad 1.41 \leqslant \lambda \leqslant 2.0 \end{cases} \qquad (5.17)$$

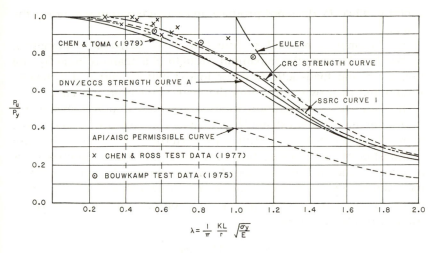

Fig. 5.9. Design curves and test data for fabricated tubular columns.

where λ is the non-dimensional slenderness ratio $\left(= \dfrac{1}{\pi} \dfrac{KL}{r} \sqrt{(\sigma_y/E)} \right)$.

The CRC column curve (Johnston, 1976), DNV/ECCS column curve for rolled tubes and welded tubes (hot finished) (ECCS, 1976; DNV, 1982) and API/AISC (1972, 1980) allowable axial force curve are shown in Fig. 5.9 together with the above-proposed curve and test data.

The DNV/ECCS curve for a tube may be obtained from

$$\frac{P_u}{P_y} = \begin{cases} 1 \cdot 0 & \text{for} \quad \lambda \leqslant 0 \cdot 2 \\ \dfrac{1 + \mu + \lambda^2 - \sqrt{[(1 + \mu + \lambda^2)^2 - 4\lambda^2]}}{2\lambda^2} & \text{for} \quad \lambda > 0 \cdot 2 \end{cases} \quad (5.18)$$

where $\mu = 0 \cdot 2(\lambda - 0 \cdot 2)$.

The CRC curve is given by

$$\frac{P_u}{P_y} = \begin{cases} 1 - \left(\dfrac{KL}{r} \right)^2 \Big/ 2C^2 & \text{for} \quad (KL/r) \leqslant C \\ \pi^2 E/(KL/r)^2 & \text{for} \quad (KL/r) > C \end{cases} \quad (5.19)$$

where $C = \sqrt{(2\pi^2 E/\sigma_y)}$.

The SSRC strength curve 1 (Johnston, 1976) is given by

$$\frac{P_u}{P_y} = \begin{cases} 1 & \text{for} \quad 0 \leqslant \lambda \leqslant 0 \cdot 15 \\ 0 \cdot 99 + 0 \cdot 122\lambda - 0 \cdot 367\lambda^2 & \text{for} \quad 0 \cdot 15 \leqslant \lambda \leqslant 1 \cdot 2 \\ 0 \cdot 051 + \dfrac{0 \cdot 801}{\lambda^2} & \text{for} \quad 1 \cdot 2 \leqslant \lambda \leqslant 1 \cdot 8 \\ 0 \cdot 008 + \dfrac{0 \cdot 942}{\lambda^2} & \text{for} \quad 1 \cdot 8 \leqslant \lambda \leqslant 2 \cdot 8 \\ \dfrac{1}{\lambda^2} & \text{for} \quad \lambda \geqslant 2 \cdot 8 \end{cases} \qquad (5.20)$$

Column strength curves of the column with D/t of 32, 48, 57·6 and 70·5 by Chen and Sugimoto (1983) are shown in Fig. 5.10a. Design pressures range from $Q = 150$ psi to 1300 psi. It is seen that the strength reduction of the column with $D/t = 32$ with an additional axial force P_{ext}/P_y is not small compared with the strength of the column with $D/t = 48$, especially in the small range of the slenderness ratio of λ (see also Fig. 5.10b). It can be seen that the effect of hydrostatic pressure on the strength of columns is significant for an additional non-hydrostatic axial load capacity with decreasing slenderness ratio, λ, for all cases considered. For relatively large slenderness ratios, where elastic buckling takes place, the hydrostatic pressure has little effect on the additional non-hydrostatic axial load capacity. This implies that for slender columns in the deep ocean, the additional non-hydrostatic load-carrying capacity may be estimated by simply neglecting the pressure effect.

To include the effect of hydrostatic pressure, Q, on the maximum additional non-hydrostatic axial load capacity, P_{extuQ}, of an imperfect long column, the modified column strength curves with pressure, Q, may be obtained simply from the case with $Q = 0$ for the case of a 1% out-of-roundness and a 0·1% out-of-straightness.

$$\frac{P_{extuQ}}{P_y} = \frac{P_{extuQ}}{P_{extyQ}} \frac{P_{extyQ}}{P_y}$$

or $\qquad \dfrac{P_{extuQ}}{P_y} = \dfrac{P_u}{P_y} \left[1 + \dfrac{1}{\alpha_u} \left(\dfrac{Q}{Q_{cr}} \right) (\lambda - 0 \cdot 4) \right] \left[1 - \alpha_p \left(\dfrac{Q}{Q_{cr}} \right)^{1 \cdot 2} \right]$ $\qquad (5.21)$

The coefficient α_u is dependent on the diameter–thickness ratio, D/t, and can be expressed conservatively as follows.

$$\alpha_u = \begin{cases} 0\cdot24\left(\dfrac{D}{t}\right) - 5\cdot12 & (32 \leqslant D/t < 48) \\[3mm] 0\cdot85\left(\dfrac{D}{t}\right) - 34\cdot4 & (48 \leqslant D/t \leqslant 70\cdot5) \end{cases} \tag{5.22}$$

5.3.3 Eccentrically Loaded Columns

The analysis of beam–columns subjected to eccentric loads applied at the ends is essentially the same as that of the axially loaded case. Herein, the maximum strength interaction curves of fabricated tubular columns for the combinations of axial load and end moment conditions are discussed according to the results of Toma and Chen (1983a) and Sugimoto and Chen (1983).

As an example, the results of the beam–columns with $D/t = 48$ are presented in terms of the additional non-hydrostatic axial load capacity, P_{ext}, and applied end moment M_A in Fig. 5.11 for the end moment conditions of $M_A/M_B = -1$ and 0. It is seen that the hydrostatic pressure has a significant effect on the interaction curves. This effect is more significant for smaller slenderness ratios. For other diameter–thickness ratios, the results also show similar tendencies.

The computed interaction curves in Fig. 5.11 are now replotted on axes of P_{ext}/P_{extuQ} versus M/M_{pQ} in Fig. 5.12. Solid lines show the modified AISC interaction equation using the terms P_{ext}, P_{extuQ} and M_{pQ} instead of P, P_u and M_p respectively, in the present AISC interaction equation. P_{extuQ} and M_{pQ} are the end points of the exact curves shown in Fig. 5.11.

Herein, the imperfections and residual stresses adopted are 1% of out-of-roundness, 0·1% of out-of-straightness and the residual stress distributions are as shown in Figs 5.4 and 5.5.

The results of the P_{ext}/P_{extuQ} versus M/M_{pQ} relations for the beam–columns with the diameter–thickness ratios of 32 and 70·5 indicate that the computed data appear to form a very narrow band for all values of hydrostatic pressure, Q/Q_{cr}, with slenderness ratio $L/r = 40$, 120 and end moment ratio $M_A/M_B = 0$, 1. Examples of interaction curves for beam-columns with $D/t = 32$ and 70·5 are shown in Fig. 5.13.

The ultimate strength interaction formula for beam–columns subjected to a combined bending moment, M, and an additional non-hydrostatic axial load, P_{ext}, including the effect of an external hydrostatic pressure, has the following form, which is a modification of the

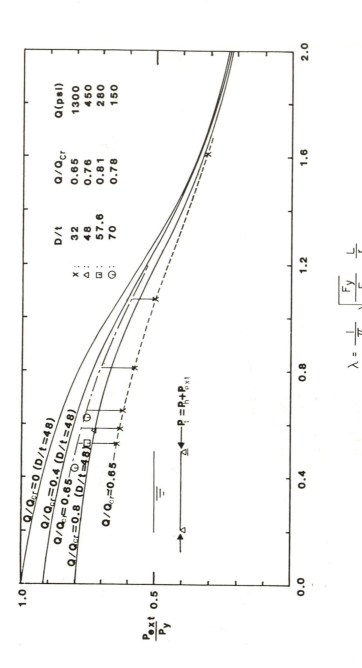

FIG. 5.10a. Column strength curves for columns with different hydrostatic pressure and diameter–thickness ratios.

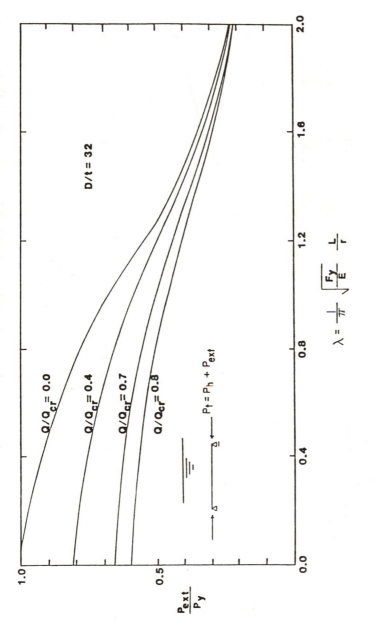

$$\lambda = \frac{1}{\pi} \sqrt{\frac{F_y}{E}} \cdot \frac{L}{r}$$

Fɪɢ. 5.10b. Column strength curves for columns with $D/t = 32$.

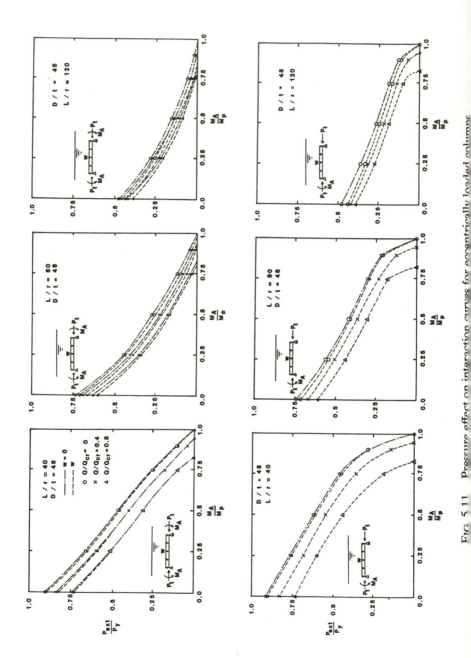

FIG. 5.11   Pressure effect on interaction curves for eccentrically loaded columns

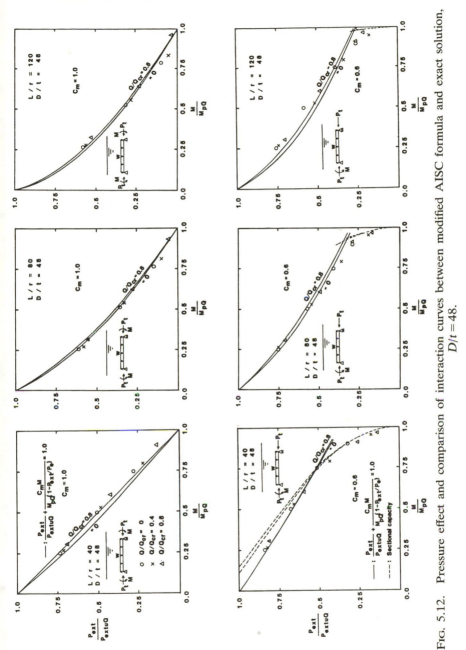

FIG. 5.12. Pressure effect and comparison of interaction curves between modified AISC formula and exact solution, $D/t = 48$.

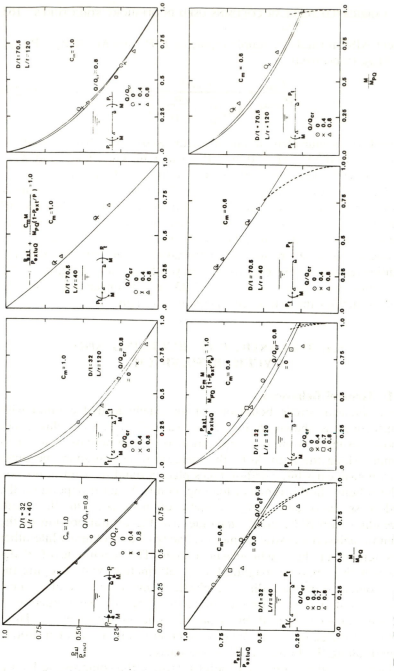

FIG. 5.13. Pressure effect and comparison of interaction curves between modified AISC formula and exact solution, $D/t = 32$, 70·5.

present AISC formula by simply replacing P, P_u, and M_p by P_{ext}, P_{extuQ}, and M_{pQ}, respectively.

$$\frac{P_{ext}}{P_{extuQ}} + \frac{C_m M}{M_{pQ}\left[1 - \left(\frac{P_{ext}}{P_e}\right)\right]} = 1 \qquad (5.23)$$

in which $C_m =$ equivalent moment factor used in the AISC specifications ($= 0 \cdot 6 - 0 \cdot 4 M_B / M_A \geqslant 0 \cdot 40$), $P_e =$ Euler buckling load, and $M =$ the numerically larger one of the two end moments M_A and M_B.

If $C_m < 1 \cdot 0$, eqn (5.23) will give $M > M_{pQ}$ when $P_{ext} = 0$, and thus a cut-off point exists where eqn (5.23) no longer applies. This cut-off point occurs when a plastic hinge forms at one end of the beam–column. For a tubular member with a 1% out-of-roundness and longitudinal residual stresses and hydrostatic pressure, the plastic hinge condition is defined by eqn (5.10). Beyond the cut-off point of the intersection with eqn (5.10), eqn (5.23) is no longer valid, so the envelope defines the estimated maximum strength.

5.4   INELASTIC POST-BUCKLING AND CYCLIC BEHAVIOUR

5.4.1   General Behaviour

Typical inelastic cyclic behaviour of an axially loaded column with imperfections is shown in Fig. 5.14. Path O–A reflects elastic behaviour resulting from the application of a compressive load to a column. Along the path A–B, the increase in deformations becomes highly non-linear while yielding takes place around the central portion of the column. In this range of loading, points A and B depend on the slenderness ratio and yield strength of material. On the load-descending path B–C, the $P - u$ moment of the central portion of the column reaches the plastic moment capacity of the column while other parts remain in the elastic–plastic region. The magnitude of P decreases with increasing magnitudes of deformation while keeping the $P–u$ moment from exceeding the plastic moment capacity of column. Experimental studies of tubular members show a rapid reduction of moment capacity, caused by local buckling in some cases. These changes in the geometry of the cross-section result in a sudden drop in strength along the branch B–C of the curve.

Elastic unloading initiates at point C, where the compressive load is

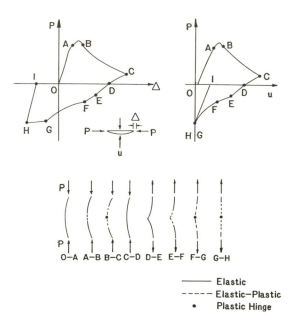

Fig. 5.14.   Typical load–displacement relationships of column.

decreased. Along paths C–D and D–E the entire column begins to behave elastically. The stiffness of this zone is much smaller than that of path O–A because of geometric changes of the column. On the path E–F, yielding will again occur near the centre portion of the column while an increasing tensile load is applied. The decrease in displacement is caused by a decrease and change of sign in the P–u moment because of tensile load. Along the path F–G, the moment at the centre part of the column reaches the plastic moment though it is of opposite sign to the moment caused by compression loads. This bending partially straightens the column as it lengthens. The tensile load required to sustain the plastic moment must increase while P–u moment is decreasing. On the path G–H, the column is fully straightened and the displacement is a purely uniaxial elongation of the column while displacement u is zero. Path H–I represents the elastic reloading zone.

The general effect of slenderness ratios of column on pre-buckling and post-buckling behaviour can be typically presented as in Fig. 5.15 in terms of elastic (u^e), plastic (u^p) and bowing component of axial shortening (u^b) (Igarashi et al, 1972).

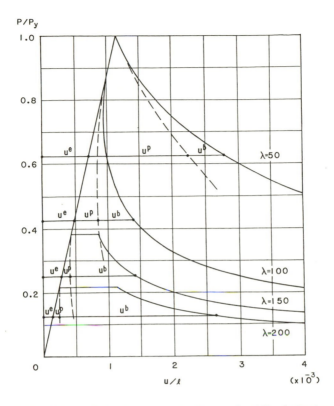

FIG. 5.15. Effect of slenderness ratio on post-buckling behaviour.

5.4.2 Analytical Method

Several methods have been developed to predict the post-buckling and cyclic behaviour of beam–columns and frames in the past. These methods are well reviewed by Popov *et al.* (1979) and Zayas *et al.* (1981). Some of these methods are briefly introduced below.

(a) Finite Element Model

The finite element model is one of the efficient analytical techniques for a linear elastic structural analysis. This technique has been extended for use in cyclic analysis of geometrically and materially non-linear problems. Basically, this method involves the subdivision of a beam–column longitudinally into a series of elements and the further subdivision of a cross-section of a longitudinal element into several elements. Fujimoto *et al.* (1972) employed the finite element method using the energy principle to study the cyclic non-linear analysis of beam–columns and K-braced frames with H-shaped cross-sectional members. Hays and Santhanam (1979) used discrete elements with spring-link mechanism for cyclic analysis of beam–columns and simple frames. They applied an α, β material model where α and β are the degradation factor and the yield growth factor respectively. Imaginary large axial springs were introduced to keep the positive definiteness of the stiffness matrix in the analysis. Smith *et al.* (1979) employed the finite element method for the buckling strength and inelastic post-buckling analysis for over 200 typical fabricated tubular columns, with particular reference to post-buckling load-carrying capacity and to the effect of initial deformations, residual stresses and certain forms of damage.

Sugimoto and Chen (1983) modified the finite segment model by Chen and Atsuta (1977) to solve inelastic post-buckling or descending branch of beam–columns and frames. This method is based on a concept similar to the finite element method with the tangent stiffness approach, which uses moment–axial force–curvature relations and axial force–moment–axial strain relations to represent the cross-sectional properties of beam–column segments. Though these finite element models have advantages in their general applicability to many types of problems, they are considered to be computationally expensive.

(*b*) *Physical Models*
Physical models provide a simpler and more specialised technique for predicting the post-buckling and cyclic inelastic behaviour of beam–columns. One of these models is proposed by Higginbotham (1973) for the analysis of pin-ended columns. In this analytical model, the column is assumed to remain elastic when loaded in compression except for a central plastic hinge location (Fig. 5.16). The moment–curvature relationships are assumed to be elastic–perfectly plastic for each axial load. The differential equations governing the lateral deflections of columns are derived to include large geometric effects. The axial shortening of this model is assumed to be the sum of the elastic shortening of the column, and the shortening due to hinge rotation. Approximating the load–shortening relation of this model, by assuming the bending moment to vary linearly from the member ends to mid-length, yields

$$\Delta = \frac{PL}{AE} - \frac{M_b^2}{L} \left\{ \frac{2}{P^2} + \frac{1}{360} \left(\frac{L^2}{EI} \right)^2 \right\} \tag{5.24}$$

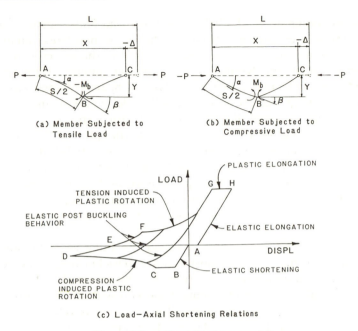

(a) Member Subjected to
Tensile Load

(b) Member Subjected to
Compressive Load

(c) Load—Axial Shortening Relations

FIG. 5.16. Higginbotham model.

Equation (5.24) in conjunction with the identities

$$M_b = M_{pm} \quad \text{if plastic rotation occurs and } P < 0;$$
$$M_b = -M_{pm} \quad \text{if plastic rotation occurs and } P > 0 \quad (5.25)$$

in which M_{pm} is ultimate plastic moment by the axial force, represent the governing equations for the force–deformation behaviour of pin-ended members.

When plastic rotation occurs at the mid-length of the member, eqns (5.24) and (5.25) are used to acquire the force–deformation behaviour. Selecting the force as the independent variable allows these equations to be solved directly for the displacement; but, if the displacement is designated as the independent variable, the correct root of a sixth-degree polynomial must be determined.

Prathuangsit *et al.* (1978) extended Higginbotham's model to study the axial cyclic behaviour of beam–columns with end restraints. Nonaka (1973, 1977) proposed a similar analytical model, but included the plastic axial deformation of the plastic hinge using the flow rule associated with a yield condition. Quadrangular and hexagonal yield conditions were used in the analysis. Igarashi *et al.* (1972) also studied the cyclic behaviour of the pin-ended column by the plastic hinge method, considering the axial deformation of the plastic hinge using the parabolic yield function and the flow rule. Toma and Chen (1982a) applied a hinge-by-hinge method to a fixed-ended column to study cyclic behaviour. These methods would be applicable to slender members which buckle elastically or nearly elastically and to cross-sections with small shape factors. A limitation of these physical models is that they are not directly suited for conventional computer structural analysis to solve arbitrary-shaped and -supported structures.

This type of physical modelling, for tubular members, and similar types of analytical solutions, were also used by Nilforsoushan (1973) and Singh (1977).

(c) Numerical Integration Method

Numerical integration or iteration methods are other applications for the study of inelastic post-buckling and cyclic analysis of beam–columns. Toma and Chen (1983b,c) applied Newmark's method for pin-ended columns using closed-form moment–axial force–curvature–axial strain relations. Han and Chen (1983b) applied iteration techniques using the influence coefficient method (ICM) for various types of end conditions. In both methods, yielding of the column segment can be processed instead of hinge concepts. The shortening in these models is assumed to be the sum of the shortening due to bowing and the shortening due to elastic–plastic axial behaviour of the segment using the axial force–moment–axial strain relationships. These models are also not suited for a conventional computer structural analysis to solve arbitrarily-shaped and -supported structures.

(d) Combined Models

Combined models are presently most commonly used for non-linear computer analysis of fully braced structures because of their savings in computer time and storage requirement. Igarashi and Inoue (1973) developed a beam–column element with plastic hinge(s) at its ends and considered the effect of bowing, where the hinge formations are checked by parabolic interaction yielding criterion and Prager's flow rule as modified by Ziegler is used for strain-hardening at hinge(s) after yielding (see Chen and Saleeb, in press). Cyclic analyses of simple frames and X-braced frames are performed by an incremental technique.

Popov *et al.* (1980) proposed a much simpler method that is applicable to non-linear computer analysis of large structural systems. Axial force–axial displacement response of a brace member is represented by the single degree-of-freedom Maison's phenomenological model matched with empirical results. The principal parameters required to model the cyclic inelastic response of a brace in their method are: effective length, yield load, yield displacement, susceptibility to local buckling (D/t), and material property characteristics. To assess the ability of their model to predict the behaviour of tubular steel frames, the two one-sixth scale models of the Southern California Example Structure tested at University of California, Berkeley were analysed. Their brace model is applicable to members with either a low or a high slenderness ratio.

The other phenomenological models that are commonly used for non-linear computer analysis of braced structures are those developed by Higginbotham (1973), Nilforsoushan (1973), Singh (1977), Marshall (1978), Roeder and Popov (1977), Jain *et al.* (1978) and Maison and Popov (1980). These models are shown in Fig. 5.17. The basis of these models is to predefine the shape of the axial force–axial displacement response of a column element that represents the brace by employing either mathematical or empirical results.

Higginbotham, Nilforsoushan and Singh used their physical theory models to compute the coefficients and parameters for their phenomenological models. Higginbotham (1973) curve-fitted the analytical results by employing second order polynomial equations to describe phases C–D, D–F and F–G of brace response (Fig. 5.16). Nilforsoushan (1973) developed a model with nine piece-wise linear segments to define the brace hysteretic loops (Fig. 5.17a). The strength and stiffness in each segment were defined by a set of input parameters. Singh (1977) developed a simpler five-segment piece-wise linear model which could give a realistic fit for members with high slenderness ratios $(KL/r > 120)$ (Fig. 5.17b). Marshall (1978) employed a seven-segment piece-wise linear model with an algorithm defining failure of a brace based on estimating the onset of local buckling (Fig. 5.17c). Jain *et al.* (1978) developed a six-segment model for members with high slenderness ratio. This model has two buckling loads, one for the first cycle and one for subsequent cycles (Fig. 5.17d) and also incorporates a feature to account for observed growth in brace length during buckling and restraightening. Roeder and Popov (1977), using a nine-segment model similar to Nilforsoushan's, introduced a feature to

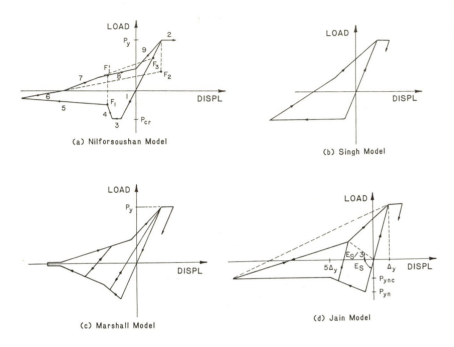

(a) Nilforsoushan Model

(b) Singh Model

(c) Marshall Model

(d) Jain Model

FIG. 5.17.   Phenomenological models.

permit gradual deterioration of the buckling load between two bounds (Fig. 5.17e). Maison and Popov (1980) also employed a nine-segment model with buckling load deterioration capabilities similar to Roeder's, and accounted for hysteretic growth in brace length during buckling and restraightening (Fig. 5.17f).

5.4.3   Numerical and Experimental Results

(a) Individual Tubular Members
Considerable experimental studies as well as theoretical studies have been performed to assess the inelastic behaviour of individual tubular members.

Jain and co-workers (1978, 1980) and Prathuangsit *et al.* (1978) performed tests and compared these with their theoretical predictions for box-shaped tubular members to study inelastic cyclic behaviour Popov *et al.* (1979, 1980) and Zayas *et al.* (1980) published experimental results of inelastic cyclic behaviour of thin-walled tubular

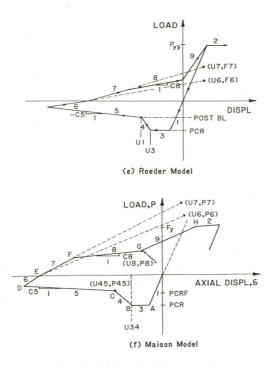

(e) Roeder Model

(f) Maison Model

FIG. 5.17—contd.

columns. Further, Sherman and his co-workers (1974, 1979, 1980) performed an extensive test programme on the inelastic cyclic behaviour of individual members. Smith et al. (1979) reported the experimental results of buckling and post-buckling performed on fabricated tubular members as well as theoretical results by the finite element method.

(b) Simply Supported Columns
Some of the results obtained experimentally and theoretically by Smith et al. (1979) are shown in Fig. 5.18 for simply supported columns.

The estimated static and dynamic collapse strengths of test specimens, defined as the ratios σ_u/σ_y of peak average compressive stresses to corresponding (static and dynamic) yield stresses are derived from stub-column tests. Experimental load–shortening curves, normalised with respect to static yield, are shown as full lines in Fig. 5.18 together where appropriate with theoretical curves shown as dotted lines.

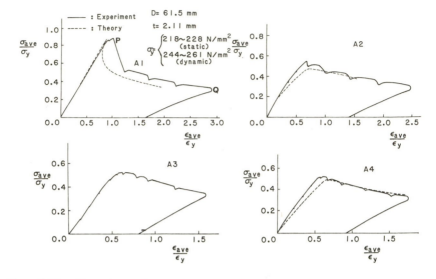

FIG. 5.18.   Experimental and theoretical load-shortening curves for simply supported columns.

Downward spikes on experimental curves correspond to stops in load application: theoretical load-shortening curves (based on static yield) should be compared with lines through the lowest points on the experimental curves. Collapse and post-collapse behaviour of each specimen is described briefly below.

Specimen A1: Collapse of this tube, which was virtually imperfection-free, occurred sharply at a load within 5% of the theoretical prediction. Post-collapse unloading (points P to Q on the experimental curve) was dynamic: this, together with elasticity of the test rig, accounts for the shift to the right of the experimental unloading curve relative to the theoretical curve. There was no evidence of local buckling following collapse and ovalisation was negligible.

Specimen A2: Collapse under eccentric load occurred slowly and in fairly close accordance with theoretical predictions: no local buckling occurred after collapse.

Specimen A3: This tube was first subjected to damage by a lateral load acting through a knife-edge: formation of a dent reduced the

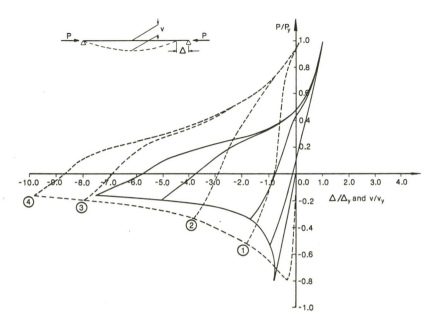

FIG. 5.19.   Cyclic behaviour of pin-ended column.

lateral load-carrying capacity of the tube to 95% of the theoretical fully plastic value. Collapse under axial load then occurred slowly with growth of the dent depth to about 2·0 t at collapse and a maximum of 3·8 t following collapse (t = wall thickness).

Specimen A4: Lateral load was applied through a padded cradle causing lateral deformation and slight ovalisation without measurable denting; maximum lateral load was 11% higher than the theoretical fully plastic value. Collapse under axial load occurred slowly and in reasonable agreement with theory; the collapse load was almost identical with that for A3, suggesting that the effect of a dent is secondary to that of lateral deformation in a thick-walled tube.

   Results of a study of typical cyclic behaviour for pin-ended beam–columns with a slenderness ratio of 80 and an initial out-of-straightness of 0·1% by Han and Chen (1983a) are shown in Fig. 5.19. There are four unloading paths starting from different points on the post-buckling branch. Each unloading curve behaves similarly. In the elastic unloading range, the reversed load–deflection (*P–v*) curves are straight lines with slightly different slopes. Next comes the elastic–plastic tensioning range, during which the plastic hinge at mid-span gradually forms. Here the slopes of the P–v curve become somewhat flat. Although the behaviour in this range differs from that in the post-buckling range, it does not show any unstable behaviour because the deflection is decreasing with increasing tension loading. Eventually the column straightens and the plastic zone spreads over the whole length of the column and all the load–deflection curves merge to the same curve. The load–shortening curves (P–Δ) behave similarly in the elastic–plastic tensioning range.

All the load–shortening (P–Δ) curves also merge together, and, at the end, the total shortening of the column reaches the same value Δ_y as the axial load reaches its ultimate value P_y. Recalling that $\Delta_y = \varepsilon_y L$, it is seen that the strain along the whole length of the column reaches the plastic strain ε_y regardless of how large a compressive strain was experienced before unloading.

The most critical section is at mid-span. The interaction curves of moment M and axial force P at mid-span for one loading cycle are shown in Fig. 5.20. It is seen that during the unloading and reversed loading ranges, the interaction between P and M is not always proportional

(c) Fixed-End Beam–Columns

The theoretical predictions based on the hinge-by-hinge method by Toma and Chen (1982a,b) are compared with tests reported by Sherman (1980). Figure 5.21 shows typical comparisons for $KL/r = 72$. Since an elastic-perfectly plastic M–P–Φ relation is used in the present study, there is a sharp change in sectional stiffness; thus, there is a sharp peak near the ultimate compressive strength. After reaching the critical compressive load, the axial load drops sharply in the present theory, while the change observed in the test is more gradual. In the tension branch, again, the theory has discontinuities at the points where plastic hinges are just formed or where an entire cross-section is just fully yielded.

Examples of a cyclic behaviour study of fixed-ended beam–columns under several cycles by Popov *et al.* (1979, 1980) and Zayas *et al.* (1980) are shown in Fig. 5.22. Analytical results are predicted using Maison's model in their analysis. The maximum compressive load carried by this specimen (cycle 3) was within 2% of the value predicted

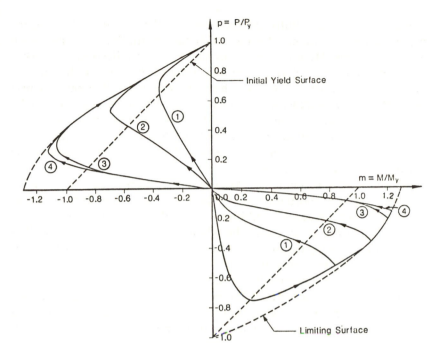

FIG. 5.20.   Interaction curve at mid-span of column.

using AISC formulas (1980). While there was some deterioration in the buckling load and energy dissipation on subsequent cycles, this was not nearly so severe as that exhibited by the pinned-end specimens. Local buckling was observed in cycle 5, first at the foot end and then at mid-span. With additional cycling, the centre hinge region deteriorated more quickly than the one at the foot end, eventually tearing open in tension.

The axial load versus axial displacement curves obtained for the fixed-end specimens are considerably different than those obtained for the pinned-end ones. As can be seen in Fig. 5.22 there is very little deterioration in post-buckling strength exhibited by the fixed-end specimens, and the initial stiffness and strength for loading in tension are much higher. Consequently, fixing the ends of the specimens, and thereby halving the slenderness ratio, results in superior energy dissipation characteristics.

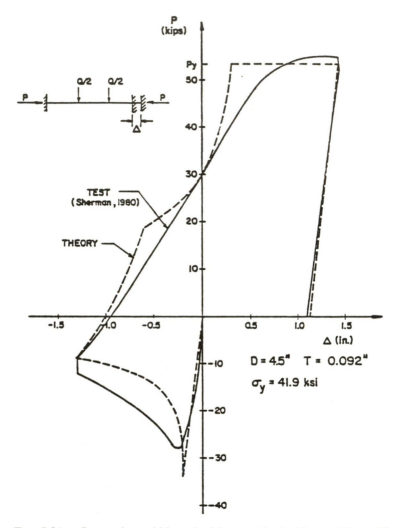

FIG. 5.21.   Comparison of hinge-by-hinge method with test, $KL/r = 72$.

(d) *Eccentrically Loaded Beam–Columns*
In Fig. 5.23 results for eccentrically loaded column with a slenderness
ratio of 61·4 and 1·5 in. eccentricity are shown and are compared with
Wagner's test (1976) and other analytical results. In the analysis, no
initial imperfection is assumed.

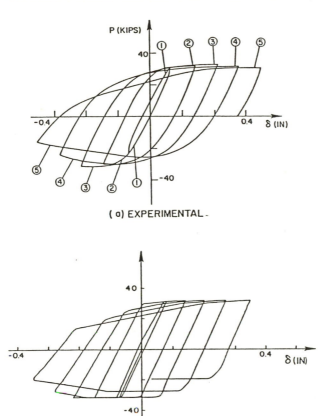

(a) EXPERIMENTAL.

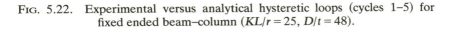

(b) ANALYTICAL

FIG. 5.22. Experimental versus analytical hysteretic loops (cycles 1–5) for fixed ended beam–column ($KL/r = 25$, $D/t = 48$).

(e) *Braced Frames*

The experimental and analytical study of tubular braces and two types of two-bay X-braced frames of one-sixth scale models of a Southern California offshore platform were tested by Popov *et al.* (1979, 1980) and Zayas *et al.* (1980). The braces and frames were subjected to imposed cyclic displacements causing buckling, post-buckling strength deterioration, tensile restraightening, and tensile stretching of the braces. Observations are presented on: when the primary buckling of the braces in frames occurred; which members were affected; the

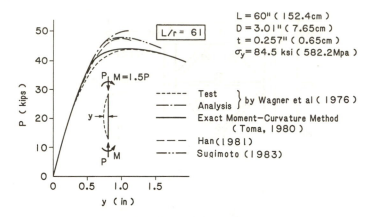

FIG. 5.23.   Axial load–deflection relationships for eccentrically loaded beam–column ($e = 1 \cdot 5$ in., $L/r = 61$).

extent of damage as it progressed through the structure; and the occurrence of local buckling in members.

In Fig. 5.24, the geometry of this frame and member number designations are shown. This braced planar frame is one-sixth scale of the prototype. The section sizes for the tubular members of the Type 1 frame are given in Table 5.1. The tube diameter-to-wall thickness ratio D/t is 48 and is representative of current practice. The principal experimental result giving hysteretic loops for the frame lateral load versus deck displacement is shown in Fig. 5.25. The maximum lateral load is 56·6 kips (251 kN) obtained during a pull cycle 9 at a displacement of 1·68 in. (43 mm). The maximum lateral load occurred during the cycle in which buckling first developed in the upper panel braces.

In each of the experiments it was observed that buckling tended to concentrate in one-half of the full length diagonal, i.e. in one brace. For example, once brace 2 buckled the axial displacement for the full diagonal concentrated in it, and brace 1 remained relatively straight. This results from the fact that once a brace has buckled, during the subsequent cycles since a brace is no longer straight, its buckling load is reduced, and it will buckle at a lower load than the adjoining straighter brace on the same diagonal.

Local buckling at plastic hinges also tends to concentrate the displacements in one brace of a diagonal pair. This in turn causes a more severe post-buckling cyclic degradation in strength of a brace as well as that of the frame.

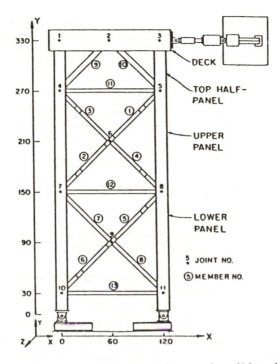

FIG. 5.24. Frame geometry and member numbers (1 in. = 25·4 mm).

The frame with braced members with D/t ratios of 33 was also tested and reported in detail. The stiffness of the analytical model is about 16% higher than the experimental value for Frame 1. This may be because of the elastic range assumptions used in the analytical models. A real structure always has initial imperfections such as initial cambers and residual stresses from fabrication and welding which can result in local inelasticity at moderate nominal stress levels. Moreover,

TABLE 5.1

TUBULAR MEMBERS

Member number or description	Tube or pipe dimensions (Nominal diameter × wall thickness: in. (m))
1, 2, 3, 4, 11, 12, 13	4 × 0·083 (100 × 2)
5, 6, 7, 8	4·5 × 0·188 (114 × 5)
Vertical pipes	12·75 × 0·281 (320 × 7)

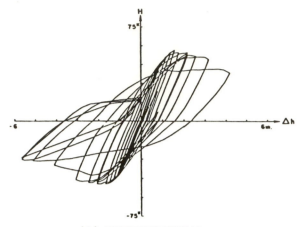

(i) EXPERIMENTAL

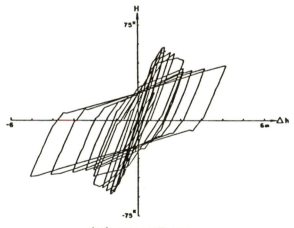

(ii) ANALYTICAL

Fig. 5.25. Experimental and analytical frame hysteretic loops (1 kip = 4·45 kN, 1 in. = 25·4 mm).

joint deformations were not directly modelled in the analyses. Movement of the supports for the experimental models was accounted for in reducing the experimental results.

CONCLUSIONS

Two major areas of the behaviour and design of fabricated tubular beam–columns and simple frames are described. The first is the maximum strength of large fabricated tubular beam–columns as affected by the presence of high external hydrostatic pressure. It is found that the external hydrostatic pressure has a significant effect on the non-hydrostatic axial load capacity for columns with short- and medium-range slenderness ratios and with small values of diameter–thickness ratios. The proposed modified AISC beam–column and section-capacity interaction equations give a good estimate for the strength of eccentrically loaded beam–columns with external hydrostatic pressure.

The second area studied is the post-buckling and cyclic analysis of tubular members and frames. It shows that the combination of the finite segment method, generalised stress–strain relationships, the incremental stiffness approach and automatic load control technique is a valid and effective method for computer-based beam–column and frame analysis in the pre- and post-buckling range under cyclic loading conditions.

REFERENCES

AISC (1980) *Specifications for the Design, Fabrication and Erection of Structural Steel for Buildings*, American Institute of Steel Construction, Chicago.

AISI (1976) *Tentative Criteria for Structural Applications of Steel Tubing and Pipe*, ed. D. R. Sherman, American Iron and Steel Institute, SP 604-876-7-5 M-MP.

API (1972) *API Recommended Practice for Planning, Designing and Constructing Fixed Offshore Platforms*, API RP2A 12th edn, American Petroleum Institute, Texas.

BOUWKAMP, J. G. (1975) Buckling and post-buckling strength of circular tubular sections, *Proc. Offshore Technology Conference*, Houston, Texas, May.

BRIGGS, M. J. and MAISON, J. R. (1978) Test of X-Braced Subassemblage, Combined Preprint for Session 45, ASCE Annual Convention and Exposition, Chicago, Illinois, October, pp. 55–87.

CHEN, W. F. and ATSUTA, T. (1976) *Theory of Beam–Columns, Vol. 1—In-Plane Behavior and Design*, McGraw-Hill, New York.

CHEN, W. F. and ATSUTA, T. (1977) *Theory of Beam–Columns, Vol. 2—Space Behavior and Design*, McGraw-Hill, New York.

CHEN, W. F. and ROSS, D. A. (1976) The axial strength and behavior of cylindrical columns, OTC Paper No. 2683, *Eighth Annual Offshore Technology Conference*, Houston, Texas, May 3–6, pp. 741–54.

CHEN, W. F. and ROSS, D. A. (1977) Tests of fabricated tubular columns. *Journal of the Structural Division, ASCE*, **103** (ST3), Proc. Paper No. 12809, 619–34.

CHEN, W. F. and SALEEB, A. F. (1982, in press) *Constitutive Equations for Engineering Materials, Vol. 1—Elasticity and Modeling, Vol. 2—Plasticity and Modeling*, Wiley Interscience, New York.

CHEN, W. F. and SUGIMOTO, H. (1983) Moment–Curvature–Axial Compression–Pressure Relationship of Structural Tubes, ASCE Structures Congress, October 17–19, Houston, Texas, Preprint SC-6.

CHEN, W. F. and TOMA, S. (1979) Effect of External Pressure on the Axial Capacity of Fabricated Tubular Columns, Final Report submitted to Exxon Production Research Co., Houston, TX, Structural Engineering Report No. CE-STR-79-1, Purdue University.

DNV (1982) Classification Notes No. 31 on Buckling Strength Analysis, Det norske Veritas, Norway.

ECCS (1976) 2nd International Colloquium on Stability, Introductory Report, European Convention for Structural Steelwork.

FUJIMOTO, M., AOYAGI, T., UKASI, K., WADA, A. and SAITO, K. (1972) Structural characteristics of eccentric K-braced frames. *Trans. AIJ*, No. 195, May.

HAN, D. J. and CHEN, W. F. (1983a) Behavior of portal and strut types of beam–columns. *Engineering Structures*, **5**, 15–25.

HAN, D. J. and CHEN, W. F. (1983b) Buckling and cyclic inelastic analysis of steel tubular beam–column, *Engineering Structures*, **5**, 119–32.

HAYS, C. O. and SANTHANAM, T. K. (1979) Inelastic Section Response By Tangent Stiffness. *Journal of the Structural Division, ASCE*, **105** (ST7), Proc. Paper 14668, 1241–59.

HIGGINBOTHAM, A. B. (1973) The inelastic cycle behavior of axially-loaded steel members, PhD Thesis, University of Michigan.

IGARASHI, S. and INOUE, I. (1973) Memorandum on the study of braced frames, Quarterly column, No. 49, Tokyo, Japan.

IGARASHI, S., INOUE, I., OGAWA, K. and ASANO, M. (1972) Hysteretic characteristics of steel braced frames, Part I, The behavior of bracing members under cyclic axial forces. *Trans. AIJ*, No. 196.

JAIN, A. K. and GOEL, S. C. (1978) Hysteresis models for steel members subjected to cyclic buckling or cyclic end moments and buckling, University of Michigan, Report UMEE 78R6.

JAIN, A. K., GOEL, S. C. and HANSON, R. D. (1978) Inelastic response of restrained steel tubes, *Journal of the Structural Division, ASCE*, **104** (ST6), Proc. Paper 13832, 897–910.

JAIN, A. K., GOEL, S. C. and HANSON, R. D. (1980) Hysteretic cycles of axially loaded steel members. *Journal of the Structural Division, ASCE,* **106** (ST8), Proc. Paper 15607, 1777–95.

JOHNSTON, B. G., (Ed.) (1976) *Guide to Stability Design Criteria for Metal Structures,* Wiley, New York, 3rd edn.

MAISON, B. and POPOV, E. P. (1980) Cyclic response prediction for braced steel frames. *Journal of the Structural Division, ASCE,* **106** (ST7), 1401–16.

MARSHALL, P. W. (1978) Design Considerations for Offshore Structures Having Non-linear Response to Earthquakes, Preprint, ASCE Annual Convention and Exposition, Chicago, October.

NILFORSOUSHAN, R. (1973) Seismic Behavior of Multistory K-Braced Frame Structures, University of Michigan, Research Report UMEE 73R9.

NONAKA, T. (1973) An elastic–plastic analysis of a bar under repeated axial loading. *International Journal of Solid and Structures,* **9,** 569–80.

NONAKA, T. (1977) Approximation of yield condition for the hysteretic behavior of a bar under repeated axial loading. *International Journal of Solid and Structures,* **13,** 637–43.

PETERSON, J. P. (1963) Axially loaded columns subjected to lateral pressure. *AIAA Journal,* **1**(6), 1458.

POPOV, E. P., ZAYAS, V. A. and MAHIN, S. A. (1979) Cyclic inelastic buckling of thin tubular columns. *Journal of the Structural Division. ASCE,* **105** (ST11), Proc. Paper 14982, 2261–77.

POPOV, E. P., MAHIN, S. A. and ZAYAS, V. A. (1980) Inelastic cyclic behavior of tubular braced frames. *Journal of the Structural Division, ASCE,* **106** (ST12), Proc. Paper 15918, 2375–90.

PRATHUANGSIT, D., GOEL, S. C. and HANSON, R. D. (1978) Axial hysteresis behavior with end restraints. *Journal of the Structural Division, ASCE,* **104** (ST6), 883–96.

ROEDER, C. W. and POPOV, E. P. (1977) Inelastic Behavior of Eccentrically Braced Frames Under Cyclic Loading, Earthquake Engineering Research Center, University of California, Berkeley, Report No. 77-18.

SANTATHADAPORN, S. and CHEN, W. F. (1977) Tangent stiffness method for biaxial bending. *Journal of the Structural Division, ASCE,* **98** (ST3), Proc. Paper No. 8637, 153–63.

SHERMAN, D. R. (1979) Experimental Study of Post Local Buckling Behavior in Tubular Portal Type Beam–Columns, Report to Shell Oil Company, University of Wisconsin–Milwaukee.

SHERMAN, D. R. (1980) Post Local Buckling Behavior of Tubular Strut Type Beam–Columns; An Experimental Study, Report to Shell Oil Company, University of Wisconsin–Milwaukee.

SHERMAN, D. R. (1983) Inelastic local buckling of circular tubes, US–Japan Seminar, *Inelastic Instability of Steel Structures and Structural Elements,* ed. Y. Fujita and T. V. Galambos, Japan, pp. 122–45.

SHERMAN, D. R. and GLASS, A. D. (1974) Ultimate bending capacity of circular tubes, *Proceedings of the Offshore Technology Conference,* Paper OTC2119, pp. 901–10.

SHERMAN, D. R., ERZURUMLU, H. and MUELLER, W. H. (1979) Behavioral study of circular tubular beam–columns. *Journal of the Structural Division, ASCE*, **105** (ST6), Proc. Paper No. 14627, 1055–68.

SINGH, P. (1977) Seismic behavior of braces and braced steel frames, Dissertation, University of Michigan, Ann Arbor.

SMITH, C. S., KIRKWOOD, W. and SWAN, J. W. (1979) Buckling strength and post-collapse behavior of tubular bracing members including damage effects. *Proceedings, 2nd International Conference on Behavior of Off-Shore Structures*, Cranfield, Beds., England, BHRA Fluid Engineering.

SUGIMOTO, H. and CHEN, W. F. (1983) Inelastic Post Buckling Behavior of Tubular Members, ASCE Structures Congress, October 17–19, Houston, Texas, Preprint SC-5.

TIMOSHENKO, S. P. and GERE, J. M. (1961) *Theory of Elastic Stability*, Chapter 7, McGraw-Hill, New York.

TOMA, S. and CHEN, W. F. (1979) Analysis of fabricated tubular columns. *Journal of the Structural Division, ASCE*, **105** (ST11). Proc. Paper No. 14994, 2343–66.

TOMA, S. and CHEN, W. F. (1982*a*) Cyclic analysis of fixed-ended steel beam–columns. *Journal of the Structural Division, ASCE*, **108** (ST6), Proc. Paper 17180, 1385–99.

TOMA, S. and CHEN, W. F. (1982*b*) Inelastic analysis of pin-ended tubes. *Journal of the Structural Division, ASCE*, **108** (ST10), Proc. Paper 1742, 2279–94.

TOMA, S. and CHEN, W. F. (1983*a*) Design of vertical chords in deepwater platform. *Journal of Structural Engineering, ASCE*, **109**(11), 2733–46.

TOMA, S. and CHEN, W. F. (1983*b*) Analytical models of tubular beam–columns. IABSE Proceedings P67/83, November, *IABSE Periodica*, 4, pp. 193–212.

TOMA, S. and CHEN, W. F. (1983*c*) Cyclic inelastic analysis of tubular column sections, *Computers & Structures*, **16**(6), 707–16.

WAGNER, A. L., MUELLER, W. H. and ERZURUMLU, H. (1976) Design Interaction Curves for Tubular Steel Beam–Columns, Proceedings of the Offshore Technology Conference, Paper OTC2684, pp. 755–64.

WAGNER, A. L., MUELLER, W. H. and ERZURUMLU, H. (1977) Ultimate strength of tubular beam–columns. *Journal of the Structural Division, ASCE*, **103** (ST1), Proc. Paper 12670, 9–22.

ZAYAS, V. A., POPOV, E. P. and MAHIN, S. A. (1980) Cyclic Inelastic Buckling of Tubular Steel Braces, Earthquake Engineering Research Center, University of California, Berkeley, Report No. UCB/EERC-80116.

ZAYAS, V. A., SHING, P. S. B., MAHIN, S. A. and POPOV, E. P. (1981) Inelastic Structural Modeling of Braced Offshore Platforms for Seismic Loading, Earthquake Engineering Research Center, University of California, Berkeley, Report No. UCB/EERL-81/04.

Chapter 6

COLLISION DAMAGE AND RESIDUAL STRENGTH OF TUBULAR MEMBERS IN STEEL OFFSHORE STRUCTURES

Tore H. Søreide and Dag Kavlie

The Norwegian Institute of Technology, Trondheim, Norway

SUMMARY

This chapter deals with collision damage on tubular members. A short description is given of general impact mechanics for the case of ship/platform collision together with a discussion of the different modes of energy absorption in tubular bracing elements.

Analytical and numerical methods for estimating the amount of damage are presented. The weakening effects from ovalisation at point of impact and local wall crippling at joints are incorporated in the numerical models.

A series of tests on lateral loading of tubular members is described with special emphasis being given to the influence from membrane force and dynamic loading on the energy absorption capability. Both axially free and axially restrained members are tested, and a considerable increase in energy absorption because of membrane action is observed. Dynamic tests are also performed in order to study the influence of impact velocity on energy absorption capability.

Laboratory tests on damaged tubes in axial compression are presented together with a numerical technique for predicting residual compressive strength of tubular members. Design curves are given showing the influence on post-damage strength of D/t ratios and column slenderness for different magnitudes of damage.

The load–displacement characteristics for the dented elements are incorporated in a three-dimensional frame analysis of a mobile platform *under functional and environmental loads. A brief description is given of a simplified non-linear frame program well suited for design use. The formulation is based on plastic hinges but includes buckling as well as large nodal point displacements.*

Examples are given for progressive collapse of simple structures as well as a typical semi-submersible platform which has been subjected to various types of damages reducing strength of elements.

6.1 INTRODUCTION

Tubular members are the most common structural components in steel offshore structures. The load carrying capacity of such elements depends on geometrical configuration, ranging from long and small-diameter members in bracing to wider elements in legs, see Fig. 6.1.

The implementation of accidental loads as a design limit state in offshore rules (see DNV, 1977) has strengthened the need for rational tools for such calculations. In connection with design and operation it is of interest to know the amount of damage of the structure as well as the residual strength in damaged condition.

Related to the prediction of damage due to impact loading, a new design philosophy is developed in the sense that structural capacity is given as energy absorbing capability rather than as ultimate load. Design criteria are given as mass and impact velocity of a striking ship or the weight and drop height of objects. The aim of the calculation is first to predict the amount of damage on the structure and second to

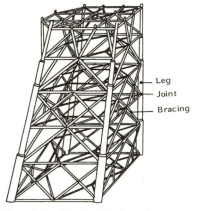

FIG. 6.1. Typical jacket structure.

consider the structure in damaged condition exposed to environmental loads. The DNV rules (1981) for mobile offshore units specify 14 MJ as impact energy for sideway collision and 11 MJ for bow or stern collision, corresponding to a supply vessel of 5000 t displacement with impact speed 2 m/s. The weights of dropped objects are related to the operational hook loads in cranes. For special purpose structures, the impact energy as given above may be modified and is subject to approval.

In order to get a representative model of a ship/platform collision, the deformation and energy absorbing characteristics of the two colliding bodies must be known. Pioneering work on the energy absorbing capability of ships has been carried out by Minorsky (1959), relating the amount of energy absorbed to the volume of damaged material. Most of the research on ships has been directed towards the protection of the reactor in nuclear powered ships (Woisin, 1976). However, recent attempts have also been made to describe the deformation process rather than the ultimate capacity (see Amdahl, 1983; Ohnishi et al., 1983).

The design of offshore platforms against collision is conservative in the sense that the striking ship is normally considered as undeformable so that the platform is designed to absorb all impact energy. For impact against a bracing element the deformation modes of the platform can conveniently be split into the following components:

(a) Local denting of the tube wall without overall bending of the member. This form of damage takes place mainly in short and/or thin-walled members. It also occurs close to the ends of tubular members and can be the result of impulsive collision loads.

(b) Overall bending without denting of the tube wall. This occurs in long members with small D/t ratios where impact loads are applied slowly and closer to mid-span.

(c) Combined overall bending of member and local wall deformation at point of impact. This is the most likely form of damage caused by lateral impact loads on members.

(d) Global deformation of platform. This response is mainly elastic, possibly with some dynamic effects involved. Normally the contribution to energy absorption from global deformation can be neglected.

The transition between the different deformation modes is difficult to define. As a local dent is created in the tube wall the neutral axis changes, a phenomenon that is associated with global beam deformation.

The extent of damage caused by accidental loads ranges from total collapse of the structure to a small amount of damage which may not have serious consequences at the time of the accident. However, such minimal damage may affect the ability of the structure to withstand extreme loads, thus having an influence on the safety. Newer general structural design codes include a progressive collapse limit state (ECCS, 1978). The philosophy behind this design limit state is to ensure that a structural system has sufficient resistance to tolerate some local damage without catastrophic consequences.

Fjeld (1979) has presented the philosophy of limit state of progressive collapse for fixed offshore structures. However, accidental loads are covered only to a small extent in present codes. The British rules (Department of Energy (UK), 1977) assume that the conventional types of structure have sufficient extra resistance to sustain accidental loads while the American Petroleum Institute code (API, 1980) contains no criteria on accidental loads but treats earthquakes as environmental load. The regulations for fixed platforms of the Norwegian Petroleum Directorate (1977) require the residual strength to be checked in damaged structures and local damage is acceptable in cases of sufficient post-damage capacity. The Norwegian Maritime Directorate has started a major research project to improve the ability to produce rational designs against accidental loads on mobile platforms (Valsgaard, 1982). This presentation describes a procedure for progressive collapse strength evaluation.

In the case of damage of a bracing element in an offshore structure, the simplest procedure for checking residual strength would be to eliminate the damaged element from the structural frame model and to perform a new linear analysis of nominal stresses. However, such an analysis is conservative in the sense that the post-damage strength of the damaged element is neglected together with the effects of stress redistribution in the structure. These factors can only be taken care of by an elasto-plastic large displacement type of analysis.

The choice of design impact situation must be made taking into consideration the probability of occurrence (see Furnes and Amdahl, 1980). The size of design vessels should be determined on the basis of the vessels intended to operate in the area, such as service vessels, tankers for offshore loading and passing ships.

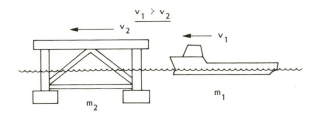

FIG. 6.2.   Collision between supply vessel and semi-submersible platform.

6.2 GENERAL IMPACT MECHANICS

Consider the situation in Fig. 6.2 where collision between a supply vessel and a mobile semi-submersible platform is illustrated. The following notation is used in subsequent derivations:

m_1 = mass of striking ship included added mass (40 per cent of vessel displacement for sideway collision and 10 per cent for bow or stern collision, see DNV, 1981)

m_2 = mass of semi-submersible platform included added mass

v_1 = velocity of striking ship immediately before collision

v_2 = velocity of semi-submersible platform immediately before collision

v_e = common velocity of ship and platform after impact

E_s = energy absorbed by ship

E_p = energy absorbed by platform

The derivation of a mathematical model of the ship/platform impact is based upon two criteria:

(a) Conservation of momentum.
(b) Conservation of energy.

The condition of momentum conservation is expressed by the following equation

$$m_1 v_1 + m_2 v_2 = (m_1 + m_2) v_e \qquad (6.1)$$

from which the common velocity after impact comes out as

$$v_e = \frac{m_1 v_1 + m_2 v_2}{m_1 + m_2} \qquad (6.2)$$

The kinetic energy before impact to some extent dissipates through plastic deformation of ship and platform. The equation for energy conservation reads

$$\tfrac{1}{2}m_1v_1^2 + \tfrac{1}{2}m_2v_2^2 = \tfrac{1}{2}(m_1+m_2)v_e^2 + E_s + E_p \qquad (6.3)$$

Combining eqns (6.2) and (6.3), the following expression for plastic energy dissipation emerges

$$E_s + E_p = \tfrac{1}{2}m_1v_1^2 \frac{\left(1-\dfrac{v_2}{v_1}\right)^2}{1+\dfrac{m_1}{m_2}} \qquad (6.4)$$

The above formula is valid for central impact. Energy absorbed by fenders is neglected together with the effect of external forces from waves and mooring system.

Corresponding expressions for ship impact against a fixed jacket type of structure are obtained by introducing $m_2 = \infty$, $v_2 = 0$

$$E_s + E_p = \tfrac{1}{2}m_1v_1^2 \qquad (6.5)$$

In most design calculations the energy absorbed by the ship, E_s, is neglected because of the lack of reliable data, leading to a conservative design of the platform structure.

6.3 DEFORMATION CHARACTERISTICS OF LATERALLY LOADED TUBES

The overall platform deformation is usually neglected when estimating energy absorption capability, and the two remaining deformation modes are local deformation of the tube wall at the point of impact and beam deformation of the bracing element. Theoretical models for these two deformation modes are described in the following, together with experiments on single tubular elements.

6.3.1 Local Deformation of the Tube Wall

The extent and form of local damage in the wall of a bracing element depends on the nature of impact. A head-on collision gives a more concentrated force than a sideway impact and results in a larger

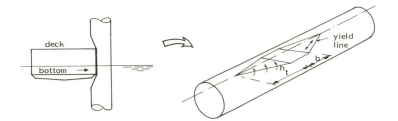

FIG. 6.3.   Plastic mechanism for sideway impact by supply vessel.

amount of local energy absorption for a given mass and velocity of the vessel. Due to this complexity it is impossible to present one single analytical model for establishing local energy absorption. Several types of model have to be considered relating to different collision situations.

For sideway impact a simple yield line model is presented by Furnes and Amdahl (1980), see also Fig. 6.3. The deformed surface is bounded by a series of yield lines and the following plastic effects are

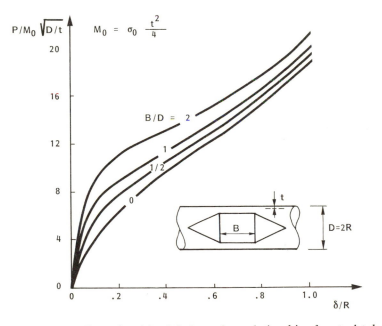

FIG. 6.4.   Non-dimensional load–indentation relationships for steel tubes.

included:

(a) Rotation of surface at yield lines.
(b) Flattening of surface between yield lines.
(c) Tension work due to elongation of generators.

The theoretical model, which is presented in a non-dimensional format in Fig. 6.4, gives fairly good agreement with experimental results for small and medium indentations. The model can form the basis for possible design curves when further verification against experiments has been performed.

6.3.2 Beam Deformation of Bracing Elements

The rigid–plastic methods of analysis (see Hodge, 1974; Jones, 1976) provide simple analytical results, often with acceptable accuracy and are appropriate for design situations. The simplest approach to the beam type of deformation is the three hinge mechanism, see Fig. 6.5.

In the case of axially restrained ends the load carrying capacity of the beam increases considerably as the beam undergoes finite deflections due to the activation of membrane tension forces. Considering the circular tubular section in Fig. 6.6 subjected to a fully plastic stress distribution under axial force N and bending moment M, the following interaction relation emerges

$$\frac{M}{M_0} - \cos\frac{\pi N}{2N_0} = 0 \tag{6.6}$$

N_0 and M_0 are the corresponding plastic capacities under pure axial

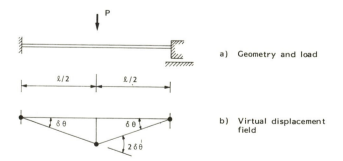

FIG. 6.5.   Collapse mechanism for bracing element.

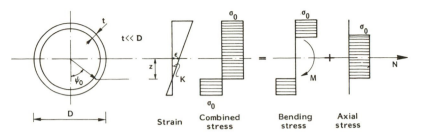

FIG. 6.6.   Strain and stress distribution over cross-section. Combined bending moment and axial force.

load and moment, respectively:

$$N_0 = \sigma_0 \pi D t \tag{6.7}$$

$$M_0 = \sigma_0 D^2 t \tag{6.8}$$

The interaction formula, eqn (6.6), is shown in Fig. 6.7.

For a central impact load P the load–deflection relation for the horizontally restrained beam in Fig. 6.5 reads (see Søreide, 1981;

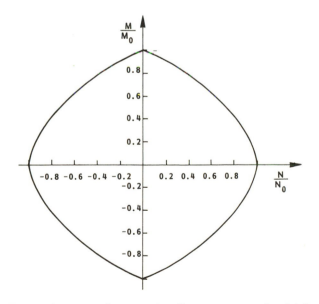

FIG. 6.7.   Interaction curve between bending moment and axial force.

Guedes-Soares and Søreide, 1982)

$$\frac{P}{P_0} = \sqrt{\left[1 - \left(\frac{w}{D}\right)^2\right]} + \frac{w}{D}\arcsin\frac{w}{D} \qquad \frac{w}{D} \leq 1 \qquad (6.9)$$

$$\frac{P}{P_0} = \frac{\pi}{2}\frac{w}{D} \qquad \frac{w}{D} > 1 \qquad (6.10)$$

where w is the central deflection at the point of impact and D is the tube diameter. P_0 is the plastic collapse load of a circular tube in pure bending:

$$P_0 = \frac{8M_0}{l} = \frac{8\sigma_0 D^2 t}{l} \qquad (6.11)$$

These expressions are based on the assumption that the ends have full axial restraint. In a real frame system like a jacket the bracing element sustains a certain degree of elastic support from adjacent elements. Such elastic restrictions can be included by extending the method of Hodge (1974) for the case of tubular members.

It is a major requirement for the validity of the present simple theory that no buckling of the tube wall takes place, so that the full plastic capacity of the cross-section is retained during deformation. Thus, restrictions must be set on maximum D/t ratios for which the rigid–plastic theory can be used. Sherman (1976) and Sherman and Glass (1976) on the basis of tests on steel tubes in bending concluded that for members with D/t of 35 or less the full plastic moment is activated and sustained during deformation. The API rules (1980) prescribe D/t less than $9000/\sigma_0$ (σ_0 is yield stress in MPa) to maintain full capacity through plastic deformation. In the range $9000/\sigma_0 < D/t < 15\,200/\sigma_0$ a limited plastic rotation capacity can be presumed.

For the clamped ideally plastic element the absorbed plastic energy at any level of deflection w is found by integration of the load–displacement expressions in eqns (6.9) and (6.10). The following energy expression emerges:

$$E = P_0 D\left(\frac{3}{4}\frac{w}{D}\sqrt{\left(1 - \frac{w^2}{D^2}\right)} + \frac{\left(1 + 2\frac{w^2}{D^2}\right)}{4}\arcsin\frac{w}{D}\right) \qquad \frac{w}{D} \leq 1 \qquad (6.12)$$

$$E = \frac{\pi}{8}P_0 D\left(1 + 2\frac{w^2}{D^2}\right) \qquad \frac{w}{D} > 1 \qquad (6.13)$$

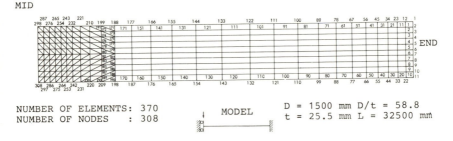

<figure>FIG. 6.8.   Finite element shell model of bracing element.</figure>

6.3.3   Computational Techniques

In order to simulate the real deformation pattern in the tubular member, a full shell analysis must be performed in which material as well as geometric nonlinearities are incorporated. Figure 6.8 shows the finite element model of a bracing element analysed by the computer program TUBBUC (Remseth *et al.*, 1978). In the central region close to the point of impact a fine mesh of triangular thin shell elements is used while the tube wall outside the local indentation area is represented by a coarser mesh of rectangular elements. The total number of elements is 370.

Strain hardening is accounted for by combining the so-called sublayer technique with the flow theory of plasticity. Geometric nonlinearity is modelled by the updated Lagrangian formulation (Remseth

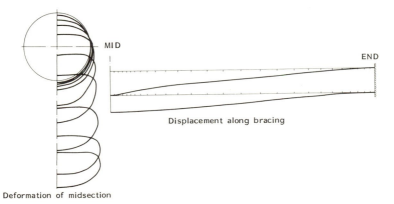

<figure>FIG. 6.9.   Deformation patterns from shell analysis.</figure>

et al., 1978) in which element strains are referred to local element axes.

The displacement pattern along the bracing element and deformation of mid-section are shown in Fig. 6.9 as calculated by TUBBUC.

It is clear that the above technique is time-consuming and costly. For design purposes a simpler numerical tool should be available. However, modification of the computational method also reduces the accuracy of the predictions. The shell analysis is very useful for studying special effects in the member performance, e.g. stress distribution close to indentation and local instability phenomena.

6.3.4 Tubular Joint

The calculation of the energy absorption capability of bracing elements requires separate studies to be performed on the deformation characteristics of tubular joints.

Most of the studies performed on tubular joints concern fatigue life or ultimate load capacity. In the study of energy absorption the total load–deformation relationship of the joint should be known so as to give realistic end restrictions when considering the single bracing element.

In the linear elastic regime of deformation the restraints from the joint on the bracing element can be calculated by a finite element shell program for different load cases such as axial tension, axial compression, in-plane bending and out-of-plane bending. However, in the non-linear range numerical shell calculations are complicated and most of the information is taken from laboratory tests.

The load–deformation behaviour of tubular joints can be represented by non-linear spring characteristics which are introduced at the element ends for horizontal movement and rotation, see Fig. 6.10.

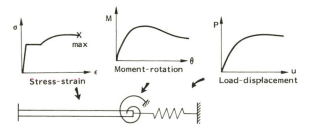

FIG. 6.10.   Stress–strain and spring characteristics.

Failure criteria can be specified as deformation limits for the springs. Typically, a joint subjected to bending may fail by buckling of the chord wall on the compression side resulting in a reduction in joint stiffness and strength. On the tension side fracture through the chord wall is the most probable mode of failure. It is clear that the combination of membrane forces and moments at the ends of the tubular elements should be checked against empirical data on tubular joint capacity. The simplest alternative is to use springs for which the load–deformation characteristics are given as input, either in the form of an ideal elasto-plastic type of relation or a general non-linear curve including unloading in the plastic regime.

Valuable information on the non-linear behaviour of unstiffened tubular joints has been presented by Yura *et al.* (1980). Capacity formulas based on experimental data are also given in design codes (see DNV, 1977; API, 1980).

6.3.5 Experimental Work on Bracing Elements

A series of tests on laterally loaded tubular members has been performed at the Norwegian Institute of Technology primarily to study two effects, namely the influence of membrane forces and dynamic loading. Both horizontally free and full axially restrained members are tested, and the increase in energy absorption caused by membrane forces is demonstrated. The effect of membrane action on the type of collapse is also investigated.

Dynamic tests corresponding to a real velocity of 1·0–2·0 m per second are performed in order to study the influence of impact velocity on the energy absorption capability.

(*a*) *Test Specimens*

Characteristic cross-sectional dimensions of bracing elements in the water plane of jackets and semi-submersibles are

$$1·0 < D < 2·0 \text{ m}$$
$$20 < D/t < 100$$
$$10 < L/D < 30$$

Geometric and material data for the models are given in Table 6.1,

TABLE 6.1
DATA FOR BRACING MODELS

Specimen	Outer diameter $D(mm)$	Wall thickness $t(mm)$	D/t	Length $L(mm)$	L/D	Yield stress $\sigma_0(MPa)$	Static or dynamic	Horizontal condition
IAI	125	2·0	61	1244	10	204	Static	Free
IAII	125	2·0	61	1245	10	211	Static	Free
IAIII	125	2·0	61	1244	10	207	Static	Fixed
IBI	125	2·5	50	1244	10	251	Static	Free
IBII	125	2·5	50	1245	10	230	Static	Fixed
IBIII	125	2·5	50	1245	10	268	Static	Free
ICI	125	3·0	41	1245	10	260	Static	Free
ICII	125	3·1	40	1240	10	328	Dynamic	Free
ICIII	125	3·0	41	1246	10	256	Static	Fixed
IDI	114	3·2	35	1240	11	318	Static	Fixed
IDII	114	3·2	35	1240	11	318	Dynamic	Fixed
IEI	88	3·0	30	1240	14	294	Static	Fixed
IEII	88	3·0	30	1240	14	294	Dynamic	Fixed
IFI	63	2·9	22	1240	20	442	Static	Fixed
IFII	63	2·9	22	1240	20	442	Dynamic	Fixed

the range of variation being

$$63 < D < 125 \text{ mm}$$
$$22 < D/t < 61$$
$$10 < L/D < 20$$
$$204 < \sigma_0 < 328 \text{ MPa}$$

where σ_0 denotes yield stress according to uniaxial tensile tests.

(b) Test Rig

The experimental set-up is shown in Fig. 6.11. The hydraulic actuator is mounted on the upper transverse beam of the rig. The test specimen is fixed to each column in the way that a steel plate is welded to the ends of the tube and this plate is then bolted to a special arrangement which allows for different boundary conditions.

A better indication of the end conditions is given in Fig. 6.12. The rollers make it possible to simulate free horizontal movement as well as full membrane restraint. In both cases the tube end is rotationally clamped, which is assumed to be close to the real situation for a bracing element.

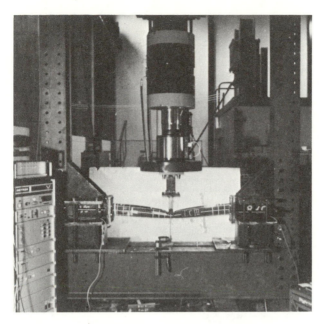

FIG. 6.11. Experimental set-up.

Displacement control of the hydraulic actuator is applied with a displacement rate of 0·15 mm/s for the static tests and 54 mm/s for dynamic testing which by scaling gives a real speed of 1·0–2·0 m/s. A rectangular indenter is used with a width (along the bracing element) equal to 50 mm.

FIG. 6.12. End of test specimen.

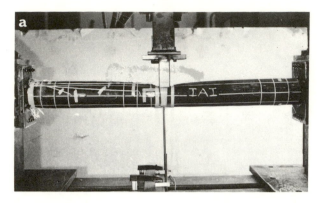

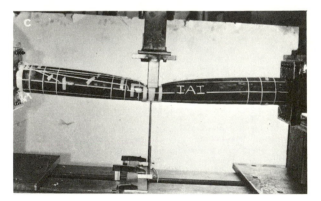

FIG. 6.13. Deformation of horizontally free specimen IAI for P/P_0 of (a) 0·50, (b) 0·69 and (c) 0·46.

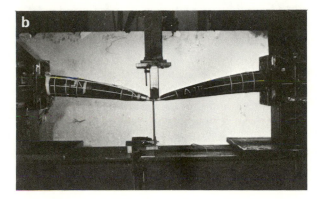

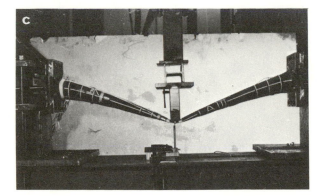

FIG. 6.14. Deformation of horizontally fixed specimen IAIII for P/P_0 of (a) 0·64, (b) 1·44 and (c) 3·50.

Strain gauges are placed close to the indenter, where local deformation is expected, and at the tube ends. Displacement transducers are mounted on each end to measure the horizontal movement and under the tube at the central section to registrate the vertical displacement of this point, which is to be compared with movement of the top point given by the actuator.

(c) Static Tests

First, attention is given to the effect of membrane forces by considering the two specimens IAI and IAIII with equal geometric and material properties. Specimen IAI has horizontally free end conditions while IAIII is clamped against axial movement. Deformed configurations at different levels of loading are shown in Figs 6.13 and 6.14 for IAI and IAIII, respectively. For specimen IAI it is seen that at maximum load carrying capacity the global deformation is small as compared to the local indentation (Fig. 6.11b). The effect of membrane forces is demonstrated by the difference in load carrying capacity. It is also seen that the stretching effect in specimen IAIII gives a much more overall ovalisation of the tube than the very local cross-sectional deformation at point of impact for specimen IAI.

Figure 6.15 shows the permanent deformation of IAI and IAIII after collapse. The axial elongation of specimen IAIII is clearly demonstrated by the difference in length between the two models. The maximum indentation for the two specimens is close to 250 mm ($2D$).

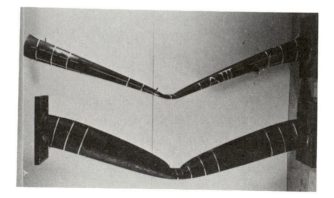

Fig. 6.15.   Permanent deformation of specimens IAI and IAIII.

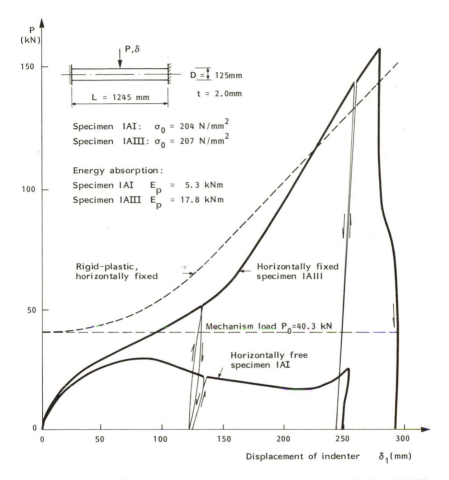

FIG. 6.16. Load–displacement curves for indenter. Specimens IAI and IAIII.

The relationships between load and displacement of indenter are given by the curves in Fig. 6.16. It is seen that the horizontally free specimen IAI reaches a maximum load of $0.73P_0$ at an indentation of about $\delta = 0.68D$ (85 mm) where P_0 is the mechanism load as given by eqn (6.11):

$$P_0 = \frac{8D^2 t\sigma_0}{L} = 40 \text{ kN} \qquad (6.14)$$

FIG. 6.17.   Local crippling of tube wall at end of horizontally free specimen
IAI.

FIG. 6.18.   Fracture at end of horizontally fixed specimen IAIII.

By further deformation of specimen IAI the lateral load reduces to $0 \cdot 40 P_0$ (16 kN). The reason for this behaviour is two-fold. First, because of the flattening of the central cross-section, the plastic section modulus is reduced. Second, local crippling of the tube wall is observed on the compression side at the ends (Fig. 6.17), an effect which also reduces the moment capacity.

In the final stage of deformation it is seen from Fig. 6.16 that the lateral load on specimen IAI rises as the first buckle at the ends closes and before the next buckle develops.

The load–displacement curve in Fig. 6.16 for specimen IAIII with membrane action is quite different. The load increases continuously and reaches an ultimate value of $4 P_0$ (157 kN) before collapse. The energy absorbed is $17 \cdot 8$ kNm for IAIII versus $5 \cdot 3$ kNm for specimen IAI. The type of collapse of model IAIII is different from the horizontally free case.

Because of the membrane action the ends of specimen IAIII are in tension all over the cross-section and no crippling occurs. Instead, the tube fails by fracture of the material close to the welds as shown in Fig. 6.18.

Although the present tests do not simulate the real behaviour of tubular joints some indications are obtained as far as type of collapse is concerned.

(*d*) *Dynamic Tests*
Consider the specimens IDI and IDII which are tested statically and dynamically, respectively with the deformation rates mentioned in 6.3.5(b). The load–displacement curves are shown in Fig. 6.19 where series 1 of curves is given for the indentation on the upper side of the specimens and series 2 is related to the displacement transducer on the opposite side of the central cross-section.

It is seen from Fig. 6.19 that the load–indentation curve (series 1) is raised by about 10 per cent because of the dynamic loading, while very little influence is obtained on the opposite side of the cross-section (series 2). This phenomenon indicates that the dynamic loading primarily effects the local deformation at point of impact with its high concentration of yield hinges, and that the increase in load carrying capacity is caused by a rise in the material stress–strain curve. However, it should be emphasised that this conclusion is representative only for the present range of impact velocity. Inertia forces may change the dynamic influence for higher velocities.

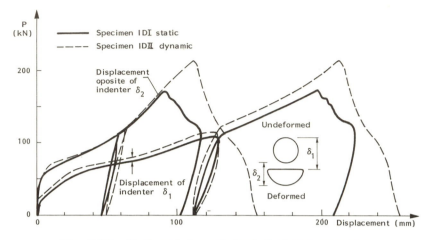

FIG. 6.19.   Static and dynamic load–displacement curves.

6.4   RESIDUAL STRENGTH OF DAMAGED ELEMENTS

The present chapter deals with axial strength of tubular members with damage in the form of local denting. The theoretical basis of a computer program for predicting the ultimate load of damaged tubes is briefly described. Comparison is made with test results and the applicability of such a program is demonstrated.

In the case of overall bending of the element without denting, a good correlation with test results has been obtained by the use of elasto-plastic beam–column analysis (see Smith *et al.*, 1979).

6.4.1   Computer Program

A tubular member that has been dented without bending has local eccentricity in the dented region as well as additional residual stresses. The influence on the buckling load of these additional local imperfections is expected to be small, since buckling is an overall phenomenon of the whole member. However, the plastic collapse load of the member may be reduced to a value much lower than the buckling load, depending on the geometry of the dent and the properties of the member.

The behaviour of the dented member stressed until its ultimate strength may be divided into three phases:

1. *Dent plastification.* When a small axial compressive load is

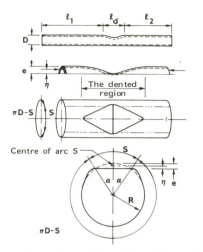

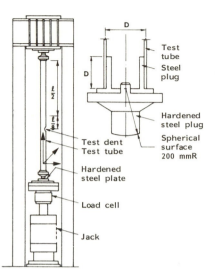

Section through the middle of the dent

FIG. 6.20. The dented tubular member.

FIG. 6.21. General arrangement of test rig and tube arrangement.

applied to a dented tubular member, axial compressive stresses develop in the tube shell. At the dent these stresses are supported by compression and bending of the dented shell. As the axial load increases plastification starts at the dent and a fully plastic hinge line is formed as shown in Fig. 6.20.

2. *Ultimate strength.* After plastification at the dent the stiffness of the dented region is reduced to a large extent. The eccentricity of the external load is magnified as plastification develops in the region close to the dent. This moment causes an overall bending of the member which also is influenced by the axial load.

3. *Post-ultimate behaviour.* After the member has reached its ultimate strength, a more complicated behaviour of the tube takes place. The incremental load–deformation relationship of the member with plastic hinge inserted is now constructed in the form of a stiffness matrix. After a plastic hinge is formed at the dent the member is divided into two beam–column elements. As deformation increases non-linear geometric effects are taken into consideration.

A computer program DENTA has been developed and a more detailed description of this program is given in Taby *et al.* (1982).

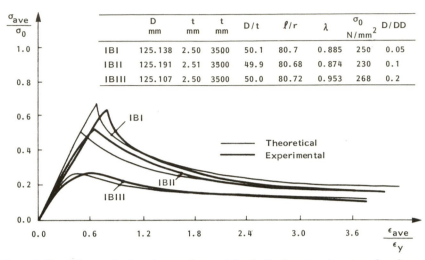

		D mm	t mm	t mm	D/t	ℓ/r	λ	σ_0 N/mm²	D/DD
	IBI	125.138	2.50	3500	50.1	80.7	0.885	250	0.05
	IBII	125.191	2.51	3500	49.9	80.68	0.874	230	0.1
	IBIII	125.107	2.50	3500	50.0	80.72	0.953	268	0.2

FIG. 6.22.   Theoretical and experimental load–displacement curves for damaged tubes.

6.4.2   Experimental and Numerical Studies

Axial compression tests were carried out on a series of 21 tubes after denting. The aim of the tests was to gain a better understanding of the behaviour of dented tubular members. The analytical models are based on this understanding and checked against the results of the tests. The tests were carried out on DIN 2391 ST 35 BK high precision tubes.

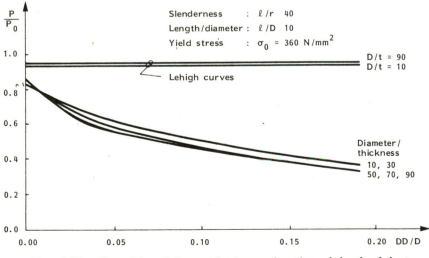

FIG. 6.23.   Capacities of damaged tubes as function of depth of dent.

Dimensions were chosen to represent, to scale, the range of tubes usually met in offshore practice. The tubes were stress relieved in order to eliminate unknown residual stresses by heating to 550°C for 1 h followed by slow cooling. The tubes were dented at 3/8 of their span in order to differentiate between buckling and plastic collapse at the dent. The experimental set-up is shown in Fig. 6.21.

Typical load–shortening curves are shown in Fig. 6.22 while ultimate loads as a function of depth of dent (DD) are given in Fig. 6.23 for different D/t ratios.

6.5 ANALYSIS OF PROGRESSIVE COLLAPSE

Mobile offshore platform structures can, in most cases, be adequately idealised by a three-dimensional frame model. The structural element may be of tubular, box or I-cross-sectional shape. A design-oriented method of progressive collapse is presented.

Ueda and Rashed (1974) have described a procedure which combines the plastic method of structural analysis with local buckling of the web for ultimate strength analysis of transverse frames in ship structures. Rashed (1980) has extended this procedure, called the Idealised Structural Unit Method (ISUM), to be used for ultimate strength analysis of tubular frame structures. The beam–column behaviour of slender members is taken care of by using an element stiffness formulation presented by Livesley (1975) where the stiffness terms are non-linear functions of axial force. Plastic hinges are introduced at locations where the element cross-section reaches its ultimate capacity. The stiffness matrix is modified to account for the plastic hinge and the load increased until the next cross-section reaches its ultimate capacity. This process continues until a complete mechanism is formed and the load cannot be increased any further.

6.5.1 Theoretical Background
The Idealised Structural Unit Method presented by Ueda and Rashed (1974) has been further developed and adapted to progressive collapse analysis of mobile offshore platforms by Aanhold and Søreide (1983). A basic feature of this approach is that the non-linear beam–column behaviour is represented with sufficient accuracy by only one element between each joint in the structure. A traditional finite element formulation would require several elements between the joints to approximate this behaviour.

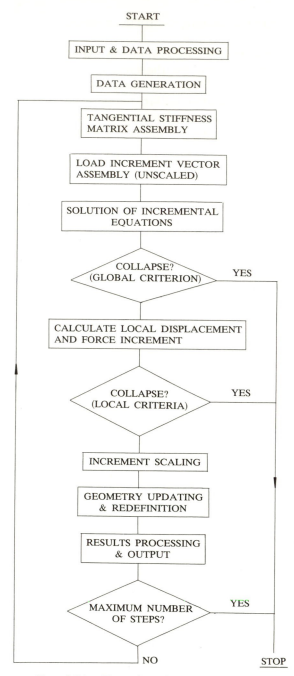

FIG. 6.24. Flow chart for analysis procedure.

The present formulation is based on energy expressions, and results in a symmetric stiffness matrix for the tangential stiffness. The structure stiffness matrix is assembled from element stiffnesses calculated in an up-dated geometry. The effect of large nodal point displacements is thus included. For a plane frame element the Livesley stiffness matrix is derived by using the following transverse displacement functions:

$$v = A_1 \cos kx + A_2 \sin kx + A_3 x + A_4 \quad \text{(compression)} \quad (6.15)$$

$$v = A_1 \cosh kx + A_2 \sinh kx + A_3 x + A_4 \quad \text{(tension)} \quad (6.16)$$

where $k^2 = |P|/(EI)$.

Incremental equations are derived from energy potentials by variations of the total energy and subsequent differentiation of the equilibrium equations (see Aanhold and Søreide, 1983). The main advantage of the derivation based on energy expressions is that it results in a symmetric matrix while the derivation by Rashed (1980) from the differential equation gives an almost identical but non-symmetric expression. A symmetric stiffness matrix saves storage as well as computer time.

The load is applied incrementally. For each load step the structure stiffness is assembled and the global displacement increment calculated. The element force increment is calculated by using the tangential stiffness matrix and the element displacement increment. At each level all elements are checked to see whether buckling or plastic capacity has been reached. If such an event is predicted the step is reduced to being the response to just reach that event. A plastic hinge is introduced in the element at the position where the capacity was reached. A modified stiffness matrix accounting for the plastic hinge is calculated and the process proceeds to the next load step. Figure 6.24 shows a flow chart for the procedure used.

The criteria for buckling will be given some further comments. Column buckling strength is defined by:

$$P_E = \pi^2 \frac{EI}{l_e^2} \qquad (6.17)$$

where $I =$ moment of inertia and $l_e =$ effective buckling length.

For I-sections and box-sections, buckling must be checked for both the y- and z-axis. The effective length l_e of the beam depends on the stiffness of adjacent elements. Some approximate expressions based on the relative stiffness of the adjacent members at each end are used by

Rashed (1980). The effective length calculated by this approach will always be less than the actual length of the element. If the rigidity in some direction is small at a nodal point this may be completely misleading. Fortunately a criterion for global buckling will, in most cases, detect failure of this type. The global buckling is detected by checking the sign of the determinant of the stiffness matrix.

Elasto-plastic buckling is accounted for by using a standard design curve for correction due to plasticity as a function of the reduced slenderness ratio (see Chen and Atsuta, 1976). For semi-submersible offshore platforms the structural members will be quite stocky which means that the corrected buckling stress is close to yield.

A cross-section that has reached the plastic capacity will remain on the plastic interaction surface and move tangentially to this surface. The present formulation does not include the possibility of elastic unloading of an element.

Figure 6.25 depicts the shape of the interaction surface for a circular

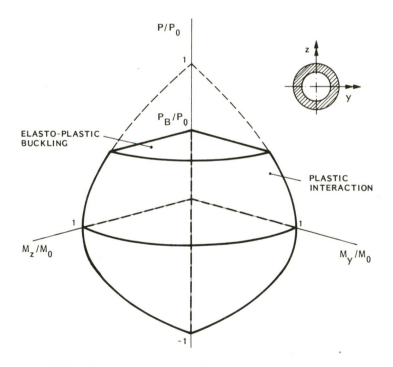

FIG. 6.25.   Plastic interaction surface for tubular cross-section.

cross-section. Note that in the compressive region a part is cut off because of the buckling criterion.

6.5.2 Numerical Examples

A computer program USFOS has been developed by Aanhold (1983) which implements the method of analysis described in the preceding paragraph. This program has been tested for a number of simple test examples as well as realistic practical design problems. One of the test examples that is of particular interest is shown in Fig. 6.26.

This frame was tested in the structural laboratory (see Zayas *et al.*, 1980) and analysed by two different non-linear computer programs based on finite element formulation. Figure 6.27 shows the comparison between USFOS and FENRIS which is a subset of Det norske Veritas SESAM-80 finite element program system (see Bergan and Arnesen, 1983). Both FENRIS and USFOS make use of the same geometry and load definition, the PREFRAME module of SESAM-80.

A second example is a semi-submersible platform with two main pontoons and six columns. The pontoons are connected by means of horizontal bracings, see Fig. 6.28. The ultimate strength of this platform has been evaluated by using USFOS. First the gravity load and corresponding buoyancy were applied in one load step. Then the wave load was incremented in steps. Two different wave load conditions were investigated; first a design wave in the transverse direction with wave trough between the pontoons (LC1). This gives a high compressive load in the horizontal transverse bracings. Secondly a diagonal wave condition giving a twisting moment in the deck structure was used (LC2).

The results are presented in Fig. 6.29. The horizontal line indicates the first plastic hinge. For the transverse load condition the platform had little extra strength beyond first yield. Analysis showed a 17·9% increase from the formation of the first plastic hinge until maximum load. For the pitch load condition the first plastic hinge formed at a load factor of 3·10 compared to 6·71 for the previous case. The ultimate load, 5·81, was, however, 88% larger than the load factor at the first plastic hinge in this case. This demonstrates that a linear analysis may give a poor indication of the ultimate strength of a redundant structure like a semi-submersible.

The next analysis carried out was to introduce various types of damage to the structure using damaged element characteristics (Aanhold and Taby, 1983). The damaged element is idealised as

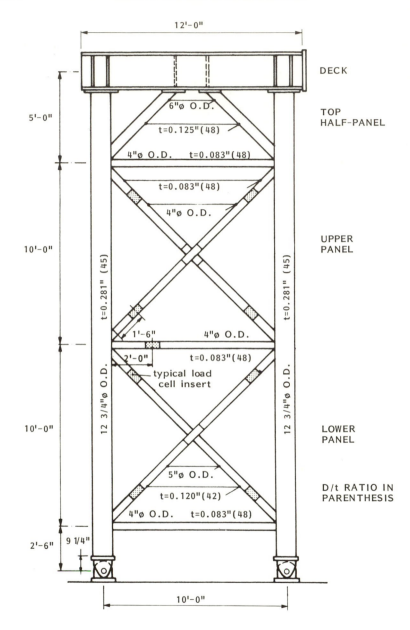

FIG. 6.26.   Plane frame tested by Zayas *et al.* (1980).

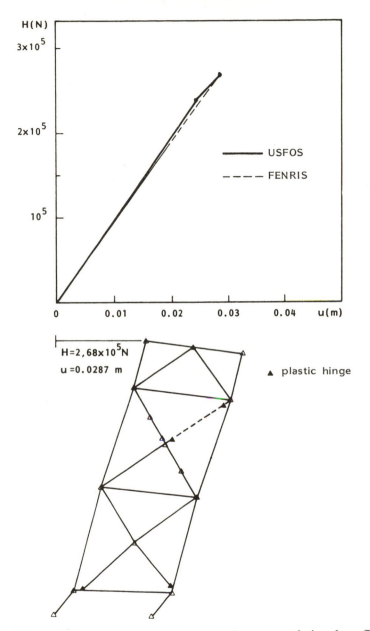

FIG. 6.27. Plastic mechanism and load–displacement relation for offshore frame.

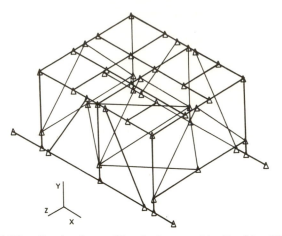

FIG. 6.28.   Semi-submersible platform as idealised by USFOS.

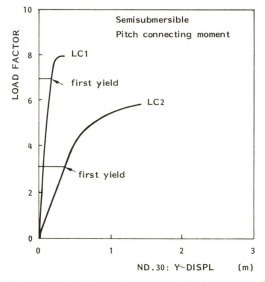

FIG. 6.29.   Load–deformation curves for intact condition.

shown in Fig. 6.30 where the dented portion is replaced by an eccentric tube of smaller diameter. The strength of the damaged element is now 50% of the original. The damage was introduced in one of the horizontal transverse bracings. As an extreme case the bracing was removed completely. The results are shown in Fig. 6.31 for the transverse load condition (LC1). The ratio between the first

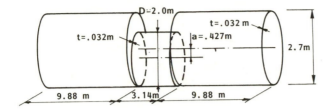

FIG. 6.30. Idealisation of damaged element.

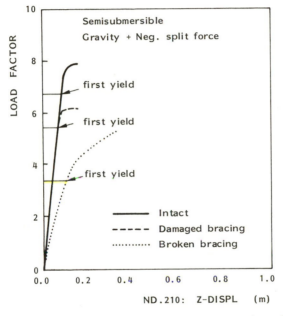

FIG. 6.31. Load–deformation curves for damaged condition.

plastic hinge and the ultimate strength is now 1·36 compared to 1·18 for the intact condition. The ultimate load was reduced from 7·91 to 6·11 for the damaged bracing. For the latter case the first yield occurred already at 3·40 giving a ratio ultimate strength of 1·55 of the load giving first yield.

The pitch load condition is not a critical load for the lower horizontal bracing, and only a slight reduction in strength was found for the damaged cases under this load condition.

The model used had 48 nodal points with 6 degrees of freedom each. A typical run with 21 load increments required 3 min CPU time on a VAX 11/780 minicomputer. This demonstrates that the analysis procedure is quite efficient and allows extensive studies without prohibitive computer costs.

Further details on the example discussed here are presented by Simons (1983). The computer programs will give an event history documenting the development of plastic hinges in the structure.

6.6 CONCLUSIONS

Theoretical methods for modelling energy absorption in tubular steel members during impact have been presented together with experimental results. It has been demonstrated how these techniques can be applied in the design against a pre-defined collision situation.

A computer program for predicting the residual strength of damaged tubes has been described and comparisons have been made with experiments. Capacities of damaged tubes as a function of depth of dent have been given as design curves.

The procedure developed for analysing progressive collapse is a useful tool at design stage. A conventional linear frame analysis gives very limited insight into the ultimate strength of marine structures. To identify what local damage may lead to a catastrophic consequence for the complete structure, a progressive collapse analysis is considered extremely useful.

ACKNOWLEDGEMENT

The work described in this chapter is partly based on theoretical and experimental studies carried out by Jørgen Amdahl and Jon Taby during their Dr.Ing. thesis studies. The authors are grateful for their contribution.

REFERENCES

AANHOLD, J. V. (1983) USFOS—A Computer Program for Ultimate Strength Analysis of Framed Offshore Structures, OTTER-report STF 88-A83004, Trondheim.

AANHOLD, J. V. and SØREIDE, T. H. (1983) Ultimate Strength Analysis of Framed Offshore Structures, OTTER-report STF 88-A83002, Trondheim.

AANHOLD, J. V. and TABY, J. (1983) Analysis of Structures with Damaged Structural Members, OTTER-report STF 88-A83003, Trondheim.

AMDAHL, J. (1983) Energy absorption in ship-platform impacts, Dr.Ing. Thesis, Division of Marine Structures, The Norwegian Institute of Technology, Trondheim.

API (1980) Planning, Designing and Constructing Fixed Offshore Platforms, API Report 2A, 11th edn, American Petroleum Institute.

BERGAN, P. G. and ARNESEN, A. (1983) FENRIS—A General Purpose Finite Element Program, 4th International Conference on Finite Element Systems, Southampton, July.

CHEN, W. F. and ATSUTA, T. (1976) *Theory of Beam Columns*, McGraw-Hill, New York.

Department of Energy (UK) (1977) *Offshore Installation Guidance on Design and Construction*, HMSO, London.

DNV (1977) Rules for the Design, Construction and Inspection of Offshore Structures, Det norske Veritas.

DNV (1981) Rules for Classification of Mobile Offshore Units, Det norske Veritas.

ECCS (1978) European Recommendations for Steel Construction, European Convention for Structural Steelwork.

FJELD, S. (1979) Offshore oil production and drilling platforms. Design against accidental loads, BOSS'79, Imperial College, London.

FURNES, O. and AMDAHL, J. (1980) *Ship Collisions with Offshore Platforms*, Intermaritec, Hamburg.

GUEDES-SOARES, C. and SØREIDE, T. H. (1982) *Large Plastic Deformation of Laterally Loaded Circular Tubes*, Division of Marine Structures, The Norwegian Institute of Technology, Trondheim, Norway.

HODGE, PH.G. (1974) Post-yield behaviour of a beam with partial end fixity. *International Journal of Mechanical Sciences*, **16**, 385–8.

JONES, N. (1976) Plastic behaviour of ship structures. *Transactions Society of Naval Architects and Marine Engineers*, **84**, 115–45.

LIVESLEY, R. K. (1975) *Matrix Methods of Structural Analysis*, Pergamon Press, Oxford.

MINORSKY, V. V. (1959) An analysis of ship collisions with reference to nuclear power plants. *Journal of Ship Research*, **3**, 1–4.

Norwegian Petroleum Directorate (1977) Regulations for the Structural Design of Fixed Structures on the Norwegian Continental Shelf.

OHNISHI, T., KAWAKAMI, H., YASUKAWA, W. and NAGASAWA, H. (1983) On the ultimate strength of bow construction (bow in collision), PRADS 83—The 2nd International Symposium on Practical Design in Shipbuilding. Tokyo/Seoul.

RASHED, S. M. H. (1980) Behaviour to Ultimate Strength of Tubular Offshore Structures by the Idealized Structural Unit Method, Division of Marine Structures, The Norwegian Institute of Technology, Report SK/R51, Trondheim.

REMSETH, S. N., HOLTHE, K., BERGAN, P. G. and HOLAND, I. (1978) Tube buckling analysis by the finite element method, *Finite Elements in Nonlinear Mechanics*, Tapir Publishing Company, Trondheim, Norway.

SHERMAN, D. R. (1976) Tests of circular steel tubes in bending. *ASCE J. Struct. Div.*, **102**(ST11), 2181–95.

SHERMAN, D. R. and GLASS, A. M. (1976) Ultimate Bending Capacity of Circular Tubes, OTC 2119, pp. 901–910.

SIMONS, J. (1983) Progressive Collapse Analysis of Semisubmersible Offshore Platforms, OTTER-report, Trondheim.

SMITH, C. S., KIRKWOOD, W. and SWAN, J. W. (1979) Buckling strength and post-collapse behaviour of tubular bracing members including damage effects, BOSS'79, Imperial College, London.

SØREIDE, T. H. (1981) Ultimate Load Analysis of Marine Structures, Tapir Publishing Company, Trondheim, Norway.

TABY, J., MOAN, T. and RASHED, S. M. H. (1982) Theoretical and experimental study of the behaviour of damaged tubular members in offshore structures. Norwegian Maritime Research, 10(2), 3–12.

UEDA, Y. and RASHED, S. M. H. (1974) An ultimate transverse strength analysis of ship structures, Journ. of the Soc. of Nav. Arch. of Japan, 136.

VALSGAARD, S. (1982) Design against accidental loads on mobile platforms, Safety Offshore Conference, Stavanger.

WOISIN, C. (1976) Die Kollisionsversuche der GKSS, Jahrbuch der Schiffbautechnischen Gesellschaft, 70.8, Hamburg.

YURA, J. A., ZETTLEMOYER, N. and EDWARDS, I. F. (1980) Ultimate Capacity Equations for Tubular Joints, OTC 3690.

ZAYAS, V. A., MAHIN, S. A. and POPOV, E. P. (1980) Cyclic Inelastic Behaviour of Steel Offshore Structures, Report EERC-80/27, Univ. of California, Berkeley.

Chapter 7

COLLAPSE BEHAVIOUR OF
SUBMARINE PIPELINES

P. E. DE WINTER, J. W. B. STARK* and J. WITTEVEEN†

*TNO Institute for Building Materials and Building Structures, Rijswijk,
The Netherlands*

SUMMARY

In deep water the loads and the deformations that a pipeline can safely
withstand are reduced by the external water pressure. The magnitude of
such reduction depends to a large extent on the pipe parameters and the
combination of loads acting upon the pipe.

In this chapter a limited survey of collapse formulae and a survey of
propagating buckling formulae is presented. Also an approximate
method for the limit state analysis of pipelines is discussed. The chapter
is concluded with a short discussion on the influence of loading sequence.

NOTATION

f Ovalisation force
f_p Yield ovalisation force $(f_p = t^2(\sigma_e/D))$
m_p Plastic bending moment of the pipe wall $(m_p = \frac{1}{4}t^2\sigma_e)$
m_r Bending moment in circumferential direction
n_a Stress resultant in the axial direction $(n_a = t\sigma_a)$
n_c Compressive stress resultant in the axial direction
n_p Yield stress resultant $(n_p = t\sigma_e)$
n_r Stress resultant in the circumferential direction $(n_r = t\sigma_r = -PR)$

'* Also, Eindhoven University of Technology, Eindhoven, The Netherlands.
† Also, Delft University of Technology, Delft, The Netherlands.

n_t Tensile stress resultant in the axial direction
t Wall thickness
u_i Displacement
x, y, z Coordinates

A Area of the cross-section of the tube
D Mean diameter of the tube
E Young's modulus
F Axial tension
F_p Yield tension (for a tube $F_p = \pi D t \sigma_e$)
I Second moment of area about the neutral axis
M Bending moment
M_p Fully plastic bending moment (for a tube $M_p = D^2 t \sigma_e$)
M_E Elastic buckling moment
N Effective axial tension
N_p Yield tension ($N_p = F_p$)
P External radial pressure
P_p Yield pressure ($P_p = 2t(\sigma_e/D)$)
P_E Elastic collapse pressure
R Radius ($R = \frac{1}{2}D$)

α Coefficient ($\alpha = 1 \cdot 17$)
β Ovalisation angle (out-of-roundness)
β_0 Initial out-of-roundness of the pipe
γ Indicates the shift of the neutral axis
ε_0 Axial strain
κ Curvature of the pipe
κ_{cr} Critical curvature of the pipe
κ_e Curvature at which yielding occurs ($\kappa_e = 2\sigma_e/ED$)
σ_a Stress in the axial direction
σ_c Compressive stress
σ_e Yield stress
σ_r Circumferential stress
σ_t Tensile stress
ψ Yield function

7.1   INTRODUCTION

One of the loading cases that occur in connection with undersea pipelines, is that due to the combined action of external pressure, bending

RADIAL PRESSURE
+
AXIAL FORCE
+
BENDING

FIG. 7.1.   Installation methods.

and tension. Such a combination is encountered during laying, trenching and also in large free spans (see Fig. 7.1). The actions may lead to severe ovalisation and finally to collapse. If the water pressure is high enough, a buckle, once initiated, may be driven along a great length of the pipeline.

A state-of-the-art on collapse and buckle propagation is presented in this chapter, together with an approximate method of analysis. The method offers the possibility for calculations in both the elastic and the plastic range. With a relatively small amount of arithmetical work limit state interaction formulae can be derived for a number of loading cases. The theory is based on the results of a MaTS project (Dutch government supported marine technological research), which is jointly carried out by TNO, Protech International and the Universities of Delft and Eindhoven.

7.2 COLLAPSE OF IDEAL PIPES

7.2.1 External Pressure Only

Buckling of circular rings and tubes under uniform external pressure has been the subject of many studies. Various solutions, which vary only in detail (E or $E/(1-\nu^2)$; t/D or $t/(D-t)$) have been presented. Bresse (1866) first published the collapse pressure formula for elastic collapse of a ring (see Timoshenko and Gere, 1961):

$$P_{\mathrm{E}} = \frac{3EI}{R^3} = 2E\left(\frac{t}{D}\right)^3 \tag{7.1}$$

Plastic collapse occurs as a result of yielding of the pipe wall in the circumferential direction. The plastic collapse pressure is

$$P_{\mathrm{p}} = \frac{t\sigma_{\mathrm{e}}}{R} = \frac{2t\sigma_{\mathrm{e}}}{D} \tag{7.2}$$

7.2.2 Combined External Pressure and Tension
The influence of tension on elastic collapse may be neglected. Flügge (1960) showed that, theoretically, the collapse pressure is not affected by axial tension. Recently, test results have been published by Kyogoku *et al.* (1981) which confirm Flügge's theory. Contrary to this the plastic collapse pressure is reduced by axial tension. The reason is that the equivalent stress, resulting from the combination of the stress in the circumferential direction and the stress in the axial direction, cannot exceed the yield stress. Holmquist and Nadai (1939) suggested the use of Von Mises yield criterion to derive an interaction formula for combined tension and pressure.

circumferential stress: $\sigma_r = -PR/t$
axial stress: $\sigma_a = F/2\pi Rt$
yield pressure: $P_p = t\sigma_e/R$
yield force: $F_p = 2\pi Rt\sigma_e$
Von Mises: $\sigma_r^2 + \sigma_a^2 - \sigma_r\sigma_a = \sigma_e^2$

Substitution in the Von Mises yield criterion gives

$$\left(\frac{P}{P_p}\right)^2 + \left(\frac{F}{F_p}\right)^2 + \left(\frac{P}{P_p}\right)\left(\frac{F}{F_p}\right) = 1 \tag{7.3}$$

7.2.3 Combined External Pressure, Tension and Bending Moment
For the elastic loading case, simple analytical solutions are not available. Numerical studies have been carried out by Fabian (1977) and Kyriakides and Shaw (1982) (see also Section 7.6). Excellent reviews of these and other results have been presented by Verner *et al.* (1983) and Juncher Jensen (1984).

For zero tension and small ovalisation the numerical results are reported to fit well with the empirical formula presented by Ikeda (1940):

$$\left(\frac{M}{M_E}\right)^2 + \frac{P}{P_E} = 1 \tag{7.4}$$

with

$$M_E = 1\cdot04ERt^2 \quad \text{and} \quad P_E = \frac{E}{4(1-\nu^2)}\left(\frac{t}{R}\right)^3$$

Several similar solutions for the elastic limit moment M_E have been published, all of which are in terms of ERt^2; they vary only as far as the multiplier constant is concerned. The multipliers suggested by

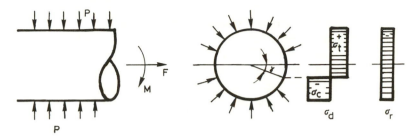

FIG. 7.2. Stress distribution for combined bending, tension and external pressure.

Brazier (1927), Reissner and Weinitschke (1963) and Kyriakides and Shaw (1982) are 1·035, 0·96 and 0·98 respectively.

For plastic collapse an upper bound interaction formula can be derived assuming the cross-section of the pipe to remain circular up to collapse. A fully plastic stress distribution is adopted, which meets the Von Mises yield criterion: $\sigma_a^2 + \sigma_r^2 - \sigma_a\sigma_r = \sigma_e^2$. Starting from the circumferential stress ($\sigma_r = -PR/t$), the axial stresses can be determined:

axial tensile stress: $\sigma_a = \sigma_t = \frac{1}{2}\sigma_r + \sigma_e\sqrt{[1 - \frac{3}{4}(\sigma_r/\sigma_e)^2]}$

axial compressive stress: $\sigma_a = \sigma_c = \frac{1}{2}\sigma_r - \sigma_e\sqrt{[1 - \frac{3}{4}(\sigma_r/\sigma_e)^2]}$

The following stress distribution is adopted (Fig. 7.2):

$$M = \int_0^{2\pi} \sigma_a R \sin\phi\, tR\, d\phi = 2R^2 t(\sigma_c - \sigma_t)\cos\gamma$$

$$F = \int_0^{2\pi} \sigma_a tR\, d\phi = Rt[(\pi + 2\gamma)\sigma_t + (\pi - 2\gamma)\sigma_c]$$

where γ indicates the shift of the neutral axis. Substitution of the axial stress components and elimination of the angle γ gives

$$\frac{M}{M_p} - \sqrt{\left(1 - \frac{3}{4}\left(\frac{P}{P_p}\right)^2\right)} \cos\left[\frac{\pi\left(\frac{P}{P_p} + 2\frac{F}{F_p}\right)}{4\sqrt{\left(1 - \frac{3}{4}\left(\frac{P}{P_p}\right)^2\right)}}\right] = 0 \qquad (7.5)$$

with $M_p = 4R^2 t\sigma_e$.

7.2.4 End-cap Effect

In the interaction formulae, presented above, the axial force F is defined as the sum of all stresses in the axial direction. For a pipe with

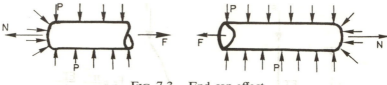

FIG. 7.3.   End-cap effect.

end caps this means that part of this force F is caused by the water pressure on the caps. The remaining external force N, the 'effective' force, will then be smaller (Fig. 7.3).

$$\frac{F}{F_p} = \frac{N}{N_p} - \frac{1}{2}\frac{P}{P_p} \tag{7.6}$$

with $F_p = N_p = 2\pi R t \sigma_e$.

Substitution of eqn (7.6) in eqn (7.5) gives the interaction formula for plastic collapse due to combined bending, tension and pressure for submarine pipelines:

$$\left(\frac{M}{M_p}\right) - \sqrt{\left(1 - \frac{3}{4}\left(\frac{P}{P_p}\right)^2\right)}\cos\left[\frac{\pi\dfrac{N}{N_p}}{2\sqrt{\left(1 - \dfrac{3}{4}\left(\dfrac{P}{P_p}\right)^2\right)}}\right] = 0 \tag{7.7}$$

7.3 THEORETICAL MODEL FOR PIPES WITH IMPERFECTIONS

7.3.1 Basic Ideas

Buckling collapse of thick-walled pipes, as being used for offshore pipelines, only occurs after large plastic deformations. Collapse in the plastic range as a result of a combination of forces, including the influence of deviations from the ideal shape, is difficult to analyse. In fact an exact analysis can only be carried out with the aid of advanced non-linear finite element computer programs. The alternative is an approximate model based on theoretical assumptions; in this chapter the latter approach is chosen.

The theoretical model to be formulated should allow the possibility of performing stability calculations in the plastic range. In addition to this, the model should be able to cover the influence of deviations from the ideal shape of the pipe. The model must be simple to understand and the amount of arithmetical work should be limited.

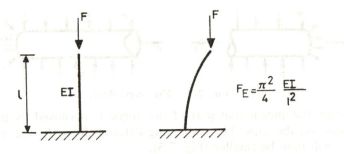

FIG. 7.4. Exact buckling load of a column.

A model which seemed to fulfil these requirements has been developed by Wilhelm (1964) for the stability analysis of portal frame structures. The method was applicable in both the elastic and the plastic range. With the same method a lower bound approximation for elastic buckling loads was developed by Vrouwenvelder and Witteveen (1975).

As an introduction to the application of this method, the calculation of the buckling load of a simple column, built in at the bottom and free at the top, will be carried out.

An exact analysis can be made by writing down the differential equation and solving it. This will result in the well-known buckling formula (Fig. 7.4). As an alternative the model in Fig. 7.5 can be used. The vertical load is placed on a pin-ended rigid element (rocker element), which is connected with the real column at the top. The buckling load simply follows from the equilibrium of the rocker element combined with the deflection (bending element) of the real column under a horizontal force f_1.

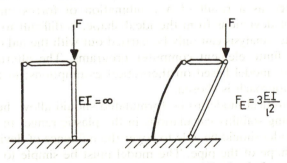

FIG. 7.5. Approximate method for the buckling load of a column.

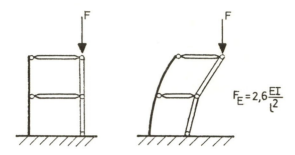

FIG. 7.6.   Improved model with two degrees of freedom.

Equilibrium of the rocker element (pin ended at both ends) requires that

$$f_1 = \frac{Fu_1}{l} \tag{7.8}$$

Deflection of the built-in column is given by

$$u_1 = \frac{f_1 l^3}{3EI} \tag{7.9}$$

Combining these equations gives

$$F = \frac{3EI}{l^2} \tag{7.10}$$

This analysis is much simpler and faster than the exact analysis, but of course, not completely accurate. The accuracy can be improved by splitting up the rocker element into several parts. By employing two parts (Fig. 7.6), the error is reduced to some 3%, however at the cost of increased calculation work.

The model also allows us to investigate the influence of an initial eccentricity (u_0) of the column. For small values of u_0 eqn (7.9) becomes

$$u_1 - u_0 = \frac{f_1 l^3}{3EI} \tag{7.11}$$

Combining this equation with eqn (7.8) gives the elastic load–deflection curve (see Fig. 7.7):

$$u_1 = \frac{u_0}{1 - F/F_0} \tag{7.12}$$

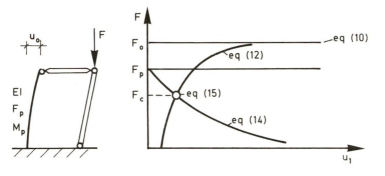

FIG. 7.7.   Model for an eccentrically loaded elastic–plastic column.

with $F_0 = 3EI/l^2$. Eccentricities cause the column to deform gradually rather than buckling, when loaded up to the critical load.

Depending on the column properties (M_p, F_p) plastic deformations may occur before the elastic buckling load is reached. For the bending element it then follows that

$$f_1 l = M_{max} \tag{7.13}$$

where $M_{max} = M_p\{1 - (F/F_p)^2\}$ for a rectangular cross-section and $M_{max} = M_p \cos(\pi/2)(F/F_p)$ for a tube. Combining eqns (7.8) and (7.13) gives the plastic load–deflection curve (see Fig. 7.7):

$$u_1 = \frac{M_{max}}{F} \tag{7.14}$$

The decreasing load–deflection curve means that the column is unstable in the plastic range. So the maximum load is attained at the

FIG. 7.8.   Formation of 'hinges' in a pipe.

intersection of the elastic and the plastic curve (see Fig. 7.7):

$$F_c = \frac{M_{max}}{M_{max} + u_0 F_0} F_0 \qquad (7.15)$$

7.3.2 Application to a Tube

From experimental simulation it was observed that almost all the deformation in the collapsed cross-section of a pipe was concentrated in four 'plastic hinges' (see Fig. 7.8). Therefore the configuration for the rocker element adopted has four rigid quarters of a circle, the adjacent rings being connected by pin joints.

From the rocker element, the ovalisation of the cross-section can be determined very simply with only one parameter, viz. the ovalisation angle β (Fig. 7.10). The bending element of the model is represented by the stiffness of the real tube, when connected only in the hinges, to the rocker element. To clarify the representation, the two rings illustrated in Fig. 7.9 show different diameters, but for analysis purposes they coincide. Primarily, the load is applied to, and supported by, the rocker element. The bending element only serves the purpose of resisting ovalisation. As far as possible it has been attempted to resort to 'manual' calculations, i.e. reduce the reliance on computer analysis. This means that derived functions must be linearised even at a very early stage, which in turn means that the model is valid only for small ovalisations. To describe the equilibrium of the model, the principle of virtual work will be used.

In the next sections, various loading cases are covered in order to demonstrate the calculation method. As an introduction, the elastic buckling load for a circular tube will be determined. Equilibrium of the

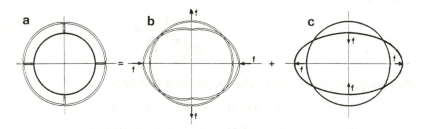

FIG. 7.9.   (a) Kinetic model with a bending element; (b) rocker element; (c) bending element.

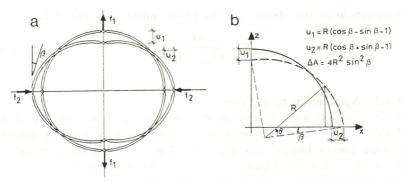

$$u_1 = R(\cos \beta - \sin \beta - 1)$$
$$u_2 = R(\cos \beta + \sin \beta - 1)$$
$$\Delta A = 4R^2 \sin^2 \beta$$

FIG. 7.10. (a) Rocker element; (b) deformation of the rocker element.

rocker element loaded as shown in Fig. 7.10 is expressed by

$$-2f_1\delta u_1 - 2f_2\delta u_2 + P\delta\Delta A = 0 \tag{7.16}$$

In eqn (7.16) δu_1 and δu_2 are the first variations of the displacement of the hinges and $\delta\Delta A$ is the variation of the area change of the cross-section. From the rocker element, it follows that for small values of β:

$$u_1 = u_2 = R\beta \rightarrow \delta u_1 = \delta u_2 = R\delta\beta \tag{7.17}$$

At this stage it is sufficient to consider first-order terms only, because the second-order terms vanish in eqn (7.16). From $u_1 = u_2$, it also follows that for the bending element, $f_1 = f_2$ must hold. The deflection follows from Timoshenko and Gere (1961):

$$u_1 = u_2 = \frac{fR^3\left(\frac{\pi}{2} - 1\right)}{4EI} \tag{7.18}$$

Elimination of u_1 and u_2 gives

$$f_1 = f_2 = f = \frac{4EI}{R^2\left(\frac{\pi}{2} - 1\right)}\beta \tag{7.19}$$

For small values of β the change of area becomes

$$\Delta A = 4R^2\beta^2 \rightarrow \delta\Delta A = 8R^2\beta\delta\beta \tag{7.20}$$

The equilibrium equation (7.16) can now be written as

$$4fR = 8PR^2\beta \tag{7.21}$$

Substitution of eqn (7.19) into eqn (7.21) gives

$$P = \frac{2EI}{\left(\frac{\pi}{2}-1\right)R^3} = 3\cdot5\,\frac{EI}{R^3} \tag{7.22}$$

The collapse load calculated with the model gives an over-estimation with respect to the exact solution ($P_E = 3EI/R^3$) of about 17%. A more accurate solution can be found by increasing the number of hinges in the rocker element.

Plastic behaviour and the effects of initial ovality on the collapse load are treated in Section 7.4.2, together with an analysis of the influence of axial tension.

7.4 COLLAPSE OF OVAL PIPES UNDER EXTERNAL PRESSURE AND AXIAL TENSION

7.4.1 External Pressure Only

For a ring and zero axial tension Timoshenko first published an expression for the critical pressure in 1933 which included initial ovality (see Timoshenko and Gere, 1961). The critical pressure was defined as the pressure which caused first yield. Later, Small (1977) and Haagsma and Schaap (1981) proposed formulae based on the formation of four plastic hinges in the cross-section.

Timoshenko's formula is given below:

$$\left(\frac{P}{P_p}\right) + \frac{P}{P_p}\left(\frac{P_E}{P_E - P}\right)6\beta_0\,\frac{R}{t} - 1 = 0 \tag{7.23}$$

Haagsma's formula is:

$$\left(\frac{P}{P_p}\right)^2 + \frac{P}{P_p}\left(\frac{P_E}{P_E - P}\right)4\beta_0\,\frac{R}{t} - 1 = 0 \tag{7.24}$$

The formula proposed by Small is more complicated. One of the reasons is the use of a different yield diagram for the interaction between bending and compression. An excellent survey of collapse due to pressure is given by Verner *et al.* (1983).

7.4.2 Combined External Pressure and Tension

In this section the theoretical model described in Section 7.3 is used to derive an interaction formula for external pressure in combination with

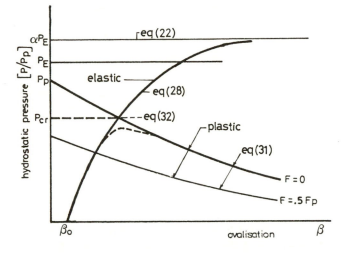

FIG. 7.11.   Pressure–ovalisation diagram.

axial tension. The effects of initial out-of-roundness will be included.
The greatest pressure that the pipe can resist, i.e. the pressure at which
collapse occurs, is attained at the intersection of the elastic and the
plastic curve (see Fig. 7.11). In reality the critical pressure will be
somewhat less, because of elastic–plastic material behaviour. For this
loading case the equilibrium equations for the rocker element are

$$F = \int n_a \, ds = 2\pi R n_a \qquad (7.25)$$

$$8PR^2\beta = 4fR \qquad (7.26)$$

For *elastic* behaviour the stiffness of the bending element, which has
an initial ovality β_0, is represented by

$$f = \frac{4EI}{R^2\left(\dfrac{\pi}{2} - 1\right)} (\beta - \beta_0) \qquad (7.27)$$

The pressure–ovalisation curve follows from the combination of eqns
(7.26) and (7.27):

$$\beta = \frac{\alpha P_E}{\alpha P_E - P} \beta_0 \qquad (7.28)$$

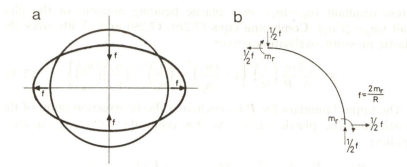

FIG. 7.12.   (a) Bending element; (b) equilibrium of the bending element.

where $\alpha = \text{constant} = 2/3((\pi/2) - 1) \simeq 1 \cdot 17$, $P_E = $ the exact elastic collapse pressure, $\alpha P_E = $ approximation by the model, and $\beta_0 = $ the initial out-of-roundness.

From the above formula it can be concluded that, in the elastic range, the ovalisation is not affected by axial force. This means that the elastic collapse pressure is also not affected by axial force. This result is in agreement with the exact solution (Flügge, 1960). Furthermore it can be concluded that the elastic collapse pressure is not affected by initial ovality.

The *plastic* pressure–ovalisation curve follows from the plastic behaviour of the bending element. Because of symmetry it is sufficient to consider the equilibrium of a quarter of the cross-section of the bending element.

$$f = \frac{2m_r}{R} \qquad (7.29)$$

The ultimate bending moment in the pipe wall in the circumferential direction is $m_r = m_p = \frac{1}{4}t^2\sigma_e$. Compressive stress in the circumferential direction and tensile stress in the axial direction reduce the ultimate bending moment. A simplified yield function which describes the interaction between bi-axial bending and extension in the pipe wall has been presented by Stark and de Winter (1983):

$$m_r = \frac{2}{3}\sqrt{3}\left\{1 - \left(\frac{n_a}{n_p}\right)^2 - \left(\frac{n_r}{n_p}\right)^2 + \left(\frac{n_a}{n_p}\right)\left(\frac{n_r}{n_p}\right)\right\}m_p \qquad (7.30)$$

where: $n_a = $ stress resultant in axial direction per unit length; $n_r = $ stress resultant in circumferential direction $(n_r = -PR)$; $n_p = $ fully plastic stress resultant $(n_p = t\sigma_e)$; m_p = plastic bending moment of the pipe wall $(m_p = \frac{1}{4}t^2\sigma_e)$. Combining eqns (7.26), (7.29) and (7.30) gives the plastic pressure–ovalisation curve:

$$\beta = \frac{\sqrt{3}}{6}\frac{\sigma_e}{P}\left(\frac{t}{R}\right)^2\left\{1 - \left(\frac{n_a}{n_p}\right)^2 - \left(\frac{n_r}{n_p}\right)^2 + \left(\frac{n_a}{n_p}\right)\left(\frac{n_r}{n_p}\right)\right\} \quad (7.31)$$

The upper boundary for P is reached at the intersection point of the elastic and the plastic curve. At this point the following equation applies:

$$\left(\frac{P}{P_p}\right)^2 + \left(\frac{P}{P_p}\right)\cdot\left\{\frac{\alpha P_E}{\alpha P_E - P}\left(\frac{D}{t}\right)\beta_0\sqrt{3} + \left(\frac{F}{F_p}\right)\right\} + \left(\frac{F}{F_p}\right)^2 - 1 = 0 \quad (7.32)$$

Because of the water pressure on the end caps, the effective tension N will be smaller. Substitution of eqn (7.6) into the above interaction formula gives

$$\frac{3}{4}\left(\frac{P}{P_p}\right)^2 + \left(\frac{P}{P_p}\right)\cdot\left(\frac{\alpha P_E}{\alpha P_E - P}\right)\left(\frac{D}{t}\right)\beta_0\sqrt{3} + \left(\frac{N}{N_p}\right)^2 - 1 = 0 \quad (7.33)$$

Equation (7.32) applies to casing, while eqn (7.33) applies to under sea pipelines.

7.5 BUCKLE PROPAGATION

If the external water pressure is small, a once initiated buckle will be limited to a local section of the pipeline. On the other hand, if the external water pressure is high enough, the buckle may be driven along a great length of the pipeline. If no structural precautions have been taken, propagation of the buckle may flatten the pipeline until shallower waters are reached.

Palmer (1975) first published a theoretical treatment of the propagating buckling phenomenon. He assumed rigid plastic material behaviour and four plastic hinges in a ring. The work dissipated in the hinges was assumed to be equal to the work done by the external pressure. Neglecting the work dissipated by deformations in the axial direction and the effect of strainhardening, a lower bound to the actual propagating pressure is found (see Table 7.1). At present, there are no publications which present a theoretical treatment including the effects of axial deformations.

TABLE 7.1
PROPAGATING BUCKLING FORMULAE

Theoretically based formulae

Palmer (1981)

$$P = 3 \cdot 14 \left(\frac{t}{D}\right)^2 \sigma_e$$

Kyriakides and Babcock (1981)

$$P = \left\{10 \cdot 7 + 0 \cdot 54 \left(\frac{E_T}{\sigma_e}\right)\right\} \left(\frac{t}{D}\right)^{2 \cdot 25} \sigma_e$$

Steel and Spence (1983)

$$P = \left\{3 \cdot 14 + 8 \cdot 29 \left(\frac{t}{D}\right)^{0 \cdot 35} \left(\frac{E_T}{\sigma_e}\right)^{0 \cdot 12}\right\} \left(\frac{t}{D}\right)^2 \sigma_e$$

Equation (7.41)

$$P = 2 \cdot 94 \left(\frac{t}{D}\right)^2 \sigma_e$$

Empirically based formulae

Mesloh *et al.* (1976)

$$P = 33 \cdot 9 \left(\frac{t}{D}\right)^{2 \cdot 5} \sigma_e$$

Kyriakides and Babcock (1981)

$$P = 14 \cdot 5 \left(\frac{t}{D}\right)^{2 \cdot 25} \sigma_e$$

Johns *et al.* (1976) and Mesloh *et al.* (1976) published an empirical formula for the propagating buckling pressure. The influence of strainhardening is discussed by Kyriakides and Babcock (1981) and by Steel and Spence (1983). Strainhardening affects the magnitude of the propagation pressure, in contrast to the onset of collapse where the magnitude of the collapse pressure is not influenced by strainhardening. The reason is that at the onset of collapse the deformations are still very small, while in the propagating buckling situation the deformations are very large.

The formula presented by Steel and Spence (1983) (see Table 7.1) covers a large number of numerical results from a computer program. The computer program is based on a theoretical model which is in essence an extension and improvement of the analysis presented by Palmer (1975).

The formula presented by Kyriakides and Babcock is based on the lowest post-buckling pressure of a ring which is also influenced by strainhardening. It is assumed that there exists a linear dependence between the lowest post-buckling pressure and the propagation pressure. An empirical expression for the propagation pressure, where strainhardening is not included, is used to determine the factor between propagation pressure and post-buckling pressure.

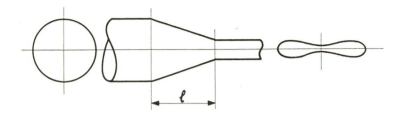

Fig. 7.13.   Assumed deformation in the propagating section.

Although the formulae by Steel and Spence and Kyriakides and Babcock appear to be quite different, the results are in good agreement for materials which display a distinct hardening effect. For pure elastic and for elastic perfectly plastic materials, however, the differences are quite severe.

There have been few published studies about the influence of initial out-of-roundness or axial force on the magnitude of the propagation pressure. Considering the propagation front to consist of a series of deformed rings an attempt is made to derive an interaction formula including the effect of initial out-of-roundness and axial force.

For calculation purposes the pipe is considered to consist of three different parts (Fig. 7.13): the undamaged part, the flattened part and the propagating part in between. Considering the propagating part to consist of a series of rings, the plastic unstable state of equilibrium will be formulated with the equations presented before (Section 7.4.2). For the propagating part with length l the equilibrium equation of the rocker element becomes

$$\int_0^l 8PR^2\beta \, \mathrm{d}x = \int_0^l 4fR \, \mathrm{d}x \tag{7.34}$$

Only cross-sectional deformation is considered. Axial bending effects in the pipe wall are neglected. This means that in the virtual work equations, the value obtained for the internal work is too low. Therefore this will give a lower bound for the propagating pressure. For convenience the deformation (β) of the rings in the propagating part is assumed to be linear between the undamaged section and the flattened section.

$$\beta(x) = \beta_1 + \frac{(\beta_2 - \beta_1)}{l} x \tag{7.35}$$

For the undamaged section (β_1) the elastic relation between external pressure and ovalisation holds (eqn (7.28)). For the flattened section (β_2) maximum ovality is assumed.

$$\beta_1 = \frac{\alpha P_E}{\alpha P_E - P} \beta_0 \qquad \beta_2 = \frac{\pi}{4} \qquad (7.36)$$

The same simplified yield function (7.30) will be used as has been done for the previous loading case. On working out the equations (eqns (7.34), (7.35) and (7.36)) the following interaction formula results:

$$\left(\frac{P}{P_p}\right)^2 + \frac{1}{2}\sqrt{3}\left(\frac{D}{t}\right)\left(\frac{P}{P_p}\right)\left[\frac{\alpha P_E}{\alpha P_E - P} \beta_0 + \frac{\pi}{4}\right] + \left(\frac{F}{F_p}\right)\left(\frac{P}{P_p}\right) + \left(\frac{F}{F_p}\right)^2 - 1 = 0$$

$$(7.37)$$

Accounting for the effect of end caps the interaction formula becomes

$$\frac{3}{4}\left(\frac{P}{P_p}\right)^2 + \frac{1}{2}\sqrt{3}\left(\frac{D}{t}\right)\left(\frac{P}{P_p}\right)\left[\frac{\alpha P_E}{\alpha P_E - P} \beta_0 + \frac{\pi}{4}\right] + \left(\frac{N}{N_p}\right)^2 - 1 = 0 \quad (7.38)$$

From the interaction formulae presented above it can be concluded that the influence of initial-out-of-roundness is small and probably may be neglected. However, there is no experimental evidence available to confirm that conclusion. In case of zero out-of-roundness the propagating pressure becomes

$$\frac{P}{P_p} = \frac{2}{3}\left\{-\frac{\pi}{8}\left(\frac{D}{t}\right)\sqrt{3} + \sqrt{\left[\frac{3\pi^2}{64}\left(\frac{D}{t}\right)^2 + 3 - 3\left(\frac{N}{N_p}\right)^2\right]}\right\} \qquad (7.39)$$

Approximation of the square root with a Taylor series simplifies this formula to

$$\frac{P}{P_p} = \frac{8\sqrt{3}}{3\pi}\left(\frac{t}{D}\right)\left\{1 - \left(\frac{N}{N_p}\right)^2\right\} \qquad (7.40)$$

For $N = 0$ the propagation pressure becomes

$$\frac{P}{P_p} = \frac{8\sqrt{3}}{3\pi}\left(\frac{t}{D}\right)$$

or

$$P = \frac{16\sqrt{3}}{3\pi}\left(\frac{t}{D}\right)^2 \sigma_e = 2.94\left(\frac{t}{D}\right)^2 \sigma_e \qquad (7.41)$$

From Table 7.1 it can be seen that this formula agrees well with the others although the low value of the constant makes this formula rather conservative.

From eqn (7.40) it can be concluded that the axial force reduces the propagating pressure. The interaction formula suggests a parabolic relation between propagation pressure and axial tension. Thus, a limited axial tensile force has only a minor effect on the propagating pressure. Larger magnitudes of axial tension, however, substantially reduce the propagating pressure.

7.6 CURVATURE AT COLLAPSE UNDER EXTERNAL PRESSURE AND BENDING

7.6.1 Pure Bending

In bending elastically as well as plastically, two failure modes have been observed:

—bifurcation buckling, where in the compressed region of the pipe wrinkles occur;

—limit load, where failure occurs because of circumferential flattening of the tube.

The bifurcation type of failure with the wrinkles in the compression side of the pipe looks very similar to failure of an axially compressed pipe. The critical elastic strain for that bending case is (Timoshenko and Gere, 1961):

$$\varepsilon_a = \frac{1}{\sqrt{[3(1-\nu^2)]}} \frac{t}{R} = 0{\cdot}6 \frac{t}{R} \qquad (7.42)$$

The critical curvature therefore has been estimated to be $\kappa_{cr} = 0{\cdot}6(t/R^2)$.

The limit load type of failure is caused by increased ovalisation of the pipe. Not only external pressure causes a tube to ovalise, but also bending. In bending, the two outer fibres are pulled, and pushed respectively towards the middle section (see Fig. 7.14). Thus, ovalisation due to bending is both dependent on the stress in the outer fibres as on the curvature. This also explains why pipe bends are more flexible than straight pipes of the same dimensions.

Brazier (1927) was the first to investigate this type of failure. Later on Reissner (1961, 1963) and others, using more refined theories,

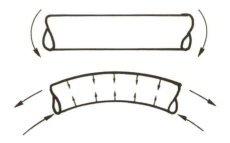

FIG. 7.14.   Bending causes ovalisation.

found similar results; these are reproduced below:

Brazier $(\nu = 0\cdot3)$ $\kappa_{cr} = 0\cdot49(t/R^2)$

Reissner $(\nu = 0)$ $\kappa_{cr} = 0\cdot48(t/R^2)$ (7.43)

Reissner and Weinitschke $(\nu = 0\cdot3)$ $\kappa_{cr} = 0\cdot50(t/R^2)$

Fabian (1977), in a very fundamental investigation, concludes that for perfectly circular tubes without axial loads, the bifurcation moment and the limit moment almost coincide. The critical curvatures, however, differ slightly as given below.

$$\text{For bifurcation: } \kappa_{cr} = 0\cdot46(t/R^2)$$
$$\text{For limit load: } \kappa_{cr} = 0\cdot50(t/R^2)$$ (7.44)

These results apply to elastic deformation only; this means that the above-mentioned formulae should not be used for pipes with $R/t \leqslant 0\cdot5(E/\sigma_e)$. For steels commonly used in pipelines (like X-60) the ratio R/t should not be less than 250. Since most offshore pipelines are relatively thick $(10 < R/t < 30)$, the ultimate curvature cannot be determined with an elastic analysis. Long before the critical curvature is reached, large plastic deformations would have taken place.

Several investigations into buckling in the plastic range have been reported. From experimental results, as plotted by Reddy (1979), it appears that the critical curvature in the plastic range can also be calculated from

$$\kappa_{cr} = c\frac{t}{R^2}$$ (7.45)

The value of c varies between $0\cdot2$ and $0\cdot4$ for the test results plotted. From the numerical studies by Fabian (1981) it appears that c is dependent on both the yield stress and the D/t ratio. The maximum value of c is reached in the elastic range where $c = 0.46$. The yield stress seems only to have a minor influence on the plastic collapse curvature. Theoretical and numerical results by Gellin (1980) and Kyriakides and Shaw (1982) confirm this. Palmer (1981) in a very illustrative and simple analysis demonstrated that, indeed, the material properties vanish.

7.6.2 Bending Under Pressure

The external water pressure decreases the ultimate curvature. Several types of interaction formulae have been mentioned, linear as well as non-linear. These are listed below:

Palmer (1981):

$$\frac{\kappa_{cr}}{\kappa^*} + \frac{P}{P_p} = 1 \tag{7.46}$$

where κ^* is the critical buckling curvature in the absence of external pressure. He points out that the data that support this formula have not been published.

Juncher Jensen (1984):

$$\left(\frac{\kappa_{cr}}{\kappa_0}\right)^{\{0.5 + 0.01(R/t)\}} + \frac{P}{P_0} = 1 \tag{7.47}$$

The critical pressure P_0 follows from Timoshenko's formula (eqn (7.23)). κ_0 is dependent on strain-hardening behaviour. For a perfectly plastic material $\kappa_0 = \kappa_e = \sigma_e/ER$, which makes this formula rather conservative for low R/t ratios. Numerical results by Fabian (1981) and Kyriakides and Shaw (1982) indicate a non-linear relationship between curvature and pressure.

In pure bending, the bifurcation type of failure will be dominant; on the other hand, pure external pressure causes a limit load type of failure. Since bending and pressure both cause flattening of the pipe, limit load type of failure may be expected over a large range of pressures.

7.6.3 Approximate Method

The cross-sectional deformation of the rocker element introduced in Section 7.3 affects a limit load type of failure. Stark and de Winter (1983) presented an interaction formula for the critical curvature under external pressure based on this approach. For the rigid plastic analysis the line of thinking is as follows:

(i)   The rocker element produces a relationship between external pressure, bending moment, curvature and the ovalisation of the tube.

(ii)   Rigid plastic analysis of the rocker element gives a yield function $\psi(M, P, f)$, which represents all loading cases (bending moment, external pressure and ovalisation force), which cause full yielding of the pipe (see Fig. 7.15).

(iii) The normality principle as conceived in plastic theory can be used to establish a relationship between curvature and ovalisation.

(iv)   The external pressure is kept constant while the curvature is increased from zero to the critical value.

Figure 7.15 represents the yield function ψ, and also shows the loading path. Making use of the normality principle the relation between the increase of curvature and the corresponding increase in ovalisation can be calculated for each point on the yield contour BC (Fig. 7.15). In point C the differential quotient $d\beta/d\kappa$ tends to ∞. This means that ovalisation greatly increases (implosion) while the curvature remains constant. Solving the differential equation which follows from the normality principle for point C gives the critical curvature.

Solving the differential equation can be substantially simplified if the yield contour (the line BC in Fig. 7.15) is straight. Then the ratio

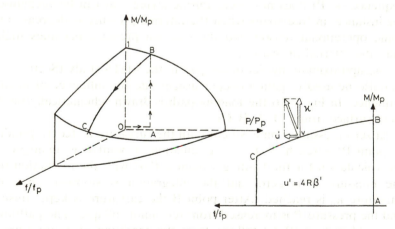

FIG. 7.15.   Section through the yield surface for load P–κ.

$d\beta/d\kappa$ is constant. For point C, where the critical curvature is attained, the following equation is found:

$$\kappa_{cr} = \frac{\frac{1}{2}t\sqrt{3}\left\{1 - \frac{3}{4}\left(\frac{P}{P_p}\right)^2\right\}^{1.5}}{R^2\left\{1 + \left(\frac{P}{P_p}\right)\left(\frac{R}{t}\right)\sqrt{3} - \frac{3}{4}\left(\frac{P}{P_p}\right)^2\right\}} \qquad (7.48)$$

The above formula relates to limit load failure only. For low external pressure it should not be expected to be very accurate, because here bifurcation buckling predominates, resulting in a lower curvature.

7.6.4 Influence of Loading Sequence

There have been few published studies about the influence of loading sequence on the collapse of pipelines. In the preceding section a specific loading sequence has been adopted, namely increasing the external pressure to a certain level and then bending, while keeping the pressure constant $(P-\kappa)$. This (idealised) sequence occurs during installation of a pipeline in deep water. One of the experiments carried out by TNO (de Winter, 1981) related to loading sequence. A substantially higher collapse curvature–pressure ratio was found, when the loading sequence was reversed $(\kappa-P)$.

Influence of loading sequence is also known to occur in other structures. Therefore, it may well be necessary to review test results and calculation methods with regard to the loading sequence used. The sequence $(\kappa-P)$ does not occur during laying, but can be recognised, for instance, in free spans when the internal pressure is decreased for some operational reason and the external pressure becomes higher than the internal pressure.

The approximate model developed in the MaTS study (Section 7.3) can also be used to gain a deeper insight into the influence of loading sequence. In Fig. 7.16 the loading path is drawn schematically on the yield surface (route O–A–B–C).

At zero pressure a pipe is bent until the curvature κ_0 (corresponding to point B) is reached. The determination of point B is analogous to the calculation for the loading sequence $P-\kappa$, with the restriction that the pressure P is zero and the integration is stopped when the curvature κ_0 is reached. After point B the curvature is kept constant and the pressure P is increased from zero until collapse. The path over the yield surface (B–C) follows from the condition of equilibrium of

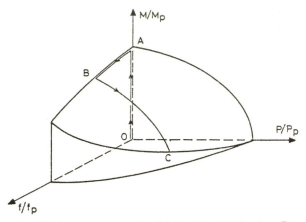

FIG. 7.16.   Path over the yield surface for load $\kappa-P$.

the rocker element and from the normality principle. The normality
principle gives, for each point of the yield surface, a linear relationship
(except on the boundary) between the increase of curvature and the
increase of ovalisation. In this case the curvature is kept constant,
meaning the curvature increment is zero; this means that the ovalisation is also maintained constant.

On the boundary of the yield surface (point C) the ultimate pressure

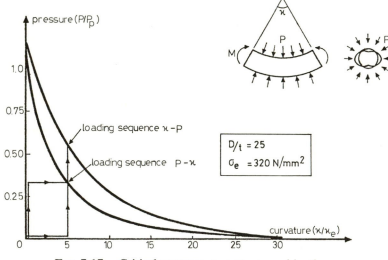

FIG. 7.17.   Critical pressure–curvature combinations.

is reached. The pressure in this point can be calculated using the deformations β and κ_0 attained in point B. In Fig. 7.17 both curves $\kappa-P$ and $P-\kappa$ are plotted together. Because of loading sequence the difference is quite large for this particular case ($D/t = 25$, $\sigma_e = 320\ \text{N/mm}^2$).

This result is important as an indicator that the model gives reasonable results and as a warning that in experimental and numerical work the real loading sequence has to be applied.

7.7 CONCLUDING REMARKS

Substantial progress has been made in recent years in the theoretical and numerical analysis of collapse of submarine pipelines. Finite element analyses and dedicated computer programs, which enable the investigation of the influence of shape deviations and the real material behaviour, have become available. We feel however that for design purposes, these results are even more useful when used in combination with simple equations and models which facilitate a good insight into the rather complex behaviour of submarine pipelines.

REFERENCES

BRAZIER, L. G. (1927) On the flexure of thin cylindrical shells and other thin sections. *Proceedings of the Royal Society, London, Series A*, **116**, 104–14.

BRESSE, M. (1866) *Cours de Mécanique Appliqueé*, 2nd edn.

FABIAN, O. (1977) Collapse of cylindrical, elastic tubes under combined bending, pressure and axial loads. *Int. J. Solids and Structures*, **13**, 1257–70.

FABIAN, O. (1981) Elastic–plastic collapse of long tubes under combined bending and pressure load. *Ocean Engineering*, **8**(3), 295–330.

FLÜGGE, W. (1960) *Stresses in Shells*, Springer-Verlag, Berlin.

GELLIN, S. (1980) The plastic buckling of long cylindrical shells under pure bending. *Int. J. Solids and Structures*, **16**, 397–407.

HAAGSMA, S. C. and SCHAAP, D. (1981) Collapse resistance of submarine lines studied. *Oil and Gas Journal*, February.

HOLMQUIST, J. L. and NADAI, A. (1939) A theoretical and experimental approach to the problem of collapse of deep-well casing. *Drilling and Production Practice*, API.

IKEDA, K. (1940) Failure of thin circular tubes under combined bending and internal or external pressure. *J. Soc. Aero. Sci, Nippon*, **7**(68), 1109–20.

JOHNS, T. G., MESLOH, R. E., WINEGARDNER, R. and SORENSON, J. E. (1976) Propagating buckle arrestors for offshore pipelines. *Proceedings of the 8th Annual Offshore Technology Conference*, Paper 2680.

JUNCHER JENSEN, J. (1984) Collapse of long, elastic–plastic pipes subjected to combined loads. *Proceedings of the 1984 European Seminar on Offshore Oil and Gas Pipeline Technology*, Birmingham.

KYOGOKU, T., TOKIMASA, K., NAKANISHI, N. and OKAZAWA, T. (1981) Experimental study on the effect of axial tension load on the collapse strength of oil well casing. *Proceedings of the 13th Annual Offshore Technology Conference*, Houston, Paper 4108.

KYRIAKIDES, S. and BABCOCK, C. D. (1981) Experimental determination of the propagation pressure of circular pipes. *Transactions of the ASME*, **103**, November.

KYRIAKIDES, S. and SHAW, P. K. (1982) Response and stability of elastoplastic circular pipes under combined bending and external pressure. *Int. J. Solids and Structures*, **18**(11), 957–73.

MESLOH, R., JOHNS, T. G. and SORENSON, J. E. (1976) The propagating buckle. *Proceedings of the 1st International Conference on the Behaviour of Off-shore Structures*, Trondheim, Norway.

PALMER, A. C. (1975) Buckle propagation in submarine pipelines. *Nature*, **254** (5495), 46–58.

PALMER, A. C. (1981) Bending buckling in submarine pipelines. *Proceedings of the 1981 European Seminar on Offshore Oil and Gas Pipeline Technology*, London.

REDDY, B. D. (1979) An experimental study of the plastic buckling of circular cylinders in pure bending. *Int. J. Solids and Structures*, **15**, 669–83.

REISSNER, E. (1961) On finite pure bending of cylindrical tubes. *Osterr. Ing. Arch.*, **15**, 165–72.

REISSNER, E. and WEINITSCHKE, H. J. (1963) Finite pure bending of circular cylindrical tubes. *Quarterly Journal of Applied Mathematics*, pp. 305–19.

SMALL, N. C. (1977) Plastic collapse of oval straight tubes under external pressure. *ASME Publication*, 77-PVP-57.

STARK, J. W. B. and DE WINTER, P. E. (1983) Plastic design of submarine pipelines. In: *Behaviour of Thin-Walled Structures* (Ed. by J. Rhodes and J. Spence), Elsevier Applied Science Publishers Ltd, London, pp. 287–311.

STEEL, W. J. M. and SPENCE, J. (1983) On propagating buckles and their arrest in sub-sea pipelines. *Proc. Instn. Mech. Engrs.* **197A**, April.

TIMOSHENKO, S. P. and GERE, J. M. (1961) *Theory of Elastic Stability*, McGraw-Hill Book Company, New York.

VERNER, E. A., LANGNER, C. G. and REIFEL, M. D. (1983) Collapse of thick wall pipe in ultra deep water. *Proceedings of the Conference on Pipelines in Adverse Environments*, Pipeline Division ASCE, San Diego, California.

VROUWENVELDER, A. and WITTEVEEN, J. (1975) Lower bound approximation for elastic buckling loads. *HERON*, **20**(4), Delft, The Netherlands.

WILHELM, P. (1964) Stability analysis of portal frame structures in the elastic and the plastic range (in Dutch). Constructies (De Vries Robbé), Gorinchem, The Netherlands.

WINTER, P. E. DE (1980) Sterkte en vervormingseigenschappen van pijpleidingen in diep water (Strength and deformation properties of pipelines in deep water), First stage of MaTS project PL-I-8, IRO, Delft.

WINTER, P. E. DE (1981) Strength and deformation properties of pipelines in deep water, Second stage of MaTS project PL-II-8, IRO, Delft.

Chapter 8

COLD-FORMED STEEL SHELLS

GEORGE ABDEL-SAYED

Department of Civil Engineering, University of Windsor, Canada

SUMMARY

The present chapter deals with the force analysis and stability of cylindrical shells made of cold-formed steel panels. It is divided into two sections: one section is concerned with barrel vaults supported along their four edges and the second is concerned with cylindrical shells simply supported along their curved edges. The theory of orthotropic cylindrical shells is applied using a formulation suitable for the special characteristics of these shells.

NOTATION

a	Length of shear panel
b	Width of shear panel
c	Corrugation pitch
f	Half depth of corrugation
k_{cr}	Constant determining the buckling load in arches
l	Half length of corrugation
m	Root of the characteristic equation
s	ϕR
t	Average thickness of corrugated sheet
u, v, w	Displacement prior to buckling in the x-, ϕ- and z-directions, respectively

247

u^*, v^*, w^* Displacement due to buckling in the x-, ϕ- and z-directions, respectively

A_s Cross-sectional area of stiffener
B_x, B_ϕ Bending rigidity in x–z- and ϕ–z-planes, respectively
$B_{x\phi}$ Torsional rigidity
D_x, D_ϕ Axial rigidity in x- and ϕ-directions, respectively
$D_{x\phi}$ Shear rigidity in the x–ϕ-plane
E Modulus of elasticity for isotropic material
L Length of the shell
M_x, M_ϕ Bending moment per unit length acting in the x–z- and ϕ–z-planes, respectively
$M_{x\phi}, M_{\phi x}$ Torsional moment per unit length acting about the ϕ- and x-axis, respectively
N_x, N_ϕ Axial force per unit length acting in x- and ϕ-directions, respectively
$N_{x\phi}$ Shear force per unit length acting in the x–ϕ-plane
p_{cr} Critical load causing buckling in shells
p_x, p_ϕ, p_z External loading per unit area of the middle surface acting in the x-, ϕ- and z-directions, respectively
Q_x, Q_ϕ Lateral shear force per unit length acting perpendicular to x- and ϕ-axis, respectively
R Radius of curvature of the shell
S Spacing between stiffeners

α Factor determining the non-linear behaviour of arches
β Factor determining the axial rigidities
$\gamma_{x\phi}$ Shear strain in the x–ϕ-plane
$\varepsilon_x, \varepsilon_\phi$ Axial strain in the x- and ϕ-directions, respectively
θ $\dfrac{1}{\pi^2}\dfrac{b^2}{Rt}\sqrt[4]{(D_x D_s t^4 / B_x B_s)}$
κ Characteristic ratio of the shear rigidity to the axial rigidities of an orthotropic shell ($= 2D_{x\phi}/\sqrt{(D_x D_\phi)}$)
λ $m\pi R/L$
μ Poisson's ratio
ρ Reduction factor of shear rigidity
σ_x, σ_ϕ Axial stress in the x- and ϕ-directions, respectively
$\tau_{x\phi}$ Shear stress in the x–ϕ-plane
ϕ_e Internal angle of arches

8.1 INTRODUCTION

This chapter is concerned with the strength and stability of barrel vaults and cylindrical shells made of cold-formed steel panels (Fig. 8.1). These shells are economical, easy to build, and have high strength-to-weight ratios.

Because of the differences in their structural performance, these shells are classified into two types which are treated separately: barrel vaults and end-supported shells.

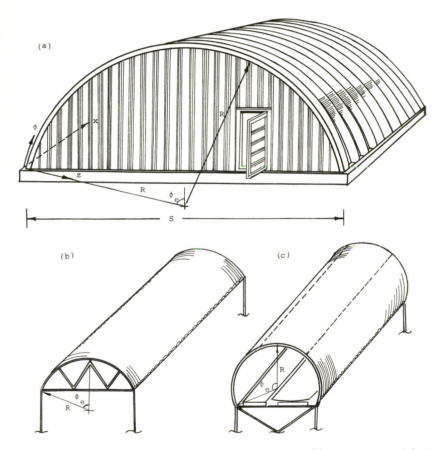

FIG. 8.1.   (a) Barrel vault; (b) end-supported roof; (c) end-supported belt conveyor.

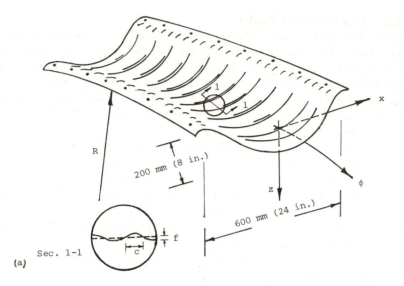

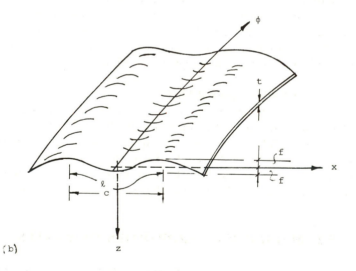

FIG. 8.2. (a) Deep U-shaped cold-formed steel panel; (b) standard corrugated panel.

8.1.1 Type I: Barrel Vaults

Herein, the single skin of sheeting is supported along the longitudinal and curved edges, Fig. 8.1a. An estimated 10 000 shells of this type are erected each year in North America with typical spans ranging from 8 m to 30 m (about 25 ft to 100 ft). The majority of these buildings are used for warehouses, grain stores and farm utility shelters. They are also increasingly being used for high human occupancy buildings such as community recreational facilities.

The barrel vaults are usually constructed from deep U-shaped cold-formed steel panels (Fig. 8.2a). The desired building curvature is obtained by developing small cross-corrugations in the lower part of the section. These cross-corrugations have a significant effect on the performance and rigidity of the panel. They improve its local buckling characteristics and reduce its bending and axial rigidity in the curved direction. Under loading, the stresses and deformations of the panel are governed by the depth of the cross-corrugation which is related to the radius of curvature of the building.

The building is made of a series of arches bolted together. End plane walls are usually built to complete the system in the form of a shell supported along its four edges. The structure may be treated as an arch or as a shell, depending on the length-to-span ratio, the longitudinal stiffness, and the loading and support conditions.

8.1.2 Type II: End-Supported Shells

Herein, single sheeting is provided with longitudinal stiffeners and is supported along the two curved ends, Fig. 8.1b. This type of structure is suitable for warehouse roofing. It can also be used for belt conveyors, Fig. 8.1c, in which the cold-formed steel panels cover the belt and act as an integral part of the load-carrying system. Standard corrugated sheets, Fig. 8.2b, are usually used for this type of shell.

8.2 MECHANICAL PROPERTIES OF PANELS

The analysis and stability problems in cylindrical structures made of cold-formed steel panels can be examined by using the finite element method, as reported by Batoz and Dhatt (1977), the finite strip method, or by applying the classical theory of orthotropic shells (Marzouk and Abdel-Sayed, 1973). In each of the above mentioned methods, the shell is represented as if being made of orthotropic material which has both membrane and bending rigidities. The determination of the appropriate elastic properties is an implicit part of the analysis in which an open profile is replaced by a planar orthotropic material.

Curvature of the sheeting in its strong direction is found to eliminate or considerably reduce the effect of distortion of the profile on the rigidity components of the panels (Davis and Young, 1978). These components, including the shear rigidities, can be readily derived using standard principles of engineering mechanics.

8.2.1 Properties of Standard Corrugated Panels

The in-plane and bending rigidities can be obtained using the following expressions for the case of standard sinusoidal (arc and tangent) profile (Abdel-Sayed, 1970; Pierce, 1976):

$$D_\phi = \frac{l}{c} tE \tag{8.1a}$$

$$D_x = \frac{Et}{(1-\mu^2)\left(6\dfrac{f^2}{t^2}+1\right)} \tag{8.1b}$$

$$D_{x\phi} = \rho\frac{Et}{2(1+\mu)}\frac{c}{l} \tag{8.1c}$$

$$B_\phi = 0{\cdot}522Ef^2t \tag{8.1d}$$

$$B_x = \frac{c}{l}\frac{Et^3}{12(1-\mu^2)} \tag{8.1e}$$

$$B_{x\phi} = \frac{l}{c}\frac{Et^3}{12(1+\mu)} \tag{8.1f}$$

in which D_x and D_ϕ = axial rigidity in the x- and ϕ-directions, respectively; $D_{x\phi}$ = shear rigidity in the x–ϕ plane; B_x and B_ϕ = bending rigidity in the x–z and ϕ–z planes, respectively; $B_{x\phi}$ = torsional rigidity; t = average thickness of the sheet; c, l and f are profile dimensions defined in Fig. 8.2b; and ρ = a reduction factor to allow for slip in the sheet connections.

8.2.2 Properties of Deep U-Shaped Panels

The U-shaped cold-formed steel panels are usually made with a width of 600 mm (24 in) and a depth of 200 mm (8 in). The depth of the cross-corrugation, $2f$, Fig. 8.2a, is related to the radius of curvature, R, of the building. It is variable over the cross-section. As an example, for the U-shape of Fig. 8.2a, f is found to be governed by the following formula (Pierce, 1976):

$$f = c\sqrt{(e/8R)} \qquad (8.2)$$

in which c = pitch of corrugation and e = the distance down from top of the overall U-shaped section at which the depth of corrugation is being calculated.

The relation between the local forces and strains in the ϕ-direction is governed by the local axial rigidity, d_ϕ, which can be calculated using eqn (8.1b). Herein, the ϕ-direction is perpendicular to the cross-corrugation.

The bending and axial rigidities of the panels are obtained by integration over the cross-section taking into consideration the reduced local rigidity, d_ϕ, of the cross-corrugated zone. Such analytically obtained results were verified experimentally by Pierce (1976).

The shear rigidity of the shell can be calculated using eqn (8.1c) after replacing c and l by the horizontal projection and actual length of cross-section, respectively.

The torsional rigidity of the open section of the panels can be approximated as follows (Hawranek and Steinhardt, 1958):

$$B_{x\phi} = 0 \cdot 4\sqrt{(B_x B_\phi)} \qquad (8.3)$$

Herein, it may be mentioned that the magnitude of $B_{x\phi}$ has little effect on the final results of the shell analysis.

Load-carrying capacity of the U-panels

Panel tests reported by Siddall *et al.* (1980) have shown that yielding in the zone of maximum corrugations takes place well before the ultimate load-carrying capacity is reached. Panel failure may be assumed when the yield point is reached in the zone of shallow corrugations or when the expected limit of plastic deformation is reached in the deepest corrugations. It was also noticed that local failure could occur by buckling of the 'web' in which the depth of cross-corrugation is very small. Because of the high residual stresses and the unpredictable nature of the local buckling, it is felt necessary to determine or confirm failure predictions by full-scale panel tests.

8.3 TYPE I: BARREL VAULTS

8.3.1 Analysis

The building with plane end walls performs as a cylindrical shell supported along its four edges. However, with the increase in the ratio of length to span of the building, its middle portion reaches a state in which it is relatively unaffected by the end walls and acts as an arch. Therefore, both the arch and shell analysis are presented here.

(a) Arch Analysis of Barrel Vaults

The pre-buckling behaviour of the arch is non-linear. The bending moment can be written as:

$$M = M_0 \delta \qquad (8.4)$$

in which M_0 = the bending moment calculated using any classical linear frame analysis or approximated by using Fig. 8.3a or Fig. 8.3b and δ = a magnifying factor accounting for the non-linear behaviour of the arches:

$$\delta = \frac{1}{1 - \dfrac{\alpha P}{P_{cr}}} \qquad (8.5)$$

in which P = the load intensity; P_{cr} = the buckling load intensity; and α = a constant dependent on the type of loading and conditions at supports. For circular arches, α is found to vary slightly with the internal angle ϕ_e and is governed by the type of loadings and by the conditions at supports. The values of α are given in Fig. 8.4a for a two-hinged arch and in Fig. 8.4b for an arch with two fixed supports.

(b) Buckling Load of Arches

The buckling load is found by Abdel-Sayed *et al.* (1981) to be governed by the following formula:

$$P_{cr} = k \frac{EI}{R^3} \qquad (8.6)$$

in which EI and R are the bending rigidity and radius of the arch, respectively, and k = a constant governed by the load distribution and by the internal angle, ϕ_e, as shown in Fig. 8.5a or Fig. 8.5b.

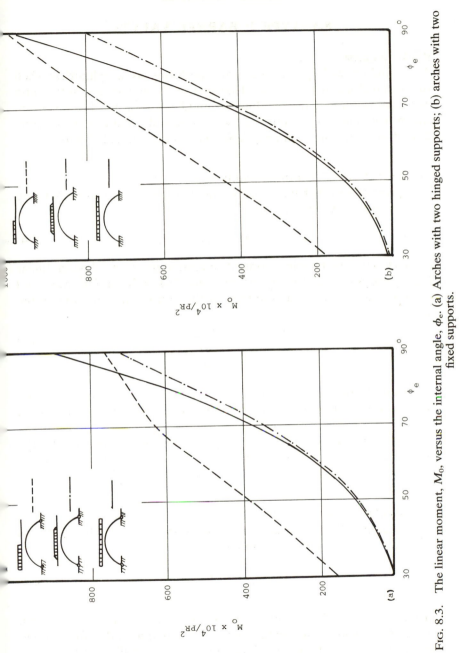

FIG. 8.3. The linear moment, M_0, versus the internal angle, ϕ_e. (a) Arches with two hinged supports; (b) arches with two fixed supports.

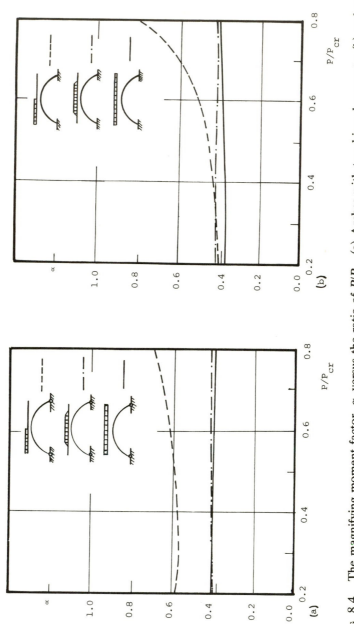

Fig. 8.4. The magnifying moment factor, α, versus the ratio of P/P_{cr}. (a) Arches with two hinged supports; (b) arches with two fixed supports.

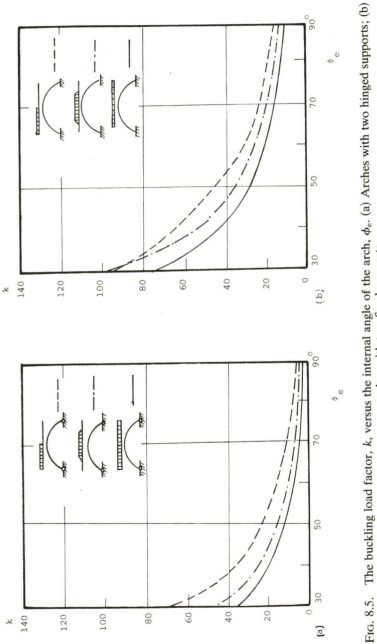

Fig. 8.5. The buckling load factor, k, versus the internal angle of the arch, ϕ_e. (a) Arches with two hinged supports; (b) arches with two fixed supports.

(c) Shell Analysis of Barrel Vaults

The shell is analysed using the theory of orthotropic cylindrical shells. The differential equations governing the behaviour of the barrel vault are formulated taking into consideration the special character of the panels, in which the rigidities in the curved direction are considerably higher than those in the longitudinal direction. The three governing simultaneous equations are given in the displacement components u, v and w in the x-, ϕ- and z-directions, respectively (El-Atrouzy and Abdel-Sayed, 1978):

$$D_x R \frac{\partial^2 u}{\partial x^2} + D_{x\phi}\left(\frac{1}{R}\frac{\partial^2 u}{\partial \phi^2} + \frac{\partial^2 v}{\partial x\, \partial\phi}\right) + p_x R = 0 \qquad (8.7a)$$

$$D_\phi\left(\frac{\partial^2 v}{\partial \phi^2} - \frac{\partial w}{\partial \phi}\right) + D_{x\phi}\left(R\frac{\partial^2 u}{\partial x\, \partial\phi} + R^2 \frac{\partial^2 v}{\partial x^2}\right)$$

$$+ \frac{3B_{x\phi}}{2}\left(\frac{\partial^2 v}{\partial x^2} + \frac{\partial^3 w}{\partial x^2\, \partial\phi}\right) + R^2 p_\phi = 0 \quad (8.7b)$$

$$\frac{B_\phi}{R^2}\left(-\frac{\partial^4 w}{\partial \phi^4} - \frac{2\partial^2 w}{\partial \phi^2} - w\right) + D_\phi\left(\frac{\partial v}{\partial \phi} - w\right)$$

$$- 2B_{x\phi}\frac{\partial^4 w}{\partial x^2\, \partial\phi^2} - B_x R^2 \frac{\partial^4 w}{\partial x^4} + R^2 p_z = 0 \quad (8.7c)$$

in which p_x, p_ϕ and p_z are the external loading per unit area of middle surface acting in the x, ϕ and z directions, respectively.

The solution of the above governing differential equations can be obtained as a sum of particular and homogeneous solutions. Herein, a particular solution is first assumed with constants which can be calculated by satisfying the three differential equations. The boundary conditions along the longitudinal edges are then satisfied by adding a solution for the homogeneous system of equations (eqns (8.7) with $p_x = p_\phi = p_z = 0$).

(i) Particular solution. While the classical analysis of cylindrical shells may replace the particular solution by a membrane solution (Marzouk and Abdel-Sayed, 1973; Davis and Young, 1978), the accuracy of the final results is improved when a particular solution is selected to satisfy the governing equations (El-Atrouzy and Abdel-Sayed, 1978). Examples of particular solutions are given in Table 8.1 for two cases of loading, namely, gravity load uniform over the horizontal projection (snow load) and radial sine load.

TABLE 8.1

PARTICULAR SOLUTIONS FOR TWO TYPES OF LOADING EXPRESSED IN FOURIER SERIES (ONLY THE FIRST TERM IS CONSIDERED)

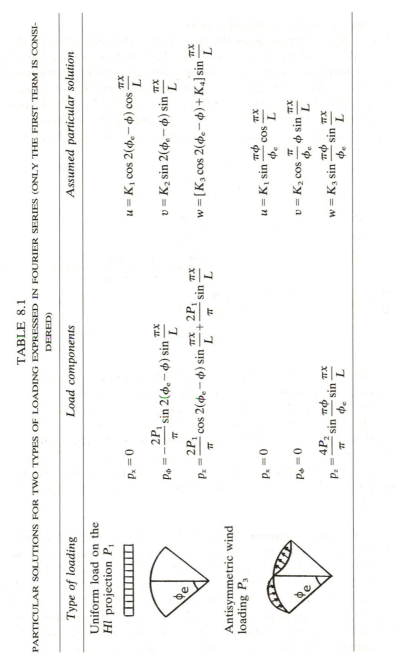

Type of loading	Load components	Assumed particular solution
Uniform load on the Hl projection P_1	$p_x = 0$	$u = K_1 \cos 2(\phi_e - \phi) \cos \dfrac{\pi x}{L}$
	$p_\phi = -\dfrac{2P_1}{\pi} \sin 2(\phi_e - \phi) \sin \dfrac{\pi x}{L}$	$v = K_2 \sin 2(\phi_e - \phi) \sin \dfrac{\pi x}{L}$
	$p_z = \dfrac{2P_1}{\pi} \cos 2(\phi_e - \phi) \sin \dfrac{\pi x}{L} + \dfrac{2P_1}{\pi} \sin \dfrac{\pi x}{L}$	$w = [K_3 \cos 2(\phi_e - \phi) + K_4] \sin \dfrac{\pi x}{L}$
Antisymmetric wind loading P_3	$p_x = 0$	$u = K_1 \sin \dfrac{\pi \phi}{\phi_e} \cos \dfrac{\pi x}{L}$
	$p_\phi = 0$	$v = K_2 \cos \dfrac{\pi}{\phi_e} \phi \sin \dfrac{\pi x}{L}$
	$p_z = \dfrac{4P_2}{\pi} \sin \dfrac{\pi \phi}{\phi_e} \sin \dfrac{\pi x}{L}$	$w = K_3 \sin \dfrac{\pi \phi}{\phi_e} \sin \dfrac{\pi x}{L}$

A general case of wind loading can be obtained from the summation of a number of sine waves (Table 8.1, Load 2):

$$p_z = \sum_m \sum_n \frac{16 p_{mn}}{\pi^2} \sin \frac{n\pi}{2\phi_e} \phi \sin \frac{m\pi}{L} x \qquad (8.8)$$

while $p_x = p_\phi = 0$.

An arbitrary gravity load:

$$p_g = \sum_m \sum_n \frac{16 q_{mn}}{\pi^2} \sin \frac{n\pi}{2\phi_e} \phi \sin \frac{m\pi}{L} x \qquad (8.9)$$

can be analysed into:

$$p_x = 0 \qquad (8.10a)$$

$$p_\phi = \sum_m \sum_n \frac{-8}{\pi^2} q_{mn} \sin \frac{n\pi}{2\phi_e} \phi \sin (\phi_e - \phi) \sin \frac{m\pi}{L} x \qquad (8.10b)$$

and

$$p_z = \sum_m \sum_n \frac{8}{\pi^2} q_{mn} \sin \frac{n\pi}{2\phi_e} \phi \sin (\phi_e - \phi) \sin \frac{m\pi}{L} x \qquad (8.10c)$$

This can also be written as

$$p_x = 0 \qquad (8.11a)$$

$$p_\phi = \sum_m \sum_n \frac{4 q_{mn}}{\pi^2} \{ \cos 2\phi_e (\cos b\phi - \underline{\cos a\phi})$$

$$- \sin 2\phi_e (\sin b\phi + \sin a\phi) \} \sin \frac{m\pi}{L} x \qquad (8.11b)$$

and

$$p_z = \sum_m \sum_n \frac{4 q_{mn}}{\pi^2} \left\{ \sin 2\phi_e (\cos b\phi - \cos a\phi) + \cos 2\phi_e (\sin b\phi + \underline{\sin a\phi}) \right.$$

$$\left. + \sin \frac{n\pi}{2\phi_e} \phi \right\} \sin \frac{m\pi}{L} x \qquad (8.11c)$$

in which $a = 2[n\pi/(4\phi_e) + 1]$ and $b = 2[n\pi/(4\phi_e) - 1]$.

A particular solution can be selected for each of the components of eqns (8.11b, c) such as the following for the underlined components:

$$u = k_{1mn} \sin a\phi \cos \frac{m\pi}{L} x \qquad (8.12a)$$

$$v = k_{2mn} \cos a\phi \sin \frac{m\pi}{L} x \qquad (8.12b)$$

$$w = k_{3mn} \sin a\phi \sin \frac{m\pi}{L} x \qquad (8.12c)$$

in which k_{1mn}, k_{2mn} and k_{3mn} are constants obtained by satisfying the governing equations.

(*ii*) *Homogeneous solution.* Considering the barrel vault to be simply supported along its curved edges, the homogeneous (bending) solution can be taken as:

$$w = C_1 e^{m\phi} \sin \frac{\lambda x}{R} \qquad (8.13a)$$

$$v = C_2 e^{m\phi} \sin \frac{\lambda x}{R} \qquad (8.13b)$$

$$u = C_3 e^{m\phi} \cos \frac{\lambda x}{R} \qquad (8.13c)$$

in which C_1, C_2 and $C_3 =$ constants and $\lambda = m\pi R/L$. By substituting eqns (8.13) in eqn (8.7), a non-trivial solution is governed by the following characteristic equation:

$$m^8 + a_6 m^6 + a_4 m^4 + a_2 m^2 + a_0 = 0 \qquad (8.14)$$

in which a_6, a_4, a_2 and $a_0 =$ constants.

The roots of eqn (8.14) can be written as follows:

$$m_1 = \pm\alpha_1 \pm i\beta_1 \text{ and } m_2 = \pm\alpha_2 \pm i\beta_2 \qquad (8.15)$$

which lead to a displacement function in the form:

$$w = \{e^{\alpha_1\phi}(A \cos \beta_1\phi + B \sin \beta_1\phi) + e^{-\alpha_1\phi}(C \cos \beta_1\phi + D \sin \beta_1\phi)$$

$$+ e^{\alpha_2\phi}(E \cos \beta_2\phi + F \sin \beta_2\phi)$$

$$+ e^{-\alpha_2\phi}(G \cos \beta_2\phi + H \sin \beta_2\phi)\} \sin \frac{\lambda x}{R} \qquad (8.16)$$

in which $A, B, C, \ldots, H$ are integration constants calculated by satisfying the boundary conditions along the longitudinal edges.

The roots m_1 and m_2 obtained using the proposed formulation, eqns (8.7), show negligible differences from those obtained using the most accurate formulation by Flügge (1932). On the other hand, a simplification of the governing equations using Donnell's approximation leads to considerable deviation in the roots when compared with Flügge's formulation (Marzouk and Abdel-Sayed, 1973). This is attributed to the very high rigidity of the panels in the curved direction in comparison with that in the longitudinal direction.

Also, the condition of equilibrium in the ϕ-direction is as follows:

$$\frac{1}{R}\frac{\partial N_\phi}{\partial \phi}+\frac{\partial N_{x\phi}}{\partial x}-\frac{Q_\phi}{R}+p_\phi=0 \qquad (8.17)$$

Donnell's assumption neglects the effect of the shear force Q_ϕ on the equilibrium in the ϕ-direction (i.e. $Q_\phi/R=0$), which is usually negligible if the shell is supported on the curved ends only. However, for long shells supported along the four edges, the effect of the arch action is dominant, especially when the bending and axial rigidities in the ϕ-direction (B_ϕ and D_ϕ) are more than those in the x-direction (B_x and D_x). In such cases, the term Q_ϕ/R should be taken into consideration in both the particular and homogeneous solutions as expressed in eqn (8.7).

The application of the theory of orthotropic shells using eqns (8.7a, b, c) was proved to be adequate when testing the behaviour of model shells made of corrugated steel sheets (El-Atrouzy and Abdel-Sayed, 1978), as well as by testing full-scale barrel vaults (Siddall *et al.*, 1980).

Effect of longitudinal stiffeners
Numerical analysis shows that unless the shell is very short ($L/S \leqslant 1\cdot5$) the shell action can hardly be observed in the case of barrel vaults with no longitudinal stiffeners. This is because of the very low axial rigidity, D_x, in the longitudinal direction. This rigidity can be increased by providing longitudinal stiffeners and assuming their effect to be uniform over the arc length. The axial rigidity is calculated as:

$$D_x = \frac{A_s E}{s}\beta \qquad (8.18)$$

in which A_s = cross-sectional area of stiffener; E = modulus of elasticity; s = spacing between stiffeners; and β = a reduction factor to account for the non-uniform distribution of the forces in the longitudinal direction. An assumed value of $\beta = 0.4$ was found to lead to analytical results of reasonable agreement with those obtained experimentally from full-scale tests with the length of shell equal to its span, Siddall *et al.* (1980). For longer shells, similar comparisons show a trend in which β should be increased with the increase in the ratio of length to span.

(*iii*) *Observation on the analysis of barrel vaults.* The following has been observed through the analysis and design of a large number of practical barrel vaults:

1. The design of barrel shells is governed by the magnitude of the moment, M_ϕ, in the arch direction as well as the axial forces N_ϕ and N_x in the curved and longitudinal directions, respectively.
2. The shell effects are much more predominant relative to unbalanced loading than to balanced loading. This is important since unbalanced load often governs the arch capacity.
3. Shell action causes relatively large shear forces in the end walls which must be designed to act as shear walls. The connections between the arches and the end walls must also be capable of transferring these shear forces. The resultant forces on the foundation are quite different from those of the arches and special consideration must be given to uplift forces which develop at the corners.
4. Care must be taken in the application of longitudinal stiffeners since their stiffness may attract greater forces than they are capable of bearing. Fairly wide spaced, heavy stiffeners seem the practical compromise.
5. An important practical concern in the analysis is to establish the base condition which may vary from fixed (arch base embedded in the foundation) to essentially hinged (arch base fastened to a typically flexible metal base plate).
6. Another practical concern relates to the presence of translucent panels within some of the arches. These not only reduce the section resistance in the area, but may cause instability of the panel surfaces immediately adjacent to the translucent panels.

8.3.2 Stability of Barrel Vaults

(*a*) *Governing Equations*

The stability of the shell is governed by the simultaneous equations in the displacement components u^*, v^* and w^* which can take place at the instant of buckling without increase in loading. These equations are found by Marzouk and Abdel-Sayed (1975) to be as follows:

$$D_x R \frac{\partial^2 u^*}{\partial x^2} + D_{x\phi}\left(\frac{1}{R}\frac{\partial^2 u^*}{\partial \phi^2} + \frac{\partial^2 v^*}{\partial x \partial \phi}\right) = 0 \tag{8.19a}$$

$$D_\phi\left(\frac{\partial^2 v^*}{\partial \phi^2} - \frac{\partial w^*}{\partial \phi}\right) + D_{x\phi}\left(R\frac{\partial^2 u^*}{\partial x \partial \phi} + R^2 \frac{\partial^2 v^*}{\partial x^2}\right) = 0 \tag{8.19b}$$

$$\frac{B_\phi}{R^2}\left(\frac{\partial^4 w^*}{\partial \phi^4} + 2\frac{\partial^2 w^*}{\partial \phi^2} + w^*\right) + 2B_{x\phi}\frac{\partial^4 w^*}{\partial x^2 \partial \phi^2} + R^2 B_x \frac{\partial^4 w^*}{\partial x^4}$$
$$- D_\phi\left(\frac{\partial v^*}{\partial \phi} - w^*\right) - R^2 N_x \frac{\partial^2 w^*}{\partial x^2} - 2RN_{x\phi}\frac{\partial^2 w^*}{\partial x \partial \phi} - N_\phi \frac{\partial^2 w^*}{\partial \phi^2} = 0 \tag{8.19c}$$

in which N_x, $N_{x\phi}$ and N_ϕ are the membrane force components in the shell at the instant of buckling. Equations (8.19a) and (8.19b) are satisfied by introducing a stress function, F, which has the following relations with the displacement components:

$$\frac{\partial^2 F}{\partial \phi^2} = D_x \frac{\partial u^*}{\partial x} R^2 \tag{8.20a}$$

$$\frac{\partial^2 F}{\partial x^2} = \frac{D_\phi}{R}\left(\frac{\partial v^*}{\partial \phi} - w^*\right) \tag{8.20b}$$

$$\frac{\partial^2 F}{\partial x \partial \phi} = -D_{x\phi}\left(\frac{\partial v^*}{\partial x} R + \frac{\partial u^*}{\partial \phi}\right) \tag{8.20c}$$

The displacements u^* and v^* are eliminated, leading to the following two simultaneous governing equations.

$$D_x \frac{\partial^4 F}{\partial x^4} + \frac{1}{R^2}\frac{D_x D_\phi}{D_{x\phi}}\frac{\partial^4 F}{\partial x^2 \partial \phi^2} + \frac{D_\phi}{R^4}\frac{\partial^4 F}{\partial \phi^4} + \frac{D_x D_\phi}{R}\frac{\partial^2 w^*}{\partial x^2} = 0 \tag{8.21a}$$

and

$$B_x \frac{\partial^4 w^*}{\partial x^4} + \frac{2}{R^2} B_{x\phi}\frac{\partial^4 w^*}{\partial x^2 \partial \phi^2} + \frac{B_\phi}{R^4}\left(\frac{\partial^4 w^*}{\partial \phi^4} + 2\frac{\partial^2 w^*}{\partial \phi^2} + w^*\right) - \frac{1}{R}\frac{\partial^2 F}{\partial x^2}$$
$$- N_x \frac{\partial^2 w^*}{\partial x^2} - \frac{2}{R} N_{x\phi}\frac{\partial^2 w^*}{\partial x \partial \phi} - \frac{N_\phi}{R^2}\frac{\partial^2 w^*}{\partial \phi^2} = 0 \tag{8.21b}$$

The buckling limit is reached if eqns (8.21a) and (8.21b) have a non-trivial solution.

(b) Boundary Conditions

The boundary conditions imposed on the middle surface of a buckled simply supported shell are as follows:

Deflection and bending boundary conditions. The four edges of the shell undergo no deflection and can be considered free from moment lateral to the shells, i.e.:

$$\text{at } x = 0 \text{ and } x = L \qquad w^* = \frac{\partial^2 w^*}{\partial x^2} = 0 \qquad (8.22a)$$

$$\text{at } \phi = 0 \text{ and } \phi = 2\phi_e \qquad w^* = \frac{\partial^2 w^*}{\partial \phi^2} = 0 \qquad (8.22b)$$

Boundary conditions in the plane of the shell. The circular edges (at $x = 0$ and $x = L$) are supported by the end walls or by edge members which are stiff in their own planes but can be displaced in the directions perpendicular to their own planes. Therefore, the boundary conditions are zero strain along each of the edges and free displacement lateral to them, i.e.:

$$\text{at } x = 0 \text{ and } x = L \qquad \varepsilon_\phi = N_x = 0 \qquad (8.23a)$$

The longitudinal edges are supported by members connected to the foundation of the shell. Therefore, no displacement can take place along these edges, i.e.:

$$u^* = v^* = 0 \qquad (8.23b)$$

The conditions, eqns (8.23a) and (8.23b), can be expressed in terms of the stress functions, F, as:

$$\text{at } x = 0 \text{ and } x = L \qquad \frac{\partial^2 F}{\partial x^2} = \frac{\partial^2 F}{\partial \phi^2} = 0 \qquad (8.23c)$$

$$\text{at } \phi = 0 \text{ and } \phi = 2\phi_e \qquad \frac{\partial^2 F}{\partial \phi^2} = D_x \frac{\partial^3 F}{\partial x^2 \partial \phi} + \frac{D_{x\phi}}{R^2} \frac{\partial^3 F}{\partial \phi^3} = 0 \qquad (8.23d)$$

(c) Deflection and Stress Function

The following series expressions are used to present the displacement component, w^*, and the stress function, F:

$$w^* = \sin \frac{m\pi}{L} x \sum_{n=1,2,\ldots}^{\infty} A_{mn} \sin \frac{n\pi}{2\phi_e} \phi \qquad (8.24a)$$

$$F = F_p + F_h$$

$$F_p = \sin \frac{m\pi}{L} x \sum_{n=1,2,\ldots}^{\infty} F_{mn} \sin \frac{n\pi}{2\phi_e} \phi \qquad (8.24b)$$

$$F_h = \sin \frac{m\pi}{L} x H_{mn}(\phi) \qquad (8.24c)$$

in which $m = 1, 2, 3, \ldots$; A_{mn} and F_{mn} = coefficients of x and ϕ; $H_{mn}(\phi)$ is a function of ϕ only; F_h is a solution for the homogeneous equation:

$$D_x \frac{\partial^4 F}{\partial x^4} + \frac{1}{R^2} \frac{D_x D_\phi}{D_{x\phi}} \frac{\partial^4 F}{\partial x^2 \partial \phi^2} + \frac{D_\phi}{R^4} \frac{\partial^4 F}{\partial \phi^4} = 0 \qquad (8.25)$$

Equation (8.24a) satisfies the deflection and bending conditions along the four edges and assumes the deflection to be in the form of a sine wave in the x-direction. Equations (8.24b) and (8.24c) satisfy the boundary conditions in the plane of the shell along the edges $x = 0$ and $x = L$. The boundary conditions are also satisfied along $\phi = 0$ and $\phi = 2\phi_e$ through the calculation of $H_{mn}(\phi)$.

Substituting eqns (8.24a) and (8.24b) into the differential equation, eqn (8.21a), leads to a direct relation between the stress coefficients F_{mn} and the corresponding deflection coefficients A_{mn}:

$$F_{mn} = \frac{1}{T_n} \frac{D_x D_\phi}{R} \left(\frac{m\pi}{L}\right)^2 A_{mn} \qquad (8.26)$$

in which

$$T_n = \frac{1}{R^4} \left(\frac{n\pi}{2\phi_e}\right)^4 D_\phi + \frac{1}{R^2} \frac{D_x D_\phi}{D_{x\phi}} \left(\frac{n\pi}{2\phi_e}\right)^2 \left(\frac{m\pi}{L}\right)^2 + D_x \left(\frac{m\pi}{L}\right)^4 \qquad (8.27)$$

Since the characteristic ratio $\kappa = 2D_{x\phi}/\sqrt{(D_x D_\phi)}$ is usually less than one in the case of corrugated sheets, $H_{mn}(\phi)$ is obtained as follows:

$$H_{mn}(\phi) = A_m \cosh n_1\phi + B_m \sinh n_1\phi + C_m \cosh n_2\phi + D_m \sinh n_2\phi$$
$$(8.28a)$$

in which

$$n_1 = R \sqrt{\left\{\frac{D_x}{2D_{x\phi}} \left(\frac{m\pi}{L}\right)^2 [1 \pm \sqrt{(1 - \kappa^2)}]\right\}} \qquad (8.28b)$$

A_m, B_m, C_m and D_m are arbitrary constants calculated by satisfying the boundary conditions given by eqn (8.23b). This leads to an expression for the stress function in terms of the displacement coefficients, A_{mn} (Marzouk and Abdel-Sayed, 1975).

The external load applied on the shell is assumed to have the form of a half sine wave in the longitudinal, x-, direction. The internal force components induced by each loading can be written in the following form:

$$N_x = \bar{N}_x \sin \frac{\pi}{L} x \qquad (8.29a)$$

$$N_\phi = \bar{N}_\phi \sin \frac{\pi}{L} x \qquad (8.29b)$$

$$N_{xy} = -\bar{N}_{xy} \cos \frac{\pi}{L} x \qquad (8.29c)$$

$\bar{N}_x$, $\bar{N}_\phi$ and $\bar{N}_{x\phi}$ are functions of ϕ only and are dependent on the load distribution in the ϕ-direction (Marzouk and Abdel-Sayed, 1975).

The expressions for w^* and F satisfy all the boundary conditions as well as eqn (8.21a). The Galerkin method is applied to eqn (8.21b) leading to a system of an infinite number of linear, homogeneous, simultaneous equations which can be written in the following matrix form:

$$(\mathbf{U} + \mathbf{KI})\{A_{mn}\} = 0 \qquad (8.30)$$

in which $\{A_{mn}\}$ is the vector composed of the deflection coefficients, A_{mn} (eqn (8.24a)), $\mathbf{U}$ is a general square matrix, $\mathbf{I}$ indicates the identity matrix, and $\mathbf{K}$ is the eigenvalues of $\mathbf{U}$, indicating the critical load.

Equation (8.30) is infinite and for calculating $\mathbf{K}$ only a limited number of deflection coefficients, A_{mn}, are considered. A computer program can be written and processed to calculate the eigenvalues and eigenvectors of eqn (8.30). Table 8.2 shows the buckling loads for shells made of standard corrugated steel for the following cases of loading:

1. Uniform distributed load (snow load).
2. Wind load in the form of a sine wave.
3. Radial pressure in the form of half sine wave.
4. Unsymmetrical radial pressure (superposition of cases 2 and 3).

(d) Observations on the Stability of Barrel Vaults
1. It has been observed that the design of barrels made of standard corrugated panels could be governed by the limit of their buckling load (Table 8.2). However, the analysis and stability study of barrels made of deep U-shaped panels show that in general their design is governed

TABLE 8.2

BUCKLING LOADS (lb/ft^2 AND N/m^2 IN PARENTHESES) OF A SHELL MADE OF STANDARD CORRUGATED SHEETS WITH $R = 3 \cdot 04$ m (120 in), $\phi_e = 90°$ AND $t = 0 \cdot 76$ mm (0·03 in)

Case of loading	L/R					
	1·0	2·0	3·0	4·0	5·0	6·0
(i) p	98·5 (4720)	51·7 (2475)	29·5 (1412)	20·3 (972)	11·7 (561)	7·16 (344)
(ii) +p −p	94·4 (4520)	33·2 (1590)	18·2 (872)	10·0 (479)	5·80 (278)	3·23 (155)
(iii) p	89·4 (4275)	47·4 (2270)	28·0 (1340)	22·4 (1074)	14·4 (690)	10·1 (484)
(iv) 1.42p p (iii) + 1/2(ii)	64·1 (3065)	28·2 (1350)	15·7 (752)	9·27 (444)	5·70 (273)	3·41 (163)

by the pre-buckling load-carrying capacity of the panels. Their buckling load limit is usually higher than their failure load due to the combined moment and axial forces, M_ϕ and N_ϕ, respectively.

2. The load applied to a shell supported along its four edges is transferred partially in the longitudinal direction and partially in the transverse direction. The ratio of distribution of the load between these two directions is dependent on the ratio of length to span of shell. Therefore, the mode of buckling-failure is governed by the ratio

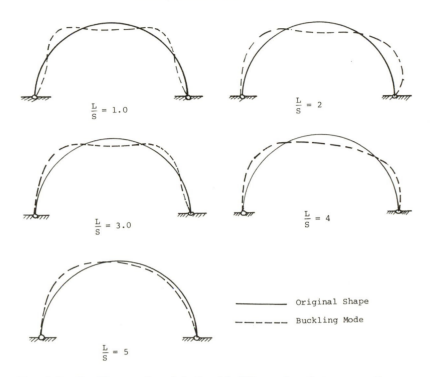

$\dfrac{L}{S} = 1.0$

$\dfrac{L}{S} = 2$

$\dfrac{L}{S} = 3.0$

$\dfrac{L}{S} = 4$

———————— Original Shape

— — — — — Buckling Mode

$\dfrac{L}{S} = 5$

FIG. 8.6. Buckling modes of shells with different length-to-span ratios.

of length to span of shell. Figure 8.6 shows the overall buckling modes of shells made of standard corrugated sheets, with $R = 3\cdot04$ m (120 in) and $t = 0\cdot76$ mm (0·03 in) and having different values of the ratio of length to span under a uniform snow load.

3. For shells having the same ratio of length to span, the critical load of uniform snow loading is found to increase with the decrease of the radius of shell, and decrease with the decrease of the central angle ϕ_e (Marzouk and Abdel-Sayed, 1975).

8.4 TYPE II: END-SUPPORTED SHELLS

8.4.1 Analysis

This type of shell is usually built using standard corrugated panels and provided with longitudinal stiffeners, Figs 8.1b and 8.1c. They can be analysed using the governing equations, eqns (8.7), or in the case of long shells, by using the approximate equivalent beam method.

(a) *Analysis Using the Governing Equations*
Herein, the system of equations, eqns (8.7), can be solved using particular and homogeneous solutions similar to those used in the case of barrel vaults (Section 8.3). Only the boundary conditions along the longitudinal edges are different. For example, for a single shell (Fig. 8.1b) the boundary conditions at $\phi = 0$ and $\phi = 2\phi_e$ are:

$$M_\phi = N_\phi = Q_\phi = 0$$

and the axial strain, ε_x, of the shell is equal to that of the stiffener:

$$(\varepsilon_x)_{shell} = (\varepsilon_x)_{stiffener}$$

It should also be noted here, that because of the absence of supports along the straight edges, the solution can be obtained with sufficient degree of accuracy by using Donnell's approximation (Davis and Young, 1978; El-Atrouzy and Abdel-Sayed, 1978). Herein, the term multiplied by $B_{x\phi}$ can be dropped from eqn (8.7b), also a membrane solution can be used to replace the particular solution. The results obtained from the analysis of an example shell are presented in Fig. 8.7.

(b) *Approximate Analysis Using the Equivalent Beam Method*
In the case of long shells (with $L/R > 3$), the solution can be adequately simplified by using the equivalent beam method. Herein the solution is followed in two steps:

(i) Beam analysis in which the shell is treated as a beam using the classical assumptions for beams, the internal force components are calculated as:

$$N_x = \frac{Mzt}{I_c} \tag{8.31a}$$

$$N_{x\phi} = \frac{VQ}{2I_c} \tag{8.31b}$$

in which I_c is the moment of inertia about the neutral axis, Fig. 8.8a, and $Q =$ the first moment of area at the point of consideration, which can be calculated from the following expression:

$$Q = 2tR^2\left(\sin \phi - \frac{\phi}{\phi_e} \sin \phi_e\right) \tag{8.31c}$$

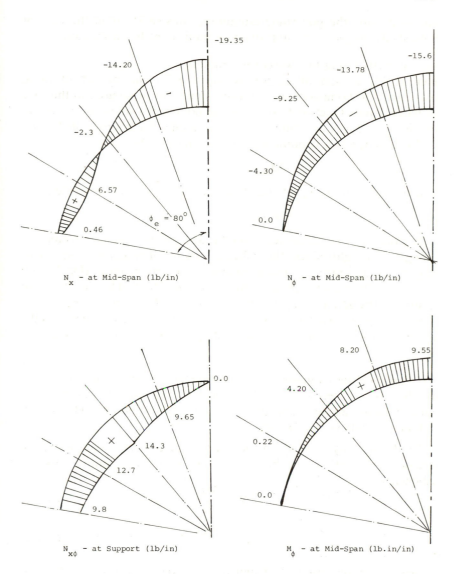

FIG. 8.7. The results of shell analysis of an end-supported shell, $L = 6 \cdot 09$ m (20 ft), $R = 3 \cdot 04$ m (10 ft), $\phi_e = 80°$, $t = 0 \cdot 8$ mm (0·03 in), standard corrugated $f = 6 \cdot 4$ mm (0·25 in) under uniform gravity load $= 73 \cdot 2$ kg m^{-2} (15 psf) (1 lb/in $= 178$ N/m, 1 lb.in/in $= 4 \cdot 45$ Nm/m).

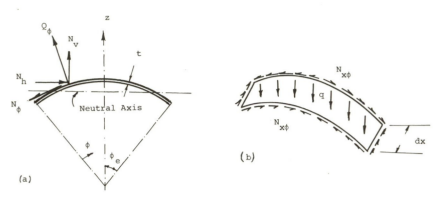

FIG. 8.8.   (a) Cross-section of end-supported shell. (b) A strip of the shell
subjected to shear and external loading.

(ii) Arch analysis in which the moment, shear and axial forces are calculated in the ϕ-direction (M_ϕ, Q_ϕ and N_ϕ, respectively). Herein, a strip dx of the arch (Fig. 8.8b) is examined, in which the equilibrium is maintained by two sets of forces—the load acting on the strip and the specific shear $\partial N_{x\phi}/\partial x$. The specific shear at any point, acting tangentially on the shell arch, can be resolved into horizontal and vertical components. The sum of the vertical components of the shear balances the load on the shell arch, while its horizontal components, which are symmetrical about the crown, balance themselves. The transverse bending moment, M_ϕ, at any point in the arch may be calculated as the algebraic sum of the moments caused by the loading and the horizontal and vertical components of the specific shears (El-Atrouzy, 1972). The beam method shows good comparison with the differential equations solution for the case of long shells ($L/R > 3$).

Because of the low rigidity of the corrugated panels in the longitudinal direction (x-direction), the deflection is large in the case of shells with no longitudinal stiffeners at the crown. The performance of the shell can be considerably improved by providing the shell with such a stiffener or stiffeners, Fig. 8.1c. In this case the analysis can be further approximated by considering the stiffeners to take the flexural tension and compression of the beam action of the shell, while the main function of the corrugated sheets is to carry the shear.

The pre-buckling behaviour of curved corrugated panels in shear is found to be the same as that of plane ones (El-Atrouzy, 1969). The latter has been subject to extensive investigations (Bryan and El-Dakhakhni, 1968). It is also shown by Abdel-Sayed (1970) that the buckling limit of curved panels is higher when compared to the buckling strength of plane panels. However, the stability of the corrugated panel could be the prime factor in determining the ultimate load-carrying capacity of the stiffened longitudinally supported shells.

8.4.2 Stability of Cylindrical Shear Panels

The stability of curved corrugated panels subjected to shear can be examined using the theory of orthotropic shells and the governing equations, eqns (8.21a, b) (with $N_x = N_\phi = 0$). Herein, the curved shear panel with length a and width b, Fig. 8.9, is examined using the coordinates x, z and s in which $s = \phi R$.

(a) Boundary Conditions
The boundary conditions imposed on the middle surface of a buckled simply supported curved panel are given in the following.

Deflection and bending boundary conditions. The edges of the shear panels undergo no deflection and can be considered free from moment lateral to the sheets, i.e.

$$\text{at } x = 0 \text{ and } x = a \qquad w = \frac{\partial^2 w}{\partial x^2} = 0 \qquad (8.32a)$$

$$\text{at } s = 0 \text{ and } s = b \qquad w = \frac{\partial^2 w}{\partial s^2} = 0 \qquad (8.32b)$$

Boundary conditions in plane of panel. The following case considers the panels to be simply supported by edge members which are stiff in

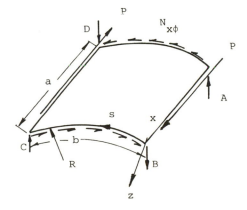

FIG. 8.9. System of coordinates and loading for a cylindrical shear panel.

their own planes but can warp in the directions perpendicular to their own planes. Therefore, the boundary conditions are zero strain along each of the edges and free displacement lateral to them, i.e.

$$\text{at } x = 0 \text{ and } x = a \qquad \varepsilon_s = N_x = 0 \tag{8.33a}$$

$$\text{at } s = 0 \text{ and } s = b \qquad \varepsilon_x = N_s = 0 \tag{8.33b}$$

These conditions can be expressed in terms of the stress function, F:

$$\text{at } x = 0 \text{ and } x = a \qquad \frac{\partial^2 F}{\partial x^2} = \frac{\partial^2 F}{\partial s^2} = 0 \tag{8.33c}$$

$$\text{at } s = 0 \text{ and } s = b \qquad \frac{\partial^2 F}{\partial x^2} = \frac{\partial^2 F}{\partial s^2} = 0 \tag{8.33d}$$

(b) *Deflection and Stress Function*
The following series of equations for deflection w and stress function F satisfy all the boundary conditions and are used to represent w and F to any degree of accuracy:

$$w = \sum_{m=1}^{\infty} \sum_{n=1}^{\infty} A_{mn} \sin \frac{n\pi}{a} x \sin \frac{n\pi}{b} s \tag{8.34a}$$

$$F = \sum_{m=1}^{\infty} \sum_{n=1}^{\infty} F_{mn} \sin \frac{m\pi}{a} x \sin \frac{n\pi}{b} s \tag{8.34b}$$

By substituting eqns (8.34a) and (8.34b) into eqn (8.21a), F_{mn} is calculated as a function of A_{mn}:

$$F_{mn} = -\Phi_{mn} \sqrt{(D_\phi D_x)} \frac{A_{mn}}{R} \left(\frac{mb}{\pi}\right)^2 \tag{8.35a}$$

in which

$$\Phi_{mn} = \frac{1}{\sqrt{\left(\dfrac{D_\phi}{D_x}\right) n^4 \left(\dfrac{a}{b}\right)^2} + \dfrac{\sqrt{(D_x D_\phi)}}{D_{x\phi}} n^2 m^2 + \sqrt{\left(\dfrac{D_x}{D_\phi}\right) m^4 \left(\dfrac{b}{a}\right)^2}} \tag{8.35b}$$

Now consider

$$N_{x\phi} = k_s \left(\frac{\pi}{b}\right)^2 \sqrt{(B_x B_\phi)} \tag{8.36a}$$

and

$$\theta = \frac{1}{\pi^2} \frac{b^2}{rt} \sqrt[4]{\left(\frac{D_x D_s t^4}{B_x B_s}\right)} \tag{8.36b}$$

Substituting eqns (8.34a) and (8.34b) into the differential equation, eqn (8.21b), and using Galerkin's approach leads to:

$$\frac{A_{m_1 n_1}}{k_s} Q_{m_1 n_1} + \sum_{m=1}^{\infty} \sum_{n=1}^{\infty} K_{mnm_1 n_1} A_{mn} = 0 \qquad (8.37)$$

in which the summation includes only those values of m and n for which $m_1 \pm m$ and $n_1 \pm n$ are odd.

Equation (8.37) represents a system of infinite number of simultaneous homogeneous linear equations which can be separated into a group of equations in which $m_1 \pm n_1$ are even numbers and then a group in which $m_1 \pm n_1$ are odd numbers. The eigenvalues can be calculated and only the minimum value is considered for the coefficient k_s.

The coefficient k_s and the relative magnitude of deflection coefficients A_{mn} are dependent on θ, a/b, t/f and f/c. Shear rigidity $D_{x\phi}$, which governs the pre-buckling behaviour of shear panels, has negligible effect on the buckling limit. This can be noticed by comparing the results when using different reduction factors, ρ. Also, it can be explained on the basis that the buckling limit is governed mainly by the bending properties of the panel and not by the membrane properties.

The above section outlines the procedure to determine the buckling limit of curved shear panels in which the longitudinal stiffeners are flexible in the direction of the panels. However, the longitudinal stiffeners could have some rigidity to restrain the panel from edge displacement in their direction.

The analysis of the case with fully restrained edges has been presented by Abdel-Sayed (1971). Herein, the boundary conditions, eqn (8.33b), at $s = 0$ and $s = b$, are modified to $\partial v/\partial x = \varepsilon_x = 0$.

The solution for this case follows a similar approach to that outlined above for the case of panels with non-restrained edges. It has been discussed in detail by Abdel-Sayed (1971).

(c) *Observations on the Stability of Curved Shear Panels*

(i) The shear strength of the curved panels increases when the longitudinal edges are forced to remain straight rather than being free to move in the curved direction of the sheets. This increase is attributed to the membrane forces developed at the longitudinal edges acting in the curved direction and thus having components perpendicular to the sheets. However, restrained curved edges have no effect on the results since there is no curvature lateral to them, in the longitudinal direction.

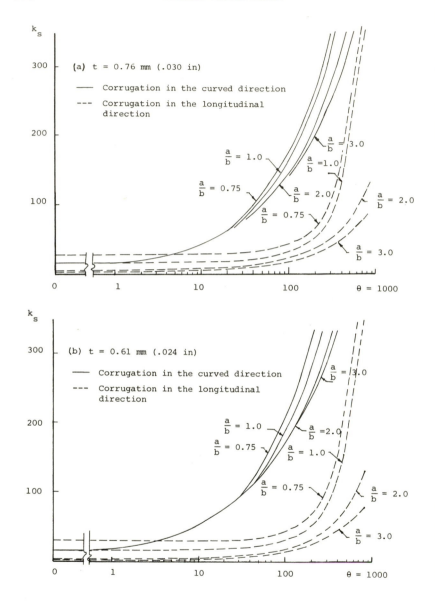

FIG. 8.10. The shear coefficient, k_s, for corrugated steel panels with non-restrained edges.

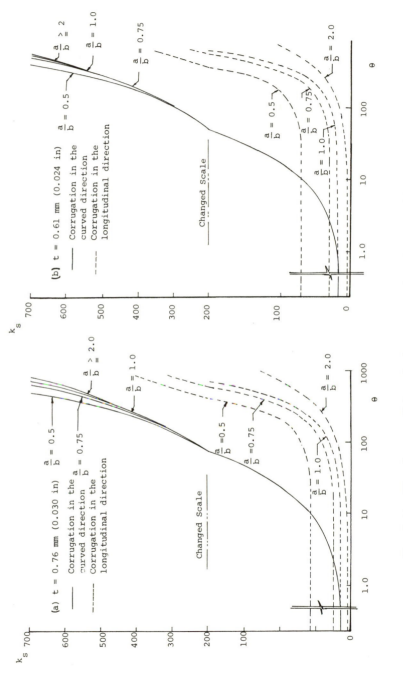

Fig. 8.11. The shear coefficient, k_s, for corrugated steel panels with restrained edges.

(ii) The experimental results reported by Abdel-Sayed (1970) show that the buckling load falls between the theoretically obtained results with the assumption of fully free or restrained edges. This is explained by the fact that both theoretical assumptions are for ideal cases and their results present the upper and lower limits to be considered for practical cases.

(iii) The most commonly used patterns of standard corrugated sheets are those designated as standard $2\frac{1}{2}$ in or $1\frac{1}{4}$ in. Considering this type of corrugation and different values of θ and a/b, the values of the shear coefficient, k_s, are calculated and presented in Fig. 8.10 for panels with non-restrained edges and in Fig. 8.11 for the case of restrained longitudinal edges. The figures are for practical use of panels with GA 20 and GA 24, $t = 0.76$ mm (0.030 in) and $t = 0.61$ mm (0.024 in), respectively.

8.5 CONCLUDING REMARKS

The theory of orthotropic shells is applied for the analysis and stability study of cylindrical shells made of cold-formed steel panels. Herein the following should be noted:

1. The governing equations are formulated taking into consideration the characteristics of these shells in which the rigidities in the curved direction are considerably higher than those in the lateral one.

2. The determination of the elastic properties is an implicit part of the shell analysis in which the open profile of the shell is replaced by planar orthotropic material. The effect of intermediate stiffeners is approximated by smearing a reduced part of their rigidities over the whole width of the shell. Also, attention should be given to the existence of openings or translucent panels, because of the stress concentrations around their edges.

3. The presented solutions are found to be valid for barrel vaults with length-to-span ratios of up to three. Beyond such ratios it is simpler and appropriate to treat the three-dimensional long barrel vault as planar arches. On the other hand, shells supported along their curved edges are considered long when the ratio of their length to radius exceeds three. The solution of such long shells can be adequately simplified by using the equivalent beam method.

REFERENCES

ABDEL-SAYED, G. (1970) Critical shear loading of curved panels of corrugated sheets. *Journal of Engineering Mechanics Division, ASCE,* December, 895–912.

ABDEL-SAYED, G. (1971) Critical shear loading of curved panels of corrugated sheets with restrained edges. *Proc. of the 1st Specialty Conference on Cold-Formed Steel Structures,* Rolla, MO, pp. 167–72.

ABDEL-SAYED, G., PIERCE, G. and SIDDALL, W. (1980) Doubly corrugated half-barrel cold-formed steel sheets. *Proc. of the 5th International Specialty Conference on Cold-Formed Steel Structures,* St. Louis, MO, November 18–19, pp. 113–43.

ABDEL-SAYED, G., SIDDALL, W. and MONASA, F. (1981) Cylindrical cold-formed steel farm structures. Preprint No. 81-526, ASCE Convention, St. Louis, MO.

BATOZ, J. L. and DHATT, G. S. (1977) Non-linear finite element analysis of orthotropic light-weight shells. IASS International Conference Light-weight Shell and Spatial Structures for Normal and Seismic Zones, Alma-Ata, USSR.

BRYAN, E. R. and EL DAKHAKHNI, W. M. (1968) Shear flexibility and strength of corrugated decks. *Journal of Structural Division, ASCE,* **94** (ST11), Proc. Paper 6218, 2549–80.

DAVIS, J. M. and YOUNG, J. G. (1978) Light gauge steel cylindrical shells. Proc. of the 4th International Conference on Cold-Formed Steel Structures, St. Louis, MO, USA.

EL-ATROUZY, M. N. (1969) Structural properties of corrugated sheets used in cylindrical shells. MSc Thesis, University of Windsor, Windsor, Ontario.

EL-ATROUZY, M. N. (1972) Cylindrical shells made of corrugated sheets. PhD Dissertation, University of Windsor, Windsor, Ontario.

EL-ATROUZY, M. and ABDEL-SAYED, G. (1978) Prebuckling analysis of orthotropic barrel-shells. *Journal of the Structural Division, ASCE,* November, 1775–86.

FLÜGGE, W. (1932) Die Stabilitat der Kreiszylinderschate, *Ing.,—Arch.,* **3,** 463–506.

HAWRANEK, A. and STEINHARDT, O. (1958) *Theorie und Berechnung der Stahlbruecken,* Springer-Verlag, Berlin.

MARZOUK, O. and ABDEL-SAYED, G. (1973) Linear theory of orthotropic cylindrical shells. *Journal of the Structural Division, ASCE,* November, 2287–306.

MARZOUK, O. and ABDEL-SAYED, G. (1975) Stability of half-barrel orthotropic shells. *Journal of the Structural Division, ASCE,* July, 1517–30.

PIERCE, G. (1976) Design Research Project on Quonset Buildings of the Type Produced by Fairford Industries in Moose Jaw, Saskatchewan, Industrial Service Division, Saskatchewan Research Council, Saskatoon.

SIDDALL, W., PIERCE, G. and ABDEL-SAYED, G. (1980) Full scale testing and analysis of circular arch skin-supported steel shell buildings. Proc. of the Annual Conference of the CSCE, Winnipeg, May.

Chapter 9

TORISPHERICAL SHELLS

G. D. GALLETLY

Department of Mechanical Engineering, University of Liverpool, UK

SUMMARY

The axisymmetric yielding failure mode in internally-pressurised perfect torispherical shells and the unsymmetric buckling mode (in which wrinkles form around the circumference in the knuckle) are discussed first and some simple formulae for predicting these failure pressures in perfect torispheres are presented. Then the more difficult problem of fabricated torispheres is considered, with particular reference to the internal pressure buckling of austenitic stainless steel ends. The predictions of a simple buckling design formula are compared with all known room-temperature experimental results and are shown to be safe. A brief discussion of Code rules for these heads is also given, together with suggestions for further work.

NOTATION

f Design stress in French Pressure Vessel Code—see eqn (9.12)

p Internal pressure

p_c Plastic collapse pressure (due to large axisymmetric deformations occurring in the head)

p_{cr} Internal buckling pressure of perfect torisphere

p_{des} Design pressure, see eqn (9.11)

p_{exp} Experimental internal buckling pressure of fabricated torisphere

p_{th} Theoretically-predicted internal buckling pressure of fabricated torisphere (eqn (9.9) with $\sigma_{yp} = F$)

r	Radius of toroidal portion (knuckle) of torisphere—see Fig. 9.3
t	Thickness of torisphere or cylinder

D	Diameter of attached cylinder
E	Modulus of elasticity
F	0·2% proof stress—see eqn (9.11)
H	Height of torisphere
N_θ	Circumferential direct stress resultant (force/unit length)
N_φ	Meridional direct stress resultant (force/unit length)
R_s	Radius of the spherical portion of torisphere
R_θ	Radius of curvature in the normal plane perpendicular to the meridian—see Fig. 9.5
R_φ	Meridional radius of curvature

2α	Included angle of spherical cap—see Fig. 9.3
θ	Polar angle
σ_{yp}	Yield point of material
σ_θ	Circumferential stress
σ_φ	Meridional stress
φ	Meridional angle

Note: $1 \text{ MPa} = 1 \text{ N/mm}^2 = 145 \text{ lbf/in}^2$.

9.1 INTRODUCTION

The dished ends used on pressurised cylindrical containers are usually torispherical in shape (see Fig. 9.1) although sometimes the ellipsoidal shape is employed. Dished ends are selected for either economic or functional reasons and some applications in which they are utilised are:

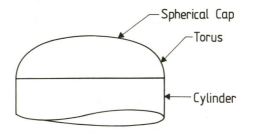

FIG. 9.1. A typical torispherical end closure.

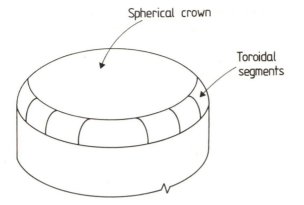

FIG. 9.2.   Crown and segment method of manufacture.

fermentation tanks in breweries, oil or gas storage tanks, water tanks, the food processing industry, fluid cokers in the chemical industry, internal bulkheads in some missiles, the primary tanks of LMFBRs and the roofs of containment structures for PWRs.

Dished ends in practice are manufactured by various means. The most common methods are (i) the crown and segment technique, (ii) pressing and spinning, (iii) pressing and (iv) deep drawing. For the very large diameter shells one has to use the crown and segment technique, in which the spherical crown portion (which may itself consist of several segments) is welded in the circumferential direction to a toroidal (or knuckle) portion; this latter consists of several curved panels which have been welded together (see Fig. 9.2). In many applications in the brewing and food processing industries (cylinder diameters up to 5 m approx.) the material of the shell is austenitic stainless steel and the ends are made by pressing and spinning in the cold condition. This forming process causes a reduction in thickness in the knuckle region of the head and can alter its mechanical properties significantly.

'As-manufactured' dished ends contain residual forming stresses and many have residual welding stresses; all have geometric imperfections of one kind or another and, for some materials, the strain-hardening effects should be considered. The 'as-manufactured' heads are thus not initially stress-free, are not perfect geometrically, nor is their response elastic. It is because of such factors that the prediction of buckling in these heads is not an easy matter. However, before considering these topics, the simpler subject of the perfect torispherical shell subjected to internal pressure will be considered first.

9.2 GEOMETRIC CHARACTERISTICS OF TORISPHERICAL SHELLS

The geometry of a torispherical shell is shown in Fig. 9.3. As may be seen, it consists of a spherical part (of radius R_s) joined to a toroidal part (frequently called the knuckle) of radius r. At the junction J, between the torus and the spherical cap, there is no slope discontinuity but there is a discontinuity in the meridional curvature. For a given D/H ratio, there are many torispheres which will satisfy the slope requirement. This may be seen from the following.

From Fig. 9.3, one has:

$$H = R_s - (R_s - r) \cos \alpha \qquad (9.1)$$

$$D/2 = r + (R_s - r) \sin \alpha \qquad (9.2)$$

where $H =$ the height of the torisphere, $D =$ the diameter of the cylindrical body, $R_s =$ the radius of the spherical cap and $r =$ the radius of the torus. From eqns (9.1) and (9.2), it is a simple matter to show that

$$r/D = \frac{(2R_s/D - H/D)H/D - \frac{1}{4}}{2(R_s/D) - 1} \qquad (9.3)$$

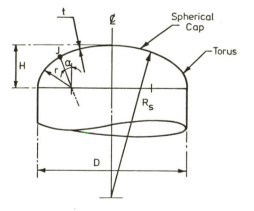

Fig. 9.3.   Geometry of a torispherical shell.

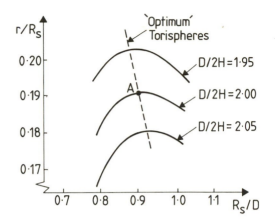

FIG. 9.4.   Illustrating the various torispherical geometries which satisfy given diameter-to-head ratios.

Once a value of H/D has been selected the values of r/D and R_s/D which satisfy eqn (9.3) can be found quite easily. The results of such a calculation, over limited ranges of the parameters, are shown in Fig. 9.4. The solid lines on this figure give the r/R_s values and R_s/D values of torispheres having the same H/D ratio. The locus of the maximum values of r/R_s (shown by the dashed line on Fig. 9.4) gives the geometries of torispheres which have been called 'optimum' by some investigators. As one example, the geometric ratios of the 'optimum' 2:1 torispherical head (point A in Fig. 9.4) are $r/D = 0.1726$, $R_s/D = 0.904$ and $\alpha = 26.50°$.

9.3 COMPRESSIVE STRESSES IN INTERNALLY-PRESSURISED DISHED ENDS

Most ellipsoidal and torispherical shells which are subjected to internal pressure have compressive hoop stresses in their knuckle regions. Compressive stresses due to internal pressure are rather unusual and, in this section, some results from the linear membrane theory of shells will be recalled to indicate how these compressive stresses arise.

A typical shell of revolution is shown in Fig. 9.5, together with the membrane forces acting on a differential shell element (it is assumed that the loading is axisymmetric and that tensile forces are positive). The polar angle θ defines the various meridians and the angle φ,

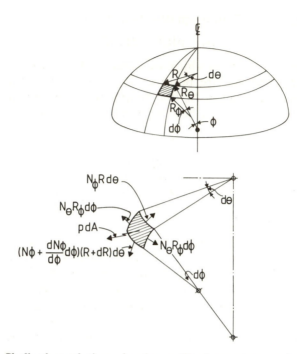

FIG. 9.5.   Shell of revolution, showing radii of curvature and direct stress
resultants (internal pressure loading).

measured from the vertical, defines the various parallels of latitude. R_φ
is the radius of curvature in the meridional plane and that in the plane
perpendicular to the meridian is R_θ (for the spherical cap in Fig. 9.3,
$R_\theta = R_\varphi = R_s$;   for   the   toroidal   shell, $R_\varphi = r$ and $R_\theta = r +$
$(D/2 - r)/\sin \varphi$).

As the shell element is curved in both the θ- and φ-directions, there
will be components of the membrane forces N_θ and N_φ along the
normal. It is a fairly simple matter to show (see Timoshenko, 1940)
that the equation of equilibrium of the shell element along its normal is

$$\frac{N_\varphi}{R_\varphi} + \frac{N_\theta}{R_\theta} = p \qquad (9.4)$$

where p is the uniform internal pressure.

The relation between the meridional membrane force N_φ and the
internal pressure p is known to be (again, see Timoshenko, 1940)

$$N_\varphi = pR_\theta/2 \qquad (9.5)$$

Substituting eqn (9.5) into eqn (9.4) then gives

$$N_\theta = pR_\theta[1 - R_\theta/2R_\varphi] \qquad (9.6)$$

For shells of revolution which are similar to the one depicted in Fig. 9.5, both R_θ and R_φ are positive. The internal pressure p is also positive. Thus, the sign of N_θ (the hoop membrane force) depends on the ratio R_θ/R_φ and it can become negative (i.e. compressive) if

$$R_\theta/R_\varphi > 2 \qquad (9.7)$$

The two radii R_θ and R_φ are independent of each other and it can be seen that if R_θ is kept constant whilst R_φ is decreased (i.e. if the curve is made tighter) then the ratio R_θ/R_φ will increase. If it exceeds 2, then N_θ will become negative and buckling in the circumferential direction becomes possible.

The foregoing application of the linear membrane theory of shells is useful in that it enables one to see fairly readily how the compressive stresses in dished ends arise. However, the linear membrane theory is not adequate for an accurate determination of the stresses in torispherical shells. To accomplish this, one needs to employ the bending theory of shells and, in many cases, it is necessary to consider the effects of large deflections when formulating the differential equations of equilibrium.

9.4 DETERMINING STRESS DISTRIBUTIONS IN TORISPHERICAL SHELLS

Many pressurised containers have large D/t ratios and undergo large deflections. In order to determine the stress distribution throughout such heads, it is necessary to use the large-deflection (non-linear) bending theory of shells. Even when the shell is in the elastic region, and one is interested in just determining the pre-buckling axisymmetric stress distribution, the non-linear theory is still required. This has been shown by several investigators and has been confirmed experimentally by Adachi (1968).

Adachi's model was a machined aluminium torispherical shell of $0 \cdot 25$ m diameter which he tested under internal pressure. Results are shown in Fig. 9.6 for the meridional (σ_φ) and circumferential (σ_θ) stresses on the outside surface. Both linear and non-linear theoretical predictions of the stresses (obtained from the bending theory of shells)

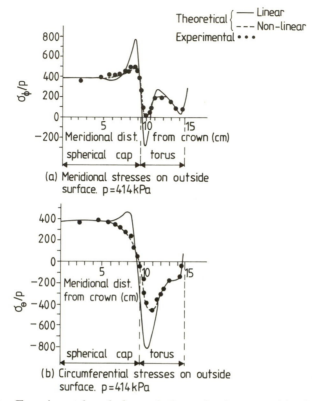

(a) Meridional stresses on outside surface. p=414 kPa

(b) Circumferential stresses on outside surface. p=414 kPa

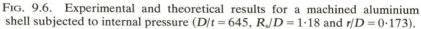

FIG. 9.6. Experimental and theoretical results for a machined aluminium shell subjected to internal pressure ($D/t = 645$, $R_s/D = 1\cdot18$ and $r/D = 0\cdot173$).

are given, together with the test results obtained from strain gauges. It is quite clear from Figs 9.6a and 9.6b that the non-linear bending theory is required to obtain good agreement with the experimental readings.

It may also be seen that the linear (small-deflection) theory predicts higher stresses than the non-linear (large-deflection) theory. One result of this is that when linear shell theories are used for calculating the buckling pressures of internally-pressurised torispherical shells, their predictions are often on the low (but safe) side.

In the example discussed above, D/t was 645 and the stresses were in the elastic range. In practice, torispherical shells are usually manufactured in the range $100 < D/t < 2000$, although shells with geometries outside these limits have been manufactured. The stress distributions throughout the heads will vary with D/t and the other geometric parameters. The magnitude of the yield stress, σ_{yp}, will often be an important variable and can affect the stress distributions considerably. However, the available shell computer programs can handle elastic–plastic material behaviour—see, for example, Bushnell and Galletly (1977).

9.5 POSSIBLE FAILURE MODES IN INTERNALLY–PRESSURISED TORISPHERES

The two static failure modes of interest in the design of torispheres under internal pressure are:

(i) elastic or elastic–plastic unsymmetric buckling, in which wrinkles occur around the circumference of the vessel in the knuckle region (see Fig. 9.7); for many steel torispherical ends in practice, it is the elastic–plastic internal buckling pressure which is the lower, and

(ii) large axisymmetric deformations occurring in the head; the pressure at which this occurs (the plastic collapse pressure) is similar to the limit pressure but a large-deflection elastic–plastic axisymmetric shell analysis is needed to determine it. The definition of plastic collapse is a little arbitrary but it is often taken as the internal pressure to cause twice the deflection at the yield point—see Gerdeen (1979).

That circumferential buckling should occur in shells subjected to internal pressure is a little surprising at first. However, when one knows that large compressive direct stresses can occur in the hoop direction in torispheres, then the possibility of circumferential buckling becomes understandable. The large displacement failure mode is also understandable but it has features that were not brought out until the fluid coker which failed at Avon, California in 1956 was analysed. Galletly (1957, 1959) performed an elastic analysis and Drucker and Shield (1959) a limit analysis. The latter showed that three plastic hinge circles developed in the head and the formation of this failure mechanism precipitated the axisymmetric collapse.

Torispherical heads can also fail in a brittle manner, e.g. the Avon vessel mentioned above—see Harding and Ehmke (1962). Ductile fracture has also occurred simultaneously with buckle formation in some small models, e.g. see Galletly (1975). However, it does not seem to have occurred in practice so far.

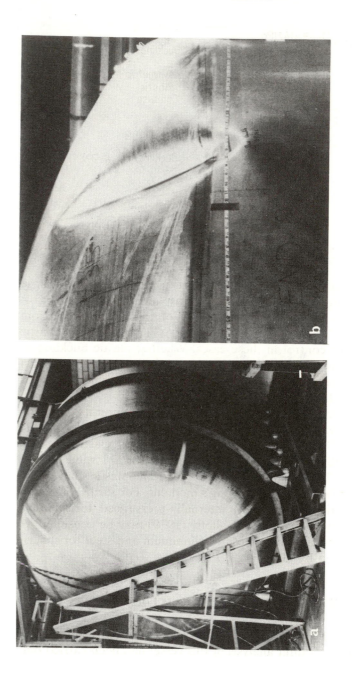

FIG. 9.7. Buckling due to internal pressure in a 3 m diameter stainless steel torispherical shell. (a) Outward buckles; (b) inward buckle.

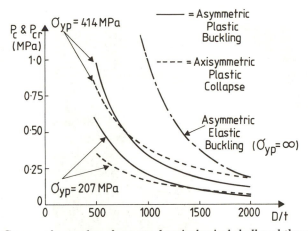

FIG. 9.8. Curves of p_c and p_{cr} for a steel torispherical shell and three values of σ_{yp}.

It is of interest to indicate how the plastic buckling and collapse pressures vary with D/t and σ_{yp}. For a torispherical shell with $r/D = 0.10$ and $R_s/D = 1.0$, approximate values of these pressures (from Galletly, 1982b) are shown in Fig. 9.8. As may be seen, elastic buckling does not control in these cases. Whether plastic buckling or plastic collapse controls (and, therefore, would occur in perfect shells) depends on D/t and σ_{yp}. As shown in Fig. 9.8, plastic collapse is more likely to occur if the yield point is low.

With aluminium torispherical ends, the elastic internal buckling pressures are only about one-third of those for steel ends (due to the lower E value). Thus, in these cases, it is possible for elastic buckling to be the controlling mode of failure in heads with D/t values in the 500–1000 range. This is also the case with thermoplastic, and other, shells which have low values of Young's modulus. For further information on the elastic p_{cr} values of internally-pressurised torispherical shells the paper by Aylward and Galletly (1979) may be consulted. A review of the buckling and collapse of aluminium and steel torispherical heads was given by Galletly (1979).

9.6 THE AXISYMMETRIC FAILURE MODE

When discussing the fluid coker which failed in Avon, California, it was mentioned that a limit analysis of this vessel had been carried out.

From the elastic and the limit analyses of the Avon vessel, it became clear that the then-current edition of the ASME Code did not treat this problem adequately. Shield and Drucker (1961) therefore analysed (numerically) a large number of geometries and obtained some design charts. These charts have subsequently been incorporated into a number of Codes.

Subsequent to this work, various investigators used shell computer programs (which permitted elastic–plastic material properties to be included) in order to calculate the axisymmetric plastic collapse pressures. These latter are the pressures at which large displacements occur and they are similar to the limit pressures. Plastic zones develop in the head in the manner shown in Fig. 9.9, which also shows an equivalent yield hinge mechanism (see, for example, Gerdeen, 1979).

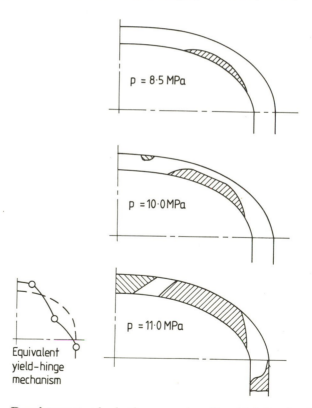

p = 8·5 MPa

p = 10·0 MPa

p = 11·0 MPa

Equivalent yield-hinge mechanism

FIG. 9.9. Development of plastic zones in ellipsoidal head subjected to internal pressure ($D/t \approx 60$).

The early shell computer programs used small-deflection shell theory but these were superseded by programs which used large-deflection theories. The BOSOR 5 program is one such program (see Bushnell, 1976) and the Liverpool group has employed it to determine the axisymmetric plastic collapse pressures. The collapse criterion chosen was the internal pressure to cause twice the yield point deflection. As discussed by Gerdeen (1979) this choice is likely to err on the low (and, therefore, safe) side.

Curves of some plastic collapse pressures for torispherical shells have been given by Radhamohan and Galletly (1979) and a simple equation incorporating the results was found using curve-fitting methods. This has the form:

$$p_c/\sigma_{yp} = \frac{12 \cdot 6[1 + 240\sigma_{yp}/E](r/D)^{1 \cdot 04}}{(D/t)^{1 \cdot 09}(R_s/D)^{1 \cdot 1}} \tag{9.8}$$

Equation (9.8) was derived for steel shells made from elastic, perfectly-plastic material and for $R_s/D \leqslant 1$. The ranges of the parameters investigated were similar to those used for the buckling study (see next section).

With regard to experimental verification of the foregoing equation, very little work seems to have been done. However, see Radhamohan and Galletly (1979) for a discussion of some relevant work done at UMIST.

9.7   UNSYMMETRIC BUCKLING OF INTERNALLY-PRESSURISED TORISPHERICAL SHELLS

In this section, the results available on circumferential buckling in perfect torispherical shells will be discussed first. Then, actual 'as-manufactured' dished ends will be considered and attention will be drawn to the factors which must be taken into account by designers of these heads. The status of the Design Codes for this problem will also be reviewed later on.

9.7.1   Buckling of Perfect Torispheres

For these shells, which contain no initial shape imperfections or residual stresses, there are several computer programs available whereby the elastic or elastic–plastic internal buckling pressures can be determined. The writer and his colleagues have used the BOSOR 5

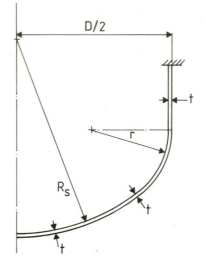

FIG. 9.10.   To'rispherical shells considered in computer analysis.

program for this purpose but there are several other programs (mainly finite element) which could also be used.

The Liverpool group has carried out parametric surveys on internally-pressurised constant-thickness torispherical shells of the form shown in Fig. 9.10. The geometric parameters which were varied were D/t, r/D and R_s/D, while the main material property to be considered was the yield point σ_{yp}. However, a few calculations were carried out on the effect of strain hardening and, while elastic, perfectly-plastic steel was the chief material of interest, some aluminium shells were also considered. The results of these calculations, in the elastic and elastic–plastic regions, are given in papers by Aylward and Galletly (1979), Galletly and Radhamohan (1979) and Galletly (1979). The ranges of the parameters covered were: $500 < D/t < 1500$; $0.06 < r/D < 0.18$; $0.75 < R_s/D < 1.25$; $207\,\text{N/mm}^2 < \sigma_{yp} < 414\,\text{N/mm}^2$. Some typical results from these computations are given in Fig. 9.11 for elastic buckling and Fig. 9.12 for elastic–plastic buckling.

Additional calculations in the range $200 < D/t < 1000$ and $R_s/D = 1.0$ have just been completed—see Galletly and Blachut (1983). Work is still continuing on this topic.

In the elastic–plastic computations, the strain hardening assumed is

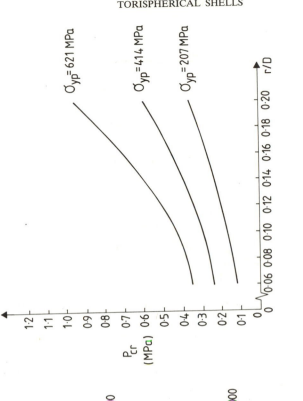

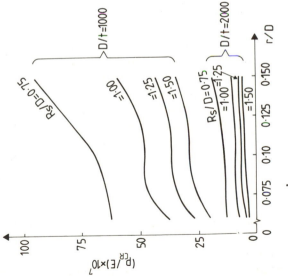

Fig. 9.12. $D/t = 1000$, $R_s/D = 1\cdot0$. Effect of r/D and σ_{yp} on the elastic–plastic internal buckling pressures of steel torispherical shells (no strain hardening).

Fig. 9.11. Non-dimensional elastic internal buckling pressures for various geometries.

of the isotropic type and the von Mises initial yield condition is used. One can employ either the deformation or the flow theories of plasticity to calculate the buckling pressures although, theoretically, the flow theory is the more correct. Some results using both theories, and BOSOR 5, are given in Galletly and Blachut (1983).

In addition to presenting curves of internal buckling pressures versus various parameters, it was thought desirable to try and derive, by curve-fitting methods, simple equations which would be of assistance to designers. These are given in the references cited above and the one suggested for the elastic–plastic buckling of perfect steel torispheres is

$$p_{cr}/\sigma_{yp} = \frac{285[1 - 125\sigma_{yp}/E](r/D)^{0.84}}{(D/t)^{1.53}(R_s/D)^{1.1}} \tag{9.9}$$

For the normal structural steels (σ_{yp} in the range 207–414 N/mm^2) a reasonable approximation of the square-bracketed term in eqn (9.9) is 0·8. Utilising this value in eqn (9.9) then gives

$$p_{cr}/\sigma_{yp} \approx \frac{230(r/D)^{0.84}}{(D/t)^{1.53}(R_s/D)^{1.1}} \tag{9.10}$$

An even simpler version of eqn (9.9) has also been suggested by Galletly (1982b). For $R_s/D = 1$, a logarithmic form is proposed in another paper by Galletly (1981a).

In order to verify the above equations one needs experimental results obtained on near-perfect torispherical shells. There have, in fact, been two sets of tests carried out which approximately fit this description. In both cases the models were small (0·137 m diameter) and were machined from solid billets of aluminium and steel. Most of the models were $\frac{1}{4}$ mm thick (some were $\frac{1}{8}$ mm), had a D/t ratio of 550 and were made of aluminium. The agreement between experiment and theory for the UMIST (Manchester) models varied from 1·05 to 0·82 while that for the Liverpool models varied from 0·98 to 0·90 (see Galletly, 1981a). Overall, the experimental/theoretical correlation in these two sets of tests was reasonably good. However, it should be noted that there were not many models in either series.

Initial imperfections in the radial direction do not appear to be very significant in this problem. This is quite different from the case of, say, externally-pressurised spheres. In this connection, it is of interest to note a typical pressure–deflection curve for internally-pressurised torispheres—see Fig. 9.13. As may be seen, the curve continues to rise

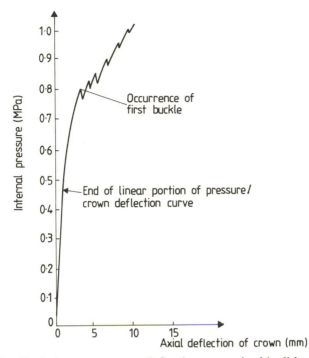

FIG. 9.13.   Typical pressure versus deflection curve of a thin dished end.

after the formation of the first buckle. More buckles appear as the pressure is raised but, overall, the slope of the pressure–deflection curve is positive, i.e. the post-buckling curve is stable.

9.7.2   Fabricated Torispheres—How They Differ from Perfect Torispheres

The torispherical ends which are used in practice differ from the perfect ones discussed in the preceding section in several important respects which will now be considered.

(a) Residual Stresses

Due to the welding or forming operations, residual stresses will be present in most dished ends in practice. With the smaller ends, which can be made from a single sheet, the distribution of residual stresses may be axisymmetric. However, with the larger heads, which usually have meridional welds, the residual stress distribution will not be axisymmetric.

While there have been a few investigations to determine the distribution of residual stresses in fabricated torispherical ends, no general conclusions can be drawn from them, especially for heads with the larger D/t ratios. Thus, insofar as a designer is concerned, he will know that residual stresses will be present in his torispherical shell but their magnitudes and distribution will not be known. This situation may change in the near future, as some investigators have recently been able to simulate the residual stresses caused by the cold bending of flat plates to form cylindrical shells—see Bushnell (1980).

(b) Initial Geometric Imperfections

The imperfections will include the following items: (i) radial deviations, causing initial out-of-circularity, (ii) the local radii of curvature of the knuckle, or the spherical cap, being different from that specified, (iii) thickness variations, particularly along the meridian; with spun heads there can be considerable thinning in the knuckle region (up to 30%).

(c) Stress–Strain Properties

In order to be able to predict the behaviour of an actual torispherical shell, one needs to know its properties in the 'as-manufactured' state. Usually, all that the designer knows is information on the material properties of the flat plate before it is involved in the forming operation. With crown and segment heads, there will be much welding and hammering; with cold spun ends, there will be the large reduction in thickness mentioned earlier. If the end is made of a strain-hardening material (e.g. austenitic stainless steel, which is frequently used in the brewing and food processing industries) then the change in mechanical properties can be considerable for cold spun ends (e.g. the 0·2% proof stress may be increased by a factor of two or more).

The question also arises as to how one should measure the mechanical properties of the head in the fabricated state—particularly in the knuckle region where circumferential buckling might occur. Obviously, owners of vessels will not want coupons cut out of the knuckle region of their vessels. With vessels which have failed in service, or in the laboratory, it is possible to obtain coupons from the knuckle. However, they will be curved in two directions and trying to straighten the coupons (for the conventional stress–strain test) may introduce additional problems. Another possibility is to take strips from the 'as-received' plate and roll them down to various thicknesses. These latter can then be used to determine various properties (e.g. the 0·2%

proof stress) and curves of reduction in thickness versus these properties can be drawn. If the designer can estimate the thickness of the
as-fabricated knuckle, then an estimate of its mechanical properties
can be made.

(*d*) *The Usual Assumptions Made in Design*
From the foregoing, it may be seen that there are several complicating
factors to be considered when trying to predict the buckling pressure of
an actual fabricated head—in comparison with a perfect theoretical
one. Due to lack of knowledge about them, the residual stresses are
usually ignored. This is also usually the case with the initial geometric
imperfections, although the fabricated ends do have to meet certain
tolerances on shape.

With heads made from materials having a non-strain-hardening
portion (e.g. mild steel) the change in mechanical properties due to
forming may not be very large and can be ignored. This is not the case
with cold spun ends made from austenitic stainless steel and the
designer will have to estimate the reduction in thickness in the knuckle
(the manufacturer's prior experience will help here) and the improved
mechanical properties. If he uses the mechanical properties of the
'as-received' plate, his design for the strain-hardened end will be safe
but not competitive commercially.

In relation to the last point, there is little guidance available to the
designer. Galletly (1981*a*,*b*, 1982*a*,*b*) has considered the buckling test
results obtained on twenty or so fabricated heads made by cold
spinning austenitic stainless steel (high-proof 304 S65). A compromise
procedure, which seemed to give reasonable results, was to multiply
the 'as-received' 0·2% proof stress by about 1·6. The results will be
discussed in the next section. However, the value of 1·6 is a tentative
one and will probably vary with the strain-hardening material used to
fabricate the dished ends.

9.7.3 Buckling of Fabricated Torispheres
In this section, the buckling of fabricated torispherical ends under
internal pressure will be considered.

(*a*) *Stainless Steel Ends*
As most of the tests have been carried out on cold spun austenitic
stainless steel heads (with diameters varying from 1·2 m to 4 m) they
will be considered first. It is unfortunate that there are so few test

results available on mild steel (i.e. approximately elastic, perfectly-plastic material) ends as, for them, strain hardening is not such an important issue.

The tests to be considered are those carried out by Kemper (1972) on production ends and by Stanley and Campbell (1981). The latter investigators carried out their tests under laboratory conditions but the ends tested by them were supposed to be production ends (the same firm (APV) made both the Kemper and the Stanley–Campbell ends). These heads were fabricated from a high-proof austenitic stainless steel (304 S65). The details of the models are given in Table 9.1 and they have been separated into two groups, i.e. pressed and spun heads and crown and segment ones. As information on all the geometric characteristics (radii of curvature and thickness) for all the heads has not been published as yet, the values given in Table 9.1 are nominal ones. In addition, to allow for the reduction in thickness during the forming operation, the nominal thicknesses in the spun heads have been multiplied by 0·9.

The minimum specified properties of the stainless steel used in the heads (304 S65) were as follows:

$$0·2\% \text{ proof stress} = 42\,500\,\text{lbf/in}^2 \ (=293\,\text{N/mm}^2 = 293\,\text{MPa})$$
$$1·0\% \text{ proof stress} = 45\,500\,\text{lbf/in}^2 \ (=314\,\text{N/mm}^2 = 314\,\text{MPa})$$

No information is available on the mechanical properties of the fabricated dished ends. However, for the SC series of heads, strips of steel were rolled down to various thicknesses and several properties were measured. The curve showing the variation of 0·2% proof stress with reduction in thickness for these heads is shown in Fig. 9.14 (the starting thickness was 3·25 mm) and, as may be seen, the effect of the cold rolling on the 0·2% proof stress is considerable. The average measured reduction in thickness in the knuckles of four of the heads was about 0·20 mm and this means that for the 0·2% proof stress there was about 482 MPa, i.e. an increase of 65% over the minimum specified value.

If the stress–strain curves of the fabricated torispheres were available, then it would be possible to use programs like BOSOR 5 to predict the internal buckling pressures (assuming no residual stresses, etc.). An attempt to do this for four of the SC-heads is described by Galletly (1981a). What will be done here (see also Galletly, 1981a,b) is to use the approximate equation derived for perfect constant-

TABLE 9.1

FABRICATED STAINLESS STEEL (304 S65) HEADS. A COMPARISON OF
THEORETICAL AND EXPERIMENTAL BUCKLING PRESSURES

Head No.	Nominal D/t	r/D	R_s/D	p_{th} (MPa)	p_{exp} (MPa)	$\dfrac{p_{exp}}{p_{th}}$
Pressed and spun heads (σ_{yp} taken as 1.6×293 MPa)						
SC3	467	0·111	1·0	1·276	1·710	1·34
SC4	467	0·074	1·0	0·903	1·365	1·51
SC5	467	0·074	0·83	1·110	1·917	1·73
SC6	467	0·074	0·78	1·193	1·917	1·61
SC16	700	0·074	1·0	0·483	0·655	1·36
SC17	700	0·074	0·83	0·600	0·738	1·23
SC8	933	0·111	1·0	0·441	0·483	1·09
SC9	933	0·074	1·0	0·317	0·428	1·35
SC10	933	0·074	0·83	0·386	0·538	1·39
SC11	933	0·074	0·72	0·455	0·593	1·30
SC12	933	0·056	1·0	0·248	0·455	1·83
K5	1160	0·083	1·0	0·248	0·228	0·92
Crown and segment heads (σ_{yp} taken as 293 MPa)						
SC1	420	0·167	1·0	1·483	1·931	1·30
SC2	420	0·167	1·0	1·483	1·917	1·29
SC14	630	0·167	1·0	0·800	0·828	1·03
SC15	630	0·167	1·0	0·800	0·738	0·92
SC7	840	0·167	1·0	0·514	0·414	0·81
SC13	840	0·167	1·0	0·514	0·566	1·10
K1	825	0·159	0·91	0·562	0·366	0·65
K2	880	0·163	1·0	0·469	0·317	0·68
K3	915	0·166	1·0	0·448	0·290	0·65
K4	730	0·162	0·89	0·621	0·483	0·78

Notes:
(i) In the above tabulation, the nominal thicknesses in the spun heads
were multiplied by 0·9 as an approximate allowance for thinning, e.g. for SC3, $D/t = 420/0.9 = 467$.
(ii) The K4 end was made from 321 S12 stainless steel. Its σ_{yp} was
taken as 259 MPa.
(iii) 1 MPa $= 1$ N/mm$^2 = 145$ lbf/in^2.

thickness heads (i.e. eqn (9.9)) and use the following for σ_{yp}:

$$\sigma_{yp} = \begin{cases} 0.2\% \text{ proof stress of the 'as-received' plate for crown and} \\ \text{segment ends} \\ 1.6 \times \text{the above } 0.2\% \text{ proof stress for cold spun ends} \end{cases}$$

It may turn out that it is better to use the 1% proof stress, rather than

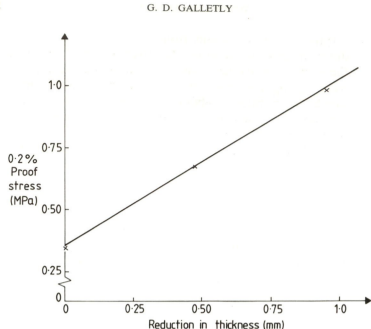

FIG. 9.14.   Stainless steel heads. Materials data from rolled strips.

the 0·2% proof stress, since the 1% value is the one usually used in Design Codes. To do this will need only a small modification to the proposed method.

The theoretically-predicted internal buckling pressures and the experimental test pressures for both the SC-heads and the K-heads are shown in Table 9.1 and it may be seen that:

(i)   For all the spun heads in the SC-series, and most of the crown and segment ones, the ratios p_{exp}/p_{th} are greater than one. This is unusual with buckling tests. The approximate manner in which strain hardening was included in the calculations, and the use of nominal geometries, probably contributed to this unusual behaviour. As the ratios p_{exp}/p_{th} are larger for the spun ends than the crown and segment ones, it is also possible that the factor which was used for cold spun ends (i.e. 1·6) should be increased.

(ii)   For all the K-ends (which were production ends) the ratios p_{exp}/p_{th} are less than one. This state of affairs is what one would normally expect from buckling tests. However, it is surprising that the results from the SC-series of ends are so different from the K-series. Both sets of ends were made by the same manufacturer and the same quality control checks were supposed to have been used for both. One point which should be mentioned about the K-series is that many ends (10–40) were made to each design and buckling occurred in only about 10% of them.

(iii) If, for design purposes, one requires a factor of safety of 1·5 on all the ends in Table 9.1, then it is necessary to divide the predictions of eqn (9.9) by $1·5/0·65 = 2·3$ to achieve this ($0·65$ is the value of p_{exp}/p_{th} for head K1 and is the smallest in Table 9.1). The ratios of p_{exp}/p_{th} in Table 9.1 would then range from 2·1 to 4·2 for the pressed and spun ends and 1·5 to 3·0 for the crown and segment ones.

(iv) If the value of 2·3 is used in eqn (9.10) then a simple equation for the design of austenitic stainless steel ends is

$$p_{des}/F = \frac{100(r/D)^{0·84}}{(D/t)^{1·53}(R_s/D)^{1·1}} \qquad (9.11)$$

where $F = 0·2\%$ proof stress of the as-received plate for crown and segment ends and 1·6 times that value for cold spun ends.

Use of eqn (9.11) should, on the basis of the available experimental evidence on 304 S65, give a design pressure for internally-pressurised torispherical ends with a safety factor of at least 1·5. This is shown in Table 9.3.

(b) Carbon Steel Ends

The number of test results on the buckling of fabricated carbon steel torispherical ends subjected to internal pressure is very small. The only ones known to the author, at the time of writing, are:

(i) an 18·3 m diameter crown and segment torispherical head reported by Fino and Schneider (1961) which buckled along a meridional weld, and

(ii) four 0·5 m diameter shallow spun torispherical ends tested recently by Roche and Alix at the Centre d'Etudes Nucleaires, Saclay, France (see Galletly, 1981b).

TABLE 9.2

CARBON STEEL HEADS: A COMPARISON OF THEORETICAL AND EXPERIMENTAL
BUCKLING PRESSURES

| Head No. | Type of head | D/t | Nominal | | σ_{yp} (MPa) | p_{th} (MPa) | p_{exp} (MPa) | $\dfrac{p_{exp}}{p_{th}}$ |
			r/D	R_s/D				
Saclay 10A	Spun	547	0·06	1·093	230	0·312	0·426	1·37
Saclay 10B	Spun	541	0·06	1·093	257	0·348	0·440	1·27
Saclay 15A	Spun	375	0·06	1·093	289	0·668	1·131	1·69
Saclay 15B	Spun	367	0·06	1·093	291	0·697	1·193	1·71
Fino–Schneider	Crown and segment	2325	0·173	0·905	248	0·109	0·086	0·79

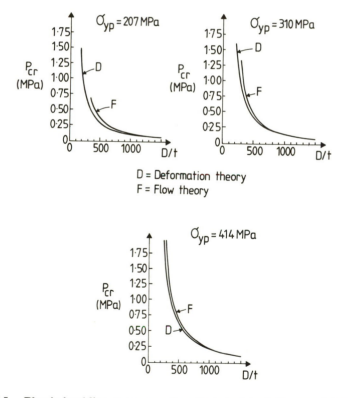

FIG. 9.15.   Plastic buckling pressures of perfect steel torispheres subjected to
internal pressure ($R_s/D = 1·0$, $r/D = 0·06$).

There are some additional tests underway but the results on these are not available as yet.

The details of the actual geometric characteristics of the Fino–Schneider head are not given in their paper so nominal values have been assumed. With the Saclay heads, the actual thickness was measured but information on the radii of curvature was not given. The data assumed herein for these heads are given in Table 9.2 and the values of p_{cr} were found from eqn (9.9). Since carbon steel is not a strain-hardening material at moderate strain levels, the mechanical properties of the cold spun Saclay ends have not been multiplied by the factor of 1·6 (which was used for cold spun austenitic stainless steel).

The theoretically-predicted internal buckling pressures and the test pressures are compared in Table 9.2. As may be seen, the Saclay spun ends have p_{exp}/p_{th} ratios greater than one, while the ratio for the large fabricated crown and segment end is 0·79. If, as in item (iii) of Section 9.7.3(a), the predictions of eqn (9.9) are divided by 2·3, then the ratio p_{exp}/p_{des} becomes 1·82 for the crown and segment end and varies from 2·9 to 3·9 for the smaller spun ends.

It should also be noted that eqn (9.9) was derived over the range $500 < D/t < 1500$. Thus, both the $D/t = 2325$ head, and the two Saclay heads with $D/t \approx 370$, are really outside the parameter ranges investigated. More information on the p_{cr} values for small values of D/t is given in the recent paper by Galletly and Blachut (1983) and, for $r/D = 0·06$, some details are given in Fig. 9.15. As may be seen, eqn (9.9) underestimates slightly the more accurate values of p_{cr} found using the BOSOR 5 computer program. In part, this explains the higher p_{exp}/p_{th} values found for $D/t \approx 370$ in Table 9.2. However, it is possible that, for mild steel also, a factor should be included in the formula, if the mechanical properties in the knuckle are enhanced during the reduction in thickness caused during the forming operation.

(c) *The Predictions of Eqn* (9.11)

It is of interest to check the design pressures predicted by eqn (9.11) when it is used for the stainless steel (304 S65) and the carbon steel internally-pressurised torispherical heads listed in Tables 9.1 and 9.2. These design pressures are given in Table 9.3 in terms of the experimental buckling pressures and it may be seen that the ratios p_{exp}/p_{des} vary from 1·5 to 4·0. The minimum value of 1·5 is very satisfactory from the safety point of view; however, the maximum value shows that some heads will be stronger than necessary.

TABLE 9.3

COMPARISON OF THE EXPERIMENTAL AND THE PREDICTED DESIGN
PRESSURES FOR FABRICATED TORISPHERES

Austenitic stainless steel				Carbon steel	
Spun		Crown and segment			
Head No.	$\dfrac{p_{exp}}{p_{des}}$	Head No.	$\dfrac{p_{exp}}{p_{des}}$	Head No.	$\dfrac{p_{exp}}{p_{des}}$
SC3	2·80	SC1	3·06	Saclay[a] 10A	3·35
SC4	3·15	SC2	3·04	Saclay[a] 10B	3·05
SC5	3·61	SC14	2·44	Saclay[a] 15A	3·99
SC6	3·37	SC15	2·17	Saclay[a] 15B	4·04
SC16	2·81	SC7	1·89	Fino–Schneider[b]	1·92
SC17	2·58	SC13	2·59		
SC8	2·28	K1	1·53		
SC9	2·84	K2	1·59		
SC10	2·92	K3	1·52		
SC11	2·77	K4	1·82		
SC12	3·82				
K5	1·91				

Notes:
1. $F = \sigma_{yp}$ for carbon steel heads.
2. F = minimum specified 0·2% proof stress for stainless steel crown and segment heads.
3. $F = 1·6 \times$ (the value in 2) for stainless steel cold spun heads.

[a] Spunhead.
[b] Crown and segment head.

9.8 CODE PROVISIONS FOR THE BUCKLING OF INTERNALLY-PRESSURISED TORISPHERES

At the present time, there are no rules in the British Pressure Vessel Code (BS 5500, 1980) covering the buckling of fabricated torispherical shells under internal pressure. An Enquiry Case on the topic is in the process of being prepared and should be published in the next update of BS 5500. In due course, design rules for the problem will be incorporated into Section 3.5 of BS 5500.

The Germans have some rules (AD-Merkblatt B3, 1977) for their special types of torispherical end, i.e. Korbbogen and Klöpper. The rules are based on a small-deflection analysis with modifications for plastic effects. The amount of experimental verification of these rules seems to be rather limited and it is also not clear what one should do with shells made from strain-hardening materials. The American Code (API, 1980) for low-pressure welded storage tanks does not consider buckling explicitly, but the allowable design stress is affected by the ratio of the tensile meridional stress to the compressive hoop stress.

The latest version of the French Pressure Vessel Code (CODAP, 1982) does contain a design equation for this buckling problem and, with the design pressure as the unknown, it reads:

$$\frac{p_{des}}{f} = \frac{106(r/D)^{0.79}}{(D/t)^{1.49}(R_s/D)^{1.09}}$$ (9.12)

where f is the design stress.

The French do not indicate how their eqn (9.12) was arrived at; however, its form is so similar to eqn (9.11) herein that it seems most likely that they have a common origin, e.g. eqn (9.9)—see also Galletly (1982b).

One difference between the CODAP equation (eqn (9.12)) and eqn (9.11) is the use of f in eqn (9.12) and F in eqn (9.11). The design stress f is, approximately, $F/1.5$. Thus, the use of eqn (9.12) will permit design pressures which are only two-thirds those given by eqn (9.11). The equation in the French Code is, therefore, more conservative than eqn (9.11) (it will be recalled that the latter equation has a minimum safety factor of 1.5).

The French Code also does not distinguish between crown and segment ends and cold spun ends. As mentioned before, the mechanical properties in the knuckle region of a cold spun austenitic stainless steel end are significantly higher than those of its crown and segment counterpart. If advantage is not taken of this fact, then the spun head design will be rather conservative.

The question of Code rules for the buckling of torispherical shells under internal pressure is still being pursued actively in several countries. In the next few years it is likely that design rules for the problem will be published in a number of Codes. A review of various design procedures (but excluding buckling) was given a few years ago by Esztergar (1976).

9.9 FUTURE WORK NEEDED

Insofar as design rules are concerned, there is a lack of adequate buckling data on fabricated torispherical ends made from materials other than stainless steel. Even for stainless steel, practically all the tests have been conducted on the high-proof 304 S65 which is not used as much nowadays as it was formerly.

Other items in need of investigation have been mentioned earlier. These include (i) how to assess the enhancement in mechanical properties in cold spun ends caused by the forming process, (ii) how significant are residual stresses, (iii) how should the mechanical properties in the knuckle region of fabricated torispheres be measured, (iv) how to estimate the amount of thinning in the knuckle of a cold spun end and caused by the forming process, (v) significance of initial geometric imperfections and the tolerances on shape which should be permitted during the fabrication of the end.

For perfect internally-pressurised torispheres, it is also of interest to investigate when buckling is the failure mode and when plastic collapse (the axisymmetric yielding mode) controls—see Fig. 9.8. Some work on this problem has been carried out at Liverpool (Galletly and Aylward, 1979; Radhamohan and Galletly, 1979) and also at Bochum in Germany by Rensch (1982). The effect of strain hardening on the internal buckling pressures is also of interest. Again, some work on this has been done, both at Liverpool and Bochum.

9.10 CONCLUSIONS

1. For perfect torispheres, whose material properties are known, it is possible to predict their internal buckling and plastic collapse pressures with good accuracy.

2. The number of experimental buckling tests on fabricated torispherical ends is very small and most of the tests used ends made from one material (austenitic stainless steel 304 S65) at room temperature.

3. The predictions of the simple buckling design formula suggested in the text (eqn (9.11)), when compared with all known experimental buckling pressures, were safe.

4. More experimental and theoretical work is needed on the stability and strength problems of torispheres.

REFERENCES

ADACHI, J. (1968) Stresses and Buckling in Thin Domes under Internal Pressure, US Army Materials and Mechanics Research Center, Watertown, MS 68-01.

AD-Merkblatt B3 (1977) Dished Ends Subjected to Internal or External Pressure, Verein der Tech. Uberwachungs-Vereine e.v. (VdTUV), Essen.

API (1980) *Recommended Rules for Design and Construction of Large, Welded Low-pressure Storage Tanks*, Standard 620, 6th edn, Rev. 2, December.

AYLWARD, R. W. and GALLETLY, G. D. (1979) Elastic buckling of, and first yielding in, thin torispherical shells subjected to internal pressure. *Int. J. Pres. Ves. & Piping*, **7**(5).

BS 5500 (1980) *Specifications for Unfired Fusion Welded Pressure Vessels*, British Standards Institution, London.

BUSHNELL, D. (1976) BOSOR 5—Program for buckling of elastic–plastic shells of revolution including large deflections and creep. *Comput. Struct.*, **6**, 221–39.

BUSHNELL, D. (1980) Effect of cold bending and welding on buckling of ring-stiffened cylinders. *Comput. Struct.*, **12**, 291–307.

BUSHNELL, D. and GALLETLY, G. D. (1977) Stress and buckling of internally-pressurised elastic–plastic torispherical vessel heads—Comparisons of test and theory. *J. Pres. Ves. Tech.*, *Trans. ASME* **99**, 39–53.

CODAP (1982) (Code Français de Construction des Appareils à Pression), Paris.

DRUCKER, D. C. and SHIELD, R. T. (1959) Limit analysis of symmetrically loaded shells of revolution. *J. Appl. Mech.*, **81**(1), 61–8.

ESZTERGAR, E. P. (1976) Development of design rules for dished pressure vessel heads. *Bull. Weld. Res. Coun.*, No. 215, 1–34.

FINO, A. and SCHNEIDER, R. W. (1961) Wrinkling of a large thin code head under internal pressure. *Bull. Weld Res. Council*, No. 69, 11–13.

GALLETLY, G. D. (1957) Stress Failure of Large Pressure Vessels—Recommendations Resulting from Studies of the Collapse of a 68 ft high × 45 ft dia. Pressure Vessel, Tech. Report No. 45-57, Shell Development Corp., Emeryville, California, March.

GALLETLY, G. D. (1959) Torispherical shells—A caution to designers. *J. Engng. Ind.*, *Trans. ASME 81*, 51–66. Also published in *Pressure Vessel and Piping Design—Collected Papers 1927–1959*, ASME, New York, 1960.

GALLETLY, G. D. (1975) Internal pressure buckling of very thin torispherical shells—A comparison of experiment and theory. *Proc. 3rd Int. Conf. Struct. Mech. Reactor Technol.*, London, 1975, Paper G2/3.

GALLETLY, G. D. (1977) Some Experimental Results on the Elastic–Plastic Buckling of Thin Torispherical and Ellipsoidal Shells Subjected to Internal Pressure, Prelim. Report. 2nd Int. Colloq. Stability Steel Struct., Liège, 1977, pp. 619–26.

GALLETLY, G. D. (1979) Buckling and collapse of thin internally-pressurised dished ends. *Proc. Instn. Civ. Engrs.*, *Part 2*, **67**, 607–26.

GALLETLY, G. D. (1981*a*) Plastic buckling of torispherical and ellipsoidal shells subjected to internal pressure. *Proc. Inst. Mech. Engrs.*, **195**, 329–45.

GALLETLY, G. D. (1981*b*) Discussion on Plastic buckling of torispherical and ellipsoidal shells subjected to internal pressure. *Proc. Instn. Mech. Engrs.*, **195**, S39–S46.

GALLETLY, G. D. (1982*a*) A design procedure for preventing buckling in internally-pressurised thin fabricated torispheres, *J. Constr. Steel Res.*, **2**(3), 11–21.

GALLETLY, G. D. (1982b) The buckling of fabricated torispherical shells under internal pressure. In: *Buckling of Shells—Proc. of a State-of-the-Art Colloquium, Stuttgart* (Ed. by E. Ramm), Springer-Verlag, Berlin, pp. 429–66.

GALLETLY, G. D. and AYLWARD, R. W. (1979) Plastic collapse and the controlling failure pressures of thin 2:1 ellipsoidal shells subjected to external pressure. *J. Pres. Ves. Techn., Trans. ASME*, **101,** 64–72.

GALLETLY, G. D. and BLACHUT, J. (1983) Plastic buckling of internally-pressurised torispherical shells. *3rd Int. Colloquium on Stability of Metal Structures*, Paris, November.

GALLETLY, G. D. and RADHAMOHAN, S. K. (1979) Elastic–plastic buckling of internally-pressurized thin torispherical shells. *J. Pres. Ves. Techn., Trans. ASME*, **101,** 216–25.

GERDEEN, J. C. (1979) A Critical Evaluation of Plastic Behaviour Data and a Unified Definition of Plastic Loads for Pressure Components, WRC Bulletin No. 254, New York.

HARDING, A. G. and EHMKE, E. F. (1962) Brittle failure of a large pressure vessel. *Proc. Am. Petrol. Inst.*, **42,** Section 3, 107–17.

KEMPER, M. J. (1972) Buckling of thin dished ends under internal pressure. *Proc. Conf. on Vessels under Buckling Conditions*, I.Mech.E., London, 1972, pp. 23–32.

RADHAMOHAN, S. K. and GALLETLY, G. D. (1979) Plastic collapse and the controlling failure modes of internally-pressurized thin torispherical shells. *J. Pres. Ves. Techn., Trans. ASME*, **101,** 311–20.

RENSCH, H. J. (1982) Elastoplastisches Beulen und Imperfektions-empfindlichkeit torisphärischer Schalen, Tech. Report No. 82-13, Institüt fur Konstruktiven Ingenieurbau, Ruhr-Universität, Bochum, December.

SHIELD, R. T. and DRUCKER, D. C. (1961) Design of thin-walled torispherical and toriconical pressure-vessel heads. *J. Appl. Mech., Trans. ASME*, **83,** 292–97.

STANLEY, P. and CAMPBELL, T. D. (1981) Very thin torispherical pressure vessel ends under internal pressure: (i) Test procedure and typical results; (ii) Strains, deformations and buckling behaviour. *J. Strain Analysis*, **16,** 171–203.

TIMOSHENKO, S. (1940) *Theory of Plates and Shells*, McGraw-Hill, New York.

Chapter 10

TENSEGRIC SHELLS

Oren Vilnay

Department of Civil and Structural Engineering, University College, Cardiff, UK

SUMMARY

A tensegric shell is comprised of a cable net and bars. The bars are arranged so that no bar is connected to or touches the others. By prestressing the bars, the net is stabilised and the shell gains its final shape.

The technical advantage of tensegric shells to overcome problems associated with large span structures is discussed. Possible patterns of bar arrangements and the design of tensegric shells are presented. Their stability conditions are formulated and the implications for indeterminate and determinate shells are discussed. It is shown that, in some cases, statically unstable tensegric shells can be made stable. The effect of external loads applied to tensegric shells is studied and it is shown that in indeterminate shells and in some loading cases the nodal displacements of determinate and statically unstable shells are because of the elasticity of the members only as in the case of ordinary reticulated shells. In most cases, however, applied loads cause large distortions in the configuration of determinate and statically unstable shells because of rigid body movements of their members.

NOTATION

a_{ij} Element ij of matrix A
$\vec{d}$ Member displacement

311

l	Member length considering external load
l_0	Member length considering prestressing
l_i	Length of member i
m	Number of the elements of the shell
n	Number of the nodes of the shell
x_i	x-coordinate of mode i
x_{ji}	$x_j - x_i$
y_i	y-coordinate of mode i
y_{ji}	$y_j - y_i$
z_i	z-coordinate of mode i
z_{ji}	$z_j - z_i$

$\tilde{A}$	Equilibrium matrix
$\tilde{A}^t$	Transposed equilibrium matrix
$\tilde{A}'$	Linear change in matrix A due to external load
$\tilde{A}^*$	Independent part of matrix A
A_m^i	Square matrix i of $m \times m$ formed from matrix A
A_0	Reference cross-sectional area
A_i	Cross-sectional area of member i
$\tilde{B}$	KA^t
$\tilde{B}^*$	Independent part of matrix B
$\tilde{D}$	$A . B$
E_0	Reference elastic modulus
E_i	Elastic modulus of member i
$\vec{F}$	Induced forces
$\vec{F}'$	Change in induced forces due to external load
$\tilde{G}$	Equilibrium matrix considering external load
$\tilde{H}$	$B^*(A^* . B^*)^{-1}$
$\tilde{K}$	Stiffness matrix
$\tilde{L}$	$E_0 A_0 AB + M$
$\tilde{M}\vec{\delta}$	$\tilde{A}\vec{P}$
$\vec{P}$	Prestressing forces
$\vec{Q}$	External load

α	Constant
α_x^0, α_x	Angle of inclination before and after loading
β	Constant
$\vec{\delta}$	Nodal displacements

10.1 INTRODUCTION

A tensegric shell is a three-dimensional assembly of linear members. The shell consists of a cable net and compression bars with each of their ends connected to the nodes of the net. The net is stabilised and the shell gains its final shape by prestressing the bars against the cable net. The bars are arranged in such a way that when the shell gains its prestressed configuration no bar touches any other, nor is connected to any other at a node. A spherical tensegric shell is shown in Fig. 10.1 and a tensegric shell in the shape of a cooling tower is shown in Fig. 10.2. An artist's impression of a swimming pool covered by a spherical tensegric shell is shown in Fig. 10.3.

There are many technical advantages in tensegric shells which can be employed to overcome the problems associated with long span structures. Tensegric shells are cost effective both in material and labour. Fabrication of the elements reduces cost and enhances ease in transport. The same type of connector is used throughout the structure. (A possible simple connector is shown in Fig. 10.4.) The foundations are simple and no anchorage to the soil is required. Because the shell is stabilised by prestressing, its erection is simple, no scaffolding is required, no special accuracy is needed and unskilled labour can be

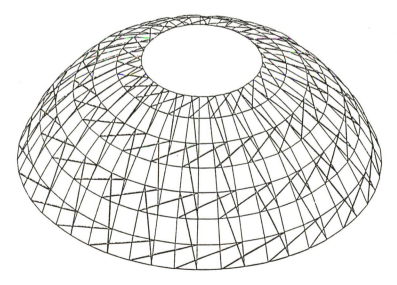

Fig. 10.1. A spherical tensegric shell.

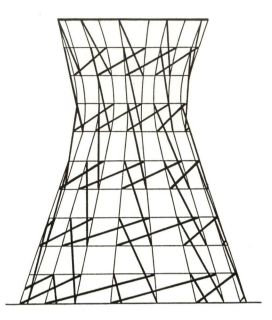

FIG. 10.2.   A tensegric shell in the shape of a cooling tower.

used. Tensegric shells are demountable which means that they can be used as temporary shelters.

Because of the fact that the tensegric shell is composed of a prestressed net, the behaviour of tensegric shells is different from that of ordinary reticulated shells. In the following pages the geometrical properties, the initial stability and the effect of external load applied to tensegric shells are investigated.

10.2   HISTORICAL DEVELOPMENT OF TENSEGRIC SHELLS

Tensegric shells are developed from tensegric bodies. The edges of these bodies are cables, prestressed by bars connected at both of their ends to the cable at the body nodes, where no bar touches another. The bars occupy the inner volume of the body. A tensegric body in the shape of an octahedron is shown in Fig. 10.5.

Snelson and Fuller (Fuller and Marks, 1973) were the first to construct tensegric bodies. Fuller coined the name tensegrity, derived

FIG. 10.3.   A swimming pool covered by a spherical shell.

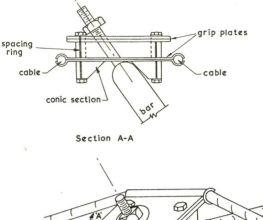

Section A-A

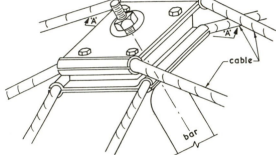

Fig. 10.4.   A possible connector in tensegric shells.

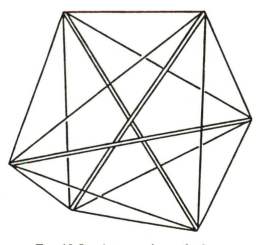

Fig. 10.5.   A tensegric octahedron.

from tension–integrity, indicating the continuous nature of the cables in these bodies. Because the enclosed volume of the tensegric body is full of bars, the functional use of the inner space is impossible.

The first attempts to shift the bars in the tensegric bodies from the centre to create a tensegric shell with free inner space, which could be of functional use, were made by Fuller (1962), who utilised the method he had used in developing the geodesic domes (Kener, 1976). However, he considered only one pattern of bar arrangement in spherical tensegric shells. Pugh (1976) developed a few other limited patterns of bar arrangements applicable to cylindrical tensegric shells.

The general principle of composing the so-called tensegric nets, which lead to unlimited types of tensegric shells, was developed by the author (Vilnay, 1977). In this chapter the tensegric nets and the way they are fitted to form shells are discussed.

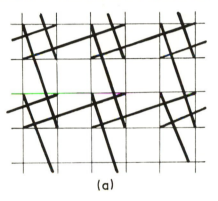

(a)

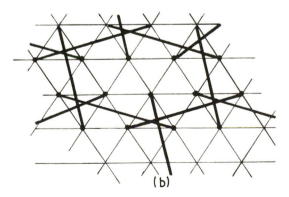

(b)

FIG. 10.6.   (a) Square and (b) triangular tensegric nets.

10.3   TENSEGRIC NETS AND THE GEOMETRY OF TENSEGRIC SHELLS

Tensegric nets are cable nets in which bars are fitted between the net nodes, one bar at a node. The bars are arranged in a typical way in which they cross each other but no bar is connected to another directly. A typical bar arrangement in the case of various cable nets is shown in Fig. 10.6. In Figs 10.6a and 10.6b the bar arrangements in the case of square and triangular cable nets are shown respectively. A similar technique is used to construct the tensegric nets shown in Fig. 10.7.

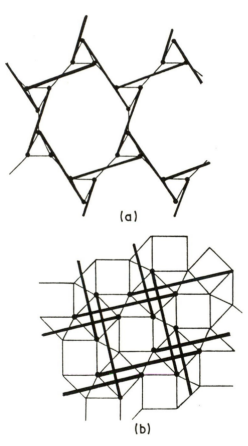

(a)

(b)

Fig. 10.7.   Other tensegric nets.

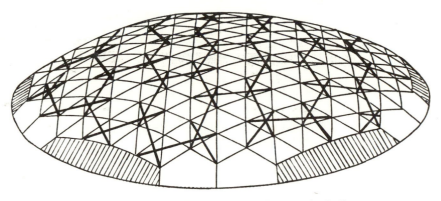

FIG. 10.8.   A shallow spherical tensegric shell.

These nets can be fitted to any required geometry of a shell. In Figs 10.1 and 10.2 the net shown in Fig. 10.6a is fitted into a dome and into a cooling tower shape, respectively. In Fig. 10.8 the net shown in Fig. 10.6b is fitted into a shallow dome and in Fig. 10.9 the net shown in Fig. 10.7b is fitted into a cylindrical shell.

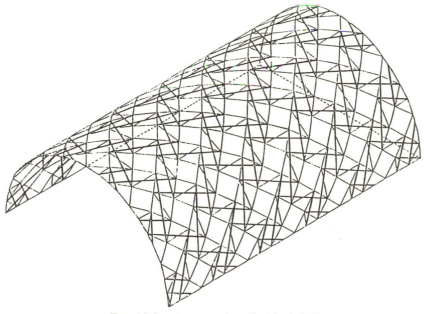

FIG. 10.9.   A tensegric cylindrical shell.

10.4 STABILITY AND PRESTRESSING
TENSEGRIC SHELL

A properly designed tensegric shell should be initially stable which implies that all the cables are straight and the net is properly stretched; in order to ensure tension in the cables, the latter should be prestressed. The prestressing should be adequate to ensure that a certain amount of tension remains in all cables under all expected loads. Thus a stable tensegric shell should be such that:

   (i)   it is prestressable, and
   (ii)   tension is induced into *all* cables by prestressing (i.e. no cable should be subjected to a compressive force).

Condition (i) is investigated by studying the equilibrium of the prestressing forces at each of the n nodes of the tensegric shell. In the case where the prestressing forces in the m elements of the shell are given by vector $\vec{P}$, the nodal equilibrium equations take the form of

$$\tilde{A}\vec{P} = 0 \tag{10.1}$$

$\tilde{A}$ is $m \times 3n$ equilibrium matrix related to the tensegric shell configuration.

Equation (10.1) and condition (i) are satisfied where

$$\text{Rank } \tilde{A} < m \tag{10.2}$$

In the case of a tensegric shell in which $m > 3n$, the so-called indeterminate tensegric shell, condition (i) is always satisfied.

In the case of a tensegric shell in which $m = 3n$, the so-called determinate shell, condition (i) implies that

$$\det(\tilde{A}) = 0 \tag{10.3}$$

In the case of a tensegric shell in which $m < 3n$, the so-called statically unstable tensegric shell, condition (i) implies that

$$\det(A_m^i) = 0 \qquad i = 1, 2, 3, \ldots, j \tag{10.4}$$

A_m^i indicates square matrix i of $m \times m$ that can be formed from matrix $\tilde{A}$. There are j matrices altogether.

Condition (ii) is studied by solving eqn (10.1). In the case of an indeterminate tensegric shell, the induced forces in at least $(m - 3n)$ members should be assumed in order to predict the forces in the rest of the members and $m - 3n$ indicates the number of independent pre-stressing states of the shell. In the case of an indeterminate tensegric shell

$$\text{Rank } \tilde{A} < 3n \qquad (10.5)$$

$m - \text{Rank } \tilde{A}$ indicates the number of members in which the induced forces should be assumed in order to predict the forces in the rest of the shell members. Thus the shell has $(m - \text{Rank } \tilde{A})$ independent prestressing states. Only where it is possible to induce tension in all cables by prestressing, will condition (ii) have been satisfied.

In the case of a determinate shell, condition (ii) implies that eqn (10.1) is not an independent set of linear equations.

One of the equations given by eqn (10.1) is a linear combination of the other equations where

$$\text{Rank } \tilde{A} = m - 1 \qquad (10.6)$$

In this case the induced force in one of the members should be assumed in order to predict the forces in the others. There are $(m - \text{Rank } \tilde{A})$ equations which are linear combinations of the rest of the equations in the case where

$$\text{Rank } \tilde{A} < m - 1 \qquad (10.7)$$

The induced forces in $(m - \text{Rank } \tilde{A})$ members should be predicted in order to find the other forces. In any case only determinate tensegric shells which satisfy condition (ii) are appropriate.

In the case of statically unstable nets, eqn (10.4) implies that the induced forces in $(m - \text{Rank } \tilde{A})$ members should be assumed before the forces in the other members can be predicted. Also, in this case, this number indicates the number of independent prestressed states of the shell.

An example of a statically indeterminate tensegric shell is shown in Fig. 10.10. The shell is spherical and provided with a rigid ring at the top; its dimensions are marked on the figure.

The shell is composed of 12 identical segments; a typical segment is shown in Fig. 10.11. In every segment there are 14 different cables marked C1 to C14 and three different bars marked b1 to b3. Thus every segment is composed of 17 different members.

In the case of symmetrical prestressing of the shell, where identical forces are induced in the corresponding member at each segment, there are 17 unknowns. These prestressing forces should satisfy the

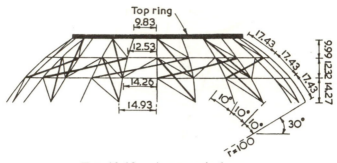

FIG. 10.10.   A tensegric dome.

three equilibrium equations at every one of the four nodes marked 3, 4, 5 and 6 in Fig. 10.11, as well as the equilibrium of the forces acting in the vertical and tangential direction on the top rig. Fourteen equilibrium equations should be satisfied at every segment. The fact that the prestressing forces induced in 17 members should satisfy only 14 equilibrium equations indicates that the shell is an indeterminate shell and thus condition (i) is always satisfied. Because the degree of redundancy is three, the three bars can be prestressed independently. In the case where bars b1, b2 and b3 are prestressed to 1·2, 1·0 and 1·2 unit force as shown in Fig. 10.12, the prestressing forces induced in the segment members obtained by using eqn (10.11) are shown there. Because there are only tensile forces in the cables, condition (ii) is also satisfied. The fact that conditions (i) and (ii) are satisfied implies that this tensegric shell is stable.

The guess of an indeterminate tensegric shell is seldom so successful

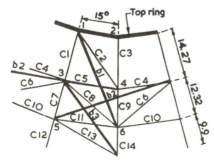

FIG. 10.11.   A segment of the tensegric dome shown in Fig. 10.10.

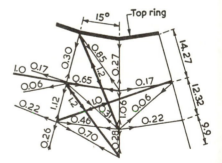

FIG. 10.12.   The induced prestressing forces in the tensegric dome
shown in Fig. 10.10.

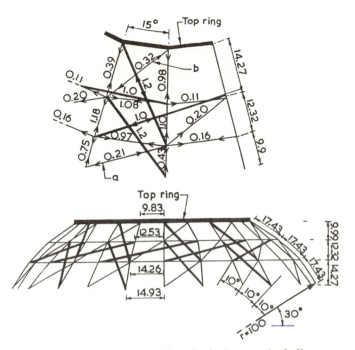

FIG. 10.13. An unstable spherical tensegric shell.

and in most cases it is difficult to guess a correct indeterminate tensegric shell. For example, in the case of the spherical shell shown in Fig. 10.13 which is very similar to the one shown in Fig. 10.10, it was found that prestressing induces compression forces in some of the cables, for example, cables (a) and (b) in Fig. 10.13; thus, this spherical indeterminate tensegric shell is not stable and cannot be erected in this geometry.

To analyse the tensegric shell shown in Fig. 10.14, the 12 unknown induced forces in the four bars marked b1 to b4 and eight cables marked C1 to C8 should be predicted. Because there are 12 equilibrium equations to be satisfied, i.e. three equations to each of the four nodes, marked A, B, C and D, it can be seen that this is a statically determinate tensegric shell.

In the case of symmetrical prestressing, the induced forces of the shell are functions of three unknowns, p_1, p_2 and p_3 shown in Fig. 10.15. These three forces should satisfy the equilibrium conditions at every node.

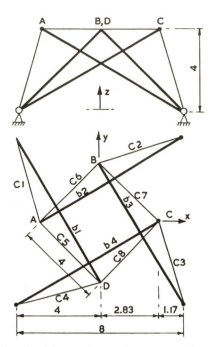

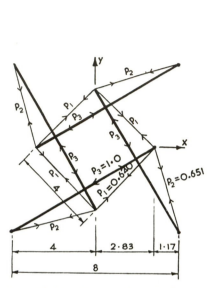

FIG. 10.14. A determinate tensegric shell.

FIG. 10.15. Prestressing of the determinate tensegric shell shown in Fig. 10.14.

The equilibrium matrix $\tilde{A}$ at a typical node takes the form of

$$\tilde{A} = \begin{vmatrix} 1\cdot414 & -0\cdot20 & 0\cdot77 \\ 0 & 0\cdot69 & 0\cdot45 \\ 0 & 0\cdot69 & 0\cdot45 \end{vmatrix} \tag{10.8}$$

It can be seen that the third row of matrix $\tilde{A}$ is a linear combination of the first and the second rows:

$$a_{3i} = a_{2i} \tag{10.9}$$

This fact indicates that det $\tilde{A} = 0$ and thus this tensegric shell satisfies condition (i) and is prestressable. By assuming prestressing p_3 to be one compression unit force, the prestressing forces induced in p_1 and p_2 are found by using eqn (10.1) to be

$$\vec{P} = \begin{vmatrix} 0\cdot64 \\ 0\cdot65 \\ -1\cdot00 \end{vmatrix} \tag{10.10}$$

and are shown in Fig. 10.15.

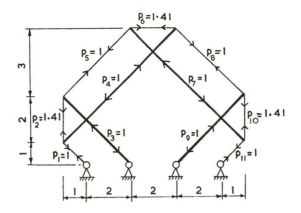

FIG. 10.16. Prestressing of a two-dimensional geometrically unstable tensegric shell.

Because prestressing induces tension in all cables, condition (ii) is satisfied. The fact that conditions (i) and (ii) are satisfied implies that this tensegric shell is stable.

Figure 10.16 shows a simple example of a two-dimensional statically unstable tensegric shell. It can be seen that there are 11 unknown induced forces in the members of the shell but there are 12 equilibrium equations to satisfy at the six nodes. The equilibrium matrix of this tensegric shell takes the form of

$$
\tilde{A} =
\begin{vmatrix}
z & 0 & 0 & z & 0 & 0 & 0 & 0 & 0 & 0 & 0 \\
-z & 1 & 0 & z & 0 & 0 & 0 & 0 & 0 & 0 & 0 \\
0 & 0 & z & 0 & z & 0 & 0 & 0 & 0 & 0 & 0 \\
0 & -1 & -z & 0 & z & 0 & 0 & 0 & 0 & 0 & 0 \\
0 & 0 & 0 & 0 & -z & 1 & z & 0 & 0 & 0 & 0 \\
0 & 0 & 0 & -z & 0 & -1 & 0 & z & 0 & 0 & 0 \\
0 & 0 & 0 & -z & 0 & -1 & 0 & z & 0 & 0 & 0 \\
0 & 0 & 0 & -z & 0 & 0 & 0 & -z & 0 & 0 & 0 \\
0 & 0 & 0 & 0 & 0 & 0 & 0 & -z & -z & 0 & 0 \\
0 & 0 & 0 & 0 & 0 & 0 & 0 & z & -z & -1 & 0 \\
0 & 0 & 0 & 0 & 0 & 0 & -z & 0 & 0 & 0 & -z \\
0 & 0 & 0 & 0 & 0 & 0 & z & 0 & 0 & 1 & -z
\end{vmatrix}
\qquad z = \sqrt{2}/2
$$

$$(10.11)$$

The elements of matrix $\tilde{A}$ are not independent as rows 5 and 12 are linear combinations of the other ten rows:

$$a_{5i} = -a_{1i} - a_{2i} - a_{3i} - a_{4i} - a_{6i} - a_{7i} - a_{8i}$$

$$a_{12i} = a_{1i} - a_{2i} - a_{3i} - a_{4i} - 2a_{6i} - 2a_{8i} + a_{9i} - a_{10i} + a_{11i}$$

(10.12)

This fact indicates that Rank $\tilde{A}$ is equal to 10. The fact that Rank $\tilde{A}$ for this shell is less than the 11 unknown forces indicates that eqn (10.2) and condition (i) are satisfied and that this shell is prestressable. By considering the independent part of matrix $\tilde{A}$ (i.e. rows 1, 2, 3, 4, 6, 7, 8, 9, 10 and 11) and assuming p_3 to be a unit compression force, the prestressing forces induced in the members are found to be

$$\vec{P} = \begin{vmatrix} 1 \cdot 0 \\ 1 \cdot 41 \\ -1 \cdot 0 \\ -1 \cdot 0 \\ 1 \cdot 0 \\ 1 \cdot 41 \\ -1 \cdot 0 \\ 1 \cdot 0 \\ -1 \cdot 0 \\ 1 \cdot 41 \\ 1 \cdot 0 \end{vmatrix}$$

(10.13)

These forces are marked on the members of the shell in Fig. 10.16. It can be seen that prestressing induces tension in all cables and thus condition (ii) is satisfied. The fact that the shell satisfies conditions (i) and (ii) indicates that this shell is stable.

10.5 THE EFFECT OF EXTERNAL LOAD

Where an external load $\vec{Q}$ is applied to a tensegric shell the equilibrium at the nodes of the shell given by eqn (10.1) takes the form of

$$\tilde{A} \cdot \vec{F} = \vec{Q}$$

(10.14)

$\vec{F}$ is the vector of the unknown induced forces in the members. In the case of an indeterminate shell there are more unknowns than equilibrium equations and the member forces cannot be predicted by only using eqn (10.14). In this case, Kener (1976) has shown that the nodal displacements and the deformation of the members should be considered. The nodal displacements $\vec{\delta}$ are related to the member displacements $\vec{d}$ by the equation

$$\vec{d} = \tilde{A}^t\vec{\delta} \tag{10.15}$$

The change in the forces $\vec{F}'$ due to these nodal displacements is

$$\vec{F}' = E_0A_0\tilde{K}\vec{d} \tag{10.16}$$

$\tilde{K}$ is the stiffness matrix and E_0 and A_0 are a reference elastic modulus and member cross-sectional area.

By using eqn (10.15), eqn (10.16) takes the form of

$$\vec{F}' = E_0A_0\tilde{B}\vec{\delta} \tag{10.17}$$

in which

$$\tilde{B} = \tilde{K}\tilde{A}^t \tag{10.18}$$

By using eqn (10.17) and by considering the prestressing forces $\vec{P}$, the total forces $\vec{F}$ are

$$\vec{F} = \vec{P} + E_0A_0\tilde{B}\vec{\delta} \tag{10.19}$$

By using eqn (10.19), eqn (10.14) takes the form of

$$\tilde{A}\vec{P} + E_0A_0\tilde{D}\vec{\delta} = \vec{Q} \tag{10.20}$$

in which

$$\tilde{D} = \tilde{A} . \tilde{B} \tag{10.21}$$

By considering eqns (10.20) and (10.1) the displacement vector is found to be

$$\vec{\delta} = \frac{\tilde{D}^{-1}}{E_0A_0} \vec{Q} \tag{10.22}$$

By considering eqn (10.19), the forces in the members are found to be

$$\vec{F} = \vec{P} + \tilde{B}\tilde{D}^{-1}\vec{Q} \tag{10.23}$$

As mentioned previously, the tensegric shells are prestressed to the extent that under all expected loads the forces in the cables, given by eqn (10.23), would always be in tension.

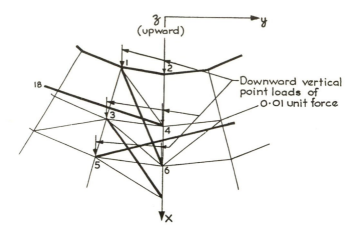

FIG. 10.17. External load applied to an indeterminate tensegric shell.

Equation (10.22) indicates that the nodal displacements of an indeterminate tensegric shell are not related to the prestressing forces and are due to the shell configuration and the elastic stiffness of the members only. In this respect, it is similar to an ordinary indeterminate reticulated shell.

Only where Rank $\tilde{A} < 3n$, the nodal displacements and the change of the induced forces (due to external load applied to an indeterminate shell) cannot be predicted by using eqns (10.22) and (10.23); in these cases, the structure behaves as a determinate but geometrically unstable one—this case is discussed later.

The indeterminate tensegric shell shown in Fig. 10.10 is loaded by equal vertical point loads of 0·01 force unit applied to all the nodes. The load on a typical segment of the shell is shown in Fig. 10.17.

As this is an indeterminate structure, the nodal displacements should be considered in order to predict forces in the members due to the external load. There are three possible displacements in each of the four nodes 3, 4, 5 and 6 and a possible vertical and tangential displacement of the top ring; thus vector $\tilde{\delta}$ has 14 elements.

Assuming equal cross-section for all the members of the shell and $E_0 A_0$ to be 10^4 force units, the forces in the shell members were analysed by using eqn (10.23) and are given in Table 10.1. It will be noted that all cables are under tension in this loading case.

By using eqn (10.22) the nodal displacements have been analysed and are given in Table 10.2.

TABLE 10.1
THE INTERNAL FORCES INDUCED IN THE INDETERMI-
NATE TENSEGRIC SHELL SHOWN IN FIG. 10.10 UNDER
THE EXTERNAL LOADING SHOWN IN FIG. 10.14

	Final induced force (force unit)
Bars	
b1	−1·193
b2	−1·201
b3	−1·021
Cables	
C1	0·279
C2	0·849
C3	0·287
C4	0·139
C5	0·643
C6	0·066
C7	1·099
C8	0·292
C9	1·058
C10	0·174
C11	0·427
C12	0·196
C13	0·700
C14	0·266

The nodal equilibrium of a determinate tensegric shell, loaded by an external load $\vec{Q}$, is given by eqn (10.14). In this case the number of unknown forces in the members is equal to the number of equilibrium equations. But the forces induced in the members of the shell cannot be predicted by using eqn (10.14) only as in the case of an ordinary determinate structure. This is because $\tilde{A}$ satisfies eqn (10.3) which implies that the elements of the kth row, a_{ki}, are a linear combination of the other matrix rows:

$$a_{ki} = \sum_j \alpha_k^j a_{ji} \qquad j \neq k \qquad (10.24)$$

in which α_k^j are constants. Thus, in the case of a determinate tensegric shell, eqn (10.14) is not an independent set of linear equations and, under most loading cases, it is not a consistent set of equations. This fact indicates that the shell cannot sustain the external load in its prestressed configuration.

TABLE 10.2
THE NODAL DISPLACEMENTS OF THE INDETERMINATE
TENSEGRIC SHELL SHOWN IN FIG. 10.10 UNDER THE
EXTERNAL LOADING SHOWN IN FIG. 10.14

Displacement vector	Nodal displacement	Displacement (unit length) × 10^2
δ_1	tan	$-0 \cdot 020$
δ_2	w_r	$0 \cdot 001$
δ_3	u_3	$-0 \cdot 018$
δ_4	v_3	$-0 \cdot 014$
δ_5	w_3	$-0 \cdot 023$
δ_6	u_4	$0 \cdot 004$
δ_7	v_4	$-0 \cdot 006$
δ_8	w_4	$-0 \cdot 002$
δ_9	u_5	$-0 \cdot 048$
δ_{10}	v_5	$-0 \cdot 031$
δ_{11}	w_5	$-0 \cdot 051$
δ_{12}	u_6	$0 \cdot 092$
δ_{13}	v_6	$-0 \cdot 014$
δ_{14}	w_6	$-0 \cdot 018$

Note tan and w_r indicate the tangential and lateral displacements of the rig and $u_i v_i w_i$ indicate node i-displacements in the x-, y- and z-directions, respectively.

Only in the cases where the determinate shell is loaded by the so-called 'fitted loads' can the shell sustain these loads in its prestressed configuration.

In the 'fitted load' case, the external load has the same symmetry as the equilibrium equations, so that

$$q_k = \sum_j \alpha_k^j q_j \qquad j \neq k \qquad (10.25)$$

In this loading case, the independent equilibrium equations take the form of

$$\tilde{A}^* \vec{F} = \vec{Q}^* \qquad (10.26)$$

in which $\tilde{A}^*$ and $\vec{Q}^*$ indicate matrix $\tilde{A}$ without row k and the vector $\vec{Q}$ without element k. Where the independent equilibrium equations are satisfied, the dependent equation (for the kth row) is automatically satisfied. In the set of independent equilibrium equations (eqns (10.26)), there is an extra unknown force in the members and the nodal displacements should be considered to determine them.

As discussed already, the relationship between the nodal displacements and the change in the member forces is given by eqn (10.17). In the case of a determinate shell, matrix $\tilde{B}$ is square. By using eqn (10.18) and considering the fact that $\det \tilde{A} = 0$, it can be seen that the columns in matrix $\tilde{B}$ are not independent. The elements of column k, b_{ik}, are a linear combination of the elements of the other columns:

$$b_{ik} = \sum_j \beta_k^i b_{ij} \qquad \text{with } j \neq k \qquad (10.27)$$

in which β_k^i are constants.

This relationship between matrix $\tilde{B}$ columns implies that it is possible to group the unknown nodal displacements given by eqn (10.17) so that

$$\vec{F}' = E_0 A_0 \tilde{B}^* \vec{\delta}^* \qquad (10.28)$$

in which matrix $\tilde{B}^*$ is matrix $\tilde{B}$ in which column k is deleted and the components of the displacements vector $\vec{\delta}^*$ are

$$\delta_j^* = (\delta_i + \beta_j^i \delta_k) \qquad j = 1, 2, 3 \qquad (10.29)$$

If $j < k$, $i = j$; if $j \geqslant k$, $i = j + 1$.

Equation (10.28) implies that for a given value of δ_k the displacement pattern given in eqn (10.30) does not induce any force into the members of the shell and thus the shell has one degree of kinematic freedom.

$$\delta_i = -\beta_k^i \delta_k \qquad \text{with } i \neq h \text{ and } i = 1, 2, 3 \ldots \qquad (10.30)$$

This is another indication to confirm that the shell cannot sustain external loads in its prestressed configuration. Only in the case where the shell is loaded by a 'fitted load', eqns (10.26) and (10.28) provide enough information to determine the induced forces in the members:

$$\vec{F} = \vec{P} + \tilde{H} Q^* \qquad (10.31)$$

$$\tilde{H} = \tilde{B}^* (\tilde{A}^* . \tilde{B}^*)^{-1} \qquad (10.32)$$

where $\tilde{A}^* . \tilde{B}^*$ is a square matrix.

The second component on the right-hand side of eqn (10.31) indicates the change in the induced forces due to the external load:

$$\vec{F}' = \tilde{H} \vec{Q}^* \qquad (10.33)$$

The change in the strain energy of the shell, U, caused by the external load is

$$U = \sum_i \frac{(f_i')^2 l_i}{E_i A_i} . \frac{1}{2} \qquad (10.34)$$

where l_i, E_i and A_i are the length, elastic modulus and area of the cross-section of member i, respectively. By using eqns (10.33) and (10.34) the nodal displacements are found to be

$$\delta_l = \frac{\partial U}{\partial q_j^*} = \sum_i \frac{f_i' l_i}{E_i A_i} h_{ij} \qquad \text{with } l = 1, 2, 3 \text{ and } l \neq h \qquad (10.35)$$

If $l < k$, $j = l$; if $l > k$, $j = l - 1$.
By using eqn (10.34) δ_k is found to be

$$\delta_k = \sum_j \delta_j / \alpha_k^j \qquad \text{with } j \neq k \qquad (10.36)$$

The fact that the nodal displacements are found by using eqns (10.35) and (10.36) indicates that they are caused due to the elasticity of the members only.

The case of an external load applied to the determinate tensegric shell seen in Fig. 10.14 is shown in Fig. 10.18. Matrix $\tilde{A}$ takes the form given in eqn (10.8). The fact that the elements of matrix $\tilde{A}$ are not independent but are related by eqn (10.9) implies that the loading cases in which

$$q_3 = q_2 \qquad (10.37)$$

are 'fitted loads'.

In the case where all the members are of the same material and with the same cross-section, matrix $\tilde{B}$ is found by using eqn (10.18) to be

$$\tilde{B} = \begin{vmatrix} 0 \cdot 354 & 0 & 0 \\ -0 \cdot 018 & 0 \cdot 12 & 0 \cdot 12 \\ 0 \cdot 043 & 0 \cdot 05 & 0 \cdot 05 \end{vmatrix} \qquad (10.38)$$

It can be seen that

$$b_{i2} = b_{i3} \qquad (10.39)$$

Hence,

$$B^* = \begin{vmatrix} 0 \cdot 354 & 0 \\ -0 \cdot 018 & 0 \cdot 120 \\ 0 \cdot 043 & 0 \cdot 051 \end{vmatrix} \qquad (10.40)$$

By using eqn (10.8) matrix $\tilde{A}^*$ is found to be

$$\tilde{A}^* = \begin{vmatrix} 1 \cdot 41 & -0 \cdot 20 & 0 \cdot 77 \\ 0 & 0 \cdot 69 & 0 \cdot 45 \end{vmatrix} \qquad (10.41)$$

By using eqn (10.31) the induced forces due to a 'fitted load' loading

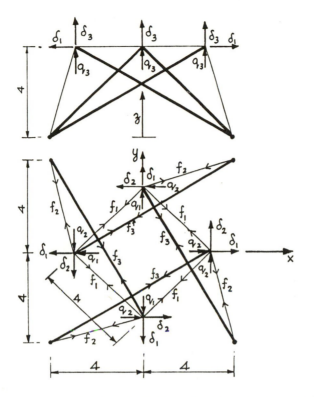

FIG. 10.18. External load applied to a determinate tensegric shell.

case are found to be

$$\begin{vmatrix} f_1 \\ f_2 \\ f_3 \end{vmatrix} = \begin{vmatrix} p_1 \\ p_2 \\ p_3 \end{vmatrix} + \begin{vmatrix} +0\cdot658 & -0\cdot046 \\ -0\cdot064 & +1\cdot131 \\ +0\cdot068 & +0\cdot175 \end{vmatrix} \cdot \begin{vmatrix} q_1 \\ q_2 \end{vmatrix} \qquad (10.42)$$

By using eqn (10.35) the nodal displacements δ_1 and δ_2 are found to be

$$\begin{vmatrix} \delta_1 \\ \delta_2 \end{vmatrix} = \frac{1}{E_0 A_0} \begin{vmatrix} +1\cdot86 & -0\cdot13 \\ -0\cdot26 & +9\cdot42 \end{vmatrix} \cdot \begin{vmatrix} q_1 \\ q_2 \end{vmatrix} \qquad (10.43)$$

By using eqn (10.36) δ_3 is found to be

$$\delta_3 = \delta_2 \qquad (10.44)$$

In the loading cases not falling within the 'fitted load' type, eqn

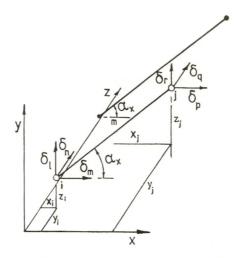

FIG. 10.19.   The displacements of a typical shell member.

(10.14) is not a consistent set of linear equations which implies that the determinate tensegric shell cannot sustain these external loads in its prestressed configuration. When such an external load is applied to the shell there will be geometrical distortion until a new configuration is achieved. The nodal equilibrium in the new configuration takes the form of

$$\tilde{G} \cdot \vec{F} = \vec{Q} \tag{10.45}$$

where $\tilde{G}$ is the equilibrium matrix considering the new configuration. In this case the change in the geometrical configuration is due not only to the elasticity of the members (as in the 'fitted load' case) but also to a rigid body movement of the members of the shell. The forces induced in the members due to the nodal displacements are given in eqn (10.19). The nodal displacement also changes the orientation of the members; the change in a typical member is shown in Fig. 10.19. Due to the nodal displacements $\cos \alpha_x^0$ given in eqn (10.46) is changed into $\cos \alpha_x$ given in eqn (10.47).

$$\cos \alpha_x^0 = \frac{x_{ji}}{l_0} \tag{10.46}$$

$$l_0 = \sqrt{(x_{ji}^2 + y_{ji}^2 + z_{ji}^2)}$$

$$x_{ji} = x_j - x_i, \quad y_{ji} = y_j - y_i \quad \text{and} \quad z_{ji} = z_j - z_i$$

$$\cos \alpha_x = \frac{x_{ji} + \delta_p - \delta_m}{l} \tag{10.47}$$

$$l = \sqrt{[(x_{ji} + \delta_p - \delta_m)^2 + (y_{ji} + \delta_q - \delta_n)^2 + (z_{ji} + \delta_p - \delta_l)^2]}$$

In the case of small nodal displacements, eqn (10.47) takes the form of

$$\cos \alpha_x = \cos \alpha_x^0 + \frac{l_0^2 - x_{ji}^2}{l_0^3}(\delta_p - \delta_m) - \frac{x_{ji}y_{ji}}{l_0^3}(\delta_q - \delta_n) - \frac{x_{ji}z_{ji}}{l_0^3}(\delta_r - \delta_l) \tag{10.48}$$

Equation (10.48) indicates that in this case $\cos \alpha_x$ is related to $\cos \alpha_x^0$ and to a linear combination of the nodal displacements. By considering eqn (10.48), matrix $\tilde{G}$ takes the form of

$$\tilde{G} = \tilde{A} + \tilde{A}' \tag{10.49}$$

in which the components of matrix $\tilde{A}$ are related to the terms of $\cos \alpha_x^0$ type and the components of matrix $\tilde{A}$ are a linear combination of the nodal displacements and are related to the rest of the terms on the right-hand side of eqn (10.48).

By considering eqns (10.48) and (10.19), eqn (10.45) takes the form of

$$(\tilde{A} + \tilde{A}')(\vec{P} + E_0 A_0 \tilde{B}\vec{\delta}) = \vec{Q} \tag{10.50}$$

Ignoring the second-order effect and considering eqns (10.1) and (10.17), eqn (10.50) takes the form of

$$\tilde{L}\vec{\delta} = \vec{Q} \tag{10.51}$$

$$\tilde{L} = E_0 A_0 \tilde{A}\tilde{B} + \tilde{M}$$

$$\tilde{M}\vec{\delta} = \tilde{A}'\vec{P}$$

In the case where $\det \tilde{L} \neq 0$, eqn (10.51) is a consistent set of linear equations. After the nodal displacements are predicted, the internal forces in the members can be analysed by using eqn (10.19). Shells in which $\det \tilde{L} = 0$ are not appropriate and should be rejected.

The elements of matrix $\tilde{L}$ consist of two components. The first is derived from matrix $E_0 A_0 \tilde{A}\tilde{B}$ and the second from matrix $\tilde{M}$. The first component is related to the rigidity $E_0 A_0$ and the second, to the prestressing forces. As matrix $\tilde{A}$ satisfies eqn (10.2), the magnitude of the nodal displacements given by eqn (10.51) depends on the relationship γ between the rigidity of the cables and the magnitude of the prestressing forces. It can be seen that in the case where $\gamma \to \infty$, the rigidity of the cables is far larger than the prestressing forces, det $\tilde{L} \to$ 0 and thus $\delta \to \infty$. In the case where $\gamma \to 0$, eqn (10.51) takes the form of

$$\tilde{M}\vec{\delta} = \vec{Q} \tag{10.52}$$

In this case, the magnitude of the nodal displacements is related to the magnitude of the prestressing forces. In order to obtain small nodal displacements, very large prestressing forces are required. The large nodal displacements associated with determinate tensegric shells are their major disadvantage.

A numerical example of the effect of the external load not falling within the 'fitted load' type is discussed below where geometrically unstable shells are considered.

In the case of a geometrically unstable tensegric shell, matrix $\tilde{A}$ satisfies eqn (10.4). This indicates that the elements of at least $(m-n+1)$ rows are a linear combination of the rest of the rows:

$$\left. \begin{array}{l} a_{ki} = \sum_j \alpha_k^i a_{ji} \\ a_{l_i} = \sum_j \alpha_l^i a_{ji} \\ \vdots \quad \vdots \end{array} \right\} \quad \text{with } j \neq k, j \neq l \tag{10.53}$$

There are $(m-n+1)$ equations, in which $\alpha_k^i, \alpha_l^i, \ldots$ are constants. In the case of a geometrically unstable tensegric shell, under most loading cases, eqn (10.14) is not a consistent set of linear equations. Only in the 'fitted load' case which satisfies eqn (10.54), the equations shrivel to a consistent set of linear equations given in eqn (10.55):

$$\left. \begin{array}{l} q_k = \sum_j \alpha_k^i q_j \\ q_l = \sum_j \alpha_k^i q_j \\ \vdots \quad \vdots \end{array} \right\} \quad \text{with } j \neq k, j \neq l \tag{10.54}$$

$$\tilde{A}^* \vec{F} = \vec{Q}^* \tag{10.55}$$

where $\tilde{A}^*$ is matrix $\tilde{A}$ in which rows $k, l, \ldots$ are deleted and $\vec{Q}^*$ is vector $\vec{Q}$ in which elements k, l are deleted. This case is similar to the case of a determinate shell under 'fitted load' and the number of unknown induced forces in eqn (10.55) exceeds the number of equilibrium equations by one and the nodal displacement should be considered. The effect of the nodal displacements on the induced forces is given by eqn (10.19). By using eqn (10.18), condition (10.53) implies that matrix $\tilde{B}$ is not independent and of the elements of columns $k, l, \ldots$, at least $(m - n + 1)$ columns are a linear combination of the rest of the columns. In the case where $\tilde{B}^*$ indicates matrix $\tilde{B}$ where columns $k, l, \ldots$ were deleted, the members forces under 'fitted load' can be found by using eqn (10.31). The nodal displacement can be found by following the same method discussed in the case of the determinate shell under 'fitted load'. The fact that in the loading cases not falling within the 'fitted load' category, eqn (10.14) is not a consistent set of linear equations indicates that the shell cannot sustain them in its prestressed geometry. Such loading applied to the shell causes partly elastic deformation and partly rigid body moment of the members of the shell until equilibrium is achieved at all nodes. If nodal displacements are small, the method described earlier for a determinate shell and given by eqn (10.51), can be used.

The nodal displacements due to an external load applied to two-dimensional geometrically unstable tensegric shells seen in Fig. 10.16 is shown in Fig. 10.20. Matrix $\tilde{A}$ of this shell is given in eqn (10.11).

In the case where all elements are of the same material and have the

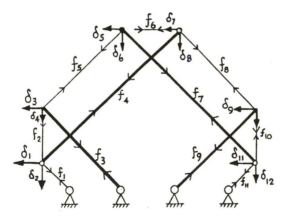

FIG. 10.20. The effect of external load applied to a geometrically unstable tensegric shell.

same cross-sectional area, matrix $\tilde{B}$ is found by using eqn (10.18) to be

$$\tilde{B} = \begin{vmatrix} a & -a & 0 & 0 & 0 & 0 & 0 & 0 & 0 & 0 & 0 & 0 \\ 0 & a & 0 & a & 0 & 0 & 0 & 0 & 0 & 0 & 0 & 0 \\ 0 & 0 & b & -b & 0 & 0 & 0 & 0 & 0 & 0 & 0 & 0 \\ c & c & 0 & 0 & 0 & 0 & -c & -c & 0 & 0 & 0 & 0 \\ 0 & 0 & b & b & -b & -b & 0 & 0 & 0 & 0 & 0 & 0 \\ 0 & 0 & 0 & 0 & a & 0 & -a & 0 & 0 & 0 & 0 & 0 \\ 0 & 0 & 0 & 0 & c & -c & 0 & 0 & 0 & 0 & -c & c \\ 0 & 0 & 0 & 0 & 0 & 0 & b & -b & -b & b & 0 & 0 \\ 0 & 0 & 0 & 0 & 0 & 0 & 0 & 0 & -b & -b & 0 & 0 \\ 0 & 0 & 0 & 0 & 0 & 0 & 0 & 0 & 0 & -a & 0 & a \\ 0 & 0 & 0 & 0 & 0 & 0 & 0 & 0 & 0 & 0 & -a & -a \end{vmatrix}$$

(10.56)

$$a = \tfrac{1}{2} \qquad b = \tfrac{1}{6} \qquad c = \tfrac{1}{10}$$

By using eqn (10.48), matrix $\tilde{A}'$ is found to be

$$\tilde{A}' = \begin{vmatrix} e & f & 0 & h & 0 & 0 & 0 & 0 & 0 & 0 & 0 \\ -e & 0 & 0 & -h & 0 & 0 & 0 & 0 & 0 & 0 & 0 \\ 0 & -f & g & 0 & i & 0 & 0 & 0 & 0 & 0 & 0 \\ 0 & 0 & -g & 0 & -i & 0 & 0 & 0 & 0 & 0 & 0 \\ 0 & 0 & 0 & 0 & -i & 0 & k & 0 & 0 & 0 & 0 \\ 0 & 0 & 0 & 0 & i & j & -k & 0 & 0 & 0 & 0 \\ 0 & 0 & 0 & -h & 0 & 0 & 0 & l & 0 & 0 & 0 \\ 0 & 0 & 0 & h & 0 & -j & 0 & -l & 0 & 0 & 0 \\ 0 & 0 & 0 & 0 & 0 & 0 & 0 & -l & m & n & 0 \\ 0 & 0 & 0 & 0 & 0 & 0 & 0 & l & -m & 0 & 0 \\ 0 & 0 & 0 & 0 & 0 & 0 & -k & 0 & 0 & m & p \\ 0 & 0 & 0 & 0 & 0 & 0 & k & 0 & 0 & 0 & -p \end{vmatrix}$$

(10.57)

In the above equation:

$e = 1/2\sqrt{2}(\delta_1 + \delta_2)$ $\qquad\qquad f = \tfrac{1}{2}(\delta_1 - \delta_3)$

$g = 1/2\sqrt{18}(\delta_3 + \delta_4)$ $\qquad\qquad h = 1/2\sqrt{50}(\delta_1 - \delta_7 - \delta_2 + \delta_8)$

$i = 1/2\sqrt{18}(\delta_6 + \delta_3 - \delta_4 - \delta_5)$ $\qquad j = \frac{1}{2}(\delta_6 - \delta_8)$

$k = 1/2\sqrt{50}(\delta_{11} - \delta_5 + \delta_{12} - \delta_6)$ $\qquad l = 1/2\sqrt{18}(\delta_7 - \delta_9 + \delta_8 - \delta_{10})$

$m = 1/2\sqrt{18}(\delta_9 - \delta_{10})$ $\qquad n = \frac{1}{2}(\delta_9 - \delta_{11})$

$p = \frac{1}{2}(\delta_{11} - \delta_{12})$

By using eqn (10.51) and considering matrix $\tilde{A}$ given in eqn (10.11), matrix $\tilde{B}$ given in eqn (10.56) and matrix $\tilde{A}'$ given in eqn (10.57), the nodal displacements due to external load can be predicted. Equation (10.51) in the case of the geometrically unstable shell shown in Fig. 10.20 is a consistent set of 12 linear equations. The fact that the set is consistent indicates finite nodal displacements due to the external load.

10.6 CONCLUDING REMARKS

In this chapter, the nature and behaviour of tensegric shells have been discussed. It has been shown that a tensegric shell is composed of a continuous envelope or a set of cables prestressed by bars, connected at both ends to the envelope, which do not touch each other. Only one type of connector is required to connect the bars to the envelope. The shell gains its shape when some of the bars are prestressed. The prestressing stabilises the shell and induces tensile forces in the envelope and compression in the bars. The tensegric shell can be transferred in a small vehicle and can be assembled and erected easily. It can be dismantled and re-assembled. Different patterns of possible bar arrangements and different types of tensegric shells following these patterns have been presented.

It has been shown that an initially stable tensegric shell should be prestressable and prestressing should induce tension in all cables. Three types of tensegric shells have been distinguished: type (i), statically indeterminate tensegric shell having more unknowns than equations; type (ii), statically determinate tensegric shells having the same number of unknowns as equations; type (iii), statically unstable shell, having more equations than unknowns. In type (i), the degree of redundancy indicates the degree of freedom in prestressing the shell, whereas in shells of types (ii) and (iii), prestressing one bar would prestress the whole shell. The fact that more than one bar should be prestressed in type (i) shells poses some difficulty in the erection process. Prestressing a second bar influences the prestressing forces in the bar already prestressed. In order to keep them at the required level the applied prestress force should be adjusted. On the other hand, in shells of types (ii) and (iii), prestressing is far simpler as it is enough to prestress only one bar and no adjustment is needed.

It has been shown that the behaviour of the shell under external loading is conditioned by its redundancy. In the case of an indeterminate tensegric shell the induced forces and the nodal displacements can be analysed as in the case of an ordinary reticulated shell. The nodal displacements due to the external load in these shells are caused only because of the elasticity of the members.

It has been shown that external load causes large displacements to geometrically unstable tensegric shells. This large nodal displacement under external load is the major disadvantage of this type of tensegric shell.

A method of analysing these nodal displacements as well as the change in the induced forces has been formulated. Only in the limited loading cases (the so-called 'fitted load' cases) the nodal displacements are because of the elasticity of the members.

It has been shown that external load causes large displacements to geometrically unstable tensegric shells. This large nodal displacement under external load is the major disadvantage of this type of tensegric shell.

REFERENCES

FULLER, R. B. (1962) Tensile Integrity Structures, Patent No. 30663521, Department of Commerce, Patent Office, Washington, DC.

FULLER, R. B. and MARKS, R. (1973) *The Dymaxion World of Buckminster Fuller*, Archer Books, New York.

KENER, H. (1976) *Geodesic Maths and How to Use it*, University of California Press, Berkeley and Los Angeles, Calif.

PUGH, A. (1976) *An Introduction to Tensegrity*, University of California Press, Berkeley and Los Angeles, Calif.

VILNAY, O. (1977) *IASS Bulletin of International Association of Shells and Spatial Structures*, **63**, 51.

INDEX